Types and Problems of Philosophy

HUNTER MEAD

California Institute of Technology

Holt, Rinehart and Winston

New York - Chicago - San Francisco
Toronto - London

TYPES

AND

PROBLEMS

OF

PHILOSOPHY

THIRD EDITION

To
B. A. G. FULLER
and
IRWIN EDMAN
In gratitude and in memory

PREFACE

To the Third Edition

IN REVISING THIS BOOK A SECOND TIME I HAVE AGAIN TRIED TO PROFIT by numerous suggestions from instructors well acquainted with it. It has of course not been possible to incorporate more than a part of these ideas without writing an entirely new book, but at least several of the suggestions made most frequently have been undertaken.

The most obvious change is a new final chapter on Humanism and Existentialism. The request for material on these two movements was the most frequent suggestion received. The two chapters on metaphysics have been substantially rewritten, particularly the sections on dualism and pluralism. The consensus of opinion seems to be that these have been the most difficult parts of previous editions, so I have tried to make them more comprehensible to students. To this end, more concrete examples have been added, and the ramifications of both dualism and pluralism into other fields have been stressed.

An extended section tracing the history of the concept of "duty" has been added, primarily as an introduction to Kant's ethical system. I am confident this will make students more sympathetic with Kant's austere and uncompromising position, since they will understand some of the views he was reacting against.

The chapter on idealism has been partially rewritten, and Berkeley in particular has been covered more adequately. There have been several suggestions for improving this chapter, and I have followed some of these insofar as it was practical. The section on mysticism has been extended, with particular emphasis upon mysticism as an epistemological position.

The glossary, already extensive, has been enlarged somewhat, primarily to include the terms utilized in the above additions. Throughout I have attempted to bring the book up to date. Philosophical ideas may not change rapidly, but references, examples and student interests certainly do change far more rapidly than most of us realize, and a conscientious author must keep this in mind as he revises.

The persons who have made helpful suggestions regarding revision are too numerous to mention, but C. N. Stockton of Bakersfield College deserves special thanks for his very detailed and extensive ideas as to how the book could be improved. Unfortunately it has not been practical to utilize more than a fraction of his excellent suggestions. Mary Ellis Arnett and Virginia Kotkin both merit sincere thanks for their secretarial assistance.

H. M.

Pasadena, January 1959

PREFACE

To the First Edition

THERE ARE TWO WELL-ESTABLISHED WAYS TO BEGIN THE systematic study of philosophy, both of which have their ardent champions. The first and perhaps more traditional method starts the student off with the history of philosophy—the chronological record of an unbroken sequence of men, schools and movements, beginning with Thales about 600 B.C. and following through until we reach thinkers still living. Probably the two principal advantages of this historical approach are (1) the student gains a sense of the continuity of the philosophical quest, and (2) he acquires a substantial body of intellectual material which can be utilized in any personal philosophical speculation he may undertake. The chief pedagogical weakness of this chronological approach is one inherent in any genetic study of a new subject: however logical the historical approach may be, it can never be the natural one for a beginner. Any spontaneous interest he may have in such a subject as philosophy always arises from contact or struggle with contemporary philosophical issues, rather than from a curiosity concerning the origin and history of philosophical concepts or an interest in what some particular historical thinker taught. Admittedly it is of real cultural value for the beginning student to learn that many of the problems which bother his mind are among the persistent issues of philosophy, but all too often the student who takes up the subject because of a genuine interest in it finds that his interest cannot survive a long analysis of ancient, medieval, Renaissance and eighteenth-century thought. His own intellectual problems are essentially contemporary problems, and his natural demand is for reasonably modern answers. He frequently feels, when pressed into a history of philosophy course, that his intellectual hunger has been offered a stone—or at best some very dry bread.

It is for this basic pedagogical reason that, despite its several advantages, the historical approach appears to be losing ground today as a first introduction to philosophy. An increasing number of teachers appear convinced that a nonhistorical initial contact with the subject is better. Usually this alternative method is built around a study of either the *types* of philosophy (that is, the chief schools and movements), as in Hocking's well-known text, or a study of the basic problems of the field, such as Cunningham's. Occasionally a more inclusive treatment, covering both the major types and the principal problems, is attempted.

As its title indicates, the present volume undertakes this combined treatment. The principal problems of philosophy are studied in terms of what I believe to be the most significant movements and schools active today. After a brief introduction which seeks to show what philosophy is and how students (along with virtually everyone else) philosophize whether they realize it or not, the relations of philosophy to its neighbors—notably science and religion—are considered (Chapters I-III). Then the two world-views which I believe to be most basic and most inclusive are described at length; these two positions, idealism and naturalism, are in fact set up as the major frames of reference within the field (Chapters IV-V). The remaining chapters then discuss the various problems of philosophy, each with its several possible solutions, in terms of these frames of reference. Thus the beginner has a few salient landmarks to guide him as he wanders through what must always be at best confusing terrain. While the professional philosopher, thoroughly at home in his field despite its great complexity, may find such an arrangement almost too simplifying, experience with numerous beginning classes has convinced me that as a first introduction such an approach has more to recommend it than any other method can claim. Whether measured in terms of either the speed with which the student comes to grips with philosophical issues or the degree of general orientation within the field attained in a single semester, I have found that such an approach best serves these purposes. This book is an expression of my conviction that the method yields pedagogical results which are definitely superior.

Writing and publishing a volume of this type involves aid from so many friends that it is impossible to acknowledge all of them individually. Several persons have been particularly helpful, however, and deserve more thanks than can be indicated by merely listing their names: Bernice and Gordon Stafford, Roscoe Poland, Marvin Headrick, John Passwater, Robert Humphreys, and Shirley Morse. Even more indispensable has been the aid of Raymond Durant and my mother, Susan H. Mead; the typing patience of the former and the critical acumen of the latter have been immeasurably helpful. Professor Raymond Iredell of Pomona College merits special thanks for advice he gave at a crucial moment regarding terminology.

H. M.

San Diego, California
January 1946

CONTENTS

Types and Problems of Philosophy

CHAPTER I

WE MUST
PHILOSOPHIZE

P HILOSOPHY IS A WASTE OF TIME." "PHILOSOPHY NEVER SOLVES anything." "Philosophy deals only with its own unreal problems— and can't even solve these." "There never was a philosopher who could endure a toothache." Remarks such as these are aimed at both the professional philosopher and the student of philosophy with such frequency that they must be considered an occupational nuisance, like chalk dust in teaching or grimy fingernails in shop work. However, just as both the teacher and the mechanic naturally resent insinuations that their personal grooming is faulty, so philosophers resent the usual implications of such remarks, that their intellectual grooming is deficient. Just as the teacher or mechanic might answer criticism with the retort, "I'd like to see you keep clean in my job!" the philosopher is often tempted to reply, "I wonder if you could do any better in my field."

But at this point the similarity ends. The critic of the chalky coat or grimy nails can always say (at least to himself), "I have enough sense to avoid such untidy occupations." No such reply can be made to the philosopher, however; as Aristotle long ago remarked, whether we will philosophize or whether we won't, we all *must* philosophize. The fastidious can perhaps avoid disorderly occupations, but no man can think logically and deeply without playing the philosopher in at least an amateur fashion. Furthermore, no one can reflect upon his experience and reach even sketchy conclusions regarding the world, life, or the nature and meaning of existence without involving (at least by implication) a whole system of metaphysics. For the professional philosopher works out

1

in detail the system of thought which lies in embryo within any naive and unconscious view of the world. The principal difference between the ideas of the trained thinker and the uncritical reflections of the philosophical innocent is a difference in the distance traveled by the two minds: the philosopher merely moves farther along the same thought-road that the uncritical thinker travels unconsciously. The philosopher usually advances more directly, since he has had more experience in avoiding blind alleys and trivial bypaths along the way. Furthermore it is likely that he sees more (at least more that is really significant) as he travels; the general route, however, remains the same.

The Inevitability of Philosophy. The reader may easily be skeptical of this description of philosophy as a universal human activity. "Nonsense!" you may say, "I've managed without philosophy these many years, and certainly I have done *some* thinking along the way!" While it is almost certain that you have done some thinking in your time—you would not have become sufficiently educated to be reading this book otherwise—it is even more certain that you have not escaped philosophizing during at least part of that time. True, you have not used the technical vocabulary of philosophy, and of course you have not been a professional who earns his living by teaching that vocabulary to college students. Nevertheless, in your own way and in your own language, you have undoubtedly been using some philosophical ideas and attitudes much of the time.

It is doubly sure that if the reader is a college student he has been philosophizing very recently, and the longer he has been in college the greater is the probability that he trembles on the edge of serious philosophical thinking at frequent intervals. If he is serious-minded, with an interest in something more than just the athletic and social life of the campus, it is probable that he has often slipped over that edge and splashed around in the pool of profound philosophical issues with some of the great thinkers of history as his unrecognized swimming companions.

One of the most startling (and perhaps ego-puncturing) experiences that the beginner in philosophy can have is to discover that the collection of vague and perhaps helter-skelter ideas which he holds on the subject of life and the universe may have a name—that on the basis of these views he can be classified as an "idealist," a "naturalist," a "hedonist," or perhaps a "pragmatist." If you are a confident personality, it is probable that you have always considered your ideas and points of view unique.

Such persons are usually surprised and even irritated by the calm ease with which the philosophy professor may be able to pigeonhole their views. On the other hand, if you are the more modest, introvertive type of student, it is likely that you have felt that your mind contained too many "crazy" ideas for its contents to be dignified by the name of philosophy. In this case you too will undoubtedly be surprised, although more pleasantly; for you too will almost certainly discover that one or several of the figures remembered in the history of philosophy have held many of these same "crazy" ideas, and have achieved fame by merely extending, integrating and articulating them. Thus both confident and unconfident beginners usually discover that they are by no means alone in their thinking. For they soon learn that there is very little new under the philosophical sun, and one has a big moment, containing either a thrill or a disappointment, when he discovers himself to be a co-thinker with Plato or Berkeley or Spinoza.

Students as Philosophers. College teachers of philosophy know that students who elect their subject do so for a variety of reasons. It is usual to discover that, among students who choose the course for some more important reason than the fact that it is reported to be easy or comes at a convenient hour, a majority make the choice because they are dissatisfied with the answers they have regularly received to certain fundamental questions. In most cases this dissatisfaction has increased sharply since entering college, because in part it comes from added knowledge and from the innumerable discussions and "bull sessions" which constitute such a large part of college life. Perhaps the most unsettling influence, however, is the growing awareness of a discrepancy between the official ideals of society or civilization and men's actual practices in the business and social world—or even on the campus. The conscientious student may realize too that his own avowed ideals often have little relation to his daily activity; he discovers that he is still paying lip service to the standards of conduct he learned at home or at church, but largely ignoring them as he carries on his present college life.

It is these contradictions and inconsistencies—intellectual, ethical, and religious—which impel many students to make their first contact with philosophy, either in class or through their own struggles for intellectual consistency. For example, every teacher is familiar with students such as Bob. Bob was raised in an atmosphere of devout Christianity, but he soon discovered that any reference to the doctrines he has always accepted without question was likely to bring frowns, sneers, or looks of acute embarrassment to the faces of his fellow students. At first Bob tended to discount such negative reactions as exceptional and unrepresentative of campus attitudes, but as his college is a typical one, it was almost inevitable that he should have to face the fact that *he* is the exception (or at least a member of the minority), and that few of his friends and classmates are restrained directly by considerations of Christian doctrine in either their thinking or their behavior. The conflict which this discovery caused in Bob's mind became particularly nagging when he realized that many students whom he particularly respected and admired—or, even worse, some of his favorite instructors—shared in this general indifference or open hostility to traditional religious faith.

In an attempt to resolve this conflict Bob did what any intelligent person would under the circumstance: he began to *think*. He secured more information regarding the origin and history of the doctrines he had always accepted as "gospel," and attempted to understand the reasons which had led intelligent and well-educated (and quite moral) persons to abandon these doctrines. He discussed the various issues involved with representatives from both schools of thought, attempting meanwhile to maintain an attitude of impartial judgment.

In this effort to settle his conflict Bob's intelligence demanded that he try to employ reason rather than emotion, since he realized that the problem is primarily intellectual, and only indirectly emotional. He decided that his family and religious teachers were not "objective" in their arguments claiming to prove the existence of God or the immortality of the soul; on the other hand he also felt that his skeptical and atheistic friends were sometimes no less prejudiced and emotional, or were merely rationalizing a rebellion against religious backgrounds similar to his own. Thus neither group seemed to offer him a reliable source of impartial, unemotional thinking, and he felt impelled to reject both as guides to the solution of his problem. Hence he was forced to attempt to formulate for himself a logical statement of what he could honestly believe on the basis of his experience and knowledge up to date.

Whether Bob knew it or not, at this point he became a philosopher. If he continues to be logical and persistent in his effort to formulate his own beliefs, it is likely that he will reach conclusions similar to those articulated in some well-established metaphysical system. But, regardless of whether he arrives at some viewpoint made famous by Aristotle or perhaps by William James, or at one which he can honestly call only his own, if his method has been logical and his approach rational, both his activity and his conclusions will merit the name "philosophy."

Ruth's case can be found on every coeducational campus. Although her training has been less strictly religious than Bob's, the moral instruction she received from her parents was thorough and definite. Her parents consider themselves "liberal," but Ruth has been taught that certain things lie outside even the most liberal boundaries of conduct. Foremost among these excluded items are any and all types of sexual activity outside of marriage, particularly for a self-respecting woman. While her parents are well-read and possess some knowledge of psychology and sociology, they have raised their daughter to believe that standards of sex morality are strict and unchanging.

By the time that Ruth has been on the campus for a semester or two, she begins to realize that, although most of the girls were raised in a moral atmosphere similar to that in her home, some of them have departed from it in theory or practice—or both. Furthermore, some of these girls are frank regarding their conduct, especially when talking with intimates, and Ruth is surprised to see that their friends do not appear to think less of them for their attitudes. Most disturbing of all (for Ruth has always been taught that such conduct inevitably leads to unhappiness, especially for a girl), she observes that these girls seem as happy and well-adjusted as most of their schoolmates.

As Ruth is intelligent and open-minded, she too attempts to think the matter through in a rational manner. An enlightened library policy permits access to reliable books on the major problems of sex and marriage, but it does not take her long to realize that the solution to her problem will not be found in such books nor derived from sorority house midnight discussions. For what she is seeking to discover is something much deeper, more complex and far more significant than any answer to the problem of sexual continence. She is attempting to discover what determines "right" and "wrong." Hitherto she has always relied on the word of her parents and teachers to determine these two classes of conduct, but she suddenly realizes that this is no longer adequate, since all their instructions were expressed in specific commandments regarding certain actions, rather than in terms of a rational criterion for "right." The fact that most people believe as her parents do seems irrelevant to her search, just as does the antiquity of this social preference for continence; she realizes that these are only various forms of authority, which can have no binding intellectual force upon minds that reject the particular authority involved. Something more basic and more rational is required.

Thus Ruth is finally in a position to begin some intellectual reconstruction. Before long she discovers that the problem of "right" and "wrong" can be solved only by going yet deeper, for she sees that these terms are dependent upon "good" and "evil." Hence her search ultimately leads to this fundamental question: "What is the good life?" Until a satisfactory answer to this most searching of all man's questions has been worked out, Ruth realizes that she can only fall back on authority of some kind as a guide to her conduct, even if it is an authority as dubious as the majority opinion of her fellow students. Perhaps her search for an adequate answer to the problem of the good life will lead her to a course in philosophy or ethics. But whether it does or not, if her private efforts carry her any place near the point we have described, she is well along the highroad of philosophy.

Of course not all students, even if they are intelligent and serious-minded, have sufficient persistence to think problems such as these through to a point where the basic philosophical issues stand clearly revealed. Bob, for example, could have cut his analysis short by deciding that nobody seems to have reliable evidence regarding the truth or falsity of religious beliefs, and consequently that "faith" becomes a purely personal matter. Ruth likewise could have turned back soon after beginning her intellectual journey by deciding that as her parents are older and wiser than she is they should be followed, particularly as their views coincide with majority opinion regarding sexual morality.

But even if our two students had reached only such elementary positions as these, each would still at least imply a philosophy which has been fully formulated and ably defended in the long history of thought. Bob, for instance, would appear to be drifting toward a relativistic skepticism of some sort, while Ruth would be resting content in an implied authoritarianism.

Some Further Examples. Or let us consider the case of Charles. While still in grammar school Charles became intrigued with that brain-teaser which everyone has met at some time or other: "If a tree falls in the middle of a forest and there is no one around to hear it, is there any sound?" Even after he had learned that the answer depends entirely upon a definition of "sound," the problem continued to fascinate him, particularly after some older person suggested that the same question could be asked regarding all our sensory experience. For example, if none feels it, is the stove "hot" or the weather "sticky"? Gradually Charles came to feel that in all experience the person is more important than the thing he experiences. Furthermore, the person is not only more important but somehow more basic and "real," so that mind or consciousness must be considered the central element in the universe. Whether he realizes it or not, Charles has hit upon the fundamental doctrine of one of the greatest and most influential schools of philosophical thought, metaphysical idealism.

Another student, Dick, is much interested in science, particularly geology, astronomy and the biological studies. From his courses in these subjects he has learned that science, even in its most inclusive generalizations and far-ranging laws, depends always and ultimately upon *facts*. He is increasingly impressed by science's ability to explain one by one the various mysteries of human experience, and he finds particular satisfaction in realizing that the boundaries of the unknown, the mysterious and the "supernatural" shrink every day. Finally he comes to feel as all of his science instructors do that, while science may never be able to tell us everything we want to know, there is already sufficient evidence to prove that *any* field yields its maximum of reliable knowledge only when approached scientifically. Dick also believes that there is nothing that lies outside the universe of nature studied by science; "nature" includes everything that exists, so there is no place for the "supernatural." When he reaches this last point of view he has (probably quite unconsciously) stumbled upon the central doctrine of another principal philosophic position, naturalism.

As a final example there is Barbara, a hard-headed, practical-minded and somewhat cynical junior who has never had much patience with theory or speculation. "Where does it get you?" is her usual vocal reaction to theoretical discussions. More recently her critical challenge has been broader in its scope, for now she is likely to ask, "Does it make any difference in the long run *which* theory you hold—and if so, just what? What's the pay-off in terms of concrete results—that's what I'm interested in!" While she would certainly be surprised (and probably annoyed) to be informed of the fact, Barbara also appears to have a theoretical position which is implied in her questions. For these suggest a crude *pragmatism* that attempts to evaluate everything in terms of results of concrete effects, and which holds that theories and speculative distinctions have meaning only insofar as they lead to differences we can directly experience.

It must again be emphasized that probably none of these five students would think of their intellectual activity as philosophizing, and it is still less likely that they would consider the result of their thought an embryonic system of philosophy. As we shall see in the pages ahead, however, organized philosophy has developed from just such thinking about these same problems. Indeed, the history of philosophy is only an unbroken succession of divergent answers to these problems (and others like them), while any philosophical "system" is little more than an integrated and very systematic attempt to answer the principal basic questions that plague the human mind whenever it begins to think deeply and inclusively.

Principal Differences Between Popular and Systematic Philosophy

There are three notable differences which separate the philosophy we call "popular" or "personal" from the kind that wins lasting fame, or even from the kind which most professional philosophers engage in. The most obvious difference is the fact that these personal philosophies are usually expressed in simple, everyday layman's language. The ideas of most of the great thinkers, on the other hand, are usually stated in a more abstract and more technical vocabulary which must be learned like the special terminology of any science. This technical vocabulary is also the greatest barrier standing between most philosophers and the general public.

Actually this difference between popular and professional types of philosophy is not as great as it seems. Once this technical vocabulary is learned, unsuspected similarities between the two begin to appear. It is a common occurrence for beginning students to say, once the instructor or the dictionary has translated some abstruse metaphysical statement into simple language, "Why didn't he say so in the first place?" The answer to this natural layman's question is that, assuming the translation into simpler language is adequate (which is not always true, for some philosophical sentences are probably impossible to put into everyday terms), it is still very awkward to state abstractions of a high order in other than abstract technical language.

The same terminological problem occurs in most fields: many of the concepts which are basic in any particular field are symbolized by what laymen consider technical terms, but the writer or speaker would have to use a whole sentence (or perhaps several sentences) in place of the single term if he were required to use only ordinary language. If the layman had to read or listen to such discourse for a brief time, he would quickly see that it is extremely inefficient to attempt to avoid all technical terms— inefficient for both the writer and his audience. What seems needed, particularly in philosophy, is greater willingness on the part of philosophers to define terms clearly and then use them with precision and consistency, and an equal willingness on the part of the students to learn the vocabulary of the field. In this particular book, it is hoped that the glossary which is included will prove the author's desire to meet his readers halfway in this matter. As in the case of all such devices, however, this aid to communication is of no value unless it is used.

The second notable difference separating popular philosophies from the professional kind is the fact that popular ones exist largely in implication, whereas the systematic thinker has made his thought explicit. A popular philosophy, particularly if formulated by a person with no knowledge of the history of philosophy, is embryonic. All the potentiality and promise of becoming a fully developed system may be present, but just as it takes a biologist specialized in embryology to perceive this potentiality in the partially formed organism, so it takes the eye of someone well experienced in systematic philosophy to discover all the possibilities latent in a partially formed philosophic position. The difference between an embryo and a mature organism is enormous, but nevertheless embryos are just as important in the scheme of things as are fully-developed adults. It is therefore fortunate that students are usually encouraged by the discovery that some famous thinker's reputation has been earned by fully developing and articulating ideas which the student can recognize as his own.

A third difference lies in the fact that the major philosophical systems embody a degree of organization and consistency which is almost certain to be lacking in private world-views. The recognized philosopher has worked out his ideas *systematically,* so that his thought constitutes a scheme for explaining the universe and for solving the problems that confront the mind when it begins to inquire seriously into the nature of its experience. Most thinking, even when it is earnest and searching, fails to achieve consistency and coherence within any very large area of thought and experience. While the systematic philosopher, like any human being, is not immune to intellectual contradiction and logical inconsistency, he does nevertheless succeed in establishing coherence and logical unity over far more inclusive areas of thought than the average man, regardless of how sincere and conscientious the latter may be as a thinker. Even when a philosophical world-view fails in other respects, it usually remains impressive as an ordered, well-structured system.

The Problem of Definition

When we attempt to organize these general ideas regarding the nature of philosophy into a formal definition of the subject, difficulties immediately appear. For philosophy is an enterprise or activity, rather than a subject or body of knowledge, and it is always harder to define an activity than a substantive or entity. Sometimes an effort is made to avoid the difficulty by suggesting that there is no such thing as philosophy: there is only philoso*phizing,* the conscious intellectual activity whereby men attempt to discover the nature of thought, the nature of reality, and the meaning of human experience. Or, it is argued, there are at most only philoso-*phies,* the various ways of looking at the world formulated by thinkers living in many different civilizations. These are varied and often contradictory, and hence (it is argued) it is absurd to regard "philosophy" as a single field or body of knowledge. Moreover, each school and each individual thinker must necessarily define the subject in a different way, and by this very definition leave out much which the representative of an opposing school would include.

This last point needs to be emphasized, for it is something the newcomer to philosophy finds difficult to grasp. He may be aware that the answer to any particular philosophical question depends upon your school of thought, but he cannot understand how the definition of philosophy as such also depends in part upon what school of philosophy the definer accepts. When we compare a school whose interests are largely metaphysical (for example, idealism) with one whose focus is upon theories of truth and verifiability (such as logical positivism) we see that this is inevitably the case. The first school will necessarily define philosophy in terms of a systematic effort to establish logically the character of reality; whereas the second, which considers "reality" a meaningless term and regards any effort to establish its character as a waste of time, defines philosophy in terms of the logical analysis of language and meaning. And so through the whole roll call of the many schools of thought: each includes within its definition primarily what is stressed in its speculative or analytical activity, and each in turn excludes what does not interest it, or what it does not feel adequate to handle.

If for the moment we side with those who prefer to regard philosophy as an activity or a process, our problem is to decide what all these various and sometimes opposed thinkers are doing when they are philosophizing. What do their mental processes have in common—what, in brief, distinguishes philosophical thinking from other types of thinking? What does the philosopher do which the scientist, the religionist, or perhaps the artist doesn't do? What are his unique or characteristic intellectual activities?

Although it simplifies our problem somewhat to think of philosophy in these functional, dynamic terms, definition is still very difficult. At the minimum there are two distinct types of thinking activity in which philosophers as a group engage, although not every philosopher engages equally in both. While these intellectual activities are not unrelated, nevertheless in both intention and method they are sufficiently different to complicate attempts at definition. Several of the chapters that follow will be concerned with making this difference clear, but here we can give at least a preliminary statement.

Philosophy's Two Great Functions

Philosophy as Analysis. The first great philosophical activity is *analysis,* or *criticism.* In this role the thinker analyzes what may be called our intellectual tools. He studies the nature of thought, the laws of logic and consistency, the relations between our ideas and reality, the nature of truth, and (perhaps most important of all) the validity of the various methods we employ in attaining "truth" or "fact" or "knowledge." He analyzes, compares and evaluates the methods of science, of religion, of art, of intuition, and of common sense. Any means which men use to attain knowledge or to organize their experience is of intense interest to the philosopher, for he perhaps more than anyone else is concerned with finding the most adequate methods for attaining certainty. In part, he examines the intellectual methods of all fields to see what he can learn from them, but he is even more concerned with evaluating these methods for their own sake. Here philosophy plays the role of master critic: the claims of knowledge or truth advanced by the various fields are investigated unsparingly in terms of the methods used, the consistency of the results, and the relation of these results to the rest of human experience.

As we shall see in the chapters ahead, this critical and analytical function of philosophy is much less understood or appreciated by most people than the better-known activity of *synthesis*. This is unfortunate, because it is these analytical activities of philosophy that have come to dominate the field increasingly in recent years, and it is in this role of analysts that philosophers today appear to be doing their most fruitful work. Most of the philosophical publications that appear in either book or journal form are really critical studies, concerned primarily with the problem and methods of knowledge. Not realizing this, the general reader who tries to study these aspects of knowledge finds himself bewildered and disappointed; instead of answers to his questions concerning life and the universe, he runs head on into highly technical discussions of the methods of science, the laws of implication, or the problem of causality. Traditionally, philosophy has been regarded as a source of answers to such questions as any thoughtful person might ask, but in modern times its energies have gone increasingly into analytical (and therefore very technical) channels. Whether this major activity of modern philosophy is also its most significant activity can be decided only after we have gained a better view of the field as a whole.

Philosophy as Synthesis. The other main function of philosophy is the more traditional one: it attempts to synthesize all knowledge and man's total experience. Here the emphasis is upon the anticipated result, rather than upon the methods or tools employed. In this synthesizing activity the philosopher seeks the most inclusive view possible regarding the nature of reality, the meaning and purpose of life, the origin, the status, and the destiny of consciousness, and other such ultimate questions. The emphasis is upon *wholeness* or *completeness*. The goal is a world-view (the German terms *Weltansicht* or *Weltanschauung* are sometimes used), a picture of the universe that will omit nothing in human experience which can help make of that inexhaustible flood of experience an ordered, integrated, and meaningful whole.

The modern philosopher is usually careful not to confuse this search for a total view of reality with the implication that any integration of history and human experience which he may formulate constitutes a *final* synthesis.[1] For it seems certain that as long as the race continues, new experiences will require new and more adequate syntheses. Each generation has to reappraise and reinterpret the cumulative experience of the race, if only because the totality of man's experience has increased still further since any previous synthesis was made. Moreover that part of the total which seems most significant to any present generation (that occurring within the preceding two or three decades) has not as yet been intellectually processed, so to speak. Hence the integrating function of philosophy is endless and must necessarily always be so. No formulation, however inclusive, can stand for long as the last word. It may endure for a few generations, although under the conditions of modern civilization very few attain even such a comparative longevity as this. The philosopher, as certainly as any intellectual worker, appears to have a permanent job.

Some Possible Definitions

It is usual to attempt to define philosophy in terms of its subject matter, and the newcomer to the field ordinarily finds these more static definitions more enlightening. As an inclusive statement which does justice to both ways of viewing the field, one definition holds that philosophy is a persistent and organized attempt "to see life steadily and see it whole." Sometimes this is taken in the sense of a systematic search for meanings and values, and sometimes as suggesting a profound probing into the nature of reality, such as the scientist makes when he investigates the

[1] In the long history of philosophy, some of the earlier thinkers were less modest regarding the finality of their synthesizing achievements. We have learned from their failures, however, and it seems unlikely that there will again soon be philosophers claiming that their system represents the final integration of knowledge and experience.

character of the physical world or the nature of organic activity. But whichever way we understand the statement, philosophy is a systematic and thorough attempt to relate the universe and human life to each other in a meaningful way. As someone has said, the aim of philosophy is "to discover the nature of the universe, our relation to it and our prospects in it, to the dual end of satisfying our heads in their demand that curiosity be answered, and our hearts in their demand that human life and human experience be rendered as significant and worth while as possible."[2]

Philosophy (particularly in its synthesizing activity) represents the effort to combine into an integrated system all knowledge and all experience, both individual and racial. It seeks to organize all truths into a unified whole, to take all those partial aspects of experience which come to us in fragmentary form from our daily living and weld them into a coherent picture. Various thinkers may call this completed picture a world-view, a reproduction of reality, a sketch of the nature of things, a blueprint of the "unknown," a diagram of "things as they are," or a representation of the Ultimate. But whatever we may call it, and whatever it may represent in our minds, the motive that prompts its formulation is everywhere and in all ages the same: to increase understanding, to satisfy the human urge to *know,* and thus to render life both more intelligible and more worth living.

Philosophy as the Love of Wisdom. The original meaning of the term "philosophy" tells much of the story. To the Greeks it was the "love of wisdom," and the philosopher was therefore the "lover of wisdom." The modern viewpoint might prefer to regard it as the search for, or pursuit of, wisdom, but the distinction is probably not important. Love usually leads to a pursuit of some kind, and the love of wisdom is no exception. The important point is that it is the desire for *wisdom* that arouses the philosopher to activity, rather than the more usual things which men strive for. To know is his passion, and understanding is the goal of his existence. It is likely, however, that he differs from many of his fellow men in the degree of understanding that is required to satisfy him. For most minds are ready to rest when they have accumulated sufficient knowledge to meet the practical demands of daily living or to permit them to feel that they have at least some insight into the meaning of human experience. The philosopher, however, is not satisfied with such a modest goal. Knowledge for him means *inclusive* knowledge—or at

[2] I have been unable to locate the source of this statement.

least such a degree of it as the shortness of life and the limitations of man's mind will permit. Philosophical wisdom implies some genuine understanding of the universe and of all human experience.

Philosophy as a Practical Pursuit. While the philosopher is forced to admit that his goal is less likely to be reached than the more modest goals for which most men strive, he denies that his pursuit is any less practical than the more ordinary human quests. For, he argues, the urge of curiosity is as basic and natural in man as any of the so-called "practical" drives for pleasure, power, or fame. If any activity which aims to satisfy desire is a practical activity, then the search for understanding or wisdom, arising as it does from one of the most fundamental human desires, is intensely practical. True, the philosopher ordinarily has more of this particular drive than most people, but no one is without it in some degree. To be human is to be curious, to be curious is to demand answers to any questions that come within the sweep of our roving minds, and therefore to be human is to philosophize. Whether we do it consciously, habitually and professionally, or only unconsciously, occasionally and as an amateur, we must to some extent philosophize merely by virtue of the fact that we are members of the species *homo sapiens*.

Summary of Definitions. To summarize these various definitions, we may describe philosophy as that activity in which men seek to understand the nature of the universe, the nature of themselves, and the relations between these two most fundamental components of our experience. Philosophy is thus an organized search for knowledge, carried on by means of systematic reflection upon the discoveries of the scientist, the findings of the historian, the insights of the artist, the poet, and the mystic, all combined with our personal and daily experience. These systematic reflections in turn require a thorough analysis of the mind's capacity for gaining knowledge, so that a basic part of philosophical activity consists of the study of the sources, the methods, and the limitations of human knowledge. Since knowledge is normally communicated and recorded, this in turn may involve an analysis of man's means of communication, particularly language.

When we are philosophizing we are trying to answer the persistent questions that all men at some time raise concerning the nature, meaning, and value of life. The subject matter of philosophy is thus the nature of existence, the nature of experience, and, finally, the relation which man and his experiencing mind have to the rest of the cosmos. The philosophical search is in essence a quest for inclusive knowledge regarding the character, meaning, and value of experience.

Philosophy's Problems

As we enter the field of philosophy it quickly becomes evident that the study of this subject primarily requires making the acquaintance of certain problems. We soon see that philosophy is organized around these central problems, and eventually we discover that they and their numerous solutions *are* philosophy. The history of the field is largely a record of the various answers that have been worked out for the same set of recurrent questions. These answers have been as numerous as the minds that have framed them, and they have been so divergent that it is sometimes hard to believe they are intended to be solutions to the same set of problems. Underneath, however, there is a core of persistent issues with which successive generations of thinkers have struggled. Societies change, civilizations rise and decline, but nearly every age and every society leaves behind sufficient records to reveal that it too has wrestled with the very old and very persistent problems of philosophy. Most of these major problems will be treated at some length in the chapters that follow, but here it may be helpful to describe some of them briefly, since in no other way can we easily gain an impression of philosophy's range and goals.

The Primary Problem. In traditional or classical philosophy the primary question has always been this: What is it—human experience—all about? If understood in its fullest significance, this question sums up (or at least involves) most of the other problems and issues with which philosophy deals. The professional philosopher usually asks this question in some more abstract form, such as, What is the nature of ultimate reality? Laymen, on the other hand, are likely to phrase it in some such fashion as this: What is the meaning of life and the universe? While this latter question requires a somewhat different answer, it too refers to the same basic central problem. However it is phrased, this is the core query around which any system of philosophy is built. And, in some form or other, it has been asked by everyone at some time during his life regardless of his intelligence, educational background or proclaimed indifference to metaphysical speculation.

The Problem of Man's Relation to the Universe. Another great problem that philosophy must attack grows out of the one we have just described. This concerns the relation between man and the rest of the universe. There are some thinkers who regard this as the most significant question that we can ask, less inclusive perhaps than the first sweeping inquiry concerning the nature of reality, but more directly linked with our daily experience. For this one concerning the relation between ourselves and our environment is perhaps more fundamental to our happiness and welfare than any other question.

In the Middle Ages, men believed that the universe (as far as it was then known) was designed solely as a backdrop for our planet, which in turn existed as a stage on which the great drama of salvation was enacted. Naturally the geocentric (earth-centered) theory of the cosmos played directly into such an anthropocentric (man-centered) view of things. This was made evident when Copernicus first launched his astronomical system in opposition to this earlier view. The major moral argument against the heretical new view was that it lowered the dignity of man by displacing him from his central role in the universe, so that he no longer appeared to be the protagonist in the whole cosmic spectacle. While modern science makes any such view of man's relation to the universe seem both egotistical and absurd, there still remain enough divergent views concerning the exact nature of that relation to give the philosophers a lively time.

The Problems of Religion

Immortality. All this in turn leads to other even more urgent problems which philosophy must acknowledge as members of its family. From a consideration of the nature of the universe and its relations to man, we are led to what is for many persons the most desperate question which either philosophy or religion has to face: *Whither* go we? To a majority of minds the puzzle of whence we came is far less important than why we are here and where we go afterwards. They are willing to dismiss the problem of our origin as a hopeless mystery, or at least as primarily of academic interest. But the problem of the purpose of life and our ultimate destiny is one that no human can avoid. Some opinion on the subject of immortality each individual must have, and here again the philosopher differs from most men only in that his views on the subject are more fully thought out, and perhaps more consistent with his total picture of reality.

Immortality as a Philosophical Issue. A serious consideration of human immortality is generally associated with religion and theology. As a consequence students are often surprised to learn that philosophy also gives earnest thought to the issue. If we recall, however, that nothing in man's experience is alien to philosophy—particularly nothing concerned with ultimate meanings and values—we will not be surprised that a question so important to both religion and morality should come under the searching gaze of the philosopher.

It is to be expected that philosophy's approach to the problem will differ significantly from religion's. For one thing, the metaphysician is far less likely to regard immortality as a "necessary postulate" of the moral life, and far more likely to follow the lead of scientific evidence in his search for an answer to the great question. He usually insists that the factual possibilities of personal survival be fully canvassed, and demands that the whole issue be discussed without a priori assumptions regarding the "necessity" of immortality or its presumed relation to ethics. Even if he believes that survival can be proved on rational grounds, or that his world-view makes it at least a thrilling possibility, the philosopher is almost certain to interpret any such existence in terms unlike those traditional in religious thought. For the theologian, the relation between earthly life and postmortal survival usually centers around such points as morality, divine justice, retribution and the like. In nearly all religions, immortality is predicated upon the assumption that it is a state which must be *earned;* this relates it to the rest of our experience primarily in *moral* terms. The philosopher, on the other hand, is more likely to be concerned with the relations between such a survival and the whole of our experience—including our moral decisions and standards, of course, but also including a great deal more. Viewing the universe in all-inclusive terms, philosophy naturally considers life less exclusively in terms of "right" and "wrong," "sin" and "salvation." Consequently it also views the matter of immortality in broad terms, seeking to relate the issue to the character of the universe as a whole, rather than to the character of man or to man's salvation.

The Problem of God. The newcomer to philosophy is usually less surprised that "God" should constitute one of the problems of the field, for the subject of deity somehow impresses us as less exclusively a religious matter than immortality seems to be. It is common, however, for beginners in philosophy to be surprised at the attitude most thinkers take toward the issue. Even after the student has learned that in this field we employ the same method of rational analysis for all problems, approaching them with objectivity and impartiality, it is nevertheless disconcerting to realize that "God" is to philosophy just one more intellectual issue. Sometimes it is difficult to persuade the beginner that it is possible (or even good taste) to approach the subject except with lowered eyes and bowed intelligence. To proclaim here that in philosophy there are no aspects of human experience that are "sacred" in the sense of being immune to rational analysis, often impresses students as hardly a decent attitude. To consider the problem of God with no more awe or emotion than we bring to an analysis of the concept of causality (for instance) seems hardly suitable to the subject. Even if the student is able to see that the philosopher's attitude implies no disrespect, but is only a kind of constitutional guarantee that "all problems are created equal," it is still unlikely that he will be able to approach the question without preconceptions. A belief in the existence of God is so strongly traditional in Western thought that any challenge of this belief, or even a serious consideration of any possible alternative to it, is to many minds inconceivable. Even when the discussion is carefully sterilized by an agreement among all parties that this is a purely academic question having no necessary relation to religious faith, it still remains difficult for some students to relax and participate freely.

However, it does not take many days in a philosophical classroom for anyone to realize that the problem of God is not only one of the most important with which philosophy deals, but also one of the most interesting and thought-provoking. It is common for students to find that what the concept of deity has lost in awesomeness it has gained in interest and intellectual challenge. If they are fortunate enough to make this discovery, they have to that extent become philosophers.

The Problem of Man's Freedom

Along with the problems of God and immortality there goes a third, that dealing with the freedom of the will. One of the most important intellectual changes resulting from the extension of the scientific viewpoint has been the diminishing areas in our experience within which a strict determinism does not prevail. Originally men regarded all of nature (and of course human nature) as basically lawless. To the primitive mind, if a rock rolls down a hillside, it is because that stone possesses a will of its own which can be exercised arbitrarily. That apparent freedom of choice and movement which man feels in himself is transferred by primitive minds to all objects and creatures. Each has an independent will, and exercises it freely. This naive view gave way, in most of the world, to the knowledge that ordinary physical objects obey mechanical laws, although it was still uncertain just what those laws were or how they operated.

The development of science altered our thinking profoundly. Galileo and his co-workers were able to formulate this crude knowledge of mechanical fact into indubitable laws. Moreover, these were discovered to be laws which admitted no exception and which implied a rigorous sequence of cause and effect. Since that time one natural process after another has been brought under the sway of scientific law and order. From the realm of material bodies the frontier has been extended to include the realm of animal life, and it is no longer assumed that motility renders null the primary principle that all change is caused by antecedent changes of some kind—i.e., that every event is determined by a cause, results in its corresponding effect.

Despite the expanding march of scientific law, one great domain, human life, has until recently been considered immune from any complete application of this deterministic principle. While men learned early that their bodies were subject to many of the mechanical laws which affect inanimate objects (gravitation, for example), they have always been impressed by the undeniable feeling that within the realm of *choice* and *volition* we are free. This feeling of freedom is so basic in human experience that most persons assume without question that while their actions may be restricted by physical factors, their wills can make choices that are independent of any antecedents. The belief in this feeling is so strong and so nearly universal that it is difficult for a person without extensive scientific or philosophical training to admit the possibility that both his actions and his choices may be as strictly determined by prior events (usually earlier choices and actions) as any other event in nature.

Free-will vs. Determinism. While modern psychology has added much weight to the deterministic viewpoint, it remains as yet an unproved hypothesis. Consequently there is ample room for philosophical controversy over the issue of free-will *vs.* determinism. Because the deterministic position is thoroughly repugnant to most persons of a strong religious or idealistic inclination, philosophical feelings probably run higher over this issue than any of the other problems of the field. To the idealistic mind, a rigid determinism extended to human life appears to negate what such minds regard as our most uniquely human capacity, that for making moral choices. The powerful arguments of the determinist (which we shall consider fully in a later chapter) do not impress persons who are predominantly idealistic as heavy enough to warrant a disbelief in freedom of the will.

Neither side of the warm free-will controversy has yet bested the other, and this remains probably the most obstreperous of philosophy's problem children. There is at least a possibility that the development of psychology may permit this age-old question finally to be settled. If so, it would be a happy day for mother philosophy, since it would again prove her contention that not all her brood are incorrigibles. Certainly philosophy would be happy to be rid of this problem, for none has caused so much turbulence.

The Ethical Field and Its Problems

The next major question with which the professional thinker must deal is the most practical of all the philosophical puzzles. One could conceivably write off the problems outlined thus far as having no pressing *practical* importance, however real and significant they may be as intellectual issues. But now we come to the most human, most intimate and perhaps most nagging of the great human problems: What is the good life? For those persons who shy away from any question which includes the term "good" lest they become involved in a debate on morals, the problem may be restated without any loss of cogency: What is the most important thing in life? Or (to use the form for which the author has a strong personal preference), What most makes life worth living?

The problem of the ultimate good, its nature and its relation to all values, constitutes one of the chief concerns of that subdivision of philosophy called *ethics*. It is probable that those chapters ahead which deal with ethical problems will prove the most interesting to a majority of readers. For example, is "happiness" the most important thing in life? If so, what is the relation of happiness to "pleasure"—the pursuit of which has traditionally been one of the mainsprings of human behavior. Could the realization of some sort of "perfection" be even more important than the attainment of happiness, or is "service" perhaps the ultimate good in life? And where do "duty" and "obligation" come in? What is the relation of each of these possible ethical ultimates to our lives as a whole, and what implications for daily living would each have should we select it as the *summum bonum* (highest good)?

It is evident that ethics is that branch of philosophy which is least likely to be accused of impracticality. For whatever we may think regarding the importance of such questions as, "Where do we come from?" or, "Where do we go?" the problem of what we should do meanwhile is completely practical. The question of what we should do with our days and what we should try to make of our lives is for all men the most inclusive and most fundamental of practical concerns. Perhaps only intellectuals can see value in speculating as to the nature of the ultimate real, but even the lowest "lowbrow" sometimes finds himself engaged in violent disputes concerning the nature of the good life and whether he ought to do this or that. If there can be no escape from philosophizing, it is doubly certain there is no release from the constant necessity of making ethical choices. The philosopher's chief contribution here is an insistence that these choices be as intelligent, as logical, and as satisfying as possible. The attempt to make them so constitutes the subject matter of *ethics*.

There are numerous other problems included in philosophy's large family, several of which are important enough to merit a separate chapter in the pages that follow. The problem of *truth* and the complex issues involved in *esthetics* will require particular attention, since these contain questions related to philosophy as a whole. It will be better, however, to postpone any mention of these until we are ready for a full consideration of their difficulties, as any brief introduction is likely to prove confusing instead of helpful to the reader.

The Goal of Philosophy

By now it must be apparent that the philosopher has set himself no simple task or modest goal. As Plato well said, he is the spectator of all time and existence. Taking all knowledge as his domain and all experience as his raw material, he aims at a synthesis from which no aspect of being, no fragment of thought, or no atom of reality, shall be missing. Everything in the universe which enters into human experience thereby also enters into philosophy. Whatever we undergo, whatever affects us, whatever makes any mark upon our consciousness is of concern to the philosopher. He can accept no ideal less than that of a total and completely unified picture of reality, and by reality he usually means the sum of all experience—past, present, future, actual and potential. Everything, everywhere, and whenever it occurs, is grist to the philosopher's mental mill.

The question of how far the human mind can go in the attainment of such a tremendous ideal must wait for subsequent chapters. At this point it will be enough to say that the philosopher is acutely aware that as yet it is only an unrealized ideal. Furthermore, it will be well to admit frankly that there are many modern thinkers who believe this goal unattainable. A large part of contemporary philosophical activity is centered on the question, What are the capacities of the mind, and exactly where do the limits of human knowledge lie? But in spite of these modern doubts concerning the ability of the mind to reach such a goal as the philosopher has traditionally set for himself, it still remains an ideal. Certainly the desire for more inclusive knowledge and increased understanding is the mainspring of every genuine philosopher's being.

Philosophy as a Universal Human Activity. From this attempt to think logically about our experience as a whole and to make it as intelligible as possible, there can be no escape. Individuals will vary as to the degree of intelligibility they seek in the welter of daily experience, but to find life tolerable we each must be able to discover *some* order and coherence in the raw material that pours into our consciousness hour by hour as life is lived through. All of us, even the least educated or the most simple-minded, are of necessity engaged in a ceaseless effort to find meaning behind apparent meaninglessness, to discover unity beneath surface diversity, and (above all) to impose some degree of order on the seeming chaos of our personal experience. Much of this effort may be unconscious or unarticulated, but we cannot escape making it. Regardless of our age, our occupation, our education, or even the civilization in which we live, this constitutes the irreducible minimum of intellectual activity on the human level of existence.

And this is exactly what the philosopher is also doing. If, as is widely believed, philosophy represents the maximum of intellectual activity, we have to conclude that both the indispensable minimum and the probable maximum of human thought are concerned with the same task: the discovery of order and meaning in the moment-by-moment flow of our experience. The chief difference between these two intellectual levels has already been suggested. The philosopher is consciously engaged in a full-time activity, while most minds are unconsciously engaged in a spasmodic activity. Both, however, are journeying on the same road. The full-time traveler naturally goes farther and sees much more along the way, but the two inescapably remain fellow travelers. Whether we will or not, we must as human beings all travel the road. How far we go, how much we discover en route, will depend on our intelligence, our temperament, and our education. From some sort of a journey, however, there can be no escape.

In the pages that lie ahead we shall not attempt to impose upon the student any particular set of answers to these great problems of the philosophical world. Instead we shall try at all times to give the most adequate summary possible of the chief answers that have been formulated by the numerous schools and their individual leaders, to the end that the reader may be aided in organizing his own views and experiences into a more coherent and more satisfying whole. It cannot be promised that answers to all the ultimate questions will be found in the succeeding chapters, but it is probable that the thoughtful student will at least find new light cast on these difficult problems. Even more important is the possibility that he may find here raw material which will contribute substantially toward the formulation of a philosophical viewpoint of his own.

CHAPTER 2

PHILOSOPHY AND
ITS NEIGHBORS

A T THIS POINT IN OUR STUDY THE READER IS PROBABLY SOMEWHAT
puzzled concerning the relations existing between philosophy
and some of the other fields of thought. It is probable that
several of the definitions we have given suggest that philosophy overlaps and even duplicates the work of at least two of its neighbors,
science and religion. For is not science concerned primarily with the
nature of physical reality and the structure of the universe? Are not
physics, chemistry, astronomy, and geology occupied with just these questions? And have they not given us reasonably full and definite answers?
What more can the philosopher do—what more can he want? As to the
all-important questions concerning the role of man in the universe and
the meaning of our experience, what purpose does religion have except
to provide us with answers? Here again, what excuse is there for the
philosopher and his work?

After the preliminary definition of philosophy which we have just
been through, probably the best means of gaining a further understanding of the field will be to approach it negatively and make clear what
philosophy is *not*. Acknowledging that the field has very important relations to both science and religion, and that it is striving for the same type
of basic answers which they seek, the differences among the three fields
are nevertheless more fundamental than their similarities. If we can gain
an insight into these differences of both aim and method, we shall have
come quite a way toward understanding both the spirit and the content
of philosophy.

Like all fields of human activity, philosophy has intimate relations with some of its neighbors and only slight contact with others. Its closest relations are with science on the one hand and religion on the other. Less intimate affiliations exist between philosophy, art, and literature, although as we have already seen there is no sphere of activity and no field of thought that is totally foreign to the philosophical quest. Everything contributes to this quest, and science and religion are singled out for special discussion in connection with philosophy only because of their relatively greater importance to it. Also it is with these two adjacent fields that the domain of the philosopher is most frequently confused. This confusion is natural, since in philosophy we are dealing with much of the same subject matter that they work with. Then too the specific problems of the three fields overlap considerably, and their vocabularies are common to a large extent. But however natural this confusion may be, it is nevertheless important to any understanding of philosophy that we eliminate it from our thinking. Its results have been particularly serious in the relations between philosophy and religion, with which we shall begin our discussion.

Philosophy and Religion

One of the most serious handicaps that the philosophical thinker labored under for centuries was the idea that philosophy and religion, because of a partial overlapping of subject matter, were intellectual Siamese twins, neither of which could go anywhere without the other. Such a linkage was particularly irritating to the philosophical twin, since religion was usually in a position of dominant authority and therefore able to set both the speed and the direction of any progress. During most of the medieval period, for example, the official relation between philosophy and religion was summed up in the freedom granted to the philosopher to reach any conclusions his intellectual activities might suggest—providing these conclusions did not oppose those of revelation and sacred theology. Probably few medieval thinkers found this restriction as galling as most philosophers would today, but it was obviously not intellectual freedom as we now understand the term. While the domination of religion over philosophy has not always been as complete as it was in the Middle Ages, the church (in both Catholic and Protestant branches) has during most of its long history been unwilling to allow speculative thinking to move freely over the whole geography of thought. If nothing else, the church has usually wanted to issue the passports for making such intellectual journeys and thus hold the power to decide who should be allowed philosophical travel. It has been less than two centuries, even in liberal democratic nations, since philosophy was able to struggle free from such bonds, and in some areas the freedom has come within the memory of men still living. Since this independence has been hard won, it is logical that philosophers as a group should consider it the most basic of intellectual civil liberties and should regard it as worth maintaining at any cost.

The Difficulty of Maintaining Independence. While philosophy has finally attained a position where it can refuse to acknowledge any duty to religion, or submit to any subordinate status under it, there have been moments when it looked as though the philosopher had jumped from the frying pan into the fire. In his struggle to free himself from religious domination, he has naturally aligned himself with the scientist, who had been through a comparable experience in achieving his own independence. Further, the magnificent development of science during the period when philosophy was fighting for its independence sometimes awed the philosopher unduly, and on occasion he tended to tie his thinking too closely to the tail of science's kite. We shall have more to say regarding this potential subordination of philosophy to science in our next chapter. But however real that danger may be, historically the chief problem has been to keep philosophical speculation unhampered by theological restrictions. We shall therefore begin our analysis of the affiliations between philosophy and its neighbors with a consideration of its relations with religion.

The Differences Between Philosophy and Religion

THE FIRST DIFFERENCE: SUBJECT MATTER

Like religion, philosophy is concerned with formulating answers to certain ultimate questions. Those questions which the two fields most clearly have in common are the origin and destiny of man, his relation to the universe in which he lives, the nature of God, man's relation to God, the immortality of the soul, the freedom of the will, and human conduct in relation to human happiness. Such a community of subject matter as these great problems represent would in itself be enough to make the two fields partially overlap. However, there are at least four things that far more definitely separate the two. In the first place, while much of their subject matter is in common, much of it is also different. Philosophy, for instance, goes deeply into the problem of the mind's capacity to deal adequately with its experience. Religion usually solves this problem by assuming two sources of knowledge, reason and faith, and does not analyze the capacities of either in any such thorough fashion as philosophy does. Again, philosophy is more occupied with scientific and semiscientific problems, such as the origin and history of the physical universe, its laws and general structure, the origin and evolution of life, the nature of causality, and so on. In general, the scope of the philosopher's activity is broader than that of the religionist, and consequently the problems which he treats cover a much wider range. It would be a fair statement to say that while the two begin with many of the same problems, it is probable that long after the religious thinker has found satisfactory answers the philosopher will be found fighting doggedly on to what he considers "more adequate solutions" to the same questions. By these he means more precise and more comprehensive answers, and philosophy is thus inclined to regard religious minds as prone to accept too easy solutions. Finally, it is likely that at any moment we discover a philosopher at work, he will be struggling with some problem which concerns the theologian only indirectly, if at all. This is to say, in general, philosophy runs well beyond theology both in its scope and in its analysis of whatever problem is under consideration.

THE SECOND DIFFERENCE: METHODS

The second differentiation between the two fields is related to the first. This concerns the methods which each employs. As we have just seen, religion is willing to accept certain propositions as objects of belief —that is, on faith—while philosophy is not. Without being sidetracked into a discussion of the logic or psychology of belief, it will be well to indicate briefly what "faith" means as the term is ordinarily employed in both religious and philosophical circles. In its usual denotation, it indicates the acceptance of a statement or doctrine as containing a truth that is not derived from either sensory sources or rational processes. Ordinarily the doctrine is considered to have a divine or supernatural origin of some kind; it is the result of "revelation," which in turn indicates any means whatever whereby men receive direct communication from the supernatural world. This source may be a book (for example, the Bible), prophetic utterances, or mystical experiences of some sort. Inevitably, however, the immediate source of the revelation is some human being, and his adequacy as the channel of communication between the divine and the merely human is also taken on faith.

It is of course true that the religious thinker employs logic and reason with excellent effect in elaborating the structure of religious thought, but they are used in an effort to add the proofs of *reason* to what he, in common with all believing persons, accepts on *faith*. In most religious thought, if a conflict or contradiction arises between the revelations of "faith" and the fruits of "reason," the latter are subordinated to the former, and the conclusions of intelligence may give way to the satisfactions which faith can give. In philosophy, on the contrary, reason and logic have the predominant role. The philosopher is quite willing (and even anxious) to formulate a world-view which will satisfy the demands of both the head and the heart; if the demands of one *must* be sacrificed, it is more likely to be the longings of the heart.

Philosophy and Reason. All this is to say that the passion of the philosopher is to *know*, regardless of the cost. If his search for knowledge and understanding yields an interpretation of experience which parallels that of most religions, well and good. But if his reasoning leads with inescapable logic to a world-view in which our lives have only such purpose and value as we can realize by our own efforts in a universe that is both unaware of our existence and indifferent to our happiness, so be it. The philosopher makes every effort to follow intelligence to whatever conclusion it leads. As far as is humanly possible, he strives to emulate the scientist and ignore the promptings of his emotions while searching for truth. Bertrand Russell has said that "the kernel of the scientific outlook is the refusal to regard our own desires, tastes, and interests as affording a key to the understanding of the world."[1] While the philosopher does not always achieve this rigorous ideal as completely as the scientist must, nevertheless his devotion to it as an ideal serves to differentiate his

[1] Bertrand Russell, "Science and Culture" in *Mysticism and Logic,* p. 42.

activity from that of the religious thinker. The author recalls once hearing a well-intentioned elderly lady ask a very tough-minded philosopher, "But can't you *reason* yourself into such a belief?" His reply was instantaneous: "Don't you mean, can't I *rationalize* myself into it?" meaning thereby doing just what both the scientist and the philosopher try hardest not to do—namely, allow his emotions, his natural human wish to live in a friendly, purposeful universe, to influence the conclusions toward which his reasoning was tending. Whatever other satisfactions life may yield to the philosopher, *intellectual* satisfaction he must have before all else. While some persons feel that any thinker who places the satisfactions of the head higher than those of the heart is scarcely human, the philosopher cannot feel that any other attitude is worthy of a thinking being.

There is an episode in one of the ancient Greek tragedies that may give insight as to the nature of this philosophical quest. Ajax, one of the not-too-bright heroes of the Greek army in their long war against the Trojans, returns home after the fall of Troy, glorying in and bragging of his exploits on the field of battle. Finally, even the tolerant Olympian deities become tired of his boastings and contrive for him a suitable punishment. One day they momentarily deprive him of his reason so that he is impelled to attack a flock of sheep, many of whom he slaughters under the delusion that he is still battling the Trojans. When he recovers his senses, he has become the laughingstock of Greece. Ajax, the great warrior, now occupies himself with slaughtering sheep! For a person of such abounding ego-drive as this ex-hero, the laughter is intolerable. After much brooding over his situation, he resolves on suicide—the conventional solution to such a problem. Unsheathing his now dishonored sword, he pauses for a final moment to try to understand what has happened to him that his heroic stature should be so pitiably reduced. Just before he falls upon his weapon he cries out to the avenging gods, "Light! Light! if only to die in!" In that final moment of his life, Ajax rose to the plane on which the philosopher tries to live at all times: the passion to know transcended all other passions, and he felt that death would be less degrading and bitter if it could be accompanied by understanding.

Contrast with the Religious Attitude. Religion can offer no parallel to this attitude of philosophy. The primary purpose of virtually every religion is to give its followers a sense of peace and harmony. It can do this best by postulating a universe in which the individual has purpose and value, and in which his life has meaning for something or someone beside himself and his immediate associates. If the religionist cannot find rational grounds for such a belief, then reason is made subordinate and faith is invoked to supply the lacking conviction. As much as the philosopher requires *intellectual* satisfaction, the religious person demands *emotional* satisfaction. Each type of mind is usually puzzled that the other can be content with such a standard of satisfaction, and each is likely to find the other party a person to be viewed askance.

THE THIRD DIFFERENCE: INITIAL ASSUMPTIONS

The next factor which serves to differentiate these great fields follows closely the two we have just described. This is the amount of assumption that each makes before beginning its intellectual operations. This includes assumptions, postulates, and presuppositions of all kinds. In philosophy, for example, much effort is made to avoid assuming anything more than absolutely necessary, while hidden or unconscious assumptions are guarded against even more scrupulously. The philosopher feels that the presence of unacknowledged assumptions is one of the greatest hindrances to clear thinking and he therefore consistently strives to purge his own thought of any trace of them.

The Problem of God as an Example. Let us take as an example the contrasting attitude of the two fields toward the problem of God. The theologian may devote volumes to discussing the nature of God, His relations to the universe and the individual human soul, etc. But however long the discussion, and however subtle the analysis of the God idea, it is predicated upon the assumption that God exists. Even when the theological analysis includes the so-called rational proofs of God's existence, there is always present an emotional conviction of that existence which is far more fundamental than any reasoned demonstration. For the religious thinker, whatever God may or may not be, however personal or impersonal He may be, and whatever His role in human affairs, one thing at least is sure: He *is*. He somehow and somewhere *exists*. Most theologians are free to admit that God, as an existent Being, is the assumption that lies behind all their thinking. The ordinary religious person, however, is seldom aware that he is unconsciously taking the existence of God as an assumed fact in any thinking he does upon the subject. In short, while the theologian usually acknowledges his basic assumption, the less educated religious mind rarely does.

Philosophy's Attitude of Detachment. In contrast to both levels of religious thought, the attitude of the philosopher is one of detachment and pure speculation. He regards the whole question of God, both His existence and His nature, as wide open. In philosophy there are no "sacred matters" that cannot be disturbed. The metaphysician is no more awed to be dealing with the concept of a Supreme Being than with any other ultimate issue that perplexes the mind of man. One of the first things the student of philosophy learns is that the very existence of this field as a significant intellectual activity depends upon the right to question any idea, concept, value, law, activity or institution within human experience. As is sometimes said humorously, even God must present His credentials at the door of the philosophy classroom.

Now this more detached speculative attitude of philosophy makes it less likely that the philosopher's conclusions will contain hidden assumptions. He checks and counterchecks his thinking frequently to make certain that some unacknowledged postulate, some presupposition, has not crept in during an unguarded moment. Ideally, he begins his thinking with no more assumptions than are absolutely necessary to carry on such intellectual activity. He would be happy if he could reduce these assumptions to two or three, such as his own existence, the existence of the external world, and the existence of some sort of knowing or experiencing relation between these two. Whether every philosopher can honestly claim that his mental baggage was originally reduced to these irreducibles is doubtful, but he can usually claim that he has made a conscious effort to acknowledge all assumptions—including even such indispensable ones as these.

Philosophy and the "Self-evident Truths" of Religion. As with God, so with the other postulates upon which any system of religious thought is built. Many religions, for instance, begin their theological structure with certain "self-evident truths." These usually concern not only the existence of God, but His omnipotence, omniscience, omnipresence, omnibenevolence, His role as creator of the universe, etc. For the believer, positive propositions concerning all of these may seem too obviously true to require proof; they appear to be "self-evident." But not to the philosopher. To him the word "self-evident" is a challenge. Immediately he sees or hears the term, he is inclined to say, "Hold on there! 'Self-evident' is not an adjective to be applied lightly. What do you really mean by it, and to whom is your statement supposed to be so obviously true as to require no proof?" Then there usually follows a comparison of the statement in question with some of the classic examples of self-evidence, such as are found in the axioms that underlie Euclid's geometry. From there the discussion moves naturally to an inquiry such as modern mathematical thinkers sometimes undertake concerning the actual self-evidence of even these classic examples. This may lead logically to an analysis of the whole concept of self-evidence, its importance as a source of knowledge, its relation to the problem of proof, and the like. But by this time the religious thinker has undoubtedly turned to what he considers more fruitful speculation, satisfied that there are enough individuals who will accept his "self-evident" propositions as really self-evident to make discourse possible.

THE FOURTH DIFFERENCE: GOALS SOUGHT

The last major difference between philosophy and religion lies in their goal or ultimate purpose. This naturally influences both the mental attitude with which their practitioners begin activity and the methods they employ. We have already suggested that the primary passion of the philosopher is to *know*, with little regard to the cost of achieving that knowledge, and with even less concern whether or not it harmonizes with his deep-seated human hopes and aspirations. On the other hand, we have suggested that the primary aim of religion is to give a sense of peace and assurance which "the world cannot give nor take away." Thus it is apparent that religion has a more practical intent than has philosophy— at least more immediately practical. It is also evident that religion will probably be important in the lives of far more people than philosophy can ever touch. Those who spend their lives in philosophical activity are always quick to insist that the urge to know is as fundamental a drive in man as the desire for peace and spiritual security. But while the two drives may be equally fundamental, it does not follow that they are equally strong in all men. To most persons the promise which religion holds out is much more attractive. They feel they must have an assurance that life is worth living, and they believe religion can give this to them more easily than its rival can. For if philosophy can offer such an assurance, it is usually only as the result of much rigorous thinking.

In sum, although the philosopher may utilize his metaphysical speculations in the formulation of a workable philosophy of life (and thus achieve the same "practical" result as the religionist), most people realize that philosophy is more concerned with theory than with practice. They suspect that the philosopher would continue his speculations just as doggedly whether or not they ever led to practical conclusions—or in fact to *any* conclusions. The primary purpose of the religious thinker, on the other hand, however theological and abstract his thought may become at times, always remains to provide an intellectual background for an exceedingly practical pursuit: the attainment of spiritual peace and emotional security.

Philosophy and Science

The relations between philosophy and its other great neighbor have in general been more harmonious and cooperative than those with religion. In spite of occasional mutual chidings and mild family arguments, philosophy and science have lived together as a mother and her brilliant son. Both have been guilty of dogmatism in unguarded moments, and like all sons, science has on occasion taken the parent to task for old-fashioned ways and ideas, or for interfering with the independent life of a younger generation. Philosophy has reciprocated by criticizing many of the assumptions and intellectual tools of science. Further, she has worried much lest her son in youthful enthusiasm make the mistake of "throwing the baby out with the bath-water" by considering as unimportant (or even unreal) all those aspects of human experience that cannot be studied in the laboratory. In general, however, the relation between the two has been one of mutual respect. This has been even more apparent since the reaction against German absolute idealism, when philosophy herself was forced to admit the mistake of trying to engage in metaphysical speculation independently of science. Since the parent has acknowledged any former error on this point, the son has regained the respect that was temporarily lost. Now, while she must draw heavily upon him for her sustenance, he is loyal enough not to complain—provided, of course, that she acknowledge the source of her income, and not try to live beyond it by claiming scientific authority for unproved theories or purely philosophical speculations.

Dual Relation Between the Two Fields. Speaking more technically, the relation between the two fields is a dual one. In our opening chapter we discussed the twin activities of philosophy as a whole, and indicated that the work of the philosopher consists of both *analysis* and *synthesis*. It is in relation to science that these complementary philosophical functions have become most clearly separated, and it is in large part the development in science that has made the analytic activity of philosophy predominant in recent years. Furthermore, it is this analysis that brings the two fields closest together and engenders the greatest amount of mutual respect. However, as this more intimate analytical function is also more technical and less directly related to the intellectual experience of most students, we will be wise to look first at the synthesizing operations of philosophy. Since this is also the more traditional philosophic activity, by beginning our consideration with it we shall be following the general history of thought.

Science as Specialization

When what we now call "the sciences" first began to leave the parental roof of philosophy and set forth to establish a life of their own, the well-marked divisions now existing were unknown. Even the term "science" did not exist. Instead, the vague, embryonic studies were lumped together as "natural philosophy." The first workers within this field were too busy attacking specific problems to worry about its eventual boundaries or to realize that there might be overlapping claims to certain parts of the unmapped domain. The situation was similar to that of the pioneers on the American frontier, where the first settlers were too busy chopping down individual trees to be concerned with the size of the forest, and too occupied working some small part of their claim to be disturbed if a neighbor felled a few trees on the farther fringe. It was only as the various parts of the scientific domain became at least roughly cultivated that the divisions we now have began to arise. Several lines of natural cleavage appeared, particularly around the common distinction between the "physical" and the "biological" sciences. Later the social studies developed and claimed the right also to call themselves sciences, so that at present there are few of man's intellectual activities that do not show the influence, if not the essential organization, of the scientific point of view.

This breaking up of "natural philosophy" into many semi-independent fields has brought many gains and some losses. The division itself was inevitable. In the late fifteenth century it was possible for a universal genius like Leonardo da Vinci to know well nearly all the sciences of his day and do original work in several of these. Even at the end of the eighteenth century Goethe could do work in several unrelated sciences, besides being an excellent statesman and the foremost poet of his nation. Such intellectual scope is now practically impossible. Each of the divisions of science, and even many of the subdivisions, has grown so complex and detailed that years of study are required to master any one of them. To make any original contribution to the field usually demands singleness of purpose maintained through a lifetime, plus a degree of specialization hardly conceivable to persons outside the laboratory. In modern times specialization has become the first law of scientific advancement.

Even when the scientist is working toward some inclusive generalization that will synthesize research done by many different minds, it is almost inevitable that the crucial experiments and special techniques required to establish this new generalization will represent a sharply focused attention upon increasingly diminished areas of nature. In fact the critical experiment which usually serves to verify any new hypothesis normally represents a more specialized and detailed control and manipulation of some particular process than has hithertofore been attempted.

An Example from Early Physics. A good example of this concentrated specialization is found in the work of Galileo as he was founding the science of dynamics around 1600. Prior to his experiments it was believed that all physical bodies are intrinsically light or heavy, and that the speed of their rise or fall depends upon this intrinsic weight, since it was assumed that objects "seek their natural places" with a power proportional to whatever intrinsic lightness or heaviness they possess.[2] However, Galileo had outgrown this vague and misleading Aristotelian physics, and was groping for a more exact formulation of the laws of falling bodies. Moreover he was seeking a statement which would not attempt to answer the question *why* bodies fall (such as previous philosophers had sought) but would instead state with certainty and precision *how* they fall.

[2] Cf. Dampier, *A History of Science*, p. 143. I have drawn the general outline of Galileo's experiment from this same source.

He knew that a falling body moves through space at a constantly increasing speed, hence the real problem was to determine the *rate* of this increase, particularly in relation to the other factors involved. After one false start (on the basis of a common-sense hypothesis that the speed increases in proportion to the distance fallen) he hit upon the idea that the speed increases with the *time* of the fall (rather than the *distance*). The next step was that which follows the formulation of any scientific hypothesis: deduce the consequences that may be expected to follow if the hypothesis is correct, and then (as the third step in scientific experimentation) work out experiments that give definite results which can be compared with those previously deduced. Galileo soon discovered that experiments with bodies falling freely were useless, since the speeds were too great to be measured by such instruments as then existed. This speed had to be reduced to a point that would permit accurate measurement, and the idea of motion on an inclined plane naturally suggested itself. However, apparently Galileo did considerable calculating and experimenting to convince himself that the laws of velocity for balls rolling down a slope were the same as those for bodies falling free the same vertical height. Once he was convinced of this identity he could plunge into his experiments without reservations. His results checked with those derived by deduction from his hypothesis (that the speed of a falling body is proportional to the time of the fall), thus proving the hypothesis.

These famous experiments marked the beginning of modern scientific method, and pointed the direction experimentation has moved ever since. More interesting for our purpose in this chapter, they revealed that Galileo had realized what every modern scientist knows, the necessity for concentrating his research by working out special and carefully delimited problems in a complete and methodical way.[3]

An Example from Modern Physics. Our second example of the scientist as a specialist concentrating on one particular and strictly limited problem likewise comes from physics. This time we turn to more recent work, carried on during a fifty-year period ending in 1933. The experimenter is A. A. Michelson, one of the world's great authorities on optics and the physics of light, who is particularly noted for his invention of the interferometer and his efforts to prove or disprove the existence of some luminiferous medium such as the ether postulated by some scientists.

Michelson's abiding interest centered in the problem of accurate de-

[3] *Cf.* Dampier, *op. cit.,* p. 141.

termination of the speed of light, and both his first and last experiments, performed more than half a century apart, were devoted to the matter.[4] Because the velocity of light is one of the most basic constants in nature, physicists have for several centuries sought to determine this speed with precision. The first measurement was made in 1675, but through astronomical observations only, so the problem of a terrestrial method for verifying or refining the original measurement (186,000 miles per second) remained. Various nineteenth-century experimenters set up systems of revolving mirrors and intermittent light sources, but the variations in result—ranging from 185,150 to 195,344 miles per second—showed that more accurate methods were needed. Michelson first worked out an improved arrangement for such measurement when he was only twenty-five years old, and came up with a somewhat refined figure (186,508) which he felt he could guarantee to be correct within .0001%. As in the other nineteenth-century experiments on the problem, the distance over which he did his measuring was comparatively short, the two mirrors being only 500 feet apart.

Some forty years later Michelson returned to the problem, this time working on a much larger scale. His two points were mountain peaks in Southern California twenty-two miles apart. The five separate trials gave an average quite close to his earlier figure, but the variation in the several readings prompted him to extend the distance even farther in a hope of still greater accuracy. Consequently he next picked out two peaks eighty-two miles apart. However, a difficulty which had been minor over the shorter distance, smoke and haze in the atmosphere, proved extremely serious over the eighty-two miles, so the experiment had to be abandoned.

When nearly eighty years old and in failing health Michelson attacked the problem for a final time. In this case he abandoned the long-distance method and sought for greater precision by performing the experiment in a vacuum. An air-tight mile-long metal tube three feet in diameter was built with special pumps for creating a vacuum in such a large container. Research was carried on with this device for three years (even after Michelson's death in 1931), and an average for the 2,885 determinations gave a speed for light of 186,264 miles per second. It is generally

---

4 *Cf.* Bernard Jaffe, *Men of Science in America*, pp. 360 ff., from which I have drawn the material for this example.

agreed among physicists that "this figure will probably stand for years as one of the soundest constants in physical science."[5]

One thing of interest in this example for our present purpose is the way in which greater and greater accuracy was sought through a variety of techniques, and finally through the virtual elimination of what had hithertofore been an uncontrollable factor, the condition of the atmosphere. It is even more important to note that, although what was sought was a constant which would constitute a basic measuring stick for all physical science, the actual problem of determining this constant was a very limited and highly specialized one, in which both the general interests of science and the particular interests of the different special sciences involved had to be temporarily ignored. While philosophy likewise has its particular technical problems, in the solution of which broad interests of the field have to be similarly ignored, this specialized concentration upon a rigorously limited problem is far more characteristic of science than of philosophy. For, as we shall see shortly, the philosopher has always been primarily concerned with general problems and inclusive issues, and specific or limited technical questions have been subordinated as means to these larger ends.

The Losses from Specialization. This excessive specialization required of most scientific workers has naturally tempted the scientist to ignore many practical concerns and social activities. In addition it has imposed a severe restriction upon the time and energy and eyesight which the worker can give to keeping abreast of the developments within departments of scientific activity other than his own. Even where the departments lie adjacent to that in which he works, or chance to be divisions in which he has a genuine interest, the restriction is unavoidable. Specialization and still greater specialization appears to be the price the great majority of scientific workers must pay for achievement within their chosen field. While hybrid divisions exist, such as astrophysics, psychophysics and biochemistry, even these apparent exceptions to the trend towards specialization usually only involve a greater degree of concentration within a slightly broader area, rather than any general synthesis of the two fields concerned. The workers within any of these hybrid areas are largely occupied with specific problems that require specialized backgrounds; outside of the two fields included they are necessarily as restricted as any group of scientific workers. The popular quip that science

[5] Jaffe, *op. cit.*, p. 380.

is the process of learning more and more about less and less has a great deal of truth in it.

In recent years it has become commonplace for humanists, advocates of liberal education and thoughtful men in general to decry such specialization on the grounds that it threatens many of the values created by civilization. Some thinkers, including some scientists, see in it a possible threat to civilization itself. Several reasons are given to justify these fears. There is first the fact that extreme specialization produces personalities which are less than whole men. The educational process required to produce scientific specialists is necessarily not a process favorable to creating broadly educated, all-round individuals. As a consequence, the scientist or technician is likely to be "trained" rather than "educated" in the sense of being prepared for living in the modern, complex world, particularly the world of people and their social problems. In view of the greater and greater role these scientists and technicians seem destined to play in national (and international) life, their narrowness of background and outlook constitutes an added threat to our whole civilization.

A second danger lies in the natural tendency for many scientists to believe that all human problems can be solved by the same methodologies they find so fruitful in their field. This does not mean that all scientists are materialists and mechanists seeking to reduce every occurrence in the universe (including man's activities) to physiochemical terms; it means rather that the specialized scientist is often inclined to believe that increased knowledge automatically resolves controversies and settles disputes. In the various sciences this is largely true, since here controversies generally arise from inadequate knowledge, which permits rival hypotheses and untested theories to do battle with one another in what amounts to a knowledge vacuum. However, in that vast area where most men live most of the time—the area of evaluation and choice-making—increased knowledge may contribute very little toward making our choices easier. As our knowledge grows, choices may in fact become increasingly difficult, since we are faced with more alternatives, or we become more aware of the ramifications and complexities involved in each decision. In short, one danger which the specialization of science may produce in its workers is a naïveté in other, nonscientific areas, particularly areas involving social action and ethico-political decisions.

And finally there is the danger that scientific specialization will produce personalities that are indifferent or unaware as regards human beings and their feelings. Such unawareness is often described as "treating people like they were machines," or "regarding people merely as physical objects." Of course other types of specialization—in fact excessive concentration in any field—may produce this blindness to human beings and their emotional needs. But in the scientist it seems particularly glaring when it occurs, since scientific workers as a class are clearly men of intelligence and good will. Unfortunately their training, while utilizing their intelligence to the full, may permit their natural social sensitivity to atrophy.

Philosophy as Generalization

If the statement that science is a process of learning more and more about less and less has considerable truth in it, then the converse statement—that philosophy is a process of learning less and less about more and more —is in many ways even truer. Where science works largely in terms of analysis and ever more detailed analysis, the essence of philosophy has traditionally been synthesis and always more inclusive synthesis. The ideal philosopher is as unspecialized in his interest and background as the scientist is specialized; breadth of interest is almost synonymous with the philosophical attitude. One of the prime prerequisites to fruitful metaphysical speculation is a mind whose range of intellectual activity is unlimited, and whose scope of knowledge is as inclusive as the limitations of human life will allow. On the other hand, insofar as it may distract the scientist from concentration upon specific problems, such a breadth of interest is likely to be a scientific liability.

Philosophy as the Complement of Science. It thus becomes clear that the primary relation between science and philosophy is a complementary one. Speaking from the viewpoint of the philosopher, one of his chief functions in the intellectual world is to counteract the specializing tendency of the scientist by a type of knowledge that is as broad as the scientist's is restricted. The two fields each give to the intellectual world at large precisely what the other lacks. More specifically, the philosopher occupies the position of intellectual receiver for all the findings of the several sciences. One of his most important functions in modern society is to pool all the facts and insights which the workers in the various fields may discover, but which they do not have the time (or perhaps the interest) to gather together into an organized system. Nor does the philosopher stop with the mere pooling of this knowledge. To change our figure, he resembles the jig-saw puzzle addict who would never be satisfied just to collect numerous pieces. He wants to put them together, partly for the satisfaction of accomplishment, but even more in order to see what sort of a pattern or picture they will make. The scientist is content (or more often, forced by the limitations of time and energy) to hack out the fragments of the total picture; at most, he puts together only a few of them to make up just part of the picture in one small corner of the whole. The philosopher is even more interested in the whole than in the fragments. He has such a passion to complete the total design that he will if necessary build around the gaps which science has not yet been able to fill, and thus by assumption, inference, and implication attempt to formulate a more complete picture of the "nature of things."

The Scientist's Attitude Toward Speculative Generalizations. As might be expected, the cautious scientific worker sometimes worries about this passion for completion which characterizes the metaphysical speculator. While the scientist admits philosophy's right to formulate a tentative total picture, he is afraid lest the enthusiastic speculator forget to indicate clearly where the solid pieces of fact end, and where the insubstantial pieces of unverified theory begin. He points out that the history of thought shows several instances of philosophers putting together pictures that were made up largely of theory-fragments, with just enough pieces of solid scientific fact to make the whole thing impressive and credible to persons who were not sufficiently critical to realize the clever though well-intended fraud involved. The scientist goes on to point out the tendency of uncritical minds to believe that, because there are some scientifically derived pieces in the picture, it therefore *as a whole* has the backing of scientific authority. This error naturally worries the scientific worker. It has usually made him shy of all metaphysical systems, since when they become discredited it appears to cast an unjustified shadow upon his own intellectual efforts and scientific integrity.

If it were only the public that is at fault in the matter, for failing to make a clear distinction between scientific fact and philosophic interpretations, the scientist would be more sympathetic towards the speculating philosopher. There is a suspicion in the scientific mind, however, that the fault lies not with the public so much as with the philosopher himself. It has sometimes been the philosopher who failed to keep the distinction clear in his own mind—not through intellectual dishonesty, of course, but as the result of something far more subtle and philosophically dangerous. For even the best of philosophers is still a human being, and therefore subject to the great human tendency to "read in" meanings that support his system. And even a lifetime of rigorous thought cannot always eliminate every trace of wishful thinking from philosophical speculation.

Science Discovers, Philosophy Interprets

Much of what we have said up to this point suggests that the ideal philosopher must be a person equipped with expert knowledge in each of the sciences. According to such a view, he would be essentially a superscientist who, needing to know everything that all the scientists know, must have in addition the traditional grounding in philosophy. Fortunately no such exhaustive training is required for fruitful thinking in this borderland between the two fields. It is necessary that the philosopher be thoroughly acquainted with both the principles and the results of each science, and that he have a sound knowledge of the logic and method of science in general. But it is not necessary that he know the special techniques employed by each science, nor the vast mass of data which they have accumulated. In short, his emphasis must be upon general results, rather than upon the detailed data leading to those results, and upon broad principles rather than upon specialized testing techniques. In addition to this general knowledge, it is always an advantage for the philosopher to have done work under laboratory conditions in at least one of the sciences, just as it is an advantage (but not a requirement) for the art critic to have done creative work in at least one artistic medium. At best, however, all that the most conscientious thinker can do concerning the sciences *en masse* is to skim off the cream as research workers milk the cow of nature. But even with this restriction, it is not unusual to encounter a philosopher who keeps up on what is happening in some branch of scientific endeavor better than do many of the laboratory workers in immediately adjacent or closely related fields.

Any philosophical pretensions to complete knowledge are of course out of the question; every speculative thinker is only too conscious that he is essentially a drone as far as the actual work of science is concerned. Nevertheless there are thinkers whose theories and sweeping views are built so solidly upon an intimate knowledge of scientific research, its problems and its results, that they merit (and usually receive) the respect of even those scientists who are most antagonistic to philosophical activity. For it is obvious that when a philosophic view is formulated upon a thorough understanding of the data of the various sciences, and (equally important) when the formulator has carefully distinguished between those facts and his devices for combining them into a coherent picture, the result can be nothing to which even the most critical-minded scientist could legitimately object.

There is another important reason why the scientist usually hesitates to criticize the habit of formulating inclusive speculative hypotheses: such general hypotheses have sometimes played a suggestive or directive role in the development of a science, particularly in its early stages. Since these hypotheses normally run beyond both past and present knowledge, and even perhaps beyond the possibility of any immediate experimental testing, speculations of this type are usually considered "philosophical" rather than "scientific," even if their content closely approximates that of a particular science.

There are various celebrated instances of philosophy playing this suggestive role in relation to science—for example, the mathematical-mechanistic concepts worked out by philosophers in the seventeenth century which helped prepare the ground for the work of men like Galileo and Newton. In the area of biological science, the idea of evolution was developed and applied to history long before it was applied to biology and geology. In fact, the evolutionary hypothesis was largely kept alive through the centuries by succeeding generations of philosophers, although most biological scientists rejected the theory right down to the time of Darwin's great work.

Of course no philosopher would pretend that all or even a large percentage of these speculative theories have been scientifically fruitful. As John Dewey has well said, there has been an overproduction of philosophical hypotheses on the far frontier of scientific knowledge.[6] But this waste or excess production has provided flexibility and freedom of move-

---

[6] See Dewey's article under "Philosophy" in the *Encyclopedia of the Social Sciences*. His general discussion of the relations between philosophy and science is particularly good.

ment in the advancement of science. The historical fact that from amid much philosophical chaff there has come a substantial harvest of ideas contributing to this advance of science has served to keep the scientist tolerant of the speculative mill which philosophers operate.

How Far Beyond Science Should Philosophy Go? There still remains the question of just how far the philosopher may go beyond the proven facts of scientific research, even when he frankly avows that he is running beyond the data available. In other words, how closely must the philosopher be restricted to his role of synthesizer pure and simple and how much dare he interpret those facts? It is sometimes said that the function of science is to *discover*, while that of philosophy is to *interpret*. In general this holds true, but there remains the problem of just how far the "interpretation" can go without becoming an independent viewpoint which no scientist (or group of scientists) would acknowledge as legitimately derived from the experimental evidence.

There is a tendency on the part of the scientists themselves to hold that *any* synthesis of scientific knowledge, even one involving no extraneous ideas or interpolated theories, is metaphysical in nature and therefore not strictly scientific. In recent years several well-known workers within the physical sciences have taken time out from their experiments to attempt just such formulations.[7] Most of their fellow scientists have remained unimpressed by such efforts, except to admit that if this synthesizing operation is to be attempted, it is probably safer to have a scientist-turned-philosopher doing the risky job than for a philosopher-turned-scientist to undertake it. Even under ideal circumstances, however, most men trained in the rigorous methods of the laboratory feel that there is always danger that speculations will creep in unacknowledged, or that inferences will become confused with facts.

The Caution of Science. The philosophers are of course delighted when some scientist risks the criticism of his colleagues to attempt such a synthesis, whether or not they are satisfied with the picture he puts together. Far from being jealous that a scientist should undertake what has been a traditional part of philosophy's work, the metaphysicians urge other workers in the various sciences to do the same thing. But it is not likely that there will be any overwhelming response. As we have already indicated, the average scientist lacks time, energy, and training for this

[7] Sir Arthur Eddington is probably the outstanding case, and *The Nature of the Physical World* his best example.

synthesizing activity. Even when he does have the necessary prerequisites, he is likely to agree with his fellow workers that such ambitious projects had better be left to philosophy. For the philosopher has a very different type of intellectual reputation to uphold; he is expected to be bold and speculative, and should he run beyond the data available in his speculations, no one will be too critical—except of course the scientist.

It is thus clear that the relations between science and philosophy-as-synthesizer are vague and shifting. In general, the scientist is not strongly sympathetic with this division of philosophical activity. In fact, if this were the only relation between the fields, philosophy would not be on much better terms with science than it has sometimes been with its other great neighbor, religion. Fortunately for neighborly relations, the other major activity of philosophy is regarded by the scientist as not only legitimate but important to the progress of his own field. Let us therefore turn to a brief consideration of philosophy in its role of analyst and critic.

The Analytical Function of Philosophy

This other basic relation between philosophy and science is far more technical than the one we have been discussing thus far. As concerns the everyday interrelations of both fields, however, it is of much greater importance, so it is necessary that we get at least some understanding of both the methods and the results involved. In discussing the synthesizing operations of philosophy as it deals with the findings of the laboratory, we have tried to convey the idea that while the philosopher works largely in terms of putting the pieces together, science is busily engaged in breaking down physical reality into smaller and smaller entities. It will therefore involve some mental adjustment as we turn to this second relation between the two fields, for now it is philosophy that performs the analysis, carrying the breaking-down process much farther than science does.

The Problem of Definition. This paradoxical situation occurs in the area of "definition" and "concept-formulation." This area is far more important in intellectual circles than one would ever suspect from merely reading the abstract terms that name it. Like any great field of thought, science (as well as each of the separate sciences) has numerous key terms by means of which it carries on its operations. These terms represent the fundamental concepts upon which the vast intellectual structure is built. The assumptions, axioms, postulates, and "general principles" of the field are all expressed in these terms, so it is not surprising that they should occur again and again whenever the discussion begins to get down to the bedrock underlying some particular corner of the scientific edifice. The most important examples in the realm of general science are *matter, energy, force, time, space, law, order,* and (most important of all) *cause.* Anyone who has read even an elementary text in high-school physics or chemistry will recall how frequently these terms appeared. They are so fundamental in science, and their use so characteristic of that field, that it is certain that any educated reader would know immediately from a glance at the list that the discussion was scientific in nature.

Philosophy's Chief Contribution to Science. Philosophy long ago discovered that everybody in science used these terms, and therefore presumably knew what they meant. Unfortunately it was often evident that they did not always mean the same thing, even when the same person used them at different times. Consequently the philosopher began to wonder just how much objective "truth" a field could claim for its discoveries if the key terms used in making them possessed no standard meanings. In spite of the great intellectual rigor of science its terminological precision has not always been comparable. The situation here has been much the same as in ordinary discourse, where we usually assume that all parties involved are employing the terms and concepts in the same way— that is, we proceed as though everyone had agreed on the exact definition of these before the discussion started. It generally takes an argument to reveal that this is not the case; only after a certain amount of wrangling and perhaps some heated name-calling do the parties agree to start over again by defining terms and clarifying concepts.

Each of the sciences has its key concepts and basic presuppositions which are taken pretty much for granted by those persons working in that field. In addition all the sciences assume, largely without question, the adequacy of our minds to secure reliable knowledge—at least through the methodologies of science. The scientist as such does not question deeply either the limits or the validity of human knowledge, and only rarely does a scientific worker ask the question which philosophy considers most basic in this whole area: What is scientific knowledge really knowledge *of*— that is, what do we actually have when we attain such knowledge? Is it a picture of reality, a facsimile representation of nature as it is, independent of human observers? Or, on the contrary, do we inevitably get only some approximation of a representation which is necessarily distorted by man's sensory apparatus and nerve structure, and ineradicably oriented toward our interests as biological creatures trying to survive and adapt in a particular environment?

If the thoughtful scientist does become aware of the problems of knowledge—that is, if he advances beyond the common-sense but philosophically naive position of taking our minds and their knowledge-gathering abilities for granted—he is likely to move to the equally uncritical position of assuming that all epistemological problems (problems concerning the nature, the limits, and the validity of knowledge) can be solved. He is likely to believe that a little analysis of the knowledge situation, plus a little patience and good will on the part of everyone interested in the problem, will quickly resolve the difficulty. The philosopher, however, acquainted with the centuries of analysis and criticism and controversy which have centered on the problems of knowing, cannot rest content with this easy assumption. The claim to know what is real and what is true may be made by any of the sciences, but philosophy has discovered that this claim, if it is to be allowed at all, can be made only after searching analysis of the human mind and its whole knowledge-seeking process.

Thus, there has grown up what is undoubtedly philosophy's greatest service to science: a critical analysis and occasional refinement of the intellectual tools of the field. While the scientist has sometimes argued in defense of his own particular use of a conceptual tool, he has in general been grateful for the analysis. There has been an increasing tendency for the scientist to hand over this chore to his analytic friend willingly, acknowledging that it will be in experienced hands. For the philosopher has had long experience in dealing with conceptual terms—indeed, he seldom works with anything else—and he is therefore in a position to undertake such analysis as something of an expert.

In a later chapter, when we consider the biological sciences in general and the theory of evolution in particular, at least two of these key concepts of science ("life," "evolution") will be analyzed fully. Until we reach that point in our presentation, it will be better not to attempt an example of the analytic process. Any instance we might give at this time would almost certainly miss its mark: to the student well-grounded in science, it would probably seem pointlessly simple; to the student lacking any scientific background, it would probably appear so abstract as to be meaningless. However, there is no likelihood of any reader completing this book without understanding what we mean when we speak of the philosopher as a supercritic or superanalyst. Beginning with our next chapter we shall be carrying on such analyses throughout the book, while the final section on God and immortality will be exclusively analytical in character. It is enough at present if we have some idea of the two contrasting functions which philosophy performs in relation to science. Those pages lying ahead of us that touch on the common problems of philosophy and its two principal neighbors will inevitably amplify and clarify this contrast.

CHAPTER 3

IDEALISM:

The World Is Friendly

B Y NOW THE READER IS UNDOUBTEDLY AWARE THAT PHILOSOPHY IS not a simple subject. He has discovered that when a problem appears almost solved, new ramifications of it crop up, these lead immediately into other hitherto unsuspected problems, which in turn lead to still others. The philosopher has been described as "the man who always asks the next question"; he is the killjoy who always spikes a potential solution with "Yes, but . . ." or "Or on the other hand, . . ." or "True, but doesn't that imply . . ." Philosophy is indeed a complex subject, probably far more so than the reader can imagine. We could at this point pervert Hamlet's famous statement, "There are more things in heaven and earth, Horatio, than are dreamt of in your philosophy" into "There are more things in philosophy than are dreamt of" by most beginning students. As that general study or science that seeks to include and summarize all other studies and sciences, philosophy can hardly escape complexity.

If we are to gain an oriented insight into the richness and complexity of the subject, some drastic preliminary simplifications will be necessary. We must risk doing violence to philosophy by ignoring differences and skipping over distinctions until only the indispensable rudiments of classification are left. For we are now ready to plunge into the vast and turbulent sea of philosophical "schools." Thus far we have avoided making more references than are absolutely necessary to the existence of this stormy sea on whose shore we have been chatting. But now the roar of clashing waves and currents of thought has become too insistent and such aloofness to their strife can no longer be maintained.

The History of Philosophy as the Conflict Between Two Great Thought Currents. This chapter and the next represent an attempt to achieve a simplified bird's-eye view of philosophy. Like all extreme simplifications, this will mean the elimination of many distinctions and the blurring of boundaries between minor schools. These can be added later as they are needed. At present it will be enough if the basic opposition between the two major metaphysical movements can be grasped clearly and permanently. In other words, the picture we shall get as we look down from our elevation will resemble a map of the oceans on which are indicated the main flows, such as the Gulf Stream and the Japanese Current. The cartographer makes no attempt to show each variation in the average, year-round movement; even where two main currents meet, the map depicts this union as smooth and apparently effortless. The whorls and eddies that result from such a junction are indicated only slightly or else ignored completely. If we sailed that ocean, however, our impression would be of something quite unlike the beautiful smooth curves of the map maker. We would be too conscious of the surface appearance of the sea to believe that there could be any deep, unchanging direction to the movement here. Where the map maker and the oceanographer show smooth simplicity, we would find clashing complexity. Yet, each would be right, for the picture is relative to the point of view.

In this chapter and the next we shall try to imitate the map maker. Later there will be some elaboration of this first drastic simplification, and at least the chief by-currents will need to be indicated. For a beginning, we shall consider only the two most significant movements. To change our figure for a moment, in studying these two schools we shall be seeking to establish a division within philosophy which is as basic to the subject as the concept of positive and negative charges is to modern physics. For these are the two main poles of philosophical thought, and around them move most of the schools and their individual thinkers.

The General Viewpoint of Idealism

A glance at the history of thought in Western civilization reveals that *idealism* has probably been the most widely held and most important type of philosophy. In modern times particularly it has been so widespread and influential that the beginning student is often surprised to discover that "idealism" and "philosophy" are not synonymous terms. The dominant position of this school, coupled with its acceptability to established authorities of all kinds, has often made its great rival *naturalism* appear as an intruder or a poor relation in the garden of metaphysics. In part, this dominant status of idealism has resulted from the affiliations between its views and those of Christianity; in part, it has come from the generally optimistic attitude toward life and the world which has characterized the occidental mind. From whatever sources the support has come, the idealistic school has long been established as the "genteel tradition" in philosophy, and its adherents have commanded the widest hearing.

This is not to imply that there is no intrinsic merit in idealism to account for its dominance of Western thought. Quite the contrary: its doctrines make a powerful appeal to both reason and emotion, and many of its advocates have been counted as among the ablest thinkers the race has produced. Furthermore, it satisfies both the head and the heart in a way that probably no other world-view can, and since it is this dual satisfaction that most men expect from philosophy, both the influence and the vitality of idealism may well be permanent. Even the opponents of idealism usually acknowledge that as a metaphysical formulation it possesses breathtaking grandeur.

The Ultimate Real Is Psychical in Nature. What, then, are the essential beliefs of this great school of thought? Ignoring for the moment all the various subschools, reduced to its essence idealism is the belief that ultimate reality is *psychical* or *spiritual* in its nature, and that the universe is the embodiment of mind or spirit. Idealism holds that if we would gain the clearest insight into the nature of reality we will not look to the physical sciences, with their emphasis upon matter and motion and force, their electrons, protons, and all the rest; instead we will turn to thought, to intelligence, to reason, and to all the spiritual ideas and values of the race. It is not that there is anything incorrect in the picture of the universe which science gives us; it is probably a very true picture— as far as it goes. But it is incomplete. Science leaves out much that the idealist holds indispensable to a true or a total picture; for example, it omits all considerations of *value,* and scarcely even acknowledges the existence of what is (for most idealists) the supremely important thing in the universe, *personality.* Furthermore, science, with its complete objectivity and impersonality, cannot avoid giving a distorted view of the nature of things. It necessarily ignores the most fundamental element in knowledge or experience: the mind or ego that does the experiencing. All perceiving or knowing obviously requires a knowing subject, but science ignores this fact and naturalism denies its central importance. Idealism argues that from this knowing, experiencing subject comes not only all meaning and value, but even all existence; hence any system which does not build upon the mind or knowing subject as central must necessarily give an inadequate (if not false) picture of reality.

A universe such as this, in which the core of reality is mental or spiritual rather than physical, is plainly a world-order closely linked with man and his activities, his hopes and ideals. It is a universe that offers assurance that man as an individual has a destiny, and that the cosmic environment is friendly to man's efforts to achieve that destiny. Idealism presents a view of "things as they are" which makes the world a place in which we can feel an intimate relation between ourselves and the universe. In such a world we can be at home both intellectually and emotionally, for we and our environment are part of the same cosmic order and have our source in the same Mind or Spirit.

Also basic in idealism is the belief that our minds and the thought-world in which they move are related to reality in a particularly intimate and significant way. It is in our rational, intelligent activity that we most closely parallel the Activity that shapes the universe. If we would know what lies at the heart of the world, we must look within ourselves. In our own minds and souls, in the character of the human personality, is to be found the clearest indication of the nature of this Activity.

The Principal Implications of Idealism. This peculiar correspondence between our minds and reality has many important implications, and it is these that give idealism its strongest popular attraction. In the first place, from the fact that our finite minds function in terms of logic, order, and coherence, we can assume that the Absolute Mind functions in the same way. And since the universe is the embodiment or creation of this Mind, it further follows that our natural environment may be expected to reveal the same characteristics of order, coherence, and logic. From this correspondence we may also assume the essential intelligibility of the universe—which, since it is the creation of Reason, naturally has reasonableness ingrained in its fundamental structure. And, finally, from this intelligibility and reasonableness we may assume the adequacy of our human minds to deal with the world in which we live; our mind is capable of understanding its world because both are fundamentally rational, and both are rational because they are dependent upon the universal Reason.

The Distinction Between "Appearance" and "Reality"

Thus far the idealist has been arguing on purely logical grounds. This much of his system is deduced from the original postulate: the universe is the embodiment of Mind or Spirit. And now, having established this much, he presses on to a bold corollary. Since the universe is rational and intelligent, there can be no permanent disorder, irrationality, or disharmony in it. It is not only rational, but it is a rational *whole*. Mind is operative throughout, and no corner or fragment of the universe which Intelligence inhabits can be immune from its sway.

Now, however logically this corollary may follow from the basic assumption of idealism regarding the mental nature of reality, it is obviously not derived from the daily experience of living men and women. Our hour-by-hour contact with the world about us reveals an actuality that has little relation to this bold speculative hypothesis. For man, life appears to be a mottled patchwork of progress and decline, conquest and defeat, war and peace, starvation and plenty, nature kind and nature savagely hostile. In the life of the individual, the universe is even less clearly rational and intelligible: frustration, pain, and defeat are as large a part of our experience as success, happiness and conquest. Even the most successful and well-ordered life reveals large splotches of apparently purposeless striving and meaningless suffering. The most idealistic part of human nature, our mind, also fails to come up to this speculative claim. It is as expert at rationalizing (finding good reasons to justify selfish or sensual actions) as at reasoning, and we as individuals are rational creatures only occasionally and irregularly. The less successful and well-ordered lives are usually a contest between pleasure and pain; to a large part of the race, life is barely tolerable, and there are millions who are kept from suicide only by a blind, animal will-to-live and a cheating hope which perpetually promises a better tomorrow that never arrives.

The Importance of the Distinction. In the face of this primary fact of human life, it is to be expected that the idealist will seek support for his position from something besides direct experience. For no one is more aware than he that if the argument is to be won it must be on other grounds than this; one will not appeal to experience when the evidence from that source is at best inconclusive, and at worst overwhelmingly negative. In order to deal with this problem of proving the universe rational and harmonious despite all the evidence to the contrary, the idealistic thinker first establishes a distinction that is all-important to his thought, that between *appearance* and *reality*.

This distinction is closely related to much of our common experience. The idealist emphasizes how often we confuse appearance and reality, either as the result of careless observation or because of inadequate thinking. Then, too, we often think we have cut through the surface appearances of things and got down to what we take to be reality, only to have this in turn reveal itself as merely the manifestation of a deeper and more basic reality—and so on until we have a whole hierarchy of "realities," each of which is only an "appearance" of a deeper actuality. But any such hierarchy implies a culminating point of some kind, so the question inevitably arises: What is the *ultimate* real? Is it not possible that it is something totally different from the surface appearance of "things as they are"? Further, since we can be mistaken so often in our everyday experience, is it not possible (and even probable) that we do great violence to the truth about reality when we allow ourselves to be impressed by the apparent disorder and irrationality in the world?

It should be pointed out that idealism goes far beyond the common-sense distinction between appearance and reality which we all constantly make. When we say, for example, that a stage set appears to be a city street lined with buildings but is in reality only painted canvas, we are comparing one observed physical thing (the canvas) with another observed or observable thing, a city street. Thus our contrast of appearance-reality stays within the framework of experience, and both elements in the contrast are equally empirical and equally open to investigation; meaningful, testable statements about each can be made and verified. In short, both the appearance and the reality are facts of experience.

Idealism sets up a much more profound and audacious distinction— namely, that between the observable or empirical world ("appearance") and the transcendental or nonempirical "reality." This means that the idealist is willing to confer on something that is not only unobserved but unobservable a greater degree of actuality than he attributes to the physical world in which we live. This clearly reverses the common-sense view that material objects are the most real things we know, in comparison with which anything "mental" or "spiritual" seems more like an appearance. The boldness of this doctrine gives idealism much of its fascination and challenge for many people.

The Problem of Evil

The various subschools within idealism have different methods of explaining this discrepancy between appearance and reality. It is important that we examine briefly at least the most characteristic of these, since their answers will reveal much regarding idealism in general. However, as this great problem overlaps a far more popular issue which idealism has to face, it will be well to consider the two together. This better known issue is the celebrated "problem of evil"—undoubtedly the toughest nut which any system of idealism has to crack.

Briefly, the problem is this: If the universe is the embodiment of Mind or Reason, how is it that our experience reveals so much that is irrational and unintelligible? How does it happen that we are frequently forced to reconcile what is obviously blind chance or tragic coincidence with Intelligent Purpose supposedly lying behind it all? If the order of things were truly rational, would we be sitting here now wrestling with the problem of evil? We never hear of the "problem of good," and we should logically expect that in a universe that is rational throughout there would be no evil to require explanation. Even more difficult is the particular form of this major problem which nearly all religions have to face: If God were all-powerful and all-wise, but not all-good, we could understand the existence of such a world as we actually have. Or if He had supreme wisdom and goodness but only limited power, we could understand. But how are we to reconcile the existence of an infinite God with the fact of evil? Either He must not care, or else He cares but is powerless to do anything about the situation. Or, as a third possibility, He possesses the necessary supreme wisdom but only limited power, which would require a sequential elimination of evil, and this would in turn need vast stretches of time for its accomplishment.

Some Religious Answers. For the theist, believing in a personal but infinite God, the problem necessarily involves an extended analysis of the nature of Deity, the relations of God to His universe, etc. Much of this analysis we shall have to consider in our two final chapters, but here it will be enough to look at the common-sense answers to these disturbing questions. The most obvious reply, and certainly the most widely accepted, is that "God's time is best": He knows what He is doing and what is best for His world and every creature in it. Admittedly His ways are not our ways, and His time is not always our time, but in the final reckoning, when all is understood and we are able to see everything in its true light, it will be shown that our suspicion as to God's indifference or impotence was unwarranted. Then we shall see that it was only the "appearance" of things that deceived us; the "reality" (which of course an omniscient God knew from the beginning) was rational, intelligible, and good. In brief, for the theist, as for the idealist, the real problem is to pierce the veil of appearances and see through to reality.

Now there are three principal solutions to the problem of this apparent evil and irrationality in the world. We can take an extreme position and say that the so-called evil is only an error within our own minds. In the Infinite or Divine Mind, there can exist only Goodness and Truth, so that any error or evil must obviously be the product of our own finite mortal minds. We have only to cast out the *thought* of evil (since it exists only in our own minds) in order to eliminate the *actuality* of evil; the idea and the actuality are identical. The second solution to the problem of evil is less extreme and more "common-sense." In this view, evil is acknowledged as real, but it is argued that if we take the long view—if we learn to see things "under the aspect of eternity"—we will realize that however genuine the suffering and misery and stupidity in the world may be, these are becoming progressively diminished. This might be called an historical approach to the problem. Its exponents believe in progress, and hold that man can, through reason and his own efforts, speed up the march of progress and carry its movement to limitless achievements, including the elimination of much of what we now regard as evil. In philosophy this viewpoint is known as *meliorism,* or the doctrine of improvability. In religion, where it is preached by many liberal churches today, it suggests that God needs our aid in the fight: that life (and perhaps the whole cosmic process) represents a relentless conflict between the forces of good and those of evil. This is a conflict in which every fighter is needed, and in which a choice for the good aids in undercutting the very existence of evil. In sum, evil is real enough, but its reality will be eliminated by the eventual triumph of the good, which can be brought about by the joint efforts of God and man.[1]

Platonism

Between the two religious (and therefore essentially practical) explanations of the appearance-reality relation there is a point of view of much greater metaphysical significance. This is *Platonism,* one of the supreme creations of philosophical speculation. While Plato's thought is not a strict idealism, since the basic elements in his system possess an extramental status (whether their nature is spiritual, material, or merely logical is one of the most controversial points in the history of philosophy), Platonism nevertheless has many features that appear in modern idealism, and it well represents the general mood and attitude of this great school.

Plato builds his system upon the contrast between appearance and reality which we are discussing. For him, the real nature of anything is the "idea" which it embodies. These ideas or essences he regards as possessing both an independent existence and a superior reality. In fact, they *are* reality: physical objects only reflect or copy this ultimate reality, which is both the essence of the physical object and its eternal, changeless prototype. Thus there exists, behind the veil of sense experience, an ideal world of essences. It is from this higher realm that all reality comes: the more completely an object embodies its underlying "idea," the more reality it has.[2]

---

[1] In American philosophy, this doctrine is particularly associated with the names of William James and John Dewey. Dewey's thought, however, must be described as *social meliorism,* since it builds upon what we are calling naturalism rather than upon an idealistic view of the world—that is, evil is to be eliminated by man's own social efforts, independent of God (who plays no part in Dewey's system).

[2] Plato specifically calls these ideal modes of reality "ideas" or "forms." In recent years this traditional view of Plato's system which I am presenting has been seriously challenged in many particulars, notably by J. A. Stewart and Natorp. The chief point of attack is the conventional view that the Forms have an existence independent of any embodiment or enactment in a concrete object. This newer interpretation would bring Plato nearer to Aristotle and the moderate realism of

The Two Levels of Reality.   But all this is somewhat condensed and abstract, so let us undertake to break it down a bit. For Plato, there are two levels or modes of reality. The first is the obvious and undeniable reality of everyday, tangible objects—of chairs, rocks, trees, mountains, and living creatures. But existence on this level does not constitute the *true* real; this lies behind the mask of apparent reality, and abides in a higher realm. (Plato is vague concerning the specific locale of this higher realm, except to suggest that it is somewhere "up in the heavens.") This realm forms an ideal order of eternal essences, which exist in a hierarchy established on moral principles and dominated by the idea of the Good. But what are these ideal eternal essences, and what is their relation to this lower, everyday world of physical or natural objects? Plato specifically calls these ideal modes of reality "ideas" or "forms," and it is the latter term that has become the preferred English word. But the word "form" has several meanings, one of which runs directly counter to Plato's intent. We are frequently asked to understand the term in the sense of the external shape or outline of a thing—that is, its over-all contour or general appearance. For Plato, however, the word means the inner structure or articulated idea which the object embodies. What is it to be anything— for example, what is it to be a house? It is this question which the Form or Idea can answer by representing the essence of a thing. The Form of the house would therefore be its plan, design or organization; a set of blueprints would reveal more of this than would a model or a series of front and side elevations, or even photographs of the completed building. For the Platonic Form is always the intangible idea or concept which physical objects may embody or partially articulate, but which they can never actually be.

The realm of true reality is consequently a realm of Forms which are eternal, changeless, perfect. These are the prototypes of all classes or species of earthly objects, and Plato implies that there is no object which does not have a Form corresponding to it, from which it derives such a reality as it has.

---

such medieval thinkers as Abelard. In addition, it would certainly link Plato more closely with modern science than he has traditionally been. However, I have felt it better to present the time-honored view of Platonic Forms—not as expressing my own view on the matter (which remains neutral), but solely to avoid confusing the student. Here, as throughout the book, my aim is clarity rather than completeness, the forest rather than the tree—even though this sometimes means ignoring some rather sizable trees.

The Forms as Concepts. The basic relation between any object and its Form is identical with that between a percept and its corresponding concept—that is, between any concrete object we experience that belongs to a class or species (indicated by a common noun, such as a book, chair, dog, etc.) and our *idea* or *concept* of that class. For example, we have all seen hundreds of books. But we each have in our mind, independent of the image or memory of any particular book, an idea of "book in general," or book in the abstract. This idea is what would immediately come to mind if we were asked, "What is it, in general, to be a book?" This is called a *concept*.

In Plato's metaphysics, this concept or the "thing-in-itself" as it is at heart and stripped of all unessential attributes, constitutes a Form or Idea. One of the key problems in the long history of philosophy has been the exact status of concepts, and nearly the whole of medieval philosophy was centered in an interminable controversy as to whether they had real existence outside of the mind. One school held that "book" as an idea had an actual existence apart from and independent of any and all physical books. Their opponents held that any concept is merely a name, a convenient handle which we create to enable us to deal with some class of objects falling within our experience. (Suppose that every tree or every dog we met in a lifetime required a separate term to name it.) Plato's position in the controversy is definite: he still remains the most famous and most influential exponent of one side of the controversy. His whole system depends upon the doctrine that concepts (or universals, to use the medieval term,) have a greater degree of reality than anything we experience through our senses. In the language of today's science and mathematics, Plato holds that the class is more real than its members.

The key point in Platonism is that the Forms not only exist, but constitute the only true reality. The earthly objects that embody them are only "reflections," "shadows," or "copies" of these eternal prototypes, possessing a limited degree of reality only by derivation—or, to use Plato's favorite term, by participation in the corresponding Idea. Here we have what has always been a cardinal belief of idealism: Reality is conceptual or rational, and consequently the best way to apprehend it is through reason and the analysis of our own mental activities. As our minds are structured, so is the real; through the conceptualizing activities of our own intelligence we gain the best insight into the nature of ultimate reality.

The Implications of Platonism. This general metaphysical doctrine of Plato is important enough in itself, but in addition it carries a most significant implication which idealists since Plato have taken pains to make explicit. If true Being is located in a realm of ideal Forms or essences which we apprehend through rational processes, then obviously sense experience and the objects of sense experience retire into relative metaphysical unimportance. The literature of idealism is full of disparaging remarks concerning the shortcomings of the senses, the inability of sensory experience to reveal truth, and the transitoriness of the objects with which the senses deal in comparison with the changeless character of the knowledge which reason reveals to us. Plato goes so far as to call the senses and their activities a handicap to the discovery of reality; sense experience is a veil between us and true "Being," for it can report to us only what happens in the realm of change, or "Becoming." Idealism thus runs contrary to what we may call the philosophy of common sense, which considers true (at least as far as it goes) the picture of "things as they are" that our senses give us. Certainly common sense is startled to be told that our sensory processes are not only inadequate but positively detrimental to a comprehension of the real nature of things. For the idealist, however, such a conclusion is not only logical but inescapable.

The Moral Tone of Idealism

This idealistic exaltation of rational activity over sensory experience is not based exclusively on logical or epistemological grounds. There is in most idealism, as in Platonism, a strong moral tone that colors most of its thinking. As we have seen, Plato's ideal Forms not only represent essences but also perfections; the Forms are not averages but ideals, and it is these which the mind longs to discover behind the veil of sense. Then, having attained an apprehension of them, the mind strives to live in terms of their perfection, insofar as the burden of the flesh and the barrier of the senses will permit. This theme of the body, with its senses and appetites, as constituting a burden, a prison, or a charnel house, recurs frequently in Platonism, and at least mild implications of the same sort are found in all schools of idealistic thought. The inevitable result of such an attitude is a tendency towards dualism. Plato's primary division of reality into a lower, derived physical world of "Becoming" and a higher realm of true "Being" easily leads to a view of life in which body is opposed to soul, matter to mind, sense to reason. An asceticism or puritanism of some sort frequently follows; the body, with even its healthy normal appetites, becomes an object of moral suspicion. Christianity, embodying a profound dualism, has naturally found much philosophical support in idealism, while Plato has been called "a Christian four hundred years before Christ."

The Idea of the Good. Plato's system culminates in the Form of the Good. While this idea is not defined with exactitude, it must be understood in a broad moral sense. The whole system is thus based upon a foundation of value; it is plain that however much concerned Plato was to show the physical universe as only a shadow or reflection of the higher intelligible world of Forms, he was even more concerned to prove that the universe is grounded in value. In this attempt to identify the Good and the Real, Plato was typically idealistic. For such thinkers, it appears to be temperamentally impossible to conceive the universe except as concerned with and directed towards the Good. Other schools of philosophy are willing to admit the possibility that reality may be either morally neutral or basically evil, but any such possibility lies outside the idealist's realm of conceivability. Thus we can forecast his answer to what some thinkers regard as the most searching question in philosophy: Is the cosmos at bottom a *moral* order or a *mechanical* order? Is the universe a vast mechanism, blind, impersonal, and morally indifferent as only a mechanism can be? Or it is basically a moral structure, in which values and ideals are supreme, and at the heart of which there is not only Reason and Purpose, but Goodness? For the idealist, the second alternative alone is possible. Any other answer would not only invalidate his whole system, but would in his opinion deal an even heavier blow to human hopes. For he feels that a mechanical world order would undercut all those values which are supremely important in human life and which constitute the mainspring of our spiritual activity. In such a mechanistic universe, man would be trying to live the good life and achieve moral purposes in a vast moral vacuum; it would be an empty cosmos that would be totally unaware of, and sublimely indifferent to, all that matters to humanity and its highest aspirations.

The Good as Cosmic. The idealists of all schools unite in clear agreement on one point: any system of merely human values—morality in a naturalistic setting, for example—would be both purposeless and meaningless. Our values and ideals have reality and validity only if they have support of the cosmos. In a mechanical or naturalistic world order they would be as empty and pointless as the universe itself. As far as humanity is concerned, such a cosmos would render both metaphysics and morality worse than meaningless: they would be a vast joke. In short, idealism finds it is impossible to separate ethics and metaphysics. It is only as we can feel sure that our moral struggles, and indeed all our values, have relation to the whole universe that they can have any significance. What naturalism has to say on this issue we shall see shortly, but meantime we may note that it is on this point that the two great schools clash most violently. For idealism, the issue is basic, and consequently no compromise is possible: either the universe is friendly to man and all his values, or else these ideals are a sardonic joke—a cosmic farce. Certainly, concludes the idealist, in such a world ideals would not be worth dying for; in fact, they would not even be worth living for.

It is sometimes pointed out by neutral observers of the idealism *vs.* naturalism controversy that the idealistic metaphysician appears to construct his system with a predetermined goal in mind: to picture a universe in which values will be not only safe but even favored by the cosmic forces. The opponents of idealism are quick to seize on this neutral judgment as evidence that idealists are less objective (and consequently less dependable philosophical guides) than the naturalists. For, these opponents of idealism argue, if we decide beforehand what sort of world we are going to find, is it surprising that we end up with an impressive picture of just such a world? The naturalist thus accuses the idealist of being so predisposed towards a value-guaranteeing cosmos as to be at best prejudiced, and at worst guilty of sheer wishful thinking, and in any case, quite unreliable as a purveyor of philosophical truth. The favorite naturalistic challenge here is, "Where would science be if it had pursued such preconceived and emotionally satisfying goals as these?" To which the idealist usually replies that he is not a scientist, and that he does not admit that the scientific attitude and general methodology are necessarily the most reliable source of truth. But we will have much more to say on these controversial matters when we look at naturalism in our next chapter, for the issue is clearly too large and too important to be dealt with briefly.

Subjective Idealism

We must be careful not to imply that idealism's interests are exclusively in the division of ethics, for many contemporary members of this school are far more concerned with epistemological and metaphysical problems. We must therefore turn from the "moral idealism" of such thinkers as Plato to the more strictly "metaphysical (or epistemological) idealism" of men like Berkeley and Hegel. Fortunately our exposition of their thought can be much briefer than in the case of Plato's. This is not because they are less significant as members of the school—in many ways they are both more typical of idealism today than the Greek philosopher—but because the general mood of their thinking is substantially the same as his. Clear moral implications will be apparent in these later men, but since it is their more technical analyses that are important to us, we shall limit our discussion to these.

Epistemological idealism, the most significant form of idealism of our day, is the belief that only mind is real. Matter, with all its manifestations, is only a mental content, and is therefore dependent upon mind for its existence. Matter has an existence, undeniably, but this can be analyzed into perceptions. To use the modern terminology, matter does not have an *objective* (*i.e.*, independent, extramental) existence, but is dependent upon the *subject* (the observing or experiencing mind) for its being. It will be noticed that we have here a change from Plato. In his system, the Ideas or Forms have an existence independent of thought. Whether or not he held these forms to have some sort of concrete or physical existence is not the important point here; what is significant is that in Platonism there is something that cannot be resolved into a mental content of either the human or the Infinite mind.[3]

The Philosophy of Berkeley. This doctrine of subjective idealism first became prominent in the eighteenth century. At this time, philosophy had become acutely aware of how difficult it was to explain satisfactorily the exact relation between "knowledge" and "reality"—that is,

---

[3] It is for this reason that Plato and his medieval successors are often called "realists"—to the endless confusion of beginning students of philosophy. If we define idealism narrowly in its eighteenth-century meaning (as in this section we are just beginning), then there is logic in using the term "realism" for the Platonic system, since it does believe in the real, independent existence of something outside of the mind.

between our experiences or perceptions, and the external, objective world of nature to which these supposedly refer. It is difficult to resist going into the fascinating story of the developments that led to this subjectivism. However, we shall perforce be satisfied with an outline of the system of subjectivism's most brilliant exponent, George Berkeley. His argument runs thus: All things which we call "matter" are objects of our experience; as such, they exist for us only as perceptions. When we say, for instance, that a tree exists, we are saying nothing except that we have a perception or an experience which we label "tree." But this experience, however vivid, does not in any way confer an independent, objective existence upon the "tree," which remains only an experience. In short, to say that anything exists is synonymous with saying that it is perceived through one or more of our senses. Berkeley's famous dictum, *esse est percipi* (to be is to be perceived), sums up the whole case: there is no existence apart from a mind that experiences the existent. In the language of modern psychology, our "tree" is nothing except a group of sensations, and sensation is subjective. Our so-called "object" therefore turns out to be only a mental experience—to exist is to be experienced—as does all matter in its various forms. Reality is thus purely mental; the whole world is mental, and there exist only minds and their perceptions.

The Common-sense Criticism of Berkeley. Berkeley's purpose in formulating his doctrine was self-confessed: to refute the materialism of his day. He felt, very logically, that when he had disproved the independent existence of matter, materialism was left without a leg to stand on. His opponents appealed to common sense, and one of them, the famous lexicographer Samuel Johnson, thought to refute the subjective idealist by a mighty kick against a stone. "Thus do I refute Bishop Berkeley!" he is supposed to have declared. But neither common sense nor stone-kicking meets that argument, as the witty Irishman quickly pointed out. All that Dr. Johnson had proved was what subjectivism had already acknowledged: that we do have bundles of sensations—in this case presumably of kinesthetic resistance and a stab of pain localized in the big toe. But does this prove the independent existence of anything, except our own conscious minds as centers of perception? Common sense argues that it is absurd to claim that an object of perception, such as a book lying on the table, ceases to exist when we go out of the room or otherwise stop perceiving it for a moment. But Berkeley answers immediately, "What are the qualities or attributes an 'existing' book would have under these circumstances?" When common sense answers, as it must, in terms of one or more sense qualities such as "green" or "heavy" or "thick" or "large," Berkeley springs the trap. For what are all of these except sense data, and as such purely mental or subjective? Existence remains, despite all that common sense can muster by way of argument, merely a bundle of sensations, and therefore mental in character.

But common sense, convinced that there must surely be some catch in such a system as this, returns with a new attack. How can Berkeley explain the consistency and the community of our perceptual world? If all existence is dependent upon the mind, why are my various perceptions of yonder tree so consistent with each other? Why, for instance, does it always get perceived as a pine instead of occasionally as an elm or a beech? Further, how are we to explain the fact that there is plenty of practical evidence that you and I both experience the same tree when we turn our eyes in a certain direction? If your tree and mine are so similar that all evidence makes them identical, there must be a single common source or cause for our perceptions. And where could this common cause lie except outside of both of our minds—namely, in the external world?

Berkeley answers by reminding us that he nowhere denies the existence of an external world, but only of a *material* world existing *independently* of all perception—that is, a world that is not an idea in some mind. In his own words,

> Indeed I hold the objects of sense to be nothing else but ideas which cannot exist unperceived. Yet we may not hence conclude that they have no existence except only when they are perceived by us; there may be some other spirit that perceives them though we do not. It would not follow, hence, that bodies are annihilated and created every moment, or exist not at all during the intervals between our perception of them.

"There may be some other spirit which perceives them when we do not." What can this other mind or spirit be? Obviously if Berkeley could prove that such a mind existed, he could better meet the demands of common sense. It does not take long to see where his argument is heading.

> But whatever power I have over some of my ideas, I find that others have not a like dependence on my will. When, for example, I open my eyes in broad daylight, it is not in my power to choose whether I shall

see or no, nor to determine what I shall see. It is likewise as to hearing and the other senses. The ideas imprinted on them are not creatures of my will. There is, therefore, some other will or mind or spirit that produces them.

These ideas which I cannot control, these ideas of sense are more strong, more lively, more distinct than those which I can control. They have, likewise, a steadiness, order, and coherence which belong not to those that are the effects of my will. They speak themselves the products of a Mind more powerful and wise than human minds.

Some truths there are so near and obvious to the human mind that a man need only open his eyes to see them. Such I take this important one to be, namely, that all the choir of heaven and furniture of the earth, in a word, all those bodies which compose the mighty frame of the world, have not any subsistence without a mind; that their being is to be perceived or known; that, consequently, so long as they are not actually perceived by me, or do not exist in my mind or the mind of any other created spirit, they must either have no existence at all or else subsist in the mind of some Eternal Spirit.

The Berkeleian hypothesis, in order to satisfy common sense, must postulate the existence of some mind other than (and greater than) our own. There is no other way that the universe can be maintained in existence, and no other way that the coherence and consistency of our perceptions can be adequately explained. So, in the single concept of "God" Berkeley has tied his whole system together. God's perception keeps the universe in existence, whether any human minds are on perceptual duty or not. God's mind also guarantees the uniformity of our perceptions: when we look out the same window every day we see the same trees and buildings outside, because their real existence depends upon God's awareness of them. We may come and go, glance out the window or not, but He steadily maintains in existence all the physical objects that drift through our experience in casual, on-again off-again fashion. Whatever else Berkeley's God may be He certainly is not casual or haphazard in His perceptual activities! He is right on the job, twenty-four hours a day, every day of the year. And of course, being omniscient, He perceives everything which exists, including much that men never have seen or will see.

The Central Role of God in Berkeley's System. It is hardly an exaggeration to say that God is as important in Berkeley's system as He is in any theological structure. By calling in the Divine Mind and Its infinite store of perceptions, he has at one stroke accomplished the following: (1)

accounted for the existence of an external world as common sense demands; (2) explained the continuity and consistency of our perceptions (God's mind takes over when we go to sleep or become engrossed in other perceptions and thus maintains all objects in existence, ready to be perceived by our finite minds when they reawaken or turn again in that direction); (3) explained the similarity of our sensations when we experience a single common object (since the object exists as a single idea in God's mind, it is not strange that we should all experience it similarly); (4) destroyed materialism by eliminating a material world independent of thought; (5) disproved atheism by making God indispensable to all existence. There is little doubt that Berkeley sincerely believed that the elimination of God from thought would destroy the universe—not to mention the Berkeleian system.

All these things Berkeley felt he had explained and proved. Philosophy had to wait another generation for Hume, the brilliant Scottish skeptic, to show that the Berkeleian logic is a two-edged sword that cuts both ways. For if we do not start with a belief in the existence of God, there is no way to prove that our perceptions have an objective support in the Divine Mind. For instance, if all existence is dependent upon being perceived, whence comes God's existence? Plainly He is not a perceptual object—unless, of course, we hang ourselves on logic by insisting that God can generate Himself by perceiving Himself.

Whatever may be our final estimate of Berkeley's system, it is clear why it is called "subjectivism" and why those idealisms that develop from it all lean heavily on logic and epistemology. All such systems base their world-view upon the undeniable fact that everything which exists appears to be inextricably linked with our perception of it. From this the idealist believes it only logical to conclude that existence as such is dependent upon perception—*esse est percipi*. As we shall see in a later chapter, the epistemological realist finds such reasoning invalid. At this point in our presentation, however, it will be more to our purpose to discuss briefly the so-called "egocentric predicament" which, although developed as an argument against subjectivism, can be thrown into the ring from a neutral corner in such a manner as to make the idealistic position more comprehensible and perhaps more acceptable.

The Egocentric Predicament. Without involving ourselves in the *conclusions* of the argument from the egocentric predicament, its premises can be stated briefly as follows: Any object, in order to become an object of knowledge, has to be an object of experiencing—that is, nothing can enter our minds without going through a relation. This is the relation of *cognition* (which means knowing, experiencing, perceiving—all in their broadest sense). Only *via* the cognitive process do things enter our consciousness. Admittedly we have no way of discovering what they would be apart from this cognitive relation—what they might be in, by, or for themselves—because obviously the moment you consider anything in an attempt to learn what its true nature is, it becomes an object of cognition. In other words, we can never get out of our minds and free of our sensory processes to meet things face to face. We cannot sneak around from behind and catch them off guard and "out of character." We are confined within our own consciousness, as lifelong prisoners of our sensory and cognitive apparatus. Hence the "egocentric predicament," from which no man ever escapes.

For the subjective idealist, the implication of this situation is clear and logically inescapable: the experiencing mind is the ultimate reality of the universe. The only things that exist are minds and their perceptions; apart from these, there is nothing. For the realist, on the other hand, the fact of the predicament is undeniable but not these implications. The realist can see no warrant for taking an unfortunate limitation of the mind and elevating it into the basis for a world-view. Admittedly, he argues, all we can know about the world is what comes to us through experience, but the inevitability of the cognitive relation does not justify conferring on that relation the ultimate metaphysical status. However, the idealist has the last word here (this being his chapter). He finds nothing "unfortunate" in the egocentric predicament; to him it indicates not a limitation of the mind, but the very nature of reality. For idealism, the problem is not to get outside our minds, for they *are* reality, and the real can have nothing "outside" it except the unreal—that is, the nonexistent.

Solipsism

It will be noted that Berkeley's system is clearly pluralistic, since it holds that reality consists of minds ("spirits" is the Berkeleian term) and their perceptions. Even the Divine Mind, important as it is in tying the system

together, constitutes only one more perceptual center, so the basic pluralism remains.

Any system which is both pluralistic and subjectivistic appears
doomed to be perpetually haunted by a ghost—a ghost, moreover, which
no invocation of the Divine Mind can permanently eliminate. This
perennial haunter of subjectivistic systems is *solipsism,* which is universally acknowledged to be the most extreme and intellectually devastating of all philosophical positions. The solipsist is a thoroughgoing subjectivist who has the courage to take the final logical step that all anti-
subjectivists feel is an inevitable one for idealists of this type. He is willing to carry his logic to its bitter end by concluding that nothing really
exists except himself and his individual perceptions. "I and my ideas (or
perceptions) are all that exist"—such is the basic position of a solipsist.
Everything else, all other persons and objects and the whole physical
universe, have existence only as they are perpetually actualized by the
solipsist's mind.

Basically the solipsist challenges anyone and everyone to prove *by
logic* a positive answer to this question: "What exists except myself and
my experience?" It is obvious that this is merely an extension of the question implied in less extreme forms of subjective idealism, such as Berkeley's. But whereas Berkeley (and in fact every idealist) asks, "How can
you prove that anything exists except as it is known to some mind?"
the solipsist sharpens the question still more by demanding, "How can it
be proved that anything exists except as it is known by *my* mind?" And
solipsism insists upon a *logical* answer; no appeal to common sense will
do, nor will any appeal to overwhelming majority opinion. Since a solipsist has already declared himself a minority of one who is so important
that his ideas and experiences confer existence on everything else that
possesses being, he is hardly impressed by the argument that most men
do not agree with him. For who are these countless millions who do not
agree? They owe their very existence to his awareness of them, so why
should their opinions outweigh the logical conclusions of the mind that
brought them into being?

Perhaps the reader now begins to understand why solipsism is a
stronger position, logically speaking, than it may first appear. Regardless
of how repugnant it may be to common sense, as long as we play the
philosophical game by the rules of strict logic (which the solipsist insists
we do) this position is hard to controvert. While Schopenhauer was

hardly a solipsist, the opening sentence of his major philosophical work gives classic expression to the essential doctrine of this school: "The world is my idea." "Exactly!" agrees the solipsist. "And I challenge anyone to prove that the world and all it contains is anything *more* than my idea."

It is useless to argue with a solipsist by pointing out the common-sense fact that the world existed long before he was born and will continue to exist long after he dies. His reply usually runs something as follows: "How do I know this—how can it be proved to me? All I *know* (and all that can be established by logic) is that I now experience an environment around me. How long that environment has existed and how long it will exist, as well as how far it extends beyond my perceptual range, are matters regarding which I *know* nothing and can *know* nothing. True, there is hearsay, rumor, even records of various kinds; but these too exist only as part of my experience. Furthermore they are not knowledge as I insist we define knowledge—namely, that which is known to me personally by direct experience on my part."

As concerns the existence of the universe after his own experience ends, the solipsist agrees absolutely with the suggestion in one of A. E. Housman's poems that the would-be suicide has only to drive home the knife he holds against his own breast and the whole universe will crash into nonexistence. Another poet, the American John Hall Wheelock, has given a beautiful statement of much the same idea in his long poem, "Mediation."[4] After brooding upon the mystery of existence and the expression of this mystery in art and literature, he says:

> Earth takes us with her: silently she swings
> Through the old orbit, bearing in her breast
> The drowsy mouth, the mouth that sings.
>
> And yet all this lives only in my mind;
> And when that darkens, the whole world will darken
> Suddenly,—the whole world go blind.
>
> All I have touched, all I have loved and known
> Will fail me,—and the breast of Life draw back,
> Leaving me in the dark alone.

[4] From *Bright Doom*, by John Hall Wheelock, copyright, 1927, by Charles Scribner's Sons.

O starry universe, hung in the clear
Bell of my mind, be living in me now!
Dwell in me for a moment here!

How often, in the many minds of men,
Have you been born, only to pass away,—
Dying with every mind again!

This is a thought that is too hard for me:
It is a bitter thing to think upon,
That, to myself, all this shall be
As if it had not been, when I am gone.

But perhaps we had better draw back too. As Hamlet has well said after brooding upon similar problems, "That way madness lies."

Objective or Absolute Idealism

It was partly as an escape from the cul de sac of solipsism that a school of German philosophers in the early nineteenth century developed the last form of idealism that we need consider. This is known as *absolute idealism*—or, more popularly, "the philosophy of the absolute." Its chief exponents were Fichte, Schelling, and Hegel, of whom the last was by far the most influential. As far as concerns idealism in both England and the United States, this absolutistic school has been extremely influential. This influence appears to have passed its zenith some time before World War I, but no one can read intelligently the philosophy, theology, or even poetry of the nineteenth and early twentieth centuries without some acquaintance with this school and its doctrines.[5]

In essence, absolute idealism is as strongly monistic as Berkeley's system is pluralistic. "Unity," "totality," "the whole," are key terms in absolutism, which represents probably the most heroic attempt yet seen to impose unity and integration upon the world and human experience.

[5] The foremost absolute idealists in America were Josiah Royce and W. T. Harris and his St. Louis School. In England the principal figures were T. H. Green, F. H. Bradley, and Bernard Bosanquet. The British poet Coleridge was also strongly influenced by Hegelian thought, and did much to make it known in literary circles.

It achieved this unity by the apparently simple expedient of identifying *nature* with *mind*. Berkeley had of course tried to do much the same thing by identifying *nature* with *experience*, but his system included too many individual minds to permit the gap between the two to be closed. Hegel's system tried to eliminate this difficulty by the concept of a total or absolute mind (usually called simply "the Absolute"), of which our individual finite minds are only fragments.

From Berkeley to Hegel. The logical steps by which this Absolute comes into being are exceedingly interesting, particularly now that we are in a position to understand its inevitable development from Berkeleian subjectivism. Like the subjectivist, the absolutist starts with what is for both schools the most significant of brute facts: the complete dependence of all existence *as we know it* upon experience. From this admitted epistemological situation, both types of idealism take a tremendous metaphysical leap to the doctrine that therefore existence is dependent upon experience—*not* just existence as we know it (that is, as far as our experience extends), but *existence as such*. But where Berkeley went on to postulate a Divine Mind to maintain (as an object of perception) the natural world in existence, the logic of absolutism leads to a concept that is somewhat more subtle and intellectually sophisticated. This Absolute is, epistemologically speaking, an all-inclusive Subject to match the universe as the total object. For, if we admit with Berkeley that *esse* is *percipi*, and that each object in the world is only an object *of* perception (or *for* experience), then we are logically compelled to postulate an overall perceptual agent to give being to the overall totality of physical objects which we call the universe. The very existence of such a universe, which our finite minds know only in fragments (that is, as individual objects), requires us to believe in an Absolute Experiencer to integrate not only all our particular experiences, but all possible experience.

Whatever may be our personal judgment of absolute idealism as the definite world-view, its logic is admittedly compelling. Once we consent to take the first friendly step with good Bishop Berkeley way back in the eighteenth century, the absolutist has us body and soul. There appears to be no escape from his relentless logic: the most innocent flirtation with *esse est percipi* leads in exorably to the all-devouring embrace of the Absolute. The realist, anxious above all to escape such an intellectual destiny, has his own way of preserving his freedom. But that is another story, which must wait for another chapter.

The Characteristics of Hegel's Absolutism. To conclude this briefest possible consideration of absolute idealism, it will be well to mention a few of its peculiarly Hegelian features which have had wide influence. In the first place, this totality or whole which is the Absolute is for Hegel no static, lifeless thing. Taking his clue (as the idealist always does) from the nature of man, and particularly from man's mental processes, Hegel makes this clue his chief key for unlocking the mystery of reality. Holding as he does that nature and mind are unified in an organic whole, it is logical for him to find in man's rational nature the essence of the Absolute: it is a universal Spirit or Reason. Further—and here we have one of his boldest projections—the whole historical or evolutionary process of the universe is only the unfolding or increasing realization of Spirit. In this increasing realization we have a dual development: Spirit is both actualizing its potentialities and becoming increasingly conscious. Every historical change, every event within time, every evolutionary development, represents a phase of the progressive development of Spirit. The highest (that is, most fully realized and most conscious) of these phases are human institutions, notably art, religion and philosophy.

There remains, then, only to effect the final union. If all existence is the expression of Absolute Spirit, and if this Absolute is thus the whole of reality, then our consciousness can be nothing other than *its* self-consciousness. Hence history, or the passage of events, and our experience, or consciousness of these events, are the two incomplete or limited halves of one universal process. They are, so to speak, the objective and the subjective aspects of the one process.[6] Thus the world-process is purposive; all that occurs works towards the realization of the potentialities that are inherent in Spirit. "To come to pass" is to actualize some further possibility of the Absolute.

Summary of Idealism

It has been most difficult to present idealism in the inclusive, generalized manner of this chapter. There has been an ever-present danger that, in

---

[6] Cf. *Philosophy: An Introduction*, by Randall and Buchler, p. 223. I have referred to this excellent little book before, and the whole of Chapter XIV, "The Emphasis on Mind," contains a most lucid presentation of the development of modern idealism.

our attempt to show the reader the philosophical forest in an over-all, bird's-eye picture, we would make the mistake of ignoring the fact that any forest is made up of individual trees, no two of which are alike. The differences between the numerous subschools within idealism are frequently pronounced, and individual thinkers vary even more widely in their views. In presenting this generalized picture of so complex a field, the hardest question to answer has been Platonic: what is it to be an idealist? In other words, stripping off all the "apparent" dissimilarities and getting down to the "reality," what is the essence of idealism?

Recapitulation. To recapitulate and conclude, idealism is that view of the world in which mind, thought, or spirit is the fundamental reality. It is a system which places the knowing subject (either the individual, finite human mind or an absolute knower of some kind) at the center of things, and then arranges the rest of the universe around this central existence. Furthermore the universe is systematically related to this central knowing subject in peculiarly intimate ways. The universe is in some manner—varying from school to school of idealistic thought—a projection or extension of the mind or spirit. Consequently there are many of the same characteristics in reality that the mind discovers as basic in itself; idealism pictures for us a universe that is purposive, rational, intelligible, and (perhaps most important of all) either good in itself or vitally concerned with the good. It is a universe in which values not only have an objective existence, but where they are realized and conserved by the universal process. Under the idealistic world-view we can even find grounds for believing that this world-process has the maximum realization of value as its primary goal. Hence, "nothing is foreclosed as impossible in the direction of our highest human aspirations";[7] for at its heart the universe is friendly to man and to his ideals.

[7] The phrase is Hocking's (*Types of Philosophy,* rev. ed., p. 333).

CHAPTER 4

NATURALISM:

The World Is Indifferent

JUST AS RELIGION FINDS ITS CLOSEST PHILOSOPHICAL AFFILIATE IN idealism, so science has its philosophical accompaniment, *naturalism*. In essence, this is the belief that the natural or "real" world—the world of human experience—is the only realm with which we can or should be concerned. This is no arbitrary limitation: the natural world establishes the boundaries of our inquiry by the fact that it is the only world which experience reveals as existing. Obviously, this fundamental belief of naturalism automatically means the rejection of other-worldliness, transcendentalism or supernaturalism in any form. No knowledge, value or ideal that cannot be referred to human experience and human welfare has meaning for the naturalistic thinker.

The naturalist usually finds the elaborate metaphysic of idealism to be a superb logical construct erected on no foundation within experience, while religion's rich pattern of hope and promise seems the product of wishful thinking built on a similar lack of foundation in fact. The naturalist is usually willing to allow the idealist, the religionist, and the mystic their doctrines, but he insists that these be regarded as matters of faith entirely, without any relation to experimental proof. The naturalist usually prides himself on his "tough-mindedness," and he is inclined to be half-amused and half-irritated at what he considers the "tender-mindedness" of the idealist, who appears unable to live without constructing a sheltering, friendly world. Naturalism accuses idealism of allowing human hopes and dreams to influence and even distort its inquiry into reality, while the naturalist is confident that his own record is spotless in this regard. But we have already said enough concerning the naturalistic view to affect many readers like a dash of cold water in the face, so it will be well to go back and lay some foundations while they catch their breath.

The Historical Status of Naturalism

The history of philosophy in the Western world extends back to approximately 600 B.C., and is therefore some twenty-five hundred years old. While this long expanse of time and change has naturally seen the rise of many schools and individual points of view, the philosopher's effort today is the same as in early Greek times: to pierce beneath the welter and flux of our day-by-day experience and discover the abiding nature of things. Now as we have already indicated, the idealistic answer to this inquiry has been the most influential and widely accepted description of reality. If we think of the philosophers as forming a continuing committee of investigation, charged with the task of discovering the nature of the ultimate real, idealism could be called the official or majority report. As such it has enjoyed the acceptance and prestige usually accorded a majority report. Through the centuries, this acceptance has acquired the added force of historical precedent, so that any opposing point of view has usually found itself in the position of an aggressor against the *status quo,* with all the disadvantages such a position usually entails.

Naturalism as the Minority Viewpoint. Looking over the history of philosophy as a whole, the naturalist viewpoint has been a minority report. This minority has varied in size from large (in early Greek and recent times) to almost negligible, and it has ranged from extremely vociferous (as at present) to nearly dead silent. But, however small, it has always been in existence, firing guerilla potshots at the entrenched positions of the idealistic majority. Sometimes the flow of naturalistic thought has been the merest trickle, too small to be noticed, and again as at present it has rolled up such a flood as to drive idealism to firmer ground. But, flood or trickle, it has constituted a current of protest and criticism against both the basic assumptions and the finished products of idealistic speculations. As the protesting group or party of the "outs," it has naturally been aggressive. Already under some degree of social stigma because of its minority status, it has had little to lose. Consequently it could plunge into the philosophical fight in headlong fashion. And, like all those who attack the *status quo,* naturalism has impressed the idealist as ill-mannered and lacking in respect for the traditional dignity of philosophy. "It isn't cricket philosophically to picket," has been a common reaction from the idealistic camp. However, the pickets have kept right on marching, until today they have won better treatment and even a large voice in the management of the philosophical concern. But the basic opposition between the two points of view still remains, and, for reasons which this chapter will attempt to make clear, probably will always constitute the most fundamental division within philosophy.

What Is the World at Heart?

In the first place, the opposition between the two poles of thought remains because the fundamental issue is not, as many persons believe, whether the nature of the ultimate real is material or mental. Instead, as we saw in the preceding chapter, it is this: Is the world-order at heart a *mechanical* order or a *moral* order? Is the universe similar to a vast mechanism, mindless, purposeless and consequently nonmoral? Or is it a moral structure, operating in terms of intelligent purpose, and in the direction of realizing values and ideals? It will be seen immediately that this is a basic divergence, which not even agreement as to the "substance" of the universe can bridge. The two schools may be able to agree (as seems likely) that energy is the ultimate world-stuff. As long, however, as one school takes this energy as essentially mental or spiritual, and tends to spell the word with a capital "E" (thereby identifying it, at least by implication, with Mind or God), while the other regards energy as science does, the split must remain.

The Status of Value. The opposition between the two schools must remain for a second reason. For idealism, value is inherent in the universe; value lies at the heart of things, and the activities and processes of the universe are working towards the maximum realization of the Good. Value is therefore something objective which man discovers as basic in the cosmos, and for the idealist nothing proves the affiliation between man and his friendly environment so plainly as this fact that humanity and the universe are both concerned with the Good. For naturalism, on the other hand, there is only as much of value and goodness in the world as we can ourselves make, working in an indifferent environment. Values exist only in relation to living organisms, and the naturalist believes that we are merely deceiving ourselves if we seek to project these ideals onto the screen of the cosmos, and pretend that it has any concern for them. For the universe remains sublimely indifferent to man's hopes and ideals; the naturalist can see no evidence that "justice," for example, has any meaning (or even any existence) outside of human affairs.

This is the old argument, ably presented by Spinoza and many other thinkers. Do we desire certain objects and ideals because they are good, or do we call them "good" because we by nature desire them, and in this way attempt to justify or rationalize our desires by giving them honorific names? For idealism, goodness inheres in certain objects or certain acts because they are a significant part of the cosmic scheme. For naturalism, these "goods" exist as such only because of our own biological natures and their needs. Both as individuals and as a race, we have needs which must be met if we are to survive individually and prosper as a species. We call "good" those objects (e.g., food), institutions (e.g., marriage) or actions (e.g., parental sacrifice) which satisfy any of these primary needs, and for naturalism that is all that the term can mean. To speak of the "Good" as something that transcends human welfare is meaningless for naturalistic thought.

The Contrasting Views Regarding Man's Nature. There is still another reason for the permanent opposition between these two schools. Despite all it may say regarding the kinship of man with a friendly universe, idealism builds its ethics upon a basic separation between "nature" and "human nature." Without lessening his emphasis upon the rational character and spiritual ground of the natural world, the idealist nevertheless argues that man, by his unique possession of a mind and a rational will, represents something apart from the rest of nature. Furthermore, human nature is not only separate; it is higher—a link, as it were, between nature and Mind, between the natural and the supernatural. Hence when (for example) the naturalist argues that there is no evidence of justice existing in the universe except as a purely human ideal, and points out that the primary law of nature seems to be something nearer "dog eat dog," the idealist remains unmoved. For he admits that nature is "red in fang and claw," but insists that man's possession of reason removes him from this primitive law of a mere battle for survival. Human nature is redeemed by its kinship with the source of Reason and Goodness, and thereby transcends its animal heritage.

In the naturalistic view, man is one of the animal species, and in spite of possessing mind or consciousness, never escapes this origin. The realm of nature is unbroken in its inclusive extent, and man is as much a part of this realm as any other species; he is no less subject to its laws, and his actions are as strictly controlled by cause and effect as anything else in the universe. Nature admits no exceptions; each species has unique abilities and characteristics, but the possession of these in no way separates it from the rest of the natural order. Nor do its unique capacities give the species a significance beyond that of other forms of life. For a rodent, the ability to gnaw would undoubtedly seem more important (and therefore of greater cosmic significance) than the ability to reason abstractly. For a deer, it would probably be fleetness that made it unique in its own eyes—and therefore of more importance in the eyes of the universe. For a fish, all values would be established in terms of liquidity and swimability.[1]

The Naturalistic View of Mind. From our preceding chapter we are now aware of the centrality of mind in the idealistic view of things. For naturalism, however, mind is only an instrument or tool. Man's survival in the struggle for existence is not aided by protective coloration, extreme speed, sharp claws, or the ability to give off a violent smell or to utter frightening roars. Other animals can outrun him, outswim him, and outfight him in unaided combat. Instead of these special abilities and equipments, man has another instrument, his intelligence, which enables him more than to compensate for his lack by inventing weapons and tools of all kinds, and by harnessing natural forces to work for him. But this remarkable mind of man's, admittedly the most flexible of all instruments of adaptation, remains nothing (as far as the rest of the universe is concerned) except an instrument of survival and adjustment.

[1] As suggested by Rupert Brooke in his delicate satire called "Heaven," in which a fish's idea of the hereafter is presented at some length. The poem is unfortunately too long to quote.

It is unique, and of overwhelming importance to man, but this does not prove that it has any more cosmic significance than the tiger's claw or the fish's fin. It is true that man can do more with his intelligence than the other animals can with their "tools," but it is likewise true that he can do more in the direction of harm as well as in the direction of "the Good." In short, the possession of intelligence only means more power and a wider range of action, not necessarily greater good.

The favorite naturalistic theme thus runs something as follows: In the beginning was nature, then by a long and very slow process of evolution, man. The human species is a development (or, if it makes the idealist happier, a flowering) of nature, but no more or less important than the other animal species, from which it is separated by differences that are far less important biologically than the needs and traits it has in common with them. The natural order is continuous, and man, despite his mental uniqueness and his general importance to himself, represents no break in that order.

"Nature" in the Naturalistic Scheme. The naturalist is sometimes accused by his opponent of making the concept of "nature" so broad and inclusive as to be meaningless, much as the naturalist accuses his opponent of stretching "mind" to cover everything and thus making it mean nothing. What naturalism intends by the term, however, is something quite different. When it calls "nature" the sole reality, and thus appears to make it identical with existence, this is not to postulate a new Absolute which shall be like "a night in which all cows are black."[2] Instead, the naturalist is postulating a universe where the transcendental can have no place. He is advocating a naturalism that shall preclude any supernaturalism. What leads him to define nature in such a way as to exclude all "other worlds" or "beyonds" from the category of existence is his profound distrust of systems which, however logical and well-constructed, have no empirical foundations.

Naturalism assumes three postulates regarding nature. These three are so basic and characteristic that they determine the whole spirit of this school of philosophy. Consequently if we understand these postulates completely, including their negative implications, we shall have a good picture of this world view. (1) First, naturalism asserts that there is only one system or order of reality, only one level of existence. By implication, this postulate eliminates all systems of dualistic metaphysics

[2] Hegel's description of Schelling's Absolute.

and makes impossible the existence of any sort of transcendental or super-natural realm. (2) Second, naturalism holds that this single order of reality consists of all objects and events in space and time, and only of these. Here again the negative implications are important: such a postulate eliminates the possibility of discourse about a deity who is "outside of time," or a transcendental realm which is "beyond space." And it also renders meaningless any statements regarding objects and events which cannot be placed within the categories of time and space. (3) And finally, naturalism holds that the behavior of this single order of existence—that is, the whole cosmic process and all the particular events which make up this process—is determined exclusively by the character of this order and can be reduced to a system of causal laws. Here too the implications are perhaps more significant, and certainly more revealing, than the postulate itself: to accept this postulate is to state that we believe the universe to be self-contained, self-sufficient, self-dependent and self-operating. It also means that we regard the universe as self-directing, and uninfluenced by any "outside" agency or "higher" power. In fact to accept this postulate is to deny the possibility that the world order, or series of natural events, can be intruded upon in any manner by any agent. This does not imply that man cannot learn how to control nature by discovering her laws and their application. Since on the naturalistic hypothesis man is himself a part of the order of nature, his interference with that order, even when most obvious (for example, moving mountains) or most basic (for example, atomic fission), does not constitute an intrusion from out-side nature such as supposed "miracles" and "divine revelations" would be.

Naturalism and Science

As might be expected, the naturalistic philosopher is devoted to both the methods and the findings of science. As we have seen, idealism admits the scientific view of the world to be true as far as it goes, but denies that it goes far enough to give ultimate knowledge. The naturalist in turn denies that we can go beyond that systematic organization of empirical data which we call "science" and still be on sure ground. As far as naturalism is concerned, knowledge (that is, any knowledge worthy of its name) must either derive directly from sensory experience, as in common sense, or be capable of eventual sensory verification, as in science.

The Confusion of Naturalism with Positivism. This limitation of knowledge to the empirical or scientific level has led to much misunderstanding of naturalism, both by its idealistic opponent and by educated persons generally. This misunderstanding has historical roots that penetrate down through the last hundred years of intellectual accumulation. As we have indicated, there are nearly as many subschools within naturalism as within idealism. Both of the larger schools have on occasion had to pay in loss of intellectual prestige for the extreme doctrines of some small subschool that was marching in its column. In the case of naturalism, the extreme group has been the *positivists.* Their founder was the French philosopher and sociologist Auguste Comte, whose main work was published more than a hundred years ago (1839-1842). The school is now virtually dead—somewhat to the relief of the more moderate naturalists who have in recent decades become weary of justifying its extremist position. Unfortunately many antinaturalists are not aware of this demise, and consequently still continue to castigate naturalism as a whole for the sins of the dead.

Positivism identified knowledge and science completely. Not only was science the final authority in all matters of truth or knowledge, but any of our experiences which did not admit of scientific investigation were relegated to the category of insignificance or even nonexistence. This dogmatic point of view, which could only have arisen when modern science was still in the full flood of adolescent confidence, naturally estranged all those persons for whom man's ethical, artistic, or religious experiences seemed to be not only real but significant. As a consequence, positivism was attacked violently, and in its violence the attack frequently included all naturalistic fellow travelers. At present, it would probably be impossible to find any thinker of prominence who would support the extreme positivistic position. The trend today is in the opposite direction. During the last half-century, there has been a steady philosophical development, within the broader boundaries of general naturalism, of a school now usually called "critical naturalism." This viewpoint, which perhaps represents the naturalistic attitude at its thoughtful best, endeavors to avoid the extremes of both positivism and nineteenth-century materialism by finding a place for all phenomenon, including the social, the moral, and the esthetic.[3] While defining everything (including mind) in terms of the natural world, and consistently assailing supernaturalism in all its forms, critical naturalism by no means identifies the domain of scientific fact with the field of total human experience. Even more important, it refuses to define nature exclusively in terms of either matter and motion, or events in space-time. It regards these as methodological concepts necessary to the work of science, but refuses to accord them a metaphysical status as sole definers of the character of nature or reality.

What critical naturalism does accept—and here it speaks for all naturalists—is the scientific attitude or approach, and particularly the frames of references used to formulate the general principles of science. It agrees that these principles must be based upon the facts of our common experience—the objective, verifiable realm that is open to all observers—and must not ignore or pretend to transcend these facts in some way.

The Law of Parsimony. To understand the full force of this last point we must consider one of the general principles of science, known as the "law of parsimony." As originally phrased by William of Occam in the fourteenth century, this principle (sometimes called "Occam's Razor") states that explanatory principles or factors are not to be multiplied beyond necessity. The purpose of this "razor" was to provide a weapon for hacking away the vast deadwood of entities, substances, causes, and so forth, accumulated by several centuries of medieval thought. Its indirect result was to clear the ground for the scientific formulations of the Renaissance, and ultimately to give the new sciences one of their most important intellectual tools. In simpler language, the principle says this: If several alternate explanations of any phenomenon are available, all apparently equal in their ability to account for the facts and all equally logical, then the ground for choosing among them shall be *simplicity.* "Nature favors the simplest method," or "Nature does things the easiest way," are popular statements of the axiom. In terms of our last paragraph, the principle of parsimony would hold that if natural causes are adequate to account for all phenomena—if scientific knowledge offers sufficient explanation—why invoke the unprovable hypothesis of idealism?

The crux of the matter is of course whether or not scientific formulations do constitute adequate answers in our quest for ultimate knowledge.

---

[3] For succinct statement of critical naturalism, I would again recommend Randall and Buchler, *op. cit.,* Chapter XVI.

To the idealist, the world revealed by the several sciences may be a true world, but it can never be the whole world. Indeed, he doubts that it is even a fair sample of reality, so how can its laws constitute sufficient explanations to satisfy us? Occam's law may be sound enough (continues the idealist), but it should be noted that we are required to select the simplest *adequate* explanation. Scientific explanations are adequate only for the purposes of science; as such they may give us a true picture of *physical* reality, but of the underlying true Real they tell us very little.

Contrasting Views Regarding "Nature." For, says the idealist, "the apparent self-sufficiency of nature is an illusion."[4] The natural world is only a mask upon reality—the whole of nature is but an appearance, a phenomenon, whose underlying noumenon is something very different. It is in this nonphysical reality that the natural world is grounded, and upon it the whole structure of the universe depends. For the naturalist, such a viewpoint is fantastic; it appears like a cosmic case of putting the cart before the horse. Naturalism takes its stand on the common-sense position: the seeming self-sufficiency of nature is genuine. The natural order depends on nothing outside itself for either its existence or its maintenance. On the contrary, everything within the universe, including man and his mind, depends upon the physical order for its existence. The universe is grounded upon itself alone, and we need assume no external source or transcendental power to give it either existence or intelligibility. The universe stands on its own feet, unsuspended by cosmic bootstraps. The question of what lies outside or beyond the universe is therefore meaningless; the term includes the sum of all existence, and how can there be anything outside of "existence"?

It is upon this issue that the basic split between idealism and naturalism occurs. For the idealist, the ultimate Real is a spiritual something lying behind the apparent reality of our common-sense experimental world of here and now. For the naturalist, this experiential world, the great natural order, is itself ultimate; therefore, following the law of parsimony, we should not assume unnecessary explanatory factors to account for it. The laws of cause and effect, as they are understood by and operate for science, are adequate explanations—adequate not only for science but also for both philosophy and practical living. Thus for naturalism, the elaborate formulations of both idealism and religion are

4 *Cf.* Hocking, *Types of Philosophy* (rev. ed.), p. 248.

undercut by Occam's Razor, and have no valid excuse for continued existence.

"But," the reader will demand, "if the naturalistic position is as adequate as its exponents claim and if idealism is unnecessary, then why has the latter flourished throughout the history of Western civilization, and why does it still maintain such a hardy growth? Surely there must be something more than tradition to keep idealism alive!" The reader is quite right, and that "something" is the fact that the naturalistic viewpoint is not adequate to everyone, or even to a majority of persons. For however well this world-view may be able to satisfy the head, it does not satisfy the heart of many people.

Nor is there much likelihood that the naturalistic view of the world will ever meet the emotional demands of most persons as well as the idealistic view can. The naturalistic school will always have to face the accusation that its members are without hearts, that they are scarcely human, and that their view is cold and somber in comparison with the warmth and security that idealism can give. As we have already suggested, this charge that the naturalist is indifferent to the demands of the heart is for most people much more serious than any possible intellectual weaknesses of the system. Most persons who come to philosophy seeking answers are willing to overlook a few breaks in logic, a few unexamined assumptions slipped in or a few gaps left unplugged, if only the general tone and trend of the answers satisfies their emotions. Idealism of course supplies this satisfaction; it and its rival may be on a par as far as logic is concerned, but not as concerns emotional satisfaction. This fact alone would be sufficient to account for the wide popularity and continuing vitality of idealism.

Metaphysical vs. Ethical Idealism

It is almost inevitable that somewhere in this chapter the reader has suddenly become aware of a paradox. Perhaps his experience is similar to that of many people: He has perhaps been called an "idealist" by friends and relatives, yet now discovers that his views concerning the universe and reality are more nearly those of the naturalist. If the basic idea around which this book is written is sound, and idealism and naturalism are the opposite poles of philosophy, how can one be in both camps without being grossly inconsistent—which the reader probably feels sure he is not.

The explanation is simpler than might be supposed, at least in the eyes of the naturalist. For the confusion arises from the fact that there are two types of idealism, distinguished by the names *metaphysical* and *ethical* (or *axiological*) idealism. It is of the former that we have been speaking up to this point. This major metaphysical view, strictly speaking, should be called *idea-ism;* unfortunately the word is difficult to pronounce, and the "l" was added long ago for euphony. As a consequence, the same term is now used to mean two different (and, to the naturalist, unrelated) concepts: first, that world-view in which idea, thought, or mind is the basic reality; and second, that system of belief or conduct in which ideals—that is, desirable ends or standards—are a primary motivation. If it were possible to use *ideaism* for the metaphysical view and *idealism* for the ethical doctrine, endless confusion would be eliminated.

The Metaphysical Idealist's Claim of a Monopoly. However, more than mere euphony is involved here. Another reason why two separate terms are not used is the fact that metaphysical idealism has tried to maintain a monopoly of the single term by a tenacious insistence that the two views cannot be separated. It argues that you cannot have an ideal system of conduct without presupposing a view of the universe that depicts the Real as mental or spiritual. In short, the metaphysical idealist insists that no ethical system can have force or even meaning unless it is underwritten by a cosmic order that is a moral order, in which the Good exists as the inmost core of reality. To this school of idealism, the phrase "naturalistic ethics" or "morality in a naturalistic setting" is a paradox. Unless there is a basic Good as the source of all things, "good" as applied to objects or actions or institutions is a meaningless term. Our ideals and standards must have some relation to higher, more inclusive ideals—to the Ideal with a capital "I"—if they are to have any value at all. As purely human standards, derived entirely from human experience and with meaning only for human affairs, they would be ineffectual and worthless.

Ethical Idealism in Relation to Naturalism. *Ethical* idealism has no necessary relation to this uncompromising viewpoint, and the ethical idealist frequently has little sympathy with it. This type of ethical thinker is frequently a metaphysical naturalist, who holds that values and ideals lose none of their meaning or their force by being "merely human." To call them human, or to label him a humanist, is no disparagement; in his philosophy there is nothing divine or supernatural, in comparison with which the natural or "merely human" rates lower. That man is capable of formulating ideals and then living his life in terms of them is to the naturalist a great and significant thing, but this significance comes solely from the human welfare and happiness which may thus be realized, and *not* from any supposed relation to the cosmic Good. Man's ideals have dignity and worth in their own right; they can stand by themselves, drawing their meaning and value from their relation to human life and its potentialities. For example, even if "justice" has no Platonic Form as its source and metaphysical guarantor, in any society composed of creatures with feelings and intelligence capable of sensing injustice, it would exist as a meaningful, dynamic ideal. In short, we frame ideals and seek to realize them because we are conscious of incompleteness and deficiencies in our own experience, rather than because we are burdened with any sense of Divine Perfection or the Ultimate Good. We formulate ideals for the same reason that we philosophize: because we are human beings who have capacities which make both activities possible, and because we live in a world that makes both inevitable.

Naturalism cannot see in either activity anything more than the natural reaction of human beings living in this world. Neither searching for ultimate knowledge nor seeking to realize ideals in our own lives implies a beneficent universe or a higher realm of "the Good, the True, and the Beautiful." The cosmos may be indifferent to our ideals and our hopes, but this is irrelevant. We strive to realize them for our own satisfaction, or for the welfare of those we know and the happiness of the ones we love. And this striving is unrelated to the concern or indifference of the universe.

The Broader Implications of Idealism

By now the reader should find the geography of the two philosophical hemispheres clear in outline. We are therefore ready to begin our study of the problems of philosophy, for now these problems and the schools that have arisen in answer to them can be better understood. We have our bearings, as it were, and from now on we can sail far out on a rough sea of speculative thought, confident that we have enough landmarks to assure us of a safe return. But for added safety and greater enjoyment on the forthcoming voyage, it will be well to take a final panoramic glance around. The landmarks may seem certain and foolproof as we stand on the shore, but while trying to steer a course through clashing waves and swirling currents they are likely to stand out less clearly.

We have seen idealism to be a doctrine of optimism and confidence. This mood of assurance is derived from a well thought-out view of reality as a realm of intellectual, moral, and spiritual values—a setting in which our own struggles to realize values and ideals take on increased significance because the universe as a whole is not only friendly towards such an effort but actively participates in it. In this *Weltanschauung* the ground of all being is Mind or Intelligence. This Intelligence, however, is no mere neutral center of rational processes. On the contrary, it is as characterized by *goodness* as by *rationality*.

Human Conduct Under an Idealistic World-view. Such a view of the world bears important implications for human conduct. First, it implies that man's rational and spiritual activities have far greater significance than the amount of time we usually devote to them would suggest. When we are most rational or most spiritual we are in closest harmony with the universe, and it is then that we reach nearest to the ultimate real. It is then that we realize our own highest selves and the chief purpose of our existence. A second implication of the idealistic world-view is the almost infinite possibility of human moral and spiritual realization it offers. We have already quoted one of America's leading idealists as stating that his school holds that "nothing is foreclosed as impossible in the direction of highest human aspiration and desire." A universe which is rational and friendly offers a hope—indeed, even a definite promise— that our deepest yearnings and highest aspirations are not vain and meaningless. Thus man's hope of immortality and expectation of ultimate justice are no mere compensatory dream. They are rather the Great Promise, justified by both our own nature and the character of the cosmos itself.

Furthermore, in a rational, intelligent universe there could be no cosmic jokes, such as man's yearning for the eternal would be if it were merely wishful thinking. The very rationality of the real excludes the possibility of such gross irrationality. The logical chain runs thus: Man possesses reason, and reason can come only from Reason. On the logical grounds already indicated, it must be assumed that the source of this intelligence is also the source of all existence; Mind is the source of all being, both human and nonhuman. And, since a world that comes from Mind must bear the character of its origin, the common rationality of both man and the world is established. But in a rational, intelligent world all parts must harmonize and integrate. If man's vision of eternal life and cosmic justice is merely the expression of an animal's desire for something it does not possess, then the universe would not be a unified whole, for man's mind and emotions would be out of gear with the nature of things. Thus the realization of our highest hopes is guaranteed by the fact that we possess enough intelligence to have these hopes and to express them.

The Naturalistic Reaction Against the Implication of Idealism

The naturalist's viewpoint is to a considerable degree a reaction against this idealistic view. As someone has said, the naturalist is impelled to metaphysics largely by a revulsion against what he considers so much bad metaphysics. The world as idealism pictures it impresses him as such a patent example of man's ability to think wishfully and dream rationally that he is driven to protest against it—but to protest against one metaphysical system is to imply another, and once the opposing system is implied its formulation becomes inevitable. Thus the naturalistic thinker is forced into metaphysical speculation, however much he might prefer to stop when he has synthesized the findings of the various sciences and intellectual disciplines. It is this reluctant entry into the metaphysical arena that sometimes prompts idealism to accuse its rival of having a purely negative approach to philosophy and its problems: the idealist is inclined to feel that naturalism is not a philosophy, but the denial of philosophy. In other words, the anti-idealist is accused of a dog-in-the-manger attitude; since he cannot formulate a complete "rational" picture of reality (that is, one which gives the starring role to Mind and guarantees man a comfortable seat in the royal box), he spitefully attacks all efforts to do what he cannot. But the naturalist stubbornly answers, "It is true that my world-view is less neat and inspiring than idealism's;

however, this is because my intellectual integrity will not allow me to fill in the gaps in the picture with such assumptions as I feel that the idealist uses. If the idealist wants to use his heart to complete a picture which no head can yet achieve, that is his privilege—but it does not prove that his system alone is worthy of being called philosophy."

The Divergent Over-All Moods of the Two Schools

But as we have already suggested, most persons are more interested in the general mood of a philosophy than in its intellectual details. It is this general over-all mood or tone of any thought system that is decisive to the layman. As we are now well aware, the moods of idealism and naturalism are even more divergent than their intellectual aspects. Idealism embodies a mood of serene confidence in the basic rationality of both man and the universe. And this rationality implies not only that reality has an order and a logical structure comparable to that of the mind, but points to the existence of purpose and direction in the cosmic process. And since this purpose or "drift of the cosmic weather" (as William James called it) is in the direction of realizing value or achieving the Good, we have only to link our individual lives and purposes with its over-all purpose to find significance and happiness in life. Hence idealism invites us to seek the rational reality which admittedly often lies well concealed beneath the less than rational appearances—and meanwhile to enjoy the serenity which faith in the existence and discoverability of such a reality has to offer.

The philosophy of naturalism, on the other hand, can offer us only the Spartan mood and high-priced exhilaration of a morning shower with no hot water. Its mood of indifferentism, of a universe in which human affairs and yearnings are no more important than the activities and desires of any other animal species, is not such as to appeal to most persons. Like those who take a cold morning shower, the naturalists will probably always remain a hardy minority, tolerated as harmless but slightly eccentric. For naturalism offers no mood of certitude and comfort, no Great

Amen resolution to the discords of life. It says, rather, what A. E. Housman sings so persistently:

> The troubles of our proud and angry dust
> Are from eternity, and shall not fail.

It is not that naturalism denies the possibility of improving our life—certainly it is committed to no pessimistic view of human nature—but rather that it insists any such amelioration must come from our own efforts expended in the world of here and now. A bit of verse by Stephen Crane expresses the point tersely:

> A man said to the universe:
> "Sir, I exist!"
> "However," replied the universe,
> "The fact has not created in me
> A sense of obligation."[5]

The Indifference of the World to Human Welfare. A figure drawn from the psychology of adjustment expresses the idea in a more practical way. As the psychologist would say, the problem of human happiness is one of adjustment; happiness is the sustained emotional tone that accompanies a condition of adjustment between the healthy organism and its environment. In short, if we would be happy, we must become integrated with the physical and social world in which we live, either by changing that environment, or (if this is impossible) by altering our aims so as to make them realizable. *But,* as we begin our process of adjustment, we must remember this one central fact: Our environment is only a passive partner in this relationship. The world lies passively around us, willing to be used to any extent that we can impose our will upon it. But to sit and wait for it to take the initiative, or show any interest in our welfare and happiness, is to reveal ourselves as both intellectually and emotionally immature.

The situation is well illustrated by a bird building her nest under the barn eaves. There stands the barn, passive and quite indifferent to the success or failure of the nest-building operation. The bird may wear her-

[5] Reprinted from *The Collected Poems of Stephen Crane*, copyright, 1899, 1926, by Alfred A. Knopf, Inc.

self out in vain; unless she can solve the problem of adapting the materials to that location, failure is inevitable. The barn will not lift a rafter or move a plank, regardless of her desires and efforts. Nothing can shake the barn from its indifference, for the same reason that nothing can move the universe from its indifferentism: both represent only the play of natural forces. In neither is there Intelligence or Spirit or Personality. In neither is there anything that can be moved by mere thought, whether this take the form of idle daydreams, elaborate systematized metaphysics, or even dignified prayers. For the naturalist, this is the core fact of man's relation to the universe in which he lives.

Naturalism Not Necessarily Pessimistic. Now this naturalistic attitude towards our world does not mean (as its exponents hasten to point out) that happiness is impossible, that life is a farce, or that the universe is a huge joke. Naturalism has as much interest in human happiness as does any other philosophy. However, it does differ from most of the other schools, and particularly from idealism, concerning the *means* by which happiness can best be attained and the maximum potentialities in human nature can best be realized. To the naturalist, such a goal can be reached only by building both our individual lives and our civilization upon a naturalistic foundation. We gain nothing by talking of a "higher law," "divine justice," "cosmic good," "Heaven," or "the Absolute"—and we stand to lose a great deal in that these vague concepts may become escape mechanisms, devices for ignoring obvious social evils, or techniques for justifying the patent injustices in our society. To think in these "inspirational" terms admittedly provides relief when we are harassed by bewildering problems, and when life seems too complicated to be understood or too hard to be endured. The naturalist would agree with the psychologist that such beliefs sometimes have therapeutic value in that they may temporarily relieve the strain of daily living. But there is always the danger that they may become organized into a systematic philosophy of escape, and thus be a detriment to the tremendous possibilities which life offers for achieving satisfaction and happiness. It is only as we organize our lives within the framework of reality—reality as we know it through sensory experience and science—that we can fully realize these possibilities. We get the most from life by facing it, not by escaping—even through the dignified medium of philosophy.

The Irreducible Character of the Contrast Between the Two Viewpoints

And now, in conclusion, what are we to make of this dramatic conflict between two points of view so profoundly opposed as idealism and naturalism? In the first place, how can intelligent men, of similar educational background and experience, living in the same society in the same era, arrive at viewpoints so divergent? For instance, how is it possible for a confirmed naturalist and an ardent idealist to move side by side through a common experience and each come out with added evidence for his own point of view? The writer once traveled through the High Sierras of California in company with such a pair of philosophically-minded individuals, and found their arguments both amusing and puzzling. In the presence of some tremendous panorama of fourteen-thousand-foot peaks the idealist would inevitably find evidence of "the Good, the True, and the Beautiful"; in the presence of natural sublimity he would always feel the purpose and design of the universe made manifest. Great mountains impelled him to great thoughts, and these in turn to the Great Thought lying behind it all. In altitude he found the Absolute; the Sierras had primary significance to him as the handiwork of God.

And the naturalist? When he had recovered from the idealist's reactions well enough to put his own into words, the divergence in viewpoint was striking. To him the scenery was equally impressive; if anything, he was even more responsive to natural beauty. But in magnificent peaks and beautiful lakes he could sense no Mind, no Design, no Purpose. Instead, they suggested the vastness of nature, its loneliness, its ageless endurance, the eternal cycle of day and night, summer and winter, sun and snow. He found no brooding Presence here, "whose dwelling is the light of setting suns," no intimations of immortality. Most frequently he was impressed by the eternality of the natural order in contrast to the brevity of man's days. In all the grandeur and beauty he felt the sternness of nature, together with the colossal indifference of the universe to man and his little life. Probably it was the word "lonely" that was on his lips most often as he described his reactions to a peak or a lake. He found such scenery bracing and stimulating, but hardly "inspiring." To live in such a setting for a few weeks blew the cobwebs out of his brain, made him aware of a pettiness of human affairs (including his own), and in general had a tonic effect—but it was the tonic effect of a dip in one of those two-mile-high lakes. In the mountains he found no Mind; their haunting loneliness was exceeded only by that of the brilliant stars that wheeled overhead in a canopy almost too bright for sleeping.

The Possible Causes of the Contrasting Attitudes. And so again the question: How can men undergo the same experience and read such divergent implications from it? For intelligence, sincerity, wisdom, or good will, it is impossible to choose between the idealists as a group and the naturalists as a group. We must look deeper than either intellectual capacity or breadth of knowledge if we would explain the fundamental opposition between these poles of philosophical thought. William James, in our own country and century, divided men into what he considered the basic classifications "tough-minded" and "tender-minded"; and this terminology has achieved wide acceptance.

James had the dual viewpoint of psychologist and philosopher. It is therefore significant that he suggested that the difference is probably one of temperament—and therefore as fundamental as any human differences that we know. Unfortunately, we know little more about either the basis or the nature of "temperament" than James did three generations ago. As of today, this area is still largely a mystery in spite of the efforts of biologists and psychologists to explore and reveal it.

Some Decision Probable. By now it is evident that the argument between these two great schools could go on forever—and probably will. Regardless of how we explain the opposition between these major poles of philosophical thought, it remains the most salient fact in the long history of speculative activity. The newcomer to philosophy may not yet be able to classify himself as "idealist" or "naturalist," but that is hardly to be expected at an early stage of one's philosophical development. It is sufficient if by now we sense the basic opposition and its principal implications. Perhaps the reader feels that both schools have strong points and telling arguments, and that one can make a selection from among these to form his own system of philosophy. Many a beginner in the field attempts to do this, but the farther he advances in philosophical study the more probable it becomes that he will be attracted to one of the two poles. In the chapters that follow, as the various problems of philosophy pass in review within the framework we have now established, the reader's own position should become increasingly clear to him.

CHAPTER 5

THE ORIGIN AND DEVELOPMENT OF LIFE

O F ALL THE PROBLEMS WITH WHICH PHILOSOPHY DEALS, THOSE that grow out of the biological sciences hold the most interest for many students. This is natural, for these problems are less abstract than many with which philosophy deals, and they involve the most interesting of all subjects, living creatures. Furthermore, they are questions that relate directly to our own history: Where did life come from? What was the form of original life? What are the changes that have come about since this origin, and how were they caused? Are transformations still going on? Is man just one more species of animal, or does he have a unique nature that can only be explained by assuming a special creation—or at least a special interest on the part of the universe? In short, we are now face to face with numerous variations on what has been called one of philosophy's three main themes: Where do we come from?

Under this single inclusive question there are three subquestions. These concern the *nature* of life, the *origin* of life, and the *development* of life. As we begin what must necessarily be a packed and meaty chapter, it will be wise to keep ourselves reminded that all the facts and theories which we meet are concerned with these three problems: (1) What is Life? (2) Where did it come from, or how did it begin? (3) What causes have brought about the infinite variety of organisms that now inhabit the earth? Students who are new to philosophy are usually more interested in the origins of life, but we shall have to concentrate rather on the other two questions. For the biologist and philosopher are both concerned more with the *development* of life than they are with its *origin,* although obviously any discussion of either of these must depend upon the views we hold regarding the *nature* of the life process.

What Is Life? We therefore logically begin with the question, What is life? The biologist prefers to ask, What is the process which we call living? However, both biologist and philosopher agree that if we can determine what differentiates living from nonliving matter, we will have moved quite a ways towards answering our first question. Before we begin to discuss the unique attributes of life, however, it is imperative that we grasp a distinction which is indispensable to the understanding of this as well as several future chapters. This is the distinction between the *substantive* and the *functional* views of life. Unfortunately, the importance of this distinction is matched by the difficulty of understanding it. For most persons, it represents such a radical departure from all previous habits of thought that they feel as if they are suddenly required to think in a new language.

The Substantive View

The substantive view of life, which nearly all of us have held since childhood and which we accordingly regard as "common sense," regards life as a substance. To prevent this statement from sounding childishly redundant, let us for the moment regard "substance" as synonymous with "thing." Thus the view involves the belief that life is a thing, an entity or a physical existent of some kind. Now the concept of substance usually includes two separate requirements. In the first place, to be a substance is to be capable of independent existence, presumably even after all qualities and attributes have vanished into nothingness.[1] Second, to be a substance is to possess permanence. Actually, this second criterion always becomes the practical test of substantiality. "For the only way we can tell that a thing is able to exist alone is to observe that it does, at some time, exist in the absence of other things with which it is usually associated. Thus unless a thing is permanent it cannot be regarded as a substance. It might conceivably be permanent without being substantial; but it could

---

[1] Cf. Dotterer, *Philosophy by Way of the Sciences,* p. 324.

not be substantial without being permanent."[2] It is obvious that "permanence" is a relative term, but in practical use it implies a fixity or stability in relation to the human life span. Thus the stars are permanent while a flower is not.

Another way to describe the substantive view is to say that it regards life as a "stuff." Many of our figures of speech imply such a concept; we speak of "wasting our life," or "pouring out one's life on the field of battle," or "giving our life for a cause," or "spending our life in futile effort." In fact, almost any term used in speaking of life, outside of the biological laboratory and perhaps the philosophy classroom, reveals the tendency to think of life as a *stuff* or *thing* of some sort—with all the permanence and independence of existence which we usually associate with "things" of various kinds. Some of the misleading effects of the substantive view of life (and, even more unfortunate, the substantive view of mind) will be discussed in our final chapter on the problem of immortality. For the present it will be enough to point out how inevitably this view leads to a belief in survival after death. For, it is usually argued, life can't just disappear; a "thing" doesn't do that. At most, things only change form, and it is therefore reasonable to assume that our lives will continue in some form after death. But more on this later.

The Functional View of Life

The usual reaction of students to the first challenge of the substantive view of life which they happen to meet is one of considerable surprise. "What else," they ask, "can life possibly be except something of this sort? Does not the fact that we have a noun 'life' indicate that there must be something substantial to correspond to it? Surely the term doesn't refer to a figment of the imagination!"

Before we present the alternate view, it will be helpful to spend a moment analyzing this last assumption that nouns always have a substantial referent. Every teacher of philosophy is frequently discouraged to discover how easily students fall into the error of such assumption, particularly when so little thought will prevent it. Fundamentally, nouns refer to *experiences* of various kinds. A majority of these are concrete: *book, chair,*

[2] *Ibid.*

dog, moon, and so forth. Other nouns represent either an illusory or imagined experience, such as *ghost, chimera, elf,* and so on. Still others indicate an abstraction or idealization: *justice, infinity, God,* for example. Still others represent an entire series of experiences, almost infinite in number, and serve merely to summarize them under a convenient heading for purposes of communication. *Mind, soul, consciousness,* and *life* are famous examples of this type of noun. Thus when we use such words we are not necessarily referring to any "thing," "stuff," or "substance." Above all, we must be careful not to assume that, because the word itself is single and suggests a unity to our mind, we may assume that its referent is therefore single, unified or substantial.

The alternative view of life, preferred by most biologists, is generally known as the *functional* or *operational* view. Instead of considering life a thing or substance, this view regards it as a *process*—or rather, as whole series of processes. "Life" thus becomes merely a convenient name which we give to the sum total of all those activities, functions, or processes which characterizes an organism. The minimum list of these functions is usually something as follows: reproduction, adjustment, self-repair and irritability (the capacity to react to changes in the environment). The functional view usually seeks to explain all of these vital processes in physical and chemical terms; it is therefore closely related to *mechanism* in biology. The substantive view, on the other hand, is nearly synonymous with *vitalism*. The last part of this chapter will be devoted to presenting the mechanism-vitalism controversy, which is the dominant philosophical issue growing out of the biological sciences. When we come to this presentation we shall have occasion to refer frequently to the contrast between the substantive and functional views. Meanwhile, however, we must consider the various theories as to the *origin* and the *development* of life. Once we have these clearly in mind, we can fruitfully return to our discussion of the *nature* of life.

The Origin of Life: Three Theories

There have been three traditional theories as to the origin of life, known respectively as *special creation, transmission,* and *archebiosis.* In recent times the last term has been largely replaced by the word "emergence," although the two concepts are not identical. Historically there have been various subtheories under these main heads, but it will be enough for our purpose to describe these three.

1. *Special Creation.* The theory of special creation is almost self-explanatory. It holds that life was introduced into a world of inanimate matter by a special creative act—presumably by God, and that this took place after an antecedent creation of the universe by the same agent. It should be pointed out that the theory as such does not necessarily imply the Biblical account of Creation given in Genesis. All that is required by the theory is the belief that *life was intentionally created in some form by an intervening agent.* Thus one could not only dismiss the Biblical account of Creation, but even hold the general theory of evolution, and still stand within the framework of this creationist hypothesis. As long as it is assumed that *some special act was required to initiate vital activity,* questions as to when, how, or by whom the creative act was performed are only minor considerations. Such an assumption also reduces all questions regarding the original form of life to secondary importance.

It hardly need be said that this special creation theory has enjoyed almost universal acceptance historically. This has been true not only among Christians, but among a majority of religious and theistic systems of thought. As far as the West is concerned, except for a few crude but brilliant suggestions among early Greek thinkers, the creationist doctrine held undisputed dominance until late in the Renaissance, when both the other theories began to be discussed.

2. *Transmission.* The transmission theory seeks to solve the problem as to how life began by avoiding it—or rather, by postponing it permanently. In brief this theory holds that life came to our earth from some other planet, perhaps some other solar system. The supposed means of transmission would be extremely small spores contained within meteorites or other bits of interplanetary matter. Certain types of spores now known are so hardy and long-lived that this method of transference from one planet to another is not as fantastic as it might appear. There is, however, a fatal objection to the theory as far as philosophy is concerned: it may explain how life came to our earth, but it makes no attempt to account for the existence of living forms on the planet from which it supposedly was transmitted. As a mere biological account of the "origin" of life this might suffice, but it can hardly be called an explanation in the ordinary sense of the term.

3. *Archebiosis.* It thus seems that we must choose between a special creation theory and some sort of *archebiosis.* This latter viewpoint is in general the position of modern science. In brief it holds that at some point in historical time, organic matter developed from inorganic matter. The theory presumes that no external force or creative power was necessary for this changeover, but that it came about by purely natural means—that is, as the result of a fortuitous combination of natural conditions. The theory does not pretend to be able to describe these conditions with exactitude, nor as yet to be able to reproduce them in the laboratory. In fact, the archebiosis hypothesis must be regarded primarily as a creed: it is not a precise explanatory formula, but rather a statement of faith that some purely naturalistic explanation of the origin of life is possible.

A hundred years ago the belief that matter could somehow become a living organism would have seemed fantastic even to scientific minds. However, beginning just about a century ago, the chemist's laboratory has produced one "miracle" after another in the form of organic compounds created from inorganic matter. Let us listen to a leading historian of science on this point:

> It had long been thought that the specially complicated substances which are characteristic of animal and vegetable tissues could only be formed under the influence of vital processes, and the belief in a spiritual interpretation of life was thought to stand or fall with the truth of this view. But in 1828 the artificial preparation of urea by Fredrich Wohler showed that one substance hitherto only found in living matter could be made in the laboratory. Other artificial preparations of natural products followed, till in 1887 Emil Fischer succeeded in building up fructose (fruit-sugar) and glucose (grape-sugar) from their elements. The distinction between organic and inorganic was thus broken down, but the so-called "organic compounds" are so many and so complex that it is still convenient to separate organic chemistry from inorganic chemistry and from physical chemistry.[3]

There is increasing evidence from recent experiments in chemical fertilization of certain species to prove a continuity between the inorganic and the organic realms. It was discovered some time ago that the ova of sea-urchins could be fertilized by other than natural means, and such species as rabbits have also been successfully fertilized by chemical

[3] Sir William Dampier, *A History of Science,* p. 270.

means.[4] Thus, while science can as yet neither precisely describe nor successfully reproduce the conditions under which life could have come into existence through exclusively natural means, it is constantly discovering new facts to emphasize the possibility (many authorities would say the *probability*) that it did begin in this manner.

The Possible Choices. We shall have more to say regarding the naturalistic theory of life origins when we discuss mechanism *vs.* vitalism later in the chapter, while the discussion of the various theories of mind and its origin in the following chapter will also throw additional light on the matter. Meanwhile it will be enough if the student sees that our answer as to how life began appears to narrow down to only two possible choices. We can either accept the doctrine of a special creation, which, whatever its theological advantages, explains very little and has no relation to modern science; or we can choose instead the as yet incomplete scientific account of life emerging from the nonliving by purely natural means without outside intervention of any kind.

Evolution Before Darwin

We now turn to a survey of the various theories regarding the *development* of life. These are concerned with explaining how the tremendous variety of forms now existing came into being. We are thus ready to attack the extremely complex problem of *evolution*, taking the term to indicate both a biological process and a general category for describing certain aspects of our experienced world.

The name of Charles Darwin looms so large in any discussion of evolution that there is always danger that the student will think that this great scientist formulated his theory single-handed in a complete intellectual vacuum. The concept of an evolutionary development of life is much older than Darwin, however, and by the time he started working on the problem the idea was widely current in intellectual circles. Some of the earliest Greek thinkers had not only believed change to be ultimate in the

---

[4] *Time* Magazine, March 12, 1934, and December 1, 1941. This purely chemical fertilization should not be confused with something far older and more common, artificial insemination, where the male sperm is *mechanically* introduced into the female reproductive system.

universe (for example, Heraclitus), but had even suggested the development of life as a gradual process in which imperfect forms are supplanted by those more nearly perfect (for example, Empedocles). By the time of Aristotle, there was the suggestion that the more nearly perfect might develop out of the less perfect. The coming of the Renaissance brought a revival of speculation concerning the possibility of some sort of development, although it was the philosophers rather than the pioneer scientists who kept the evolutionary pot boiling. Bacon, Descartes, Leibniz, and Kant all tossed ideas into the kettle. Meanwhile the scientists were slowly amassing facts which were eventually to provide Darwin and other nineteenth-century thinkers with sufficient foundation to make the evolutionary hypothesis something more than the philosopher's toy.

It is interesting to note that the weight of scientific opinion was against the hypothesis almost up to the time Darwin's theory was published. Fortunately, however, by the opening of the nineteenth century enough biologists and botanists had come out in favor of some form of developmental theory to have put the idea before the scientific world— although hardly before the ecclesiastical world. Erasmus Darwin (1738-1802), grandfather of Charles, had suggested that all living animals had been produced from what he called "a single living filament," and Buffon in France had come out in favor of a direct modification of animal forms by environmental conditions.[5]

Lamarck's Theory. It was to Lamarck (1744-1829), however, that the credit must go for the first unified and really logical theory of evolution. Like Buffon, he believed in the modifying effect of external conditions upon the organism, and from this belief came his famous doctrine of the "inheritance of acquired characteristics." In essence this doctrine holds that a change in environment will modify the bodily structure of a species. To use the classic illustration, Lamarck's theory held that the giraffe's long neck came from the constant stretching of successive generations to reach scant or tender vegetation that grew just beyond reach. This constant stretching supposedly resulted in the modification of individual organisms, and these modifications (very small in any single instance) were increased by inheritance.

It should be noted that Lamarck's theory, logical and "common-sense"

[5] Dampier, *op. cit.,* p. 294. I cannot resist injecting a recommendation of this history of science, both for its treatment of our special problem here and for scientific problems in general, particularly as they relate to philosophy.

as it was, remained only a speculative hypothesis without direct evidence to support it. However, it did suggest fruitful lines of research for the biologists to follow in performing the vast amount of spade work that was necessary before a really scientific hypothesis could be formulated.

Darwin and Natural Selection

It was Charles Darwin's glory to have made this scientific formulation, thus bringing together the twin streams of scientific research and philosophical speculation. Both by temperament and training he was the perfect biological naturalist. Even as a young man he had been convinced that there is a development of new *species* in nature, just as there is a development of new *varieties* both in nature and in domestic breeding of plants and animals. The traditional view was that although the *varieties* might be modified through either breeding or environmental conditions, the various species were, as they had been created, immutable. Darwin's conviction left him faced with two problems: he had to find some logical explanation for the supposed development of new species, and he had to collect more evidence than yet existed that such a modification of "immutable" species actually takes place. Fortunately he found a possible explanatory mechanism early in life, so that his double problem was reduced by one half. When only twenty-nine he discovered the idea he was searching for in the writings of the British economist Malthus. As described in his own words, the result was one of those great insights that have been so important in the history of science:

> In October 1838 I happened to read for amusement Malthus on Population, and being well prepared to appreciate the struggle for existence which everywhere goes on from long continued observation of the habits of animals and plants, it at once struck me that under these circumstances favorable variations would tend to be preserved, and unfavorable ones to be destroyed. The result of this would be the formation of a new species. Here I had a theory by which to work.[6]

With this insight as a guide, Darwin then spent twenty-one years amassing the biological evidence to support his hypothesis. Finally, in

[6] Quoted by Dampier, p. 295.

1859, appeared *The Origin of Species,* one of the most thought-shattering books ever written. In it the vast array of evidence is presented so clearly, and the fundamental hypothesis is argued so convincingly, that we have not only the classic presentation of the evolutionary point of view, but also one of the outstanding examples of the scientific mind in action. Almost immediately many scientists were convinced by Darwin's evidence, and within a few years the evolutionary hypothesis had won the acceptance of a majority of the scientific minded. Unfortunately the task of getting it accepted by persons outside of scientific circles was something much more difficult. The Church was especially prejudiced against the theory, since it appeared both to contradict the Biblical account of creation and to degrade man to the level of an animal species. Fortunately Darwin, himself shy and introvertive, had two powerful champions in Herbert Spencer and Thomas Huxley. The latter particularly was an admirable controversialist, and called himself "Darwin's bulldog." "With magnificent courage, ability, and clearness of exposition, he bore the chief brunt of the attack made from all sides on Darwin's book, and again and again led successful counterattacks on his dicomfited foes."[7]

The Three Factors in Natural Selection. Further scientific discoveries have brought many changes in the details of Darwin's work, yet it deserves study as something more than merely an historical landmark. Like any scientist, he was looking for a method that would explain *how* species modifications took place. Believing that he possesed enough evidence to be sure that such changes actually occur, his primary search was for the mechanism which brought them about. He discovered that the causal process involved three separate factors: the struggle for existence, variations among individuals within the species, and the transmission of these variations through heredity. It is imperative that we understand these three.

1. The struggle for existence is almost self-explanatory. Owing to the enormous fecundity of nature, far more organisms are born than can be supported by the natural environment. The resulting competition for food, added to the danger from natural enemies which haunts most animal life, makes existence a continuous struggle for survival. Clearly, this is a life-and-death matter: the victor survives, the loser perishes. There is no second prize, no higher court for the loser to appeal to. The struggle is

[7] Dampier, *op. cit.,* pp. 298-299.

grim and deadly, and it is continuous throughout the life of the individual.

2. In this unceasing struggle, many individuals are favored and many are handicapped. These advantages and disadvantages come from variations or individual differences that exist within any species. Darwin could not explain the cause of these variations, but their presence was an undoubted fact. (He believed them to be exceedingly minute, and it is regarding this point that one of the most significant post-Darwinian changes in the theory has occurred.) Whatever their cause, they serve to give the favored individual greater speed or strength, sharper claws or fangs, better protective coloration, or some other physical feature that has survival value. As a result, his probability of survival is increased, and with this his chance of winning the competition for mates. Here again, the individual organism that is handicapped by the wrong kind of variation may find there are no consolation prizes in the struggle. He may either starve or be devoured, or else his life may be sterile because he cannot win a mate.

3. However, the mere possession of a chance variation that has survival value for the individual is not enough to explain modifications in species. Obviously such variations must be transmissible through inheritance. Otherwise, no matter how great the advantage might be to the individual, his offspring would revert to the norm of the species, and we would be right back where we started. The whole evolutionary hypothesis plainly depends upon whether or not such variations can be handed on through the ordinary mechanism of heredity. Fortunately for the hypothesis the transmission of both beneficent and lethal variations has been shown by observation and experiment to be a fact. Thus, even if these changes were as minute as Darwin believed, the cumulative result of many generations of such variations might easily be a new species.

Lamarck vs. Darwin. The three factors we have described constitute what is known as the law or principle of *natural selection*. There are two things about the principle that must be emphasized, particularly as they are as true today as when Darwin's book was published in 1859. First is the divergence from Lamarck's theory, with which Darwin's hypothesis is popularly confused. In place of Lamarck's inheritance of *acquired* characteristics—that is, those resulting from exercise and habitual response —Darwin postulates the inheritance of chance variations which happen to have survival value. Thus we do not inherit what muscles or skills our parents may have acquired by *practice,* but we can and often do inherit variations in bodily structure which either of our parents acquired *by birth.* This difference is due to the two types or systems of cells which we possess; these will be described in a moment. The second thing to note in the principle of natural selection is the adjective "natural." In Darwin's system we have a fully worked-out explanation of species modification in which no outside interference of any kind is assumed. The whole process is explicable in the purely naturalistic terms which we have just described. Any external or "supernatural" agency is unnecessary.

It was probably this elimination of any need for an intelligent or purposive agent in the process which did most to arouse moral and ecclesiastical opposition to Darwin's work. It seemed to suggest that God was less necessary in the scheme of things than previously had been thought. However, it will be better if we wait to consider all the implications of the evolutionary hypothesis under one heading later in the chapter.

Evolution Since Darwin

In the hundred years since the publication of Darwin's epochal work there have been numerous changes in details of the evolutionary theory, although its general outline is still accepted as foundational to the biological sciences. Most of these changes have come as a result of our increased knowledge of the mechanisms of heredity. One of the most fruitful results of the publication of *The Origin of Species* was that it served to increase greatly the amount of experimental work in biology. At present our knowledge of the laws of heredity has reached a point where technical terms like gene, chromosome, mutation, dominant, and so forth, are a part of any educated person's vocabulary. In a book of this type it will not be feasible to go into this difficult but fascinating field, particularly as numerous brief and lucid expositions of the mechanics of heredity are available in any college library.[8] However, regardless of technical difficulties, there are two radical changes which have been made in the evolu-

---

[8] For example, Dotterer's *Philosophy by Way of the Sciences,* Chapter VI, particularly section 4, and Patrick's *Introduction to Philosophy* (revised edition), Chapters X and XI. The latter is a good antidote for students whose naturalistic predilections may have given them excessive confidence in mechanistic methods.

tionary hypothesis since its original Darwinian formulation that must be considered.

Weismann's Discovery.   The first of these discoveries represents not so much a modification of the Darwinian theory as an extension and enrichment of it. It was Weismann who made the tremendously important discovery that the body has two separate and virtually independent systems of cells. Most of our physical organism is composed of *somatic* or *body* cells; these are affected by use and exercise, and consequently are the habitat of Lamarck's "acquired characteristics." The second of these cell systems is that of the germ-cells. These have what amounts to immortality, for the germ-plasm has a continuity that extends from the first human being (and possibly the first living organism) right down to you, the reader of this page. Thus each individual has his origin not from the modifiable body cells of his parents, but from the immortal germ-cells of which his parents are only the carrier or repository. The most significant fact is that these germ-cells, stored or carried by the somatic cells, are completely independent of changes in the latter. Thus Lamarck's theory would appear to be left with no heredity foundation to stand on, since heredity depends entirely upon the transmission of the germ-cells, which are affected only by their own independent variations.

Darwin made the same mistake that Lamarck had made in assuming that species changes came from a modification of somatic cells. Fortunately, however, in the Darwinian system this was not central to the whole theory, as it was in Lamarck's. Consequently, Weismann's discovery only led to a refinement of Darwin's hypothesis, whereas it appeared to give its Lamarckian predecessor a fatal blow. One of the most impressive features of the original Darwinian formulation has been the number of changes it has been able to survive. Later discoveries have modified it, but the essentials of the hypothesis remain.

The Discovery of Mutations.   The second discovery proved a much more severe test than Weismann's had been. In 1900 the Dutch experimenter De Vries completed research which temporarily threatened to undermine Darwin's theory entirely, much to the delight of the numerous anti-evolutionists still active at that time. Once again, however, the original hypothesis has been modified to include the new knowledge, and thereby has secured a new lease on life. We have seen that the original statement of the theory postulated the inheritance of variations with survival value; these were believed to be minute variations of chance occurrence. In a famous series of experiments with the evening primrose, De Vries discovered that changes sometimes occur that are so great as to constitute a wholly new type. Furthermore, some of these will breed true. These major changes he called *mutations,* in distinction from the tiny variations assumed by most earlier workers. Thus a new variety, and possibly even a new species, could come into existence all at once, instead of as the result of a slow accumulation of small variations. Before this important discovery, evolutionists had found it necessary to postulate enormous stretches of time for the accumulation of enough true-breeding favorable variations to account for all the myriads of different species now inhabiting the earth. Thanks to the lowly primrose and its erratic breeding habits, the need for such vast ranges of evolutionary time appears to have been eliminated. Thus, instead of weakening the Darwinian hypothesis, the over-all effect of this discovery of mutations was to make it even more logical and credible.

It was not particularly difficult to fit this new discovery into the original theory. For, once the mutations had occurred (and De Vries was as much in the dark concerning their precise cause as Darwin had been in the case of his "variations") their survival or nonsurvival followed the principles of natural selection, which we have already discussed. Since 1900, much paleontological evidence has accumulated to reinforce De Vries' discovery.

The Arguments for Evolution

While the general theory of evolution is now accepted as the foundation of modern biological science, its acceptance outside of scientific circles is not yet complete. As far as most educated persons are concerned, the once flaming controversy regarding "evolution *vs.* the Bible" now seems almost as much a matter of history as the similar battle that raged regarding the heliocentric *vs.* the Biblically supported geocentric theories of the solar system. However, it is more than merely historical interest that prompts us to summarize the arguments of creationism *vs.* evolutionism. By doing this we can best see the philosophical implications of each point of view, and it is these that particularly interest us.

In presenting a summary of the case for each side, we shall distinguish between "scientific" arguments and "moral" arguments—each term to be understood in its widest sense. As might be expected, the evolutionist places more emphasis upon the scientific evidence, while the creationist argues primarily from the moral standpoint. Each, however, has arguments from both realms, and we must weigh these against one another. It will be more logical to begin with evolutionism, since its advocates have traditionally carried the burden of proof.

The Seven Principal Arguments. The scientific arguments for the general evolutionary position reduce to some half dozen or so.[9] (1) Most impressive to many minds is the evidence from *paleontology.* Fossil remains present us with relatively complete series of forms leading from one type of organism to something very different. In such a series of fossils, the differences between the members of the series are usually small enough to make the belief in a gradual development almost inescapable. Particularly celebrated are the fossil forms showing the development of the little eohippus or "dawn horse" into our modern horse. Observing the series in a museum is similar to watching a motion picture film that depicts the opening of a flower: the little skeleton grows larger by jumps, the number of toes decreases and gradually forms a hoof, and so on. (2) The argument from *embryology* is equally impressive to many persons. It points out that the further back we go in the development of the embryo, the greater the similarities between those species which the evolutionist believes to be related. To take the classic example, the embryos of human and anthropoids are far more alike in the third month of gestation than they are in the last. In the second place, the embryo goes through stages of development that correspond in a general way with those which the evolutionary theory believes the species has gone through. In the case of the human, the most conspicuous of these embryonic stages include the appearance of gill slits, a tail, and more ribs than the normal adult possesses. These stages are usually passed through quite rapidly, but instances of a prolongation beyond birth are not unknown, as when an individual is born with enough extra vertebrae to form a distinct tail. This series of supposed "flash-backs" is called a *recapitulation,* for in it the species development appears to pass in brief review. (3) Closely related to the argument from embryology is the evidence from *compara-*

[9] While this series of arguments is public domain and frequently appears in much the same form as here, I feel that the best presentation is in Dotterer, *op. cit.,* and I should like to acknowledge indebtedness to this source.

tive anatomy. This points out that experience has taught us that physical resemblance usually means that there is a common ancestry—so, when we meet two persons who look very much alike, we assume a kinship between them. Thus when we discover close resemblances in either structure or function among different species (for example, men and apes), it is logical to suspect a common ancestry. (4) The *analysis of the blood* of various species has revealed a closer similarity between those which evolutionists had held (on other evidence) to be closely related than between those thought to be distantly related. Men and apes are again the best example, for tests show that the blood of these two species is more closely akin than the blood of either is to that of any other species. (5) The argument from *vestigial organs* is one with which we are all familiar. It emphasizes the fact that even adult organisms may have anatomical "vestiges," such as the vermiform appendix, which have no use and may even be a liability. The creationist hypothesis can offer no explanation for these vestigial organs, but on the evolutionary theory they would be hand-me-downs from an ancestral creature to whom they were of use. (6) Many students are particularly impressed by the argument from *geographical distribution,* which points out that those islands or land masses which geology believes to have been isolated longest (for example, Australia and the Galapagos Islands) usually have the greatest number of rare or "freak" species on them. This is what we should expect, according to the evolutionary hypothesis, since clearly those regions that were separated earliest from the rest of the world would have the most time to develop species unlike those found elsewhere. (7) Finally, there is the argument from *controlled experiment.* Plant and animal breeding offers the most obvious examples, such as the famous experiments of Luther Burbank. We have already referred to similar work by De Vries, where precise controls have been applied to effect considerable modification in species.

The evolutionist usually admits that no one of these arguments standing by itself is completely convincing, but he believes that standing together and reinforcing each other as they do, their cumulative effect is overwhelming. In brief, claims the exponent of the theory, these seven points involve a group of observed facts that are far better explained by my hypothesis than by that of the creationist. And, since my hypothesis does integrate and explain all the relevant facts better, it should therefore be adopted and its rival rejected.

The Creationists' Scientific Arguments

The scientific arguments of creationism are to a large extent negative, in that they constitute an attack on the position of the evolutionist rather than a positive viewpoint.[10] (1) First, they claim, there are serious gaps in the supposed evolutionary series, especially between man and animal, and between chemical compounds and organisms. The latter break is particularly apparent, and there has not been much progress in bridging the gap. (2) There is very little, if any, direct evidence of evolution—that is, observable instances of an actual modification taking place. The whole theory must therefore remain unproved and, until such observations are reported, unprovable. (3) The evolutionist can offer no satisfactory account of the origin of life; all his arguments presuppose life as already existing, which is clearly an evasion of a most fundamental issue. (4) And finally, argues the creationist, the evolutionary theory represents an oversimplification of data that are extremely complex. The word "evolve," for example, is made to cover a multitude of factors. It is a mask for our ignorance as to the means by which such development could actually come about.

In rebuttal, the evolutionist admits that there are very real gaps in many of the developmental series, but he points out that these are gradually being filled in as scientific progress continues. In any case, they are certainly less wide than they formerly were. As regards the origin of life, he admits ignorance, but argues that an honest confession of ignorance is infinitely better than the fantastic and childish—not to say superstitious— account of origins which many creationists propose. In the next place, the lack of direct observational evidence for evolution is no more serious than in the case of another great hypothetical construct, the atomic system of modern physics. Both theories represent the best attempt to do what every scientific hypothesis must do: explain all the relevant facts in the simplest, most logical, and most adequate manner possible. And finally, if the issue is to be settled on the basis of direct observational evidence, can the creationist present a case of the *creation* of a new species being observed by anyone?

[10] These negative arguments are in part drawn from Conger, *A Course in Philosophy*, pp. 310-31?

The Moral Arguments

In considering the moral arguments for each side, it will be well if the creationist speaks first, since most of his heavy ammunition comes from the moral realm. (1) While the argument is now heard less often than formerly, most creationists still are bothered by the fact that the Darwinian account of the origin of species does not square with the Biblical account. (2) The evolutionary picture, including man, seems to degrade the human race. Man no longer appears to be the final (and favorite) creation of God, but just one more species of animal. (3) As we have already suggested, the theory of evolution, offering as it does a purely naturalistic explanation of biological phenomena, appears to eliminate the need for Purpose or the Creative Will in the universe. In fact, the whole theory suggests one more attempt to eliminate the supernatural from man's thinking. (4) The hypothesis can offer us no picture of either a purposed beginning or a desirable ending to life on the earth. The several sciences seem to suggest that our earth will eventually be drawn into the sun by loss of angular momentum, or will lose its heat from the gradual cooling of the sun, or perhaps meet catastrophe from collision with some other astronomical body. If this is a true picture of our ultimate destiny, then man and his ideals seem utterly futile. (5) Finally, the theory of evolution, implying as it does that our ideals have evolved as our physical structure has, suggests a purely natural origin for man's moral being. Again the supernatural is excluded, and again a mechanistic-materialistic account of even man's spiritual nature is suggested.

The Evolutionist Replies. On his side the evolutionist also has some moral ammunition, a large part of which has been manufactured for the express purpose of replying to the objections of the creationist. (1) The conflict of the Darwinian account with that in Genesis is usually admitted quite frankly, but it is pointed out that the same objection was raised against the Copernican system of astronomy when it was first formulated in the sixteenth century. And, just as it has been possible to give up the astronomy of the Bible without discrediting its spiritual authority, so it is possible to give up the biology of the Bible without diminishing its moral power. (2) The evolutionist can see no degradation in our having come *up* from lower forms of life. The glory is not in what we have come *from*, but what we have developed into. (3) The naturalistic explanation of our origin does not necessarily eliminate God from the picture, even as Creator. Evolution—or, more precisely, natural selection—may be viewed as the means by which the Divine Purpose is achieved. Many modern idealists and religious thinkers have appreciated this, and regard the whole evolutionary process as the "grand strategy" whereby Mind realized itself in the physical realm. (4) The evolutionist admits his ignorance as to origins (as we have seen), and refuses to acknowledge that his hypothesis has any intention or responsibility as far as the end or goal of life is concerned. However, he does feel that his view makes life and human history a challenging adventure, which is something that a predetermined destiny cannot offer.

Evolution and the Problem of Evil. In addition to these replies, the exponent of evolution has one great moral argument of his own. This concerns the problem of evil, which will rear its head in several of the chapters that follow. Dotterer gives a succinct summary of the situation as the advocates of evolution see it (Dotterer used the term transformism in place of evolutionism):

> The most serious objection to the special creation hypothesis arises, however, from a consideration of the presence of evil in the world. In particular, what account can the special creation hypothesis give of the origin of disease germs? Can we really suppose that God deliberately made the micro-organisms which produce pneumonia and infantile paralysis and bubonic plague and cerebrospinal meningitis, and all the other horrid and loathsome diseases which play havoc with the flower of the human race?
>
> If, in order to avoid the difficulty arising from the existence of so many species of pathogenic bacteria, we suggest that they were not originally pathogenic, we admit the radical modifiability of species, and thus *in principle* accept the transformist point of view. For if we admit that noxious species have arisen by natural descent, how can we deny that other species may have arisen in the same manner?[11]

It should be clear by now that the controversy between creationist and evolutionist resolves into a battle between naturalism and supernaturalism. The naturalistic philosopher quite properly regards the Darwinian hypothesis as one of his biggest guns, since it is largely by means of this theory that it has been possible to extend naturalistic thought over the biological, psychological and social fields. The creationist, on the

[11] Dotterer, *op. cit.*, p. 166.

other hand, is necessarily a supernaturalist, since the very concept of a special creation requires an outside (that is, supernatural) agent or power of some kind. As far as the various philosophical schools are concerned, the over-all effect of evolutionism has been to strengthen naturalism enormously. Conversely, it has probably been the largest single factor forcing supernaturalism to go on the defensive, and even the idealist has often found it necessary to revise his thinking to make room for the new theory and its implications.

The Controversy Between Mechanism and Vitalism

Now that the war between creationism and evolutionism has largely been won by the latter, at least as far as science is concerned, the mechanist-vitalist argument has become the most active area of controversy within the vague field called "the philosophy of the biological sciences." In each generation, the war apparently has to be fought in a new area; just at present the main scene of battle is in the subdivision of the biological field called "psychology." However, it will be more enlightening to examine the mechanism-vitalism argument in relation to the whole field of biology.

A Brief Statement of the Two Positions. *Mechanism* in biology is just what the name implies: the attempt to extend the mechanistic view of the universe to include living beings. It holds, in brief, that an organism is completely explicable on mechanical principles—that is, by the laws governing matter in motion. In more precise and more scientific terms, biological mechanism holds that the organism is a physiochemical system, the behavior of which can be analyzed into those types of reactions studied in the laboratories of both physics and chemistry. Thus the mechanist acknowledges no significant difference between the organic and inorganic realms; behavior upon the organic level represents only a much more complex form of the reactions characterizing the behavior of inorganic matter. Mechanism denies that any new nonphysical factor or principle appeared in nature coincident with the appearance of life. Biology thus becomes only an extension of physics and chemistry into a realm involving more complex phenomena than these two sciences usually study. However, since the field of biology is continuous with that of these two older sciences, it requires no radically new principles or fundamental concepts.

Vitalism believes that neither our present knowledge of physics and chemistry nor any future exhaustive knowledge of their laws can be adequate to account for organic phenomena. The vitalist holds that with the appearance of life in the universe, some genuinely new factor or principle was introduced into nature. Further, this "vital" principle is held to be nonmechanical, nonmaterial, nonchemical. Thus in its essence, vitalism is the doctrine that the phenomena of life are *sui generis*—that is, in a unique class or category—and consequently differ fundamentally from physicochemical phenomena. The vitalist finds in living organisms something both new and completely different from what can be discovered elsewhere in the natural order—something which no mere increase in complexity and no multiplication of already existent factors can account for. This presumed new addition to nature is virtually impossible to define, since (as we have just indicated) it is *sui generis;* and that which is wholly unique is incapable of being defined, since all definition must be in relation to something else within our experience. Various exponents of vitalism have given this indefinable factor different names, such as "vital force," "life force," "entelechy," "*élan vital,*" "psychoid," and so forth. Others have attempted to describe its presumed nature in terms of the differences that separate organic from inorganic activity, but in the last analysis this factor remains mysterious and indescribable.

The Arguments for Each Side

Each side in the controversy has strong arguments. We shall hear the mechanist first, since vitalism is largely a criticism of the simplifications and inadequacies (real or supposed) of the mechanistic position.

1. Mechanistic Arguments. (*a*) To begin with, the mechanist points out that the general viewpoint and method of science is mechanistic. It is particularly significant that the most exact sciences, those which come nearest to the ideal of all scientific activity, are physics and chemistry. Both are organized in terms of mechanistic causation. Further, the more precise a science becomes, the more mechanistic it becomes. Thus we are justified in assuming that as the biological sciences develop towards increased exactitude, they too will become more mechanistic in their explanations.

(b) There are certain general relations between biology and the other sciences that point towards a mechanistic interpretation of life processes. For example, all organisms obey the laws of matter and the "conservation of energy" principle. Perhaps more impressive is the fact that many specific vital structures and processes can be broken down into mechanical or chemical structures and processes. Probably the best example of this is the chemical analysis of cells, which reduces them to such constituent parts as proteins, peptones, and the like; these in turn are reduced to very complicated combinations of hydrogen, nitrogen, carbon, and so on.

(c) The mechanist can draw much support from the fact that historically there has been a steady extension of mechanistic explanation to biological activities, including some that were formerly believed to be immune to such an approach—for example, response to stimuli. Although it must be acknowledged that there are many organic activities that have not yielded to mechanistic explanation, there is a possibility (some would say a probability) that these also will eventually open up to such an approach. As has been well said, the mechanist is a man of faith—in mechanistic methods. And, with the record of achievement that he can now show, who can deny his right to this faith?

(d) The mechanist makes much of the fact that it has been possible to produce artificial structures that successfully imitate organisms. Even more striking to most students are the instances of artificial fertilization mentioned earlier in the chapter, whereby through either mechanical or chemical means the need for the male sperm has been eliminated. To many minds these imitations of living forms or processes, even though not yet numerous, constitute the strongest possible argument in favor of mechanism. For, it is argued, if we can do this much now by duplicating life processes, what will the future bring forth?

2. *Vitalistic Arguments.* But the vitalist has strong arguments also, one or two of which either eliminate, or at least seriously weaken, some of the points made by the mechanist. (a) In the first place, vitalism argues that physical and chemical concepts by themselves are inadequate to deal with such complex phenomena as living organisms. The gap that separates mechanical behavior (for example, that of a falling body) from human behavior (for example, that of performing a delicate surgical

operation) is tremendous—so vast, in fact, that it cannot possibly be reduced to mere quantitative difference. It is impossible to believe, continues the vitalist, that any addition of factors, or any multiplication of the possible combinations, would be enough to unify the two groups of behavior. And even if the difference could be reduced to increased complexity, the mechanistic account would still be inadequate. The organization of matter (that is, the structures) which the mechanist would require for his explanation would have to be so complex as to be fantastic— even inconceivable.

(b) In the second place, "living" includes many processes, such as breathing and self-repairing, which can be explained only teleologically— that is, in terms of a purpose or goal of some kind. Obviously mechanism and teleology are incompatible concepts: the mechanistic hypothesis explains everything in terms of efficient causes (antecedent events), while teleology implies a final cause—that is, a goal or envisioned result. As far as organic structures are concerned, this goal appears to be a "norm" or typical form which every species has and which every individual member of the species seeks to realize. As concerns vital processes or bodily functions, the same thing is true: for each part of the organism, and even for the organism as a whole, there is a functional "norm" towards which its behavior tends.

(c) Perhaps the most inclusive of the vitalistic arguments is also the one most difficult for the mechanist to answer satisfactorily. This is the fact that the organism is an organized *whole* which behaves in ways which no engine or mechanism does. All organic behavior represents a process of adjustment, by which the organism seeks either to get in step or stay in step with its surroundings. Cunningham describes this relation very well when he says, "The movement of the amoeba towards food or away from an injurious substance, for example, is in the service of the individual life as a whole; its activity has some sort of reference to its future welfare."[12]

It is this organized, purposive activity which best differentiates living from nonliving behavior, and the vitalist holds that no mechanistic explanation, even that of an omniscient mind, could be adequate to account for vital activities. The presumption of a "life force" or "vital agency" of some kind is therefore inescapable.

[12] Cunningham, *Problems of Philosophy*, p. 229.

The Bases for a Decision

In trying to decide between mechanism and vitalism, certain things should be kept clearly in mind. First, it seems evident that any issue as fundamentally scientific as this should be settled, insofar as possible, on the basis of scientific evidence. We have seen that the evidence up to date is inconclusive; some authorities feel that we probably have enough data available to make mechanism definitely acceptable, but others are more cautious. Lacking final proof, we shall have to do the next best thing: adopt as a working hypothesis that position which we feel has the stronger evidence to support it. However, since the absence of definite scientific proof for either side of the controversy makes the matter primarily a philosophical issue, we should strive to base our decision on intellectual grounds, rather than on emotional preferences. The mechanist cannot resist pointing out that vitalism undoubtedly has more organized support from certain schools of philosophy than it has from scientists. While vitalistic biologists are not wanting, it has been the philosophical dualists, and above all the idealists, who have kept the issue alive. For it is to be expected that those philosophies which conceive of Spirit as the Ultimate Real, or (in the case of dualism) as one of the two irreducible Ultimates, should find mechanism intolerable. The mechanistic interpretation seems too closely affiliated with naturalism and materialism for it to be acceptable to the idealistic-minded.

Scientific Evidence vs. *Emotional Appeal.* Standing outside the controversy for a moment and trying to view the whole issue objectively, it seems fair to advise students who find vitalism attractive to examine their motives in order to make certain that it is not religious or emotional considerations that are prompting the choice. There is of course no rule against our making decisions on emotional grounds, but in philosophy, as in science, the ideal should be to form our judgments on intellectual grounds. It is quite possible to be a vitalist on the basis of intellectual considerations, as is proved by the existence of a hardy minority of biologists holding this position. However, since it is even easier to be a vitalist on *emotional* grounds, the student who has any loyalty to the spirit of philosophy will examine his motivations before he makes his decision.

The second thing which we must keep in mind as we evaluate the two positions is the historical trend involved. We must remember that vitalism has been the standard or "official" view for centuries, whereas mechanism is a comparative newcomer in the field of modern thought. In view of this comparative youth of the mechanistic position, its achievements become impressive. Slowly but constantly it has invaded territory which appeared impregnable, forcing the vitalist to give up a bit of ground here, an important position there. At the present time, it is widely admitted in intellectual circles that vitalism is on the defensive. However, it would be completely misleading to interpret this to mean that vitalism is weak, much less moribund. In spite of the accomplishments of the mechanistic method, the exponents of mechanism still have a great distance to go before they can claim a complete victory. As is often said, although vitalism is on the defensive and has yielded considerable ground, it is still strong because it has so much ground to yield.

The Trend Toward Unification in Science. And, finally, it should be pointed out that the trend towards mechanism in biology is part of a general movement towards unification in the sciences. Looking back over the history of science, one feels that this unifying movement was implicit from the moment that modern science became self-conscious in the persons of Francis Bacon and Galileo. However, it can hardly be claimed that these early pioneers were aware of any such trend, for only within the last century has it become an announced goal among scientific thinkers. But, intentional or unintentional, the unification has progressed steadily.

Since physics and chemistry were the first sciences to come of age, and consequently were the first to achieve precision through a full utilization of quantitative methods, it was inevitable that they should become the standard or ideal which all the other sciences sought to attain. Physics particularly became the ideal science; its precise and elegant formulations of the principles of mechanics were soon the despairing dream of workers in newer, less organized fields. In the attempt to achieve a comparable rigor and definition, the other sciences naturally copied the methods of physics; its deterministic approach and mechanistic techniques were transferred wholesale to the newer, untamed areas of nature's domain. Although it soon became evident that many of these methods would have to be modified before they would be suitable to the new fields, the general mechanistic approach remained the ideal scientific method.

And, in spite of the many changes within physics, including innumerable refinements in its methods, the general mechanistic viewpoint is still basic to science. A biological mechanist is thus a worker in the life sciences who is attempting to extend this general method to his own particular field, in order both to achieve greater precision in the analysis of biological phenomena and also to relate his field more closely to the whole body of science. Thus, as a scientific ideal, the mechanistic approach in biology is excellent. Theologians, idealists, and dualists may object to it on moral grounds, but to the scientists their objections are irrelevant. The only valid question as far as either the scientist or the philosophical naturalist is concerned is this: Is mechanism adequate as an account of organic behavior? We already have our answer—or rather, our answers. For the mechanist, it is an adequate account, or at least it promises to be adequate in the not-too-distant future; for the vitalist, it is not adequate now and cannot be in the future. In sum, the vitalist holds that, however satisfactory mechanistic method may be in physics, chemistry, astronomy or geology, it breaks down as soon as we attempt a transfer to biological phenomena. To repeat, vitalism holds that the advent of life into the universe involved the introduction of a wholly novel, qualitatively distinct factor; and to explain this vital factor, wholly novel concepts are required.[13]

[13] Within recent years there has been developed a third position within biological thought which tries to mediate between the extremes of vitalism and mechanism. Known as the *organismic* view, it regards mechanism as inadequate and vitalism as scientifically worthless (because it postulates an unprovable "psychoid" or "vital force"). It is the atomistic character of the mechanist's analysis which distresses the organicist particularly. For such a position implies that the whole is merely the sum of its parts—*i.e.,* that the parts came first and that the organism is only an assemblage of these. Further, mechanism implies a local determination, as though parts act independently of the whole.

The organismic position is wholistic. It regards the whole (*i.e.,* the organism) as more than the mere sum of its parts (*i.e.,* cells, glands, organs, etc.) *not* in the vitalistic sense of a mysterious "plus" which is superadded to the parts and ties them together, but in the sense that wholes exist first and determine the parts. The organism is not an aggregation of cells. The organism produces cells, and not vice versa. "In other words, the whole is not to be deduced from the parts, nor does part work on part to make the whole, but what occurs at any given position within the whole is determined by the structure of the whole," as J. F. Brown in his *Psychology and the Social Order,* points out that where mechanism regards man as a machine, and vitalism regards him as a machine, *plus* an entelechy or "soul," the organismic view is more convincing scientifically in that it regards the human organism as a system of energy. Incidentally, Brown's presentation (pp. 27-30) may be recommended as a succinct statement of the three positions, although as an advocate of the organismic he will probably impress both mechanists and vitalists as unfair to their respective points of view.

Idealism vs. Naturalism in Biology

In glancing back over our chapter as a whole, we see a clear trend towards that fundamental opposition between idealism and naturalism described in the two preceding chapters. It is plain that as concerns both the origin and development of life there are two radically opposed schools of thought. Although we cannot identify creationism with idealism (for the idealist must come to terms with modern science, just as philosophers of every school must), we find that even when he accepts the evolutionary hypothesis, the idealist reads into the developmental process a plan or purpose or "strategy" of some sort. Thus, in the eyes of the naturalist, he affiliates himself with supernaturalism much as the creationist does. Both idealist and supernaturalist postulate a power or agent which is outside the ordinary operations of nature. The creationist, for example, makes this power something which not only designs and has purposes, but intrudes upon the natural order to realize these designs. The modern supernaturalist resembles the idealist in his views on this issue—in fact the two schools are so close on this point as to be indistinguishable. Both accept the general evolutionary position, but both place tremendous emphasis upon the *instrumental* character of the evolutionary process. Evolution (including astrophysical and geological change, as well as biological development) is regarded as merely the means or creative process by which Mind has produced mind and Spirit has developed spirit—that is, as a great tool which the Divine or Absolute Mind has employed to produce human minds, and thus indirectly to produce value or goodness.

It is logical and probably inevitable that the idealist should view evolution in this light. Committed as he is to a belief that the universe is spiritually grounded and value-directed, it is natural to hold that all cosmic processes are ultimately value-producing in character. It is this profound and pervasive belief which has permitted idealists to accept evolution, whereas many of their more narrowly theistic contemporaries have found it a serious stumbling block to religious faith.

The naturalist of course accepts completely the evolutionary viewpoint, and does not need to find purpose or strategy in the process to render it acceptable. Naturalism can face the doctrine that the organic has emerged from the inorganic, and that life has developed from lowly forms into the vast array of species we now have, without postulating a

Power, a Purpose, or a Person standing behind the process. This clearly goes back to the third of naturalism's three general postulates which we outlined in the preceding chapter. This postulate states that the behavior of the universe, both as a whole and in all its details, is determined exclusively by the character of the universe itself, operating as a single self-contained and self-dependent order. Hence the naturalist views evolution as a wholly natural process, not only in its specific mechanisms but in its initiation as well. This obviously eliminates both an intervening, initiating agent and a goal which the process is supposedly working toward.

In short, for idealism (and for those theisms which have come to terms with the evolutionary theory) evolution is teleological: it operates to realize a goal or purpose. Thus its basic dynamic is a pull from in front —that is, a future state or goal activates the developmental process. For naturalism, on the contrary, the dynamic is that of a *vis a tergo*, or force from behind (that is, everything occurs as a consequence of past occurrences). In this area naturalism is strictly deterministic, holding that evolutionary changes are a result of strictly natural causes, which means antecedent events that were themselves produced by forces contained within a self-operating universe.

The relations of naturalism and idealism respectively to the mechanist-vitalist controversy are obvious. Although it is possible for a thinker to be both a vitalist and a naturalist, this would be a rare combination. This combined position could hold, for example, that the mysterious "life force" or "entelechy," however completely it may evade physiochemical analysis, is still natural in the sense that it represents no intruded element from outside the order of physical nature. But this theoretically possible position appears to attract few thinkers; vitalists in biology are generally idealists. This fact suggests an intriguing question: which came first, their vitalism which led to an inclusive world view; or their idealism, which rendered acceptable only a vitalist theory?

It is even less likely that we will find many thinkers who combine mechanism in the biological sphere with idealism in the philosophical. Such a combination of viewpoints is again theoretically possible; one could hold that while the ground of all existence is mental or spiritual, the life process can be fully accounted for by physical analysis. But, since the strongest motive impelling thinkers toward an idealistic metaphysics is usually the need to formulate a world system which will give first place to man's mind and spirit, it would indeed be strange that a person seeking to justify the primacy of spirit in the universe would begin by postulating a purely physical and mechanistic foundation for life itself. In other words, since "mind" and "spirit" are dependent upon vital processes operating in organisms, it would be strange logic to argue that these processes themselves are wholly physical in character. For this would be an acknowledgment that the ground of existence is material, which is of course contrary to idealism's most basic postulate regarding the nature of reality. Whatever may be the outcome of the mechanist-vitalistic controversy, it seems certain that the idealist will continue to support the vitalist doctrine as long as it is intellectually possible to do so.

Meanwhile we must move on and meet some of the rest of philosophy's family of problems.

CHAPTER 6

MIND:

Mystery, Myth, or Mechanism?

THE MATTER OF DEFINITIONS IS PROBABLY THE MOST CONSTANT and irritating methodological problem in philosophy. Every field of intellectual activity has to wrestle with the problem of getting its terms adequately defined, but philosophy has a particularly difficult time of it. In part this is because, as we have suggested earlier, the philosopher is by temperament usually an extreme individualist—a man would hardly take on the whole universe and all human experience as an intellectual problem if he were not a very rugged individualist. In greater part, however, this confusion is due to the nature of the subject matter. The philosopher is working entirely with concepts, most of which are extremely abstract. Consequently he is always laboring in a rarefied intellectual atmosphere, where the air sometimes is so thin as barely to support activity.

When we turn to an analysis of *mind,* we meet this problem of definition in all its magnitude. This is particularly unfortunate, because "mind" is one of the most important categories of philosophy. It constitutes one of the major frames of reference within the field, but it is difficult to find more inclusive frames of reference to which it in turn can be linked and by which it can be defined. We thus have a category or major classification of experience which is so unique as to exist in something of a metaphysical vacuum. As the logician would say, mind is *sui generis,* in a class by itself. But, since the concept of mind is fundamental in the philosopher's realm of discourse, we must secure some comprehension of its meaning.

Distinction Between Mind and Brain. To begin with, students are nearly always confused regarding the exact relation between "mind" and "brain." Fortunately, as far as terminology is concerned, this distinction is not hard to get clear in our mind. For illustration, the preceding sentence ended with the word "mind"; it is not likely that the reader had any difficulty understanding "the distinction is not hard to get clear in our *mind.*" If instead the sentence had concluded with the word "brain," it is almost certain that the reader would have been a bit startled. For the brain is a physical organ. It is located in space, has a weight of around fifty ounces (in the adult white male), and has a definite functional relationship with the rest of the organism's physical structure. Most of us have seen brains, preserved in jars on the laboratory shelf, or in their more normal location within the cranial cavity of some frog or cat under dissection in the biology classroom. In brief, brains are physical objects, just as tangible and "objective" as a chair or a rock. As such, they are subject to all the laws affecting physical objects (such as gravitational attraction), plus those holding for organic matter (such as decomposition). Thus it would have meant very little if the sentence above had spoken about the necessity of "getting the distinction clear in our *brain.*" For we do not get distinctions clear *in* physical objects, but *about* them. If, on the other hand, the sentence had said something about "a hole in the brain," the statement would have made sense.

What, then, is *mind?* Few terms are used more often in intellectual discussion, and we have described one world-view (idealism) that builds upon mind as the ultimate reality. If the mind does not occupy space or have weight, is not affected by mechanical or physical laws, and cannot be localized within a definite spatial area, what is it? And *where* is it? And what are its relations to the realm of physical objects, including both the body and the entire natural order?

These major questions, together with numerous minor ones, are the subject matter of our present chapter. First, we shall consider the leading views of the nature of mind itself. Then we shall turn to the problem of the relations between the mind and the body, particularly that part of the body known as the central nervous system, which includes the brain. Next, we must explore that borderland between the problem of mind and the problem of knowledge, in which the basic issue is the relation of the mind to the external world which it experiences. And finally, we must briefly become strictly metaphysical and speculate concerning the relation of mind to reality in general. As can be seen, we have a full chapter ahead of us.

The Substantive View of Mind

There have been many views concerning the nature of mind, nearly all of which are still held today by larger or smaller groups of thinkers. Fortunately for our analysis, these numerous views reduce rather easily to four or five primary positions, and it will be sufficient in an introduction to philosophy if we grasp these clearly. First, and far most important historically, is the *substantive* view.[1] As the term suggests, it holds that the mind is a substance—that is, a *thing* or *entity*. However, the general concept of substance does not imply *material* existence, but rather *independent* existence, as we saw in the preceding chapter: substance is that which exists in and by itself, and not as a mode of something else. It is that which receives modifications, but does not depend on these modifications (or on relations of any kind) to give it existence. Thus, whatever relations mind may have to the body or to the external world, it does not (in this substantive view) depend on these relations for its existence. As a spiritual substance it is self-sufficient and self-existent.

This view of mind has been so influential in Western thought that one may predict that at least nine out of every ten students will hold it when they begin the study of either philosophy or psychology. It is the traditional position of Christianity, and harmonizes perfectly with what we shall shortly see to be the most popular of all metaphysical positions, "common-sense dualism" (Chapter 10). Indeed, we could quite logically call this view "common-sense substantialism": we naturally think of our mind as a nonphysical entity which unifies our moment-by-moment experiences. We think of it as that which *has* these various experiences— that which perceives or thinks or wills. We conceive it as the substratum that underlies all mental events, the agent to which they happen and to

[1] I am aware that Morris, in his *Six Theories of Mind*, draws a distinction between what he calls the *substantive* and the *substantial* views. However, the separation is very difficult to maintain, and quite beyond the grasp of most beginning students.

which they belong. In everyday speech, mind is "that which experiences." It is "common sense" to believe there is a core that is permanent and essentially changeless, in which these experiences inhere and by which they are unified. Usually the advocates of substantialism have employed the word "soul" rather than the more modern term "mind"; but whether it is Plato or the contemporary idealist who is speaking, the concept is very similar. Separateness (from the body), unity, and substantiality have been the key words of this school, and to these there has usually been added a logical fourth: immortality.

Hume's Criticism of Substantialism. While there were objections raised against this substantive view almost before Plato finished defining it, it was not until the eighteenth century that these attacks became critical enough to put substantialists on the defensive. Hume, the great Scottish skeptic, was acute enough to see that however logical or religiously satisfying belief in a spiritual substance may be, there is nothing in our actual experience to justify such a doctrine. The thinkers immediately prior to Hume, notably Descartes and Berkeley, had held that knowledge of our own mind or self is the most certain and fundamental knowledge that we can have. Descartes, reasoning from his famous *"Cogito ergo sum,"* "I think, therefore I exist," had made the supposed self-evidence of a substantial mind the foundation of his whole system. These pre-Humean thinkers had thus made introspection or self-knowledge the starting point of all intellectual inquiry. Hume, with his tongue in his cheek, agreed to the introspective test, then proceeded to apply it critically to the favorite subject of the substantialist—namely, the mind itself. The results were entirely negative: he could find no substantial entity of any kind. His argument is such a beautiful example of critical reasoning that it has become one of the most quoted passages in philosophical literature.

> There are some philosophers who imagine we are every moment intimately conscious of what we call our *self*; that we feel its existence and its continuance in existence; and are certain, beyond the evidence of a demonstration, both of its perfect identity and simplicity. . . . For my part, when I enter most intimately into what I call *myself*, I always stumble upon some particular perception or other, of heat or cold, light or shade, love or hatred, pain or pleasure. I never can catch *myself* at any time without a perception, and never can observe anything but the perception. When my perceptions are removed for any time, as by sound sleep, so long am I insensible of *myself*, and may truly be said not to exist. . . . The self is nothing but a bundle or collection of

different perceptions, which succeed each other with an inconceivable rapidity, and are in a perpetual flux and movement. . . . The mind is a kind of theatre, where several perceptions successively make their appearance; pass, repass, glide away, and mingle in an infinite variety of postures and situations. . . . But the comparison of the theatre must not mislead us. They are the successive perceptions only, that constitute the mind.[2]

Having thus knocked all the stuffing out of the substantive view of mind, Hume formulates what has come to be called the *actualist* view. This theory develops logically out of such reasoning as we have just quoted: the mind is merely an aggregate or collection of experiences, a "bundle of perceptions" that are tied together by certain laws of association. There is no inner core, no spiritual substratum serving to unify the various mental events. There are only the events themselves, linked haphazardly by what Hume calls "customs and habit." Regardless of how logical or esthetically satisfying it would be to postulate a unifying agent or entity at the heart of our experience, Hume is adamant: neither introspection nor any other method of knowing reveals any such thing. Actually, our minds are only these constantly shifting experiences, loosely tied together through association.

Kant's View of Mind. Immanuel Kant, although awakened by Hume's analysis from a dogmatic belief in the substantive viewpoint, could not rest content with Hume's somewhat anarchistic conclusions. He therefore moved on to formulate a modification of the Humean position which has been widely influential. To Kant, the traditional substantive position is not so much contrary to experience as it is logically self-contradictory. For substantialism holds that we can know our mind or self as an object of knowledge in exactly the same way we know anything in the external world. But, argues Kant, it is impossible for the self to be at once both subject and object in a knowing relationship. Myself *as subject* I can never know, but only myself *as object*. We can know only the "me" in ourselves, never the "I." And when we look at the "me" which is knowable, we discover just what Hume discovered: a continuous succession of mental states or "experiences."

Kant's objection to Hume's analysis was its failure to give sufficient emphasis to the *unity* of the mind. The laws of association alone—contiguity, succession, and resemblance—are not enough to transform a con-

[2] *A Treatise of Human Nature*, Book I, Part 4.

glomerate bundle of sensations into a whole of any kind. For example, association requires memory, and memory in turn presupposes something that does the remembering. While Kant called this unifying factor by the nebulous name of "the synthetic unity of apperception," it will be sufficient for our purpose to understand it as an agent which is neither a substance nor an entity, but rather an organizing or unifying principle that does far more than merely "tie together" the aggregate of sensations and mental events. Further, this principle or agency is active, and consequently very different from the passive, static entity conceived by Plato and most substantialists since Plato's time. While various names have been used for this Kantian view of the mind, "transcendental" and "organic" are the most acceptable. For convenience we shall adopt the latter term, since it serves to emphasize the unified, organic character of the mind.

In conclusion, it should be noted that Kant's view is a compromise position. It tries to build a theory of mind that will be true to our actual observation of minds through introspection, and which will also do justice to the peculiar unity which seems to characterize our minds as they are known to another observer. By postulating a unifying agent, Kant thought he was able to satisfy both requirements—even if it necessitated hiding our ignorance concerning the character of this agent behind an imposing term. The modern logical empiricist (as we shall see in Chapter 11) argues that unverifiable existences such as this have no more place in philosophy than they do in science, but Kant was operating within the philosophical traditions of his time when he assumed such a hypothetical unifying agent.

The Materialistic View of Mind

At the opposite pole from the substantive view of the idealist there is what we may call the *identification theory* of the extreme materialist and most contemporary behaviorists. The central thesis of this school is simple: "mind" and all its activities consist of extremely complex movements in the brain, general nervous system, and (sometimes) other bodily organs. In other words, psychical phenomena are identical with physical phenomena; mental events are merely certain bodily changes, notably those involving the central nervous system. Thus, consistent with the general materialistic position, there is no such thing as a "psychical realm"; the mental is nonexistent as such, and the term "mind" or "mental" has justification only as a convenient classification for certain kinds of *physical* occurrences.

The Monistic Implications of Materialism. Even this brief statement of the materialistic hypothesis is sufficient to make it evident that we are in the presence of a doctrine that is not only extreme, but in an entirely different category from the three views previously discussed. We have, in fact, a view that is metaphysically different, as will be pointed out fully in a later chapter (Chapter 9). The first three views, however much they differ from one another, all imply a *dualistic* view of reality. All assume a qualitative distinction between the mind and the body: whatever the exact nature of the mind, it is something separate from the physical structure of the body. Even Hume's extreme position implies a qualitative distinction between the sensations or perceptions, which when bundled together make up the mind, and the physical brain or nervous system that houses these aggregates. Again, Kant's "synthetic unity of apperception," whatever else it may be, is definitely psychical or spiritual in character. And since the substantive view is defined as the doctrine that mind is a *spiritual* entity or substance, the dualistic implications of this position are even more apparent.

In contrast to these three views, materialism holds a strictly monistic doctrine: mind *is* the complex and subtle changes within the nervous and glandular system, and that is all. There is no qualitative difference involved, since the material or physical realm is all that exists. Activity (which means movement of some sort) within certain parts of the physical realm constitutes what, for convenience, we call "mind." In short, "mind" is a handy name for a convenient methodological fiction, but does not indicate a separate entity or agent.

The Reductive Fallacy. We have called the materialistic position "extreme," but its outraged opponents (particularly the idealists) call it much stronger names. Even the naturalist, who might be expected to be as sympathetic as anyone, usually feels that materialism is here guilty of what is known as the reductive fallacy. This is that error in thinking to which extreme doctrines, both spiritualistic and materialistic, are peculiarly liable. In the present case, it involves the claim that mind is "nothing but" matter. While probably all contemporary psychologists would hold that mental phenomena cannot exist except as antecedent bodily conditions exist, only extreme behaviorists would argue that therefore the mental is "nothing but" the physical, under another name. For, as we shall see later when we get deep into the problem of metaphysics, any such identification of the two categories of existence does violence both to our experience and to language. However much mental phenomena may *depend* upon physical phenomena for their existence, the two classes of experience are not the same and no reductive simplification of the kind that materialism attempts will serve to achieve identification of one with the other. Granted that without the physical the mental could not come into being (a position maintained by naturalists and denied by idealists), nevertheless once the mental *has* achieved this dependent being, it represents an entirely different quality of existence. The mind may not have metaphysical priority (as the idealist would claim), but a qualitatively distinct existence it clearly does have.[3]

The Functional View of Mind

In an effort to formulate a view of mind that will do justice to our experience, and at the same time harmonize fully with modern science, the *functional* theory has been proposed. Unfortunately for our present purposes, the functional view is usually difficult for students to grasp unless they are well grounded in psychology before they undertake the study of philosophy. Thanks to our brief discussion of functionalism in the preceding chapter, however, the concept will not be entirely strange.

The functionalist begins with the criticism of materialism's reductive fallacy which we have just given. Rejecting all three of the dualistic views (particularly the substantive), as well as the extreme monism of materialism, functionalism acknowledges that there can be no thought without a brain, *but refuses to identify the two as a consequence of this fact.* To acknowledge the *dependence* of X upon Y is not equivalent to reducing X to C, nor is it warrant for concluding that therefore X is unreal. What we have in "mind" (argues the functionalist) is a *group* or *set of functions,* rather than either a mere physical brain or a simple spiritual

---

[3] We shall discuss this issue at some length in Chapter 9 when we contrast spiritualistic and materialistic monisms.

substance. For to call the mind a spiritual entity or substance is to say nothing; such a concept has too little relation to our experience for the term to mean anything. On the other hand, to say that mind is brain is to talk nonsense—or more precisely, to talk no-sense: such a statement does not lie outside the field of experience (as does that of the substantialist) but rather contradicts our experience, which is plainly of two types or realms of existence.

Mind Is What Mind Does. In short, for the functional view, mind *is* what mind *does.* The best comparison here is from the field of physics. To the physicist, electricity can be defined only in terms of its behavior. No scientist can tell us what electricity is "in itself"; he can answer such a question only by an enumeration of what electricity can do. For physics, electricity is what it does: it is definable only in terms of *function.* Consequently any scientific definition of it must also be strictly functional. And so with many of the other basic concepts of science. "Energy," for example, is defined as the capacity for doing work; its "nature" *is* this capacity or work-performing function, and this is all that physics knows about it or needs to know. Of electricity or energy as they are in themselves— that is, apart from their function—science knows nothing. The very concept of a definition of either which was not functional would be meaningless to science. In fact most scientists would agree with the modern logical empiricists who insist that it is linguistic nonsense even to talk about the nature of electricity "in itself," since any theories regarding this supposed nature are unverifiable.

The functional view of mind tries to extend this same approach to the psychological and philosophical field. It holds that the mind consists of certain activities and capacities of the organism. Mind *is,* to a large extent, what the organism *does.* In addition to our bodily activities, such as digesting and breathing, there are mental activities: thinking, feeling, remembering, etc. Mind is the sum or totality of these activities, and hence is one aspect of the organism's total activity or *behavior.* It should be noted, however, that this functional view does not regard the mind as "something" which engages in these special, nonbodily activities. There is no central core or unifying agent, no "personality" standing behind these activities as a scaffolding on which they hang. For the personality is no less functional than the mind. Indeed, we can define the personality as the social aspects of mind: It is the sum of those aspects of the mind which are apparent to other "personalities." In the normal individual, these various aspects or activities are integrated or unified, but the "person" or "self" is not to be thought of as a separate agent that *has* these aspects or *engages* in the activities. It and they are one and the same. To repeat, mind *is* what mind *does*.

The Mind-Body Problem

From this thorny problem concerning the *nature* of mind we logically turn to a consideration of the relationship between mind and body. Although psychology has in part taken over this special field, philosophy still has a lively interest in the issue. Also, in spite of the developments within psychology, the problem is by no means solved, so the philosopher can still legitimately throw his speculations and theories into the already merrily boiling mind-body kettle.

The several views regarding this relationship divide readily into two types, monistic and dualistic. Of these two classes, the dualistic views have been far more influential historically. This is to be expected, for, as we have already indicated, dualism is the common-sense point of view. Further, Christianity is by implication strongly dualistic, and as far as Western philosophy is concerned, those views of mind which harmonize best with Christian doctrine have usually made most headway. As far as concerns common sense, we so obviously appear to be a combination of body and mind that the reduction of one to the other (which any monism requires) seems unthinkable. In an effort to utilize both the common sense and the experience of the student, we therefore begin our presentation with the dualistic theories.

Interactionism. The most inclusive and most influential dualistic theory of mind-body relation is *interactionism*. In brief, it holds that mind and body represent two independent orders of existence, neither of which can be reduced to the other, but each of which is capable of acting upon or influencing the other. This theory has the great advantage of appearing to agree with our day-by-day experience. For we can decide to raise an arm (that is, have a purely "mental" experience regarding a material object) and lo! the arm rises. On the converse, we have all experienced the effect of fatigue, illness, or drugs upon our mental processes; when the body is upset in any way, thinking is usually disturbed or distorted.

These are such commonplace experiences that it is sometimes difficult for students to see the possibility of any view except interactionism. Unfortunately, there are several very serious objections to the interactionist position. It is these weaknesses, one or two of which many thinkers regard as fatal, that have led to the establishment of rival theories. Virtually all these alternate views have been formulated in an attempt to avoid the objectionable elements in interactionism, so it is necessary that we get a clear picture of this doctrine and the principal objections which have been raised against it.

The Arguments Against Interactionism.   The first weakness in interactionism is the fact that we are completely ignorant as to how the supposed interaction takes place. Granted that it appears possible for me to will that my arm be raised and then execute that volition, even modern psychology can tell us very little about how the thought affects the muscles and tendons that are required to do the actual lifting. Our ignorance on the matter is almost as deep as when dualism was given classic expression by Descartes in the early seventeenth century. He held the now absurd theory that the pineal body (a gland located in the middle of the brain) was the junction or "gate" where the unextended, noncorporeal ideas switched over to an impulse in the extended (space-occupying) physical body. Conversely, this pineal gland was the means whereby a bodily event (for example, a pin prick) became transformed into a sensation or an "idea."

The second major objection to interactionism is its inconceivability. To many noninteractionists, Descartes' view is no more absurd than the idea that two things as dissimilar as mind and body can actually interact in some manner. The qualitative difference between them is too fundamental for us even to conceive how a reciprocal causal effect would be possible. There is no apparent mystery in the way that two physical objects may affect each other (as by impingement, for example), and certainly the effect of one mental event upon another is a common occurrence—as when a smell (which is a sensation) brings back a memory (which is an image). But to think of a mental event bringing about a change in a physical object, or vice versa, is clearly absurd.

The Interactionist Replies.   The interactionist has prompt answers to these first two objections to his theory. Taking them in reverse order, he points out that "inconceivability" is no argument at all: the history of science is crowded with instances where something regarded as inconceivable turned out to be a fact. For the medieval mind, it was unthinkable that men could live on the underside of the world, since obviously they would fall off—and besides, who could live hanging to the earth by his feet, like a fly to the ceiling? Later, it was "inconceivable" that man should ever be able to fly, for how could a medium as thin as air "conceivably" support an object as heavy as a human body? In sum, points out the interactionist, the only proof of factuality is *fact*. We may argue logically that such and such cannot possibly occur or exist, but if our sensory experience reveals that it *has* occurred or *does* exist, neither its illogicality nor its inconceivability will be able to alter that fact.

Further, the supposed "mystery" of how an interaction of the material and the mental could take place is no argument. For there are numerous events within the natural order that are thoroughly "mysterious." Probably no scientific law is more firmly established than Newton's general formula of gravitational attraction, yet neither Newton nor we know how it is possible for physical objects hundreds of millions of miles apart to affect one another. While Einstein has advanced some fascinating suggestions as to *why* this phenomenon of "action at a distance" takes place, the essential *how* of the process is still a deep mystery. It is "inconceivable" that objects should be able to affect each other without either coming into direct mechanical contact or setting up movements in some known medium capable of transmitting them, as the air or a fluid can transmit waves. However, there can be no doubt of the *fact* of gravitational attraction, mysterious as this effect may be. And such (concludes the interactionist) may be the case with psychophysical interaction: whether we can either "conceive" of it or satisfactorily explain it, as a brute fact it appears to be undeniable. Both logic and psychology must consequently make their peace with the fact, whether they are happy about it or not.

Mechanism and the Conservation of Energy Principle

A far more serious objection to interactionism, at least in the eyes of the scientifically minded, is the apparent violation of the conservation of energy principle which the theory seems to imply. This principle is one of the most fundamental and inclusive that science has formulated. In brief, it states that the amount of energy in any physical system is constant. This energy can be transformed, or even dissipated throughout the whole system so that internally it would be at rest, but the total amount of energy can neither be increased nor decreased. Now the theory of mind-body interaction appears to run counter to this principle. To use our same example, if I decide to raise my arm and then execute that decision, what began as a purely psychic event terminates in a physical event. In such a case, it would appear that a certain amount of energy has been added to the physical system of the body from out of nowhere. If on the converse, some change in the material world, such as a clanging bell clapper, terminates in a sensation or perception of sound within my consciousness, physical energy would seem to have vanished into the physical nothingness of "mind." In either case, the principle of conservation appears to be violated.

Here again the interactionist has ready answers, although these may not seem as satisfactory as those made to the previous objections. First, he replies that a causal relation does not necessarily involve a transfer of energy.[4] All that is required to establish causality between two objects or events is some kind of necessary dependence of one upon the other. This dependence may or may not involve energy transference. Second, the interactionist statement of the mind-body relation does not exclude the possibility of an actual transfer of energy. It may be that psychic energy is transformed into physical energy, and vice versa, so that neither the creation nor the destruction of energy is involved. In other words, the interaction hypothesis does not require that we assume two closed systems; the organism may be viewed as a total system, of which the body and the mind are only parts.

The Theory of Parallelism

Whatever may be our final evaluation of the interaction hypothesis, no one can deny that it makes a strong appeal to common-sense experience. Our next theory of the relation between body and mind turns its back on common sense, and by this drastic means attempts to eliminate some

[4] On this point, cf. Cunningham, *op. cit.*, page 289. Cunningham's whole discussion of the body-mind problem may be recommended as unusually lucid.

of the objections to the other views. This is *parallelism*. The term is almost self-explanatory: mind and body represent two separate, independent and causally unrelated series of events, existing side by side in perfect parallel. The exponents of this view acknowledge that every mental change has its corresponding physical change, and that these always and necessarily accompany one another in closest conjunction. What makes this doctrine unique is its denial of *any causal relation between the two*. However inevitable the accompaniment, it is not an effective one; mind and body are two closed circuits, with no influence upon each other. As someone has suggested, they are like two partners in a perpetual ghostly minuet that never ends in an embrace.

The Objections to Parallelism. As might be expected, parallelism has taken a severe beating from its critics. "Absurd" is the adjective probably most often applied to the doctrine. Yet it was advocated by two of the greatest figures in modern philosophy, Spinoza and Leibniz, and has able supporters even today. The most cogent objections to it would appear to be these. In the first place, the principle of biological evolution is apparently violated. According to this principle, only those things survive in the struggle for existence which have functional or survival value —that is, that aid the organism in achieving a better adaptation to its environment. Hence the parallel hypothesis would make mind completely inexplicable, since it has no effect upon either the body or its physical environment. Why then should mind have continued to exist, and to increase in capacity and importance throughout the course of evolution?

In the second place, it is objected that the implications of parallelism are absurd. Its logical result can only be a *panpsychism* of some sort—the doctrine that there is "mind" in all things and everywhere in the natural order. For if there is the inevitable reciprocal accompaniment of physical and mental events as held by the theory, not only does every mental event have its corresponding physical event, but every physical occurrence must have a psychic correlate of some sort. Thus not only would all bodily changes (for example, peristalsis or the growth of cells) have a conscious accompaniment, but even purely material events in nature, such as the decomposition of rocks, would require a psychic parallel of some kind. Some parallelists have been frank to acknowledge these panpsychic implications—Leibniz, for instance—but others have shrunk from this logical consequence, which to most nonparallelists appears inescapable.

The Position of Leibniz. Probably the most consistent advocate of parallelism among the major philosophers was this same Leibniz, a seventeenth-century German mathematician and metaphysician. The intellectual impasse to which the theory led him, as well as the desperate means he was forced to employ to escape the consequence, reveal the unsatisfactoriness of such a viewpoint. Like all its exponents, Leibniz was faced with the problem of explaining *how* this parallelism came into being, and also (if possible) *why* there should be the perpetual but futile accompaniment. His solution is perhaps the only one that can be advanced: God established the twin realms of mind and matter, and then linked the two permanently in a kind of "pre-established harmony." Leibniz used as analogy his famous figure of the two clocks. It is conceivable that an expert clockmaker would be able to make two timepieces that were so well constructed and perfectly adjusted to one another that, once they had been started together, they would be able to mark off the passing hours in perfect synchronism. There would be no influence of one on the other, no causal relation of any kind—none would be needed—yet their movements would parallel each other's permanently. Tick matching tick, strike coinciding perfectly with strike, they would function side by side in absolute parallel. And so with the twin realms of body and mind. God has fitted their independent series of events to coincide perfectly: the pre-established harmony never fails, and the phenomena of the two realms match in absolute parallel throughout their existence.

Epiphenomenalism

Dissatisfaction with both interactionism and parallelism has led to the development of various other views, all of which can be regarded as protests against these first two doctrines. One of these protesting positions is also dualistic, but most of the rival views attempt to achieve a monistic solution to the mind-body problem.

The dualistic alternate is *epiphenomenalism*. Despite its forbidding name, the theory is relatively simple, and enjoys considerable acceptance at the present time. Originally it was formulated as a materialistic view of mind, and as such was very popular with advocates of nineteenth-century materialism. Even today, for reasons which will be evident as soon as the theory is explained, its exponents come exclusively from the naturalist-mechanistic side of the fence. In brief, it holds that the relation between mind and body is a causal one, but that this is not a reciprocal causation as in interactionism. The influence is one-directional only: bodily changes bring about mental changes, *but not vice versa*. Psychic activity is merely a by-product; the basic process is purely physical. The mind thus becomes only an ineffectual accompaniment or shadow of bodily activity. As Bergson states it, on this view mind is only a halo dancing above the brain processes. A more famous analogy is that of the shadow cast by a revolving wheel; the shadow has no effect upon either the wheel or its movement, but is itself entirely dependent upon them for both its existence and its character. Santayana thus describes mind in a striking phrase as "a lyric cry in the midst of business." The basic and really important thing is the bodily activity; the conscious accompaniment represents only a nonfunctional adornment of this activity. And, the epiphenomenalist adds, just as we are frequently more impressed by the picturesque or the ornamental than we are by the essential, so here we tend to read far more significance into this "lyric cry" than is warranted by a cold weighing of the facts.

Epiphenomenalism and Science. The greatest advantage of this semidualistic theory of epiphenomenalism has been its fruitful effect upon both psychology and physiology. It has encouraged its advocates to seek purely bodily explanations for mental phenomena, and operating on this hypothesis, much fruitful experimentation has been carried on. In fact, the epiphenomenalistic hypothesis has been so rewarding as a methodology that one hesitates to attack it, although we must remember that its success as a methodological hypothesis does not prove its adequacy as an over-all metaphysical position. For example, the evolutionary argument we have used against parallelism would be just as cogent against the present doctrine. If only that survives in the struggle for existence which aids the organism in the scramble for means of subsistence and species perpetuation, and if mind or consciousness is only a "lyric cry" in the midst of that struggle, then why has it continued to exist and to increase in importance in human affairs? Thus, to give a summary valuation of epiphenomenalism, we may conclude that as a working hypothesis underlying a scientific methodology, its value has been proved by its results; as an over-all view of mind, however, it has proved somewhat less satisfactory.

The Views of Spinoza and Leibniz

In the epiphenomenalism just considered we have a dualism that be-comes, for all practical purposes, a methodological monism. In the next theory which we must consider, we have the first of two positions which claim to be monistic. Both of these have been formulated to avoid the difficulties that appear inescapable in any dualistic solution of the mind-body problem. In one of these, however, the solution seems as artificial as that offered by parallelism. This is the *double-aspect* theory, associated particularly with the name of Spinoza. In brief, it holds that mind and body are but two contrasting aspects of a single underlying ultimate. They are like the two sides of a sheet of paper—or, to use a better analogy, like the convex and concave surfaces of a curved piece of glass. In other words, whether we call an event "physical" or "mental" will depend upon the aspect we are observing it under—that is, in what relations we are viewing it—just as our decision as to whether the glass should be de-scribed as concave or convex will depend upon the relations in which we consider it.

Objections to the Double-Aspect Theory. Although the exponent of this hypothesis that mind and body are only twin attributes of a single ultimate substance can avoid the criticisms leveled at parallelism, he runs into difficulties of his own. Holding mind and matter to be the same reality, he does not need to introduce a farfetched explanation such as Leibniz used. He does, however, have to make his peace with common sense, which usually argues thus: The figure of convex and concave curves is very neat, but hardly an explanation of the fact that all our experience includes two very dissimilar realms of existence. To *call* them one and the same is possible, but to *prove* them single is clearly impossi-ble. Further, it may be objected that such an identification of the two realms is hardly an explanation. It attempts to bypass the whole mind-body problem by denying that it exists: if the two are at bottom only one, there could hardly be any difficulty concerning their relation to each other.

Contemporary minds frequently feel that the double-aspect theory is as desperate in its monistic way as parallelism is desperate dualistically. In each case, common sense is outraged, and beginning students usually find it a toss-up as to which doctrine seems more futile. Certainly neither offers any explanation that science can use as a fruitful hypothesis, and while this fact alone is not enough to eliminate them from philosophical consideration, it does load them down with a heavy burden of proof. Whether or not they are able to carry this burden is a question we must leave to the reader.

Panpsychism. The other attempt to achieve a monistic solution of the mind-body problem has already been referred to as *panpsychism.* The essence of this doctrine involves the extension of consciousness, or at least some type of psychic activity, throughout the universe. This is not merely to postulate an all-inclusive Mind of some sort, as many types of idealism do, but rather to ascribe psychic processes to every part of the natural order. Thus the panpsychist ordinarily regards the whole of nature as composed of psychic centers, each of which is similar to the human mind. The result may be called a spiritual atomism. As in the systems of both the older materialist and the modern physicist, reality thus becomes a congregate of an infinite number of atoms. Unlike these more usual forms of atomism, however, panpsychism holds the ultimate units to be essentially mental or psychical in character. Leibniz is again our classic example; in his system, the universe is composed of an infinite number of "monads," or centers of perception. The degree or level of perception in these centers varies all the way from the omniscience of God, the "monad of monads," down to the "swooning monads" that make up physical matter. These have only *petites perceptions,* or unconscious mental states, but their essence nevertheless remains fundamentally psychical. In this Leibnizian system, as in all panpsychistic thought, the basic doctrine is "mind present in all things"—or, more briefly, "mind everywhere."

Again, we clearly have before us a solution of the body-mind problem which makes few concessions to common sense. And like both parallelism and the double-aspect theory, this new viewpoint is scientifically sterile. In fact, panpsychism is hardly a theory that can be proved in the usual sense of the word. If you assert that yonder rock is alive and sentient I can hardly argue. All I can reply is that you are not employing words in their usual sense, and that you are turning your back on our indisputable common-sense experience, which finds a difference between rocks and the more obviously sentient things we call animals. Admittedly, like the exponent of the double-aspect theory, you have "solved" your problem by eliminating it. As to whether or not the intellectual price of this solution is too high, each thinker will have to decide for himself. Without intending to prejudice this decision, it may be pointed out that the consensus of opinion has held that the price is very steep.

Mind as Emergent

One last view of mind in relation to body remains to be considered. We have postponed it until the last for two reasons. First, it is perhaps the most promising theory now current in this turbulent domain and, second, it is a view that appeals both to the scientific mind and to the common-sense background of the beginning student. Thus the exasperation which the reader may have felt toward some of the more extreme or more desperate theories will be soothed, and we may hope to conclude our chapter without leaving the student so irritated or bewildered that he will not want to go on to further problems of philosophy.

This last theory of mind is not exclusively a view of the relations between the bodily and the mental, but rather a view as to the status of mind in the natural order. It builds directly upon the theory of emergence which was mentioned in our last chapter. In fact, the link between the two doctrines is so close that what we are about to describe is frequently called the *emergency theory* of mind. Extending the hypothesis that life came into being or "emerged" when a new and more complex pattern of nonorganic elements was formed—that is, when a new level of organization resulted in the appearance of new modes of response—the present theory holds that mind is similarly the result of a more complex organization of bodily (more specifically, neural) structure. In other words, as the structure of the neural mechanism became more complicated, and as there developed a central nervous system linking all parts of the organism, there "emerged" from this new level of integration a new type of response. Consciousness—or more broadly, mind—came into existence as a direct consequence of this involved organization, and therefore depends upon this neural structure for its continued existence.

The Implications of Emergence. It is interesting to consider some of the implications and ramifications of the emergence theory. For one, there are probably no exponents of this view who suggest that this new level of neural organization came into being for the *purpose* of making possible the appearance of mind in the universe. Mind is considered an *effect* of the organization, not a cause. This obviously links the emergence theory with the naturalistic world-view. In fact, this theory is the special darling of the naturalist, since it claims to offer a purely naturalistic explanation to what is for the mechanist, materialist and naturalist a particularly ticklish problem—namely, how did mind enter the cosmos? A second implication of the emergence theory is its suggestion of epiphenomenalistic leanings. Occasionally these leanings become more than mere suggestion. Several advocates of the theory admit that if mind has appeared late in evolutionary history, and only as a consequence of increasing complexity and specialization of function within the nervous system, then obviously its causal significance cannot be very great. Such an admission puts us back into epiphenomenalism, with the objections raised against that theory still to be met. In general, however, those thinkers favoring the emergence doctrine usually incline toward some form of interactionism. However dependent mind may be upon a new level of neural integration for its existence, it can still be regarded as capable of affecting the body. Its dependent origin is no proof of its causal impotence. Again, there are exponents of the emergence theory who prefer the materialistic hypothesis; they argue that at most the result of the evolutionary development of the nervous system can only be a new set of bodily reactions. If for convenience we decide to call these new reactions "mental," no harm is done—unless, of course, we thereby imply the emergence of something *qualitatively* distinct from other bodily reactions and functions.

It thus becomes clear that the emergence theory is not so much a point of view concerning the nature of mind as an explanation of its origin. As has been said of a well-known modern philosophy, the theory is like a corridor with several doors opening off it. Members of a variety of sub-schools within naturalism can all get to their individual rooms through this one corridor. However, there is one thing of which we can be certain: It is not likely that any idealist will be found wandering down this emergence corridor. For while it would be logically possible to hold that our individual human minds—finite mind with a small "m"—has emerged in the manner just described, the idealist would be compelled to hold that emergence was only the *means* whereby the universal Mind inserted itself into the realm of the physical. For idealism could hardly believe that this late appearance of mind in the evolutionary process was the first appearance of Mind in the universe. Even if biological research should some day prove the emergence hypothesis beyond doubt, the idealist still could (and almost certainly would) continue to believe that emergence was only the mechanism or strategy by which Mind realized itself in the organic realm. He would hold, consistent with his general world-view, that emergence is only a methodological and not a cosmological concept. The theory may tell us *how* mind came into being, but neither why this occurred nor what the mind's relation to reality may be.

Summary. It will be well to pause and glance back over the ground we have covered in this chapter, for the problems of mind are admittedly among the most difficult in philosophy.

We began by clarifying the popular confusion between "brain" and "mind," showing that the former is part of the physical world and possesses all the attributes of any material object, while mind appears to require special categories that apply only to it. Following this we presented the traditional or substantive view of mind, which considers it a unique spiritual substance that has independent being and does not in any way depend upon relations (to the body or the external world) for its existence. We noted how easily such a concept of mind leads to dualism or idealism, as well as to a belief in the primacy of the spiritual realm and the immortality of the soul.

Next we noted Hume's criticism of this substantive doctrine, a criticism based upon a strictly empirical approach to the problem, and one which can find no experiential basis for belief in an independent spiritual substance. Kant's reaction to Hume's revolutionary attack upon the traditional view came next, and we observed how the great German thinker formulated a compromise doctrine which gave full place to both the a priori and sense-derived elements of the mind.

The materialistic view, completely contradictory to the common theory of mind as spiritual, was next analyzed. Here we placed particular emphasis upon the apparent inadequacy of at least the more extreme position of earlier materialists, who have been widely accused of the reductive fallacy which would reduce mind to "nothing but" matter in another guise. From here we turned to a viewpoint of mind, very popular among psychologists, which insists upon an operational or functional definition. This theory holds that mind should be described solely in terms of what it *does*—that is, how it functions—and argues that any attempt to get behind mental operations to discover the nature of "mind in itself" should be abandoned as both futile and unnecessary.

The last half of the chapter analyzed the various solutions of the mind-body problem. First came the common-sense position of *interactionism*, which promises much but actually gives so many new problems that it has become unacceptable to many thinkers. The desperate effort of *parallelism* to avoid these problems attendant upon any interaction theory was described, together with the powerful reasons that have prompted a widespread rejection of the theory. Next we considered *epiphenomenalism* (so popular with nineteenth-century scientists and materialistic philosophers), which grants a real but purely accompanimental existence to mind while denying it either causal efficacy or cosmic significance.

Then followed in quick succession the *double-aspect* and *panpsychistic* attempts to solve the problem, for the patent inadequacies of both these doctrines made it unnecessary to devote much time to them. Finally we turned to the *emergence* theory of mind, which today stands as the most promising answer to the age-old body-mind problem. We noted its current popularity among contemporary scientists, but noted also that it left many more philosophical individuals dissatisfied because it tells us only how the mind came into being and has little to say regarding either its nature or its place in the total scheme of things.

It is probable that many readers will be disappointed in the results of our survey of mind, since there is obviously no clear-cut or majority viewpoint which the student can take over ready-made for his own. Instead, as with all the great problems of philosophy, we find a variety of positions, many of which contradict one another and none of which seems completely adequate. Such an outcome is inevitable, however, particularly in a book of this type where the aim is to introduce the reader to the types and problems of philosophy, rather than to impose one particular type or one prepared set of answers. We are primarily interested in providing those students new to philosophy with the raw materials for constructing their own world-view, for in any final evaluation a philosophical position possesses significance only in so far as it is our own.

CHAPTER 7

TRUTH:

Pilate's Problem—and Ours

O NE OF THE MOST DRAMATIC—AND CERTAINLY ONE OF THE MOST philosophical—moments in the New Testament story of Christ occurs when the bound Jesus is taken before Pilate, the Roman governor of Judea, for examination. In the course of the dialogue between the examiner and the accused, Pilate asks, "Art thou a king, then?" to which comes the famous reply: "To this end was I born, and for this cause came I into the world, that I should bear witness unto the truth. Everyone that is of the truth heareth my voice." Pilate's reply is even more famous: "What is truth?" he asked, thereby revealing a certain philosophical attitude that is as timely today as twenty centuries ago—and probably far more common now than it was then.

This is not to suggest that the Roman procurator saw all the implications of his sweeping query. Nor is it likely that he foresaw he was to attain a dubious immortality in the history of human thought by asking it. He did reveal a certain hard-headed skepticism, however, which has earned the respect of modern philosophers. It is hard for us who have the Christian tradition as a background to view Pilate without prejudice. We must remember, however, that his time was one of social ferment. There were numerous reformers, radicals, and prophets in Palestine at that time, all preaching "the truth." It is not surprising that he had become just a little weary of hearing the term tossed about so freely and carelessly. He was aware that not everybody who bore witness to the truth had the same story to tell, and it was natural that he should wonder just what truth might be. We as Christians may feel that he was blind not to recognize the truth when it appeared in the personality of Jesus, but his cynical attitude was the natural one for a man of his position.

It is also the natural attitude for anyone in the position of the professional philosopher. For he too has met many exponents of many systems, all claiming to have hold of "truth," and nearly all being surprised when anyone challenges their claim with Pilate's searching question. In his reading, the philosopher has worked through to an understanding of many systems, all claiming to be built upon "truth," with few of them even modest enough to admit that theirs might be only a partial truth. He has reached a point where he claims a well-earned right to ask, "What is truth?" Unfortunately, at this point Pilate's attitude and the philosopher's must part company: the philosopher cannot dismiss the problem with a shrug of the shoulder, or by turning those who claim to bear witness to the truth over to their enemies for execution. The persistent question must be faced, and every effort made to solve it.

The Complexity of the Problem. The problem of truth is one of the most complex that philosophy has to consider. For not only are there many "truths," but people rarely mean the same thing when they describe a statement as "true." A little analysis will reveal that many of those arguments that end with one or both parties shouting "Liar!" reach this unhappy conclusion, not because of deliberate falsification or even unintentional error, but because the basic disagreement lies in the fact that one party is using one theory or standard of truth, while the other is appealing for support to a wholly different concept. It is thus no wonder that the disputants cannot see eye to eye; they are not even speaking the same language, even though they may be using the same words. For, as seems scarcely necessary to point out, it is meanings and not sounds that constitute the essence of language. If I say "true" and mean one thing, while you say it and intend something else, we are wasting time to talk further—unless, of course, we can stop and analyze our differences in an effort to discover a reasonable source of agreement which will make further discourse possible.

To do this is to play the philosopher. Certainly when we ask seriously, "What is truth?" we are well aboard the train of speculative thought. And, it might be added, if we are really serious in our question, we shall be aboard that train for some time. To reach a destination that will offer a comfortable stopping place is no Sunday afternoon ride, no holiday jaunt for the intellectual tourist. It is a long journey and a hard one.

The Correspondence Theory of Truth

As suggested in Chapter 1 on the major problems of philosophy, there are three primary concepts of truth, usually known as the "theories of truth." The first of these is the one to which everyone pays at least lip service, and represents what we usually think we mean when we label a statement "true." This is the *correspondence* theory. It defines as true that statement ("proposition" or "judgment" are the technical terms preferred by philosophers) which corresponds with fact or objective reality. For example, if I say, "The book is on the table in the next room," the statement is true *if* the book actually *is* in that location. In other words, the actual location of the book is a *fact,* and if my statement corresponds with the objective order of existence in which the book, the table and the next room all have definite relations to each other, then the statement is true. It describes a factual situation, and thus embodies truth.

All this sounds quite simple and obvious, despite a few technical terms sprinkled here and there. To call my words "true" when they accurately describe things as they *are* seems foolproof; how can there be any argument on the subject? Indeed, what else *could* we mean by "true"? Isn't it the ideal of every declarative sentence to describe things as they are, as precisely and factually as possible? Certainly, answers the philosopher, that is indeed the ideal of every honest statement. But there is one little point to consider: How do we know that our ideal declarative sentence does what it is supposed to do? What are the means of checking up on statements to be sure that they do their supposed job? If I say that my statement does set forth an objective fact and you say that it doesn't, we are right back where we started: we are likely to start calling each other "liar" all over again. In other words, what is the court of final appeal for determining the factuality of any proposition?

Limited Applicability of the Theory. There is another difficulty in this apparently simple correspondence theory of truth. What use is it in a field where there are no "facts" in the sense of things established and capable of universal verification? For example, to the believing mind, the miracles attributed to a saint or a religious founder are "fact," while to the skeptic they are superstitious myth. The philosopher is forced to side with the skeptic here and deny factuality to reported miracles from past ages, not necessarily because they appear contradictory to modern science, but because he feels that the term "fact" had better be reserved for those things which are open to public verification. As another instance of the inadequacy of the correspondence theory, let us consider the field of mathematics. It is possible to construct a complete system of mathematical thought that has little relation to "common sense," and which may even run counter to it. In such a case, the word "fact" can have little meaning; to insist that mathematical propositions must correspond with things as they are is absurd, since "things as they are" in mathematics may mean relations that exist only in the mind of the person formulating the system.

So where are we? It is evident that the correspondence theory of truth, far from being foolproof as most persons assume, has reliability only when used carefully in certain realms. Even where it does apply to a situation, there must be supplementary means for proving that our statement, "The book is on the table in the next room," does represent or embody fact. In other words, our first problem is to establish positive standards for determining factuality. Until we do this, the claim that such and such is a "fact" is as meaningless as to claim that so and so is "true." Everyone who announces that he is giving you the "facts" isn't necessarily doing so. It is very probable that your informer has only the vaguest notion as to what a fact is. We sometimes hear of "hard facts" or "solid facts" or "positive facts," or even "absolute facts." The implication behind these qualifying adjectives is sound: all too often so-called facts are neither hard, solid, positive, nor absolute. To the analytical mind, they may not be facts at all, but only assumptions, postulates, hypotheses, theories, or claims of various kinds, afflicted with a severe case of wishful thinking.

Sensory Verification as a Test of Truth

The most important means of establishing the factual relationship between statements and the objective order of things is *sensory verification*. If one or more of our senses can be called in to prove that things are as we say they are, then most of us would regard the truth of a statement as established beyond any argument. If I say, again, "The book is on the table in the next room," and we go in and see that it is in the place specified, certainly there can be no doubt as to whether or not my words are true. But the philosopher has more dodges up his sleeve which must be shaken out before we can all agree that here we have an undoubted instance of "truth." What are we to do, for example, when two or more of our senses don't agree in their report, as when a stick *looks* bent in the water but *feels* straight, or a substance looks solid but isn't? We have all experienced the deceptions that our senses can play on us; illusions of various kinds are too common for anyone to argue that sensory verification alone can always establish objective fact.

Hallucinations. Even more significant philosophically are those phenomena which the psychologist classifies as *hallucinations*. The term is broad, and includes various kinds of "visions," religious ecstasies, and trances. In an *illusion* we have an actual sensory reaction to an external stimulus which is mistaken (that is, misinterpreted) by the senses—in other words, an experience which has a basis in the objective order external to ourselves. In hallucinations, on the other hand, there is no outside source which causes the experience. It rises from conditions within our own organism, such as an excess of alcohol causing "pink elephants" or severe hunger causing visions and trances. While the pink elephants and purple snakes are of no particular metaphysical significance, other hallucinary experiences may be. Many persons, for example, find much "truth" in the religious ecstasies of various saints or even in their own mystical experiences; they find in the visions of Joan of Arc and Saint Teresa proof of the existence of a supernatural order.[1] If an individual has had some kind of mystical experience himself, it is usually impossible to shake his belief in the existence of a supernatural realm or supernatural being. He says, quite naturally, that the vision was as real to him as any sensory experience ever was or can be. He knows that God exists, or that ultimate reality is "One," just as certainly as he knows that you his questioner exist, and for exactly the same reason: he has seen you both, felt your presence, perhaps heard you both speak. He can no more doubt the objective reality, the actual truth of what he has experienced than he can question any other "fact" which his senses have revealed. He *knows*, because he has *perceived*.

The philosopher finds himself in a very delicate position here. To doubt the objective reality of mystical "facts" would be to cast a suspicion over much of the content of religious belief. On the other hand, to grant

[1] It should be noticed that such an evaluation of these experiences automatically means that the religious believer does not agree with the psychological definition of them as hallucinations without any external cause.

these "facts" the same epistemological status as the objects of universal, everyday experience seems impossible. There is always the danger that if we open the door and admit the content of religious visions to the realm of the factually real, then the door is also wide open to every subjective experience; even the fantasies of the insane would have some right to claim reality. On the contrary, if we exclude from the category of reality any experience that cannot meet the test of universality (that is, which cannot be shared by everyone), then we have closed the door on some of the most significant insights of the race. Joan of Arc, for example, may have been only a psychotic visionary. The fact remains, however, that St. Michel was as real to her as her grazing sheep, and that on his instructions she abandoned her sheep-tending and went to save France.

And so again our question: How reliable is sensory verification as proof of the truth of a statement?

Sensation vs. *Common Sense.* There is another reason for not putting unlimited faith in sensory verification as the proof of correspondence between our ideas and reality. This is the confusion which frequently arises between true sensory verification and its counterfeit, so-called "common sense." Modern science offers a good example of this confusion. "Common sense," for instance, tells us that the oak table top is hard and solid; certainly it offers ample resistance to our sense of touch. Modern physics, however, describes this same table top as anything but solid. It is instead a mass of atoms, which in turn consist of a central core of electrical energy surrounded by one or more negative charges called electrons, moving in their orbits at tremendous speeds. Neither the central proton nor the encircling electrons are considered to be "solid" in any common-sense meaning of the term, while the space separating the nucleus from the peripheral charges is probably relatively comparable to the space which separates the planets from the sun in our solar system.

Although a good deal of this atomic system remains a theoretical construct, there is enough experimental evidence to prove that it is probably more than a mere theory. However, "experimental evidence" means sensory verification, so we thus have a neat paradox on our epistemological hands. For here we have direct or primary sense evidence ("common sense") that the table top is solid, and at the same time we have experimental or indirect sense evidence that the table top is not solid. Just how much stock can we take, therefore, in sensory verification as proof of "truth"?

The question cannot be answered in one statement that will do justice to the views of every philosophical school. For here, as in so many of the problems of philosophy, our answer will depend upon the school of thought to which we belong. In general, however, we can say that sense evidence is of tremendous significance as *one* of the criteria of truth, but not reliable as the *only* test. Some schools put much stress upon it, insisting that, despite its admitted inadequacies, sense experience remains the most dependable single determiner of the truth or falsity of our statements. The rationalist, on the other hand, values sensory experience only as a subordinate test of truth, placing little or no faith in it as an independent, self-sufficient proof. All schools agree, however, in according it a place as one of the criteria of truth; exactly how large a place is the great question.

The Contrasting Reactions of Idealism and Naturalism

Idealism. As might be expected, idealism and naturalism are on opposite sides of the fence in this question. Idealism, with its emphasis upon the mind and its rational activities, has always stressed the reasoning, conceptualizing aspects of thought and experience. As a result of this emphasis, this school has tended to distrust the senses as sources of knowledge and revealers of the real. For the senses can report only the *appearance* of things, or phenomena. Hence our sensations have no necessary relation to the underlying reality. Indeed, they frequently stand as a barrier to contact with the real, for their report may be so "sensational" as to be distracting, or so distorted as to be completely misleading. As Plato said, we are imprisoned in our bodies and their sensory apparatus. Since we are entirely dependent upon this apparatus for our knowledge of the external world, we know only as much as sensation is capable of bringing us—which means only phenomena or appearances. The idealist holds that if it were not for our reason, which is able to pierce through the welter of sensation to the underlying reality, we would be hopelessly cut off from any ultimate knowledge or truth. This is for idealism the chief function of reason: to organize our sensations, threshing them to get out the ontological wheat, and then from this process of abstraction, by generalization and conceptualization, to formulate a "true" picture of the real.

It is not surprising, therefore, that idealism should tend to regard "truth" as the result of a perpetual contest between sensation and reason —with reason necessarily victorious before "truth" can emerge. This dualism of reason *vs.* sense (or, more fundamentally, the mental *vs.* the physical) is implicit in all metaphysical idealism. Sometimes it remains only implicit, but more often the fundamental opposition is made very clear, as in Platonism, where it becomes the basis for a vast metaphysical-epistemological-ethical-esthetic system in which the philosopher seems to become indeed "the spectator of all time and all existence."

Naturalism. Naturalism holds the reverse to be true: sensory experience, in spite of its admitted deficiencies, is a far more reliable means of contacting reality than the abstractive, conceptualizing processes of the mind which the idealist so much admires. No naturalist, however, is naive enough to suggest that raw, blind sensation can by itself give us much knowledge or "truth." He acknowledges that the mind must organize its sense data before they can become intelligible; he agrees with Kant's famous statement that "precepts [i.e., sensations] without concepts are blind." Nevertheless the naturalist remains at heart an empiricist, giving the ultimate authority to experience—and this of course means *sense* experience. He holds that ideas, concepts and all the products of rational activity should in the end be evaluated by the acid test of experience. Thus the naturalist is always suspicious of the idealistic and rationalistic systems, with their tendency to build upon reason at the expense of sense experience. He feels that empirical proof is the only check upon man's vast ability to imagine, dream and rationalize. If we make the mistake of relegating empirical evidence to a subordinate role in the search for truth or reality, then what is there to prevent "reason," with its capacity for making things look the way we want them to look, from offering us a dream-born counterfeit of the real? Sense data must be the final court of appeal. If these data do not fit our "rational view of things," then instead of dismissing the data as "appearances," it is the view which must be changed.

The Coherence Theory of Truth

It thus becomes evident that the correspondence theory of truth fits better into the naturalist world-view than into the idealistic scheme of things. The second great theory of truth, however, fits snugly into the idealistic position. This is the *coherence* theory. In brief it holds that a statement or proposition is true if it harmonizes with other established truths or with our knowledge as a whole. The best example here is the field of mathematics. In Euclid's geometry, for instance, we have a system that is deductively derived, step by step, from the original axioms and postulates. Once these are taken as true, the rest of the system follows logically, almost inevitably. We move in an unbroken chain of strictest reasoning from the original axioms to the *Q.E.D.* that ends the proof of a theorem. On conclusion we have a completely integrated piece of logical thought, which in turn coheres with a whole system of reasoning.

In such types of deductive thought, it is obvious that truth and error are determined by whether or not the proposition in question harmonizes with the system of which it is supposed to be a part. Here coherence becomes the sole criterion of truth: a statement is untrue only if it fails to integrate with the whole of our knowledge or belief.

Again, as in the case of the correspondence theory, our first reaction to such a standard is probably favorable. There seems no obvious objection to the theory, and we have heard the ideal of logicality praised often enough to make us impressed by such a goal as a completely coherent system of thought—particularly if it is so grandiose as to include all of our knowledge and experience, as in metaphysics. But there is a serpent in this epistemological paradise also, as the philosopher (usually an empiricist) hastens to point out. This is the fact that in the coherence theory, and in all deductive systems built upon it, we do not have "truth" at all, strictly speaking. We have only logical consistency, more properly called *validity*, which has no necessary relation to fact, objective reality, or the external order of nature. We have here only a species of logical order and coherence, quite capable of existing in a vacuum as far as objective reality is concerned.

Difference Between "Truth" and "Validity." Students who have been through a course in logic will recall some of the absurd conclusions to their syllogisms which were, however, entirely valid as far as the rules of logical thought are concerned. It is usually only in the logic class that one learns to distinguish sharply between "validity" and "truth to fact." Let us consider an example drawn from the borderland between philosophy and theology. The theist builds his system upon certain assumptions, such as the existence of God, His omniscience and omnipotence, the immortality of the soul, the freedom of the will, and so on. These constitute the premises from which his reasoning begins. Starting with these, he deductively formulates an elaborate structure of thought, embracing all human experience and the destiny of both the individual and the race. This theistic system leads to certain conclusions, which appear to follow logically and inevitably from the assumptions or premises with which the chain of reasoning began. But these conclusions follow logically *only from these particular original assumptions*. If we start from another set of premises (for example, the nonexistence of God, the mortality of the soul, universal determinism, and so forth), we will just as logically and inevitably get an entirely different set of conclusions. Both sets would be valid, both would be warranted (in fact, required) by the premises with which we began. But which, if either, would be "true"—and what would be meant by "true"? If we are thinking in terms of the correspondence theory, then obviously that set of conclusions is truest which best states the facts of objective existence. But when these conclusions involve such propositions as "God is good," "The universe is a great Spirit," "The universe is a vast, soulless machine," and the like, what value can the correspondence theory have? In short, how can we ever prove the correspondence between such statements and objective fact? Or, to ask an even more fundamental question, what constitutes a "fact" in this domain? If we follow our earlier suggestion and reserve the term "fact" for those experiences which are capable of universal verification—that is, which can be experienced by all observers—is it possible to speak of "facts" at all in connection with either philosophy or religion?

The Limitations of Logical Validity

The relation between "validity" and "truth" can best be illustrated by examples from mathematical and logical reasoning. For example, if we have the equation $x = y$, followed by $y = z$, it is valid to conclude that therefore $x = z$. We reach this conclusion, however, without any knowledge of the meaning or value of the symbols. We therefore have no knowledge regarding the "truth to fact" of our conclusion, because we do not know what factual meaning $x = z$ has.[2] We can be sure only that, given the two premises $x = y$ and $y = z$, we can draw the valid conclusion $x = z$. To take another example from deductive or formal logic, consider the following syllogism:

> All oak trees have rough bark
> This tree is an oak
> Therefore, this tree has rough bark

Obviously the conclusion is valid, but it is true to fact only if the two premises are also true to fact. If someone can prove that not all oaks have rough bark, or if we can successfully challenge the "fact" that this particular tree in question is an oak, then however sound and valid the syllogism may be as a piece of reasoning, its conclusions cannot possibly be true—that is, true to fact, or correspondent with the objective order of nature. On the other hand, let us rearrange this same syllogism slightly so that it reads:

> All oak trees have rough bark
> This tree has rough bark
> Therefore, this tree is an oak

A glance will reveal that the conclusion is now invalid, since there is nothing in the premises that states that only oaks have rough bark. The reasoning is inconclusive: from these two premises we can conclude "Therefore, this tree may be an oak"; there is no way, however, that we can derive from them a categorical statement, "Therefore, this tree is an oak." And the conclusion as it stands will remain invalid, even if it happens to be true to fact. In other words, if it happens that this tree *is* an oak, it is so by coincidence and not because of a logical necessity arising from the given premises.

Such is the distinction between "truth to fact" and "validity." As already stated, the coherence theory of truth has the advantage of sim-

---

[2] Hence the point of Bertrand Russell's remark that mathematicians do not know what they are talking about—and don't care.

plicity in that it concerns itself only with validity and consistency. If a system of thought coheres logically, nothing else is needed to make it acceptable—according to this theory. It is a great advantage to have such a simple standard, particularly since (as we have already indicated) it is usually possible to reach agreement as to what is consistent with any system as a whole and what is not. Unfortunately, the obvious weaknesses of this theory are such as to far outweigh its advantages. As a result, it is used as the exclusive criterion of truth in very few fields, notably in mathematics.

Principal Weakness of the Coherence Theory. The most glaring weakness of the theory has been implied in the preceding paragraphs. Without the restraining necessity of requiring that our conclusions square in some provable way with objective fact, it becomes possible to erect the most impressive and complex structure of thought upon premises which may have nothing to recommend them except the fact that they are to our selfish advantage (as in systems of political or economic ideology), or that they conform to our longing for a view of the world which will give us assurance and hope. The primary danger is that the uncritical person may be so impressed by the finished structure and its conclusions (particularly if they satisfy his desire for emotional assurance or ethical justification) that he fails to notice the foundations upon which the whole is erected. Often if an analyst can lay bare these foundations, a mind that has hitherto accepted the whole system will reverse itself and reject the whole because the initial premises are not acceptable. More often such a mind will dig around and try to lay more acceptable premises of its own as foundations, and then move the whole thought-structure intact over onto the new underpinning. Occasionally a mind that has seen the initial premises exposed as unacceptable assumptions, and has admitted that they are unsatisfactory or perhaps even absurd, will still stubbornly argue that any system that is so impressive and which reaches such beautiful, heart-warming conclusions must be true regardless of its foundations. Obviously, when any person has such a "will to believe" as this, it is probable that we are wasting our time even to discuss the question of truth with him. When the intellectual structure under which he still insists upon taking shelter has stood for centuries, it is usually doubly useless to try to show the uncritical believer that it is built upon no factual, objective foundations that can meet the correspondence test of truth.

The Pragmatic Theory of Truth

It would not be fair to imply that a person is acting arbitrarily when he chooses the coherence theory as against the one of correspondence, or that he is thinking solely in a wish-fulfilling manner. There is a probability that, consciously or unconsciously, he is appealing to the third great theory of truth to make a decision between the two we have thus far discussed. This third is the *pragmatic* concept of truth.[3] In essence, it holds that the only significant test of truth lies in its workability—that is, the fruit it bears and the results it leads to. Thus, for the pragmatist, a statement is true if it expresses a fact or describes a situation upon which we can act and secure the anticipated results. Our old friend, "The book is on the table in the next room," is really a plan of potential action: it signifies that *if* I go into the next room and look on the table, I will find the book. If I do act upon this plan and do find the book in the place indicated, then the statement becomes true—or more accurately acquires truth.

Now the general idealistic view of truth is something very different. While the subschools within idealism have somewhat divergent doctrines, as a group they regard truth as something that should logically be spelled with a capital letter. It is directly related to the ultimate real; as we have seen, one of the characteristic doctrines of idealism has been the fusion of "the Good, the Beautiful, and the True" to constitute the real. Consequently "truth" has an independent existence, and our experience with it is always in the nature of a discovery. Truth exists, and we discover it; hence it constitutes an absolute of some kind. For the pragmatist, however, there is no such thing as absolute truth in the sense of something that possesses an independent, self-sufficient existence. It is rather something which we *make*. Needing conceptual aids to deal with our experience, we formulate judgments of various kinds. It is only as we go into action on the basis of these judgments that they *become* true. Any statement is thus for the pragmatist essentially an *hypothesis* to be verified by acting upon it and observing the results.

Pragmatism and Science. Pragmatism has as its chief source the

[3] The leading names in pragmatism in America are William James (d. 1910) and John Dewey (d. 1952). F. C. S. Schiller (d. 1937) of England is usually linked with the two Americans.

methodology of science. As far as "truth" is concerned, science is pragmatic. After a scientist has framed his hypothesis to explain the data under consideration, the standard method of verification is to set up a critical experiment which will give definite "yes or no" results. The worker is able to forecast the results which the experiment may be expected to yield (if the hypothesis is true) from his knowledge of the field and its proved principles. Thus when the experiment is performed and he "puts the question to nature and compels her to answer," the truth of the hypothesis depends entirely upon whether or not it yields the results anticipated. The whole structure of science is thus built upon workability: an hypothesis which works or bears results is accepted as true.[4]

The pragmatist, like everyone else, is much impressed by the achievements of modern science. Since these have come from the employment of this practical, nonidealistic, workaday theory of truth, it is natural that some school of philosophy should suggest the extension of this theory to cover all our experience. For it seems logical to assume that any theory which has proved so fruitful in one field would also prove valuable in others. The principal attacks against this pragmatic extension have come from the absolute idealists, and have centered upon its supposed claim that workability *alone* is the test of truth. Some of the early pragmatists were perhaps guilty of oversimplifying the problem of truth, and in their pioneering enthusiasm did attempt to establish a theory in which this one test of workability should by itself determine the true and the untrue. The mature pragmatism of our own day, however, has profited by these criticisms and refined its doctrine to eliminate any such excess.

Pragmatism's Auxiliary Aids in Determining Truth. Most pragmatists realize that, while workability may be the most important test of truth, there can be additional support from other sources. The first of these auxiliary aids turns out to be our old friend "coherence": we cannot hold our truths or beliefs in atomistic isolation; they must harmonize as a whole. (An old-line pragmatist would probably argue in favor of this harmonious consistency on the grounds that our truths will "work better" if they form a coherent system.) The second aid that pragmatism calls

---

[4] There are other requirements of a good hypothesis. We have already emphasized the importance of the principle of parsimony—the simplest hypothesis is favored—and in addition such criteria as inclusiveness and what the mathematician calls "elegance" must be considered. This last is a combination of neatness, logicality, unity, and what is colloquially called "patness"—in other words, "elegance" is a difficult term to define.

in on occasion is peculiarly characteristic of this school.[5] When we cannot choose between two statements on the basis of empirical evidence, coherence, or the "cash value" of immediate results, then we are justified in deciding which of the two propositions is "true" by the amount that each can contribute in the way of "higher values," or "life values." Our beliefs, particularly those dealing with our experience as a whole, are capable of influencing our attitude toward life and the world in which we live. They can make life seem either futile or well worth living; they can give us either emotional security and "peace of mind" or the opposite. Thus when we have to decide which of two contradictory statements is "true"—for example, "The soul is immortal" and "The soul is mortal"— it is obvious that we will get little help from workability or coherence, and none whatever from sensory verification. We must choose between the two statements on some other basis. In such cases, the test of which proposition does most to realize "higher life values" becomes not only valid but probably inevitable.[6]

It should be pointed out that pragmatism never justifies the choice of one statement as true over another on grounds of "higher values" alone. It is only when the other criteria fail to determine its "truth" that we are warranted to turn to this last test as the court of final appeal. If empirical results, "cash value," or coherence make the decision for us, any appeal to "higher values" would look suspiciously like intellectual dishonesty. It is only when the other tests either are not applicable or end in an indecisive stalemate, that we can allow our spiritual well-being and emotional needs to determine the decision.

The Various Tests of Truth

The reader by now probably feels more sympathetic with Pilate when he asked his immortal question concerning the nature of truth. However,

[5] Notably of William James, who gave it more emphasis than recent pragmatists have done.

[6] Throughout this presentation of pragmatism, I have been following James rather than the more recent men. While there are important differences within pragmatism, here as everywhere throughout the book I have been trying to give beginning students clarity instead of confusion, and for that reason have thought : best to ignore the family differences within the school.

we are by no means out of the woods. Thus far we have discussed the three chief *theories* of truth, plus one of the *tests* of truth, sensory verification. There are several other such tests to be considered, all of which are as popular and probably as important as sensory verification. Many persons would prefer to call these "sources" of truth rather than "tests," but the term is not important so long as we understand their relation to the central problem.

Authority. Next to sensory verification, probably the most used test of truth is *authority*. We depend upon authority so frequently that we are hardly aware of it. While it is true that the moral and ecclesiastical authorities of an earlier day have largely broken down, new ones of a different type have taken their place. For instance, instead of the authority of the Church, we now depend far more upon science for our "truth." Whether or not the newer authority is more adequate as a general guide for life is fortunately not a question that we have to settle here. The main point is that we are probably as dependent upon sources outside ourselves for our truths as we ever were. We may be confident that science is a more reliable authority, but the fact remains that it too is an outside source as far as most persons are concerned. We may point out the pragmatic results of science as evidence of its reliability, or we may emphasize its absolute insistence upon objective verification as our warrant for accepting its authoritative claims. Or perhaps we have dabbled in the laboratory ourselves enough to have confirmed the truths of some one of the sciences. However, even the professional laboratory worker does not have the training and time to make such verifications except in his own field. We may argue that, having checked some of the statements of science through our own experiments, we are justified in assuming that other scientific facts are equally "true." This means, however, that we are taking these other facts on authority, however reliable it may be.

The Role of Authority in Education. Most of us do not have the opportunities of even the amateur scientist for verifying our authorities. And the same is true in all fields of human activity. The amount of knowledge which is ours by direct experience is, for the educated person, probably the lesser part of his total knowledge. The more educated we become and the more our background broadens, the more authorities we inevitably depend upon, for higher education involves an increasing amount of theoretical knowledge and vicarious learning. The kindergartner learns largely by doing, in activities of various sorts; the advanced college student learns largely by reading abstracts and summaries of the activities of other men. However efficient this advanced method may be as a mode of learning, it places a tremendous emphasis upon authority. And what is true of formal education is true of all fields. In a civilization as complex and myriad-minded as ours, nearly everything we do involves second-hand experience. Our news sources are excellent examples, while in such fields as medicine, economics, and so forth, we are nearly helpless before the parade of authorities, of various sorts and of varying degrees of reliability.

The problem thus becomes one of distinguishing between the various types or grades of authority, and sometimes between conflicting expert opinions within the same field. However, as each field has its own standards, it is outside the scope of this book to attempt any detailed evaluation of the types of authority. It will be enough if the reader has an increased realization of how inescapable authority must be in determining what we shall and what we shall not regard as "truth." The uncritical mind is so easily imposed upon by "authority" (usually the most recent it has read or heard), and so easily tricked into believing the knowledge thus gained to be its own and therefore infallible, that the philosopher frequently despairs of ever separating "truth" from "opinion." Socrates and Plato both wrestled with the problem of achieving this separation, and then willed it to philosophy as a permanent heritage. As far as everyday, practical "truth" is concerned, authority stands in importance immediately after sensory verification and workability. "What is truth?" As Pilate was apparently well aware, it is to a large extent what the leading authority says it is. He acknowledged this fact by accepting the disposition of the case before him recommended by those who, under Hebraic law, were the proper "authorities."

The Test of Social Agreement and Inner Certainty

Closely linked with the test of authority is another which, under some circumstances, may be even more cogent than the Church once was or than science is today. This is the test of *social agreement*. To a considerable extent, "truth" is what everybody says it is. To have to be told that *"Everybody* knows that is true!" is always to imply that we are either deficient in learning or subnormal in intelligence—or both. While social agreement exercises a powerful influence over our judgments of "truth" in all fields, it is most potent in the realms of custom, social usage, and morality. For most people, the fact that a custom or an ethical standard is accepted very widely offers good grounds for regarding it as "true." Indeed, to many persons it is always a shock to hear anyone challenge the truth of a widely held moral viewpoint. Universal acceptance—or even majority acceptance—is for such minds an adequate guarantee of truth.

The philosopher, however, has long made a specialty of challenging the force of social agreements. He takes satisfaction in pointing out the notorious ephemerality and inconsistency of these, even when the agreement is universal. The impermanence of ordinary social customs and usages is too obvious to require philosophical comment. However, when ethical standards become dominated too strongly by mere social agreement, philosophy sees a serious danger. Most moral progress has come from a tiny minority of persons who were not overawed by the vast force of social agreement—the martyrs, the reformers, the abolitionists, who found no relation between truth and majority opinion. To such ethical pioneers, "truth" is something which is self-sufficient and independent of mass acceptance.

These lonely, courageous spirits have always tested their "truth" by some other standard than social agreement. Sometimes it has been authority—the authority of the Bible, or of some prophet or leader. In other instances they have argued from the coherence theory of truth: certain practices or standards impressed them as inconsistent with the larger moral ideals professed by the society in which they lived, or perhaps as incompatible with the teachings of Christ. At other times the pragmatic theory has been used for support: the actual results of the practice were evil, regardless of the elaborate ethical rationalizations formulated to justify it. Slavery offers the classic example of a practice that was first attacked largely on pragmatic grounds.

The Mystical or Intuitive Standard.   More often than to any of these tests of truth, however, the moral pioneer has appealed to another which we have scarcely mentioned. This is the *mystical* or *intuitive* standard— an "inner light" or deep-seated conviction which seemed more compelling, more charged with unmistakable certainty, than all other truth tests combined. It need hardly be said that, as far as philosophy is concerned, this criterion is too personal and subjective to permit much analysis. The philosopher must admit both the fact of such experiences and the effect which they have upon the individual, but beyond that there is little to say. Even the psychologist does not have much to offer, except to suggest two points which must be considered in evaluating the validity of such experiences. The first of these is negative: the feeling of inner certainty by itself is quite unreliable, as proved by the fact that the insane are probably more "certain" as to the truth of their convictions than any other group of human beings. On the positive side, however, we must hasten to point out that in the last analysis this inner feeling of certainty is present in every truth experience, regardless of the theory or test of truth we are consciously employing. Even in the case of sensory verification (apparently the most foolproof and universally valid standard), what do we ultimately depend upon to prove that we "see" or "smell" or "hear" what we think we do? Is it anything other than this same inner feeling of certainty? To return to our example of Joan of Arc: Is it not probable that she was as certain that she "saw" the Archangel and "heard" his command to go save France as she was that she saw the sheep grazing around her and heard their bleatings? Is not the proof of anything which we experience as "real" established by this same test of inner certitude? Basically, is the reader's certainty that he sees the book he is now reading any greater than Joan's when she saw St. Michel, or any greater than that of the paranoic with a persecution mania who sees enemies lurking in every shadow? Admittedly the book can meet other tests which neither St. Michel nor the paranoic's "enemies" can—universal verification being the most important. But that is beside the point. To submit the book to hundreds of other observers for confirmations of its objective existence would only result in a hundred other certainties equal to the reader's and to Joan's and to the paranoic's.

The feeling of inner certainty is thus at the same time the most basic subjective test of truth, and the least reliable test. The best solution of this paradoxical situation appears to be this: Admittedly, there can be no truth experience unless this intuitive feeling of certainty is present, but by itself the feeling is unreliable. It must be present, but it must be well-accompanied. It is the means for certifying the other more objective criteria; it is an instrument for realizing the other tests of truth, but not a valid test when standing by itself.

A Final Evaluation of the Truth Theories

After an analysis of truth such as we have now been through, the question naturally rises, "Is there any truth—that is, any truth as most people understand the term, and as I understood it before reading this chapter?" This is a question which every reader will have to answer for himself, and in part, his answer will depend on what he thinks to be generally understood by the term. If truth is regarded as something absolute and static, then probably a majority of readers will now be ready to doubt that there is any such thing. If, on the other hand, we understand the term to mean something which is relative and dynamic, then certainly most of us would agree that it exists. Some readers may feel that, in spite of the criticisms we have leveled at each test and theory as it has passed in review, at least one of them has survived the ordeal well enough to constitute a dependable standard of truth.

The Composite Standard. It is probable, however, that most students will agree that the only adequate evidence of truth must come from a composite of all the various theories and tests. That is to say, (1) if a proposition can be shown through sensory verification to correspond with objective reality; (2) if it coheres with all our other knowledge and "truths"; (3) if when we act upon it we secure anticipated results; (4) if there is a high degree of social agreement concerning these first three; (5) if all the authorities involved agree, and finally (6) if underlying and permeating all these there is an inner certainty and common-sense conviction concerning the experience, then it is probably safe to assume that we have told of *truth*. Perhaps even this will not be the kind that ought to be spelled with a capital "T," but it should at least offer something we can depend on and build our lives around.

But, in the words of a cynical popular expression, this is "nice work, if you can get it." Most of us would be quite willing to build our lives around such well-established truths, but they are few and far between. Furthermore, instances of truth as well authenticated as this are generally too simple to solve our more pressing problems. For instance, our old standby, "The book is on the table in the next room," could probably meet all these tests, as could most simple, matter-of-fact statements dealing with the temporal and spatial relations of physical objects. Even the basic classification of such objects rarely presents serious truth-problems.

If I say, "This book is green," the truth or falsity of the statement can be established definitely—provided, of course, that I am not talking about a book of doubtful or off-shade color, that I do not require the agreement of color-blind individuals, or that I myself am not color-blind.

The Limitations of the Composite Standard. Unfortunately, only a part of the propositions which we have to evaluate as "true" or "false" can meet all the criteria. For example, let us take the judgment, "Suicide is never justified." How shall we decide whether or not the statement is true? Any sensory verification is obviously out of the question, as is also any appeal to the correspondence theory. The pragmatic test is also useless, unless we possess the type of mind that finds force in the irrelevant universalization, "Suppose everybody committed suicide!" The test of authority is binding only on those who accept the particular authority in question; the stern injunction of the Catholic Church against suicide, for example, is binding only on Catholics. The coherence theory might be helpful, but this will depend upon our whole background of knowledge and experience. We can require that the statement, "Suicide is never justified," square with all our other truths and principles, but since each person's collection of truths and principles is different, this would make our judgment of "true" or "false" purely subjective. But, since the only remaining test, social agreement, is useless—the diversity of opinion regarding suicide is notorious—perhaps the coherence theory is most dependable after all. But meanwhile, where has our beautiful composite theory of truth gone? Obviously, it is only in the field of sense experience that we can hope to secure agreement and derive interlocking support from all the various theories and tests of truth. This would seem to imply that it is only in the field of sense experience that we can get any incontrovertible or absolute truth. As far as the rest of human experience is concerned, it appears that we are confined to that criterion, or combination of criteria, of truth which experience proves to be most satisfactory.

There is an even more disturbing possibility that grows out of this discussion. For does it not also suggest that perhaps *all* truth is purely personal—that each man makes his own truth, living in a private world of his own "truths" which may overlap the private truth-world of another individual, but which can never be completely identical with it? In short, can there be any general or universal truth, much less any absolute truth?

The Pragmatist's Last Word. Perhaps it is the pragmatist who has the last word here. He would see nothing shocking in the existence of individual systems of truth. For each man will, consciously or unconsciously, formulate a system of truths which reasonably well meets the three requirements for truth demanded by pragmatism. First, his system will be reasonably coherent, and consistent enough to satisfy whatever sense of logical consistency he may possess; second, it will correspond with the external world well enough to work; and most important of all, it will be satisfactory and workable as a whole. It will get results, maintain or advance his welfare, satisfy his interests and desires, and in general enable him to get along in the world. Probably a more ideal system—more coherent, more correspondent, more workable—would get better results and consequently be "truer." But, as every nation is supposed to get the kind of government it deserves, so does every man get the system of truth he deserves: a system which works for him and satisfies his demands upon life and the world about him. To misappropriate and slightly misquote a famous line from Keats, the pragmatist would conclude,

"That is all the truth ye know on earth, or need to know."

CHAPTER 8

EPISTEMOLOGY:

What Can We Know?

IT IS ALMOST CERTAIN THAT MANY READERS WILL BE DISSATISFIED with the results of our analysis of the truth-problem in the preceding chapter. These results may appear inconclusive and relativistic, or perhaps the whole issue seemed to end in an implied skepticism. One may be tempted, as are many students after discussing the problem, to demand, "But I want to *know!* Of what good is philosophy if it can't answer my questions? Haven't the philosophers decided for sure whether there *is* any genuine truth, and if we can know it or not?"

It will clear the air if we become frank on this point and take the student into our confidence. The problem of truth, complicated and difficult as it is, is only one part of a much more inclusive question. This is the epistemological problem: What can we know, or what are the limits of knowledge? Naturally, any issue as basic as this involves subordinate questions concerning the *sources* of knowledge, the *types* of knowledge or "ways of knowing," methodologies, and so forth. The core query, however, is one we have already met in our introduction to the problems of philosophy in Chapter 1: What can we know, and how do we know it? There has recently been current a colloquial greeting, much used in certain social groups: "What do you know for sure?" It would be difficult to phrase the epistemological inquiry more tersely, except that the philosopher is interested in the capacities of the human mind in general, rather than with the content of any individual mind. Thus he is really asking, "What can we as a species know for sure?"

There are several schools of thought here as on all the problems of philosophy. All that we can attempt in an introductory volume is to present the most important of these points of view, and then let the reader make his own decision as to which solution of the epistemological problem appears most satisfactory. Perhaps he will select a single answer, or perhaps he may try to combine several into a more inclusive solution. We may make our decision on the basis of what we have been taught since childhood, or through a temperamental preference of some kind—or possibly on the basis of a reaction *against* what we have been taught since childhood. However, regardless of the standard by which one judges the various theories of knowledge and makes a choice from among them, the decision will be strictly personal.

The Personal Character of Knowledge. There are always some minds which are startled to be told that they make their own knowledge. To the philosopher, however, this conclusion seems inescapable. Consciously or unconsciously, each of us holds an epistemological theory; we each decide to what sources of knowledge we will give priority: sense experience, authority, reason, intuition, and so on. Perhaps the reader has grown up in a religion which places great emphasis upon authority. If he has, it is probable that he will continue to accept authority of some kind as the primary source of knowledge—unless, of course, he has revolted against that early training; in this case it is probable that he will lean toward sensory experience and reason as ultimate sources. In other words, it seems impossible to avoid the conclusion that, just as we each make our own "philosophy of life" or "view of the world," so do we each to a large extent create the content of our individual world of knowledge. Taking the term "philosophy" in its broadest sense, this is as it should be. For our philosophy is only the sum of all our various opinions about life and human experience, and among these opinions our views concerning the limits of knowledge and the bounds of certainty have maximum importance.

Relation Between the Knowledge Problem and the Theories of Truth. The sources of knowledge which we have just enumerated—sensation, authority, reason, and intuition—suggest that the problem of knowledge is closely connected with that of truth. While this is so, the two are not identical. The epistemological problem is both more inclusive and more fundamental. In view of this fact, it may be wondered why we did not discuss it first. The reason is largely pedagogical; it is easier to arouse interest in the problems of truth than in the problem of knowledge. Indeed, it is not always easy to make the philosophical beginner see that there is any epistemological problem. He has heard arguments regarding "true" and "untrue" long before he heard of philosophy, but there are very few situations in ordinary life which lead to a discussion of "knowing" and "not knowing." We may accuse a person of not knowing what he is talking about, but a considerable degree of intellectual sophistication is required to suggest asking our opponent what the sources of valid knowledge are, whether or not he is using only those which are valid, and how he knows that he knows anything for sure.

All this is only to say that we take our knowledge very much for granted. The attitude of most persons is what the philosopher calls "uncritical" or "epistemologically naive." We assume quite naturally that our minds are adequate to deal with experience (more precisely, with the objects of experience), and while we are accustomed to an occasional challenge as to how we know such-and-such to be true, we are surprised almost to the point of shock if anyone asks how we know *anything*. The effect upon the person who asks himself this question seriously for the first time is usually only a shade less disturbing than when he is first asked seriously how he knows that he exists. Both questions challenge assumptions that are so indispensable to thinking, and so well-supported by common sense, that the mere asking of them seems absurd. Yet both are asked by the professional thinker in complete good faith, and finding a satisfactory answer to the problem of knowledge is perhaps modern philosophy's most critical task.

Epistemology and Modern Philosophy

It is customary to date the beginning of modern epistemological thought from the publication of John Locke's *Essay Concerning Human Understanding* in 1690. This epochal work represents the fruits of long speculation begun when the author was still a young man. In the preface to the *Essay*, Locke describes how a group of friends were in the habit of gathering together to discuss philosophical issues. There seems to have been some dissatisfaction with the results of these sessions, for, writes Locke, ". . . it came into my thoughts that we took a wrong course, and that, before we set ourselves upon inquiries of that nature, it was necessary to examine our own abilities, and see what objects our understandings were or were not fitted to deal with." In this modest way there began an inquiry that was to affect all the subsequent history of philosophy. Locke, urged by these same friends, began working on the problem seriously; eventually he published the first modern work on epistemology.

As the quotation suggests, Locke felt that this problem of the capacities of the mind was preliminary to any metaphysical speculation. Most modern thinkers have agreed with Locke on this matter, arguing that no inquiry in philosophy can hope to be fruitful until we have first determined the adequacy of our tools of inquiry. Today, philosophers sometimes seem too much concerned with the epistemological problem. Believing that we must settle on some kind of theory of knowledge before we can fruitfully turn to the special problems of logic, ethics, metaphysics, and esthetics, modern speculative thinkers have developed what is known as "critical philosophy," which centers all philosophical activity around the epistemological problem.

Some Unfortunate Results of the Epistemological Quest. Ideally, an insistence upon this preliminary analysis represents a sensible attitude, but it must be admitted that some of the results of such caution have been very unfortunate. The general effect on modern philosophy has been to render it intellectually morbid. Thinkers become so absorbed in the purely technical problems of the field that they tend to lose contact with those larger questions with which philosophy has traditionally been concerned. Philosophy comes to be like the hypochondriac who turns so much attention to himself that the minor fluctuations in the state of his health assume an exaggerated importance, looming larger in his mind than the really significant events that occur in the outside world. The philosophical mind similarly becomes extremely *self*-conscious. Instead of seeking to make significant judgments concerning the nature of reality, or the meaning of human experience, it devotes itself to making judgments about its own judgments. Instead of looking at the world with the candid, extraverted attitude of the Greeks, modern thinkers are intellectually introverted; where classical philosophy was fundamentally objective, that of our age is primarily subjective.

Another unfortunate result of this extreme concern with the knowing process has been to estrange the general public from philosophy. The problems of epistemology are peculiarly technical, requiring a special vocabulary and a special background of knowledge. In consequence, a majority of contemporary books dealing with philosophy are unintelligible even to readers of education and broad interests. It is only the professional philosopher who can really get into these works or who, once in, can come out the other end with anything to show for his trouble. Thus we have a vicious circle: as philosophical writing has become increasingly less meaningful to the general reader, he has read less and less of it; consequently most writers in the field have stopped taking the non-professional reader into account as they write. This in turn has given the philosopher less incentive to attempt to gain significant insights into the general problems of human experience. Whether or not he can justly be accused of inhabiting an ivory tower, there is no doubt that the philosopher today spends most of his time in the philosophical workshop. Like the scientist, he has become primarily a research man concerned with technical and very specialized problems.

Is Epistemology Necessary?   As a reaction against this excessive technicality and subjectivity of contemporary philosophy, the newcomer to the field is sometimes tempted to bypass the problem of knowledge. He is likely to argue that all we need to assume is (1) the existence of the external world, (2) the existence of our own minds, and (3) the possibility of some kind of a cognitive (that is, knowing) relation between these two. He may feel that we can assume that this relation between the inner world of knowledge and the outer world of things is adequate, since on the evolutionary hypothesis we would not have survived as a species unless our cognitive processes gave us a satisfactory contact with the world in which we live. If our minds were not competent to deal with reality, if our senses gave us any seriously distorted picture of "things as they are," the human race would not have lasted as long as it has. Since the race has survived and increased numerically, the adequacy of the knowing process would seem to be proved. What reason can there be, therefore, for doubting the common-sense view of knowledge? Is not the philosophical innocent quite justified in claiming that his senses and his reason combine to give him a trustworthy picture of the external world?

This epistemological simplification of the philosophical novice is always tempting. Certainly it would eliminate many of the controversies that plague philosophy today. If it were acceptable, the thinker's problems would be materially reduced in number and those that remain would be greatly simplified. Unfortunately no such easy way out is available. We cannot get anywhere in philosophy without the epistemological problem rearing its head, and when we attempt to scotch the serpent with the beginner's neat little formula, the serpent refuses to be impressed. Even the briefest introduction to philosophy must therefore include the presentation of some of the more important solutions that have been proposed to the problem of knowledge.

The Sources of Knowledge: Authoritarianism

To begin with, there are a few fundamental ways of knowing and the various schools of epistemology can be conveniently classified in terms of the emphases they place on these. The first of these means to knowledge is *authoritarianism*.[1] Its central doctrine is that the ultimate source of knowledge is *authority* of some kind: the church, the state, tradition, or the expert. In part our problem here overlaps that of authority in relation to truth, which we discussed in the preceding chapter, but the epistemologist carries the analysis much farther.

Why Authority Is Inadequate. It will be best to begin our analysis of authority as the source of ultimate knowledge by announcing in advance what the results of that analysis will be. As far as philosophy is concerned, authority is valueless as a solution to the epistemological problem. The reasons for this conclusion begin to appear as soon as we ask what constitutes authority, and by what criterion we should select one authority as against another. These are questions that no authoritarian can avoid, because the intensely practical question of "which authority?" rises frequently. When we find ourselves in the presence of two or more claimants to the throne, there must be some criteria for deciding between the rivals. As we shall see, this criterion must always be some standard outside of the rival authorities themselves. In short, while it is possible that authority is the ultimate source of knowledge, this seems extremely unlikely, since it never carries its own certification of finality. Its own statement, "I am authority," is not enough; there must be something independent of all authority—real or pretended—to help us separate the

---

[1] It is almost impossible to discuss the various ways of knowing without borrowing from the classic work in the field, W. P. Montague's *Ways of Knowing*. My indebtedness in the present chapter will be apparent to anyone who knows Montague's work.

gold from the dross. Our analysis of authoritarianism consequently becomes a study of the extra-authoritative criteria to which its proponents have appealed for support of their position. Let us examine these and see why philosophy finds most of them invalid.

THE TESTS OF AUTHORITY

1. Antiquity. One of the standards most frequently used for choosing between rival authorities is *antiquity*. That source of knowledge which is the most ancient is the surest, and all claimants for the role of ultimate authority are to be judged by their age. Thus the most ancient regime, the oldest church, the hoariest custom are most likely to represent the truth and the right. "The old ways are the best ways," and "Whatever is, is right"—or at least is most likely to be right.

This criterion is based upon two assumptions, one valid and the other conspicuously invalid. The acceptable assumption is that the older the doctrine or institution, the more it has been tested by time, and its very age proves that it has met that test successfully. Successive generations of men have found it true, so consequently it is more likely to be so than what has undergone only a brief testing period. This might be called a variant of the "survival of the fittest," and most thinkers have agreed that, *all else being equal,* it may be a valid test of knowledge. In other words, a doctrine or institution that has survived for a long time can claim a greater likelihood of being legitimate authority *only* if there has been free competition among the rivals, so that the survivor really is the fittest. If, however, the authority has enjoyed a monopoly and has been in a position to maintain its status by the suppression of all competition, then age is no guarantee that any authority is a valid source of knowledge. And, the philosopher points out, this has been the situation throughout most of human history: almost inevitably authorities of various kinds have used their position to eliminate opposition, and thus maintain themselves in power. Consequently, few if any claims to legitimacy on the basis of age alone can be allowed.

The other assumption upon which the argument from antiquity rests is seen to be invalid the moment our attention is directed to it. Indeed, we are moved to wonder that men have ever been tricked into so obvious an error. It is frequently asserted by the authoritarian that "as old age is wiser than youth, we should honor the opinions of our ancestors." As

W. P. Montague has pointed out, this is a fallacy to which conservative minds are particularly liable. To quote from his analysis of the error:

> If our ancestors were now alive they would be very old, and their opinions, as the outcome of generations of experience, would indeed be worthy of reverence. But when our ancestors uttered the opinions which are now hoary with age and which we are asked to revere, they were as young in years as ourselves, and the world in which they lived was much younger in the matter of racial experience. Their opinions, however old they may be, express the childhood of the race, not its maturity. And the age of an opinion or dogma actually affords a presumption against its truth rather than in favour of it.[2]

2. *Number.* The second extra-authoritarian standard for deciding between conflicting claims is that of *number.* The formula is simple: The doctrine or authority which is accepted by the largest number of persons is the true one. Another form of the same argument is what might be called the gospel of universality, which holds that any belief that enjoys universal acceptance is almost necessarily true. Or, in terms of our present problem, an authority which is acknowledged everywhere is the most reliable as a source of knowledge.

The assumption upon which this criterion is based is essentially the same as that of antiquity; the more minds that accept a doctrine, the greater the number of tests it has to meet, and therefore the more likely it is to be true. On its face this appears dependable, but further thought will reveal weakness. Mere number can have significance as a determiner of truth only if these numerous judgments have been reached independently. In court, for example, the number of witnesses who report the same evidence becomes significant only if we can be sure that their opinions were arrived at independently of one another. The same holds true of expert opinion of all kinds; the number of experts that can be summoned in support of a case adds weight only to the extent that these views have been reached independently.

In our day, even in a democracy where majority rule can sometimes be all-powerful, we are usually cautious about asserting any necessary relation between mere numbers and truth. This much we seem to have learned from history, which is replete with instances of majorities having been wrong, and even with cases of universal belief being erroneous. The

[2] *Ways of Knowing,* p. 44.

"fact" that the earth was flat, once believed universally and without question, is the stock example. Furthermore even the most dogmatic authoritarian is usually aware that he probably holds some doctrines that represent a minority viewpoint, and he is naturally unwilling to have this particular doctrine evaluated by any mere counting of noses. Thus today most of us realize that the use of a numerical criterion for establishing authority is only a convenience of democratic government.

3. *Prestige.* The third test for determining authority is that of *prestige.* This involves the subordinate problem of expert opinion, since the expert in any field is the man who has by some means or other acquired enough prestige to be considered an authority. This third test is probably the most influential of all, because every mind is influenced by prestige, however immune it may be to the criteria of *antiquity* and *number.* Our practical problem is not how to eliminate the influence of prestige from our thinking, since this is probably impossible, but how to use it intelligently and legitimately.

The major danger in this situation is the natural tendency to transfer prestige from one field to another. While no department of human affairs is immune from this fallacious borrowing, the most flagrant cases in our day usually appear in relation to the sciences. The authority of the scientific expert is so great, both among his fellow-scientists and the general public, that when he presents an opinion on any subject we are likely to be impressed. Even if the subject is one on which the scientist has no special knowledge, it is difficult not to transfer the reputation he has gained in his own field to some other domain. It need hardly be said that any legitimate authority such an opinion may have depends upon how closely related the two fields in question may be. If an expert physicist makes statements on the subject of chemistry, these are probably worth listening to respectfully; if he expresses an opinion in the biological sciences, the relation is less close, and consequently the "authority" is less likely to be significant. Should he have an opinion in the social sciences, it is quite likely to be just an opinion, carrying no weight whatever as authority. Frequently a man's training and experience in one field will actually work against his ability to form authoritative judgments in some other field. Scientific training, for example, may handicap an individual's judgment in the artistic and literary fields. Or, to take another frequent example, the ability to make money in our economic system obviously does not equip one for making authoritative evaluations in the arts, letters, sciences, education, or even political theory. Yet the great extent to which persons of wealth have been accepted as authority in any and every field of thought was, until very recently, one of the most characteristic aspects of American culture.

Still more widespread has been that exploitation of prestige called testimonial advertising, whereby screen and radio stars, athletic heroes, and popular idols of all kinds endorse cigarettes, soaps, cereals, and so forth. In practically no case does the endorsement carry any legitimate weight, because the relation between the endorser and the product is identical with that between the ordinary consumer and the same product. When movie star Miss X announces that she smokes Z cigarettes exclusively, she is of course expressing nothing more than a personal preference, which is probably no more critical or analytical than that of the average smoker. The implication which the advertiser seeks to carry into the minds of the public is that her taste in cigarettes is on a level with her reputation as a screen personality. Whether or not he is successful is a question we must leave to those charged with the responsibility of making up advertising budgets. Judging by the amount of money spent on this type of advertising, sponsors must be convinced that the appeal to the authority of prestige is remunerative.

The Universal Influence of Prestige. As already suggested, no person is entirely immune to the force of prestige. We nearly all have some idol, hero, or thinker who influences us in our thinking and living, and whom we tend to follow even in trivial matters, or in decisions in which the "hero" has no special qualifications which might offer us fruitful guidance. Sometimes this prestige centers around a book or an institution or a cult, so that the Bible, or the church, the club, or the political party, becomes the authority for determining even the minor details of daily life. The problem here is not how to escape the influence of all authority, which is impossible, but how to select that which is most reliable and valid as a source of knowledge. If some authority we must follow, whether we will or not, how shall we determine which it ought to be?

The philosopher comes in at this point to say what appears to be the inescapable last word on the relation of authority to the general problem of epistemology. He points out that whatever may be the value of authority in religion or in government, so far as our search for the *ultimate* source of knowledge is concerned, authoritarianism must be rejected. As we have seen, every authority sooner or later has to face the question.

"Why is your word any more final than that of some rival claimant?" And always the answer must be in nonauthoritarian terms; the appeal must be to something lying outside the original authority. Even if some other authority is cited as support, the issue is only postponed. Since there can be no infinite regress in this matter, eventually the chain of authorities leads us back to some extraneous source. At the end of the series we always discover an individual who derived his knowledge either from ordinary experience, or from a mystical, supernatural revelation of some kind. Of these two, the ordinary experience may have been one of several kinds: it may have been (1) sensory perception, (2) reasoning from this sensory experience, (3) reasoning from a priori or self-evident truths of one kind or another. These constitute the sources of knowledge upon which all authority must ultimately depend; consequently our epistemological search must turn to them.

The Sources of Knowledge: Mysticism

The extraneous source of knowledge to which the religious authoritarian is likely to turn is a mystical or supernatural experience of some kind. Such experiences are usually called revelations, and it is upon these that most systems of religious thought are based. It is not necessary that these experiences be the authoritarian's own. In fact they are more likely to have happened to some prophet, cult-founder, or inspired seer whose authority the religious authoritarian accepts.

The acceptance of these revelations as valid epistemological foundations implies that man has two distinct sources of knowledge: (1) ordinary or natural (usually sensory perception and reasoning based upon this perception), and (2) extraordinary or supernatural. The extraordinary type subdivides into several kinds, but all are usually included under the general term "mystical experiences."

Mysticism may be defined as the belief that men's most reliable source of knowledge or truth is a supersensory, superrational faculty. This faculty is sometimes identified with "intuition," but since this term is used so loosely in popular speech, most contemporary mystics prefer to regard the epistemological source they rely on as something apart. They regard it as a distinct and unique instrument for apprehending reality. Moreover, all mystics agree that man's most important activity is the cultivation of this unique inner experience. They also agree that its revelations have priority over all other sources of knowledge. The experience is, epistemologically speaking, absolute.

Nature of the Mystical Experience. What is this "inner experience" that is central in the mystic's pattern of life and which gives him his most significant knowledge? Unfortunately, although many mystics have tried to describe this experience, they nonetheless insist that it is basically beyond description. Their floundering efforts at description seem to prove their contention. In part this is because the experience is so unlike all other experiences; in part also it is because the occurrence is usually so overwhelming. Consequently, in spite of the large body of mystical literature, we actually know very little about the central experience that has produced this literature. However, most of us have had moments of intuition, "inner light," or unexplainable conviction that are similar enough to the mystic's experience to make a description of his experience fairly intelligible. What keeps most of us out of the category of "mystic" is not the complete lack of comparable experience, but rather our failure (due to temperament or training) to take these experiences seriously, much less to make them central in our lives.

Most mystics would insist that these semimystical experiences which many of us occasionally have are not the genuine thing. If they were, mystics hold, they would have been powerful and significant enough to acquire right-of-way over all other events, both previous and subsequent. This is precisely what happens in the case of the true mystic.

Nevertheless, in its most common form, the experience does have definite resemblance to certain moments we nearly all have on rare occasions. These are the moments when everything seems to fall into place: the usual chaos and hectic disarray of our lives suddenly seems to reach a point of pause or climax, and all the scrambled pieces of the jigsaw puzzle we call "life" suddenly appear to fit together into a meaningful pattern. Or, if the pattern is not entirely clear and questions still remain, events at least seem to bring us to a moment of arrested activity. We stop, struck by the conviction that there *are* answers to our questions and solutions to all problems—a conviction that our lives do make sense and do have an order of some kind.

Perhaps this mood is most likely to strike us in the presence of nature, particularly of impressive natural beauty. Many poets have written of such moments, but none better than William Wordsworth, who was himself a pantheistic mystic. He tells of how, amid natural beauty,

> . . . I have felt
> A presence that disturbs me with the joy
> Of elevated thoughts; a sense sublime
> Of something far more deeply interfused,
> Whose dwelling is the light of setting suns,
> And the round ocean and the living air,
> And the blue sky, and in the mind of man;
> A motion and a spirit, that impels
> All thinking things, all objects of all thought,
> And rolls through all things. . . .

Some people have similar experiences in the presence of great works of art, or when listening to certain music. Others may have it as a consequence of some emotional experience involving other persons, as when one watches a sleeping child or lover. The experience is primarily that of *synthesis*—that is, an integration of large areas of life and meaning. If we verbalize such an experience when it occurs our words are usually something like, "This is what life means!" or perhaps, "This is the purpose of life!"

And so with mysticism. A mystic's experience is likely to differ from the kind we have just outlined both in intensity and in inclusiveness. It may differ, too, in arising at irrelevant times and places, rather than as a consequence of some emotional or aesthetic situation. And it of course differs in its effect upon the individual's life, since a mystic is likely henceforth to date all the events of his life history as occurring before or after this experience took place.

Whether or not we accept mysticism as the most adequate way of knowing will obviously depend upon whether or not we accept the mystical experience itself as genuine. While such an experience may take many forms, most of the outstanding mystics of history have reported it to be an essentially indescribable but overwhelming feeling of the *oneness* or *unity* of all things. As such, the experience frequently has pantheistic implications, since it appears to identify God with the universe. Sometimes the mystical experience has been a direct contact with God, so intimate as to constitute a temporary union or identification. Mystical literature is full of references to "The One," and the term may mean either God or the totality of existence in which God and the universe are fused in some manner.

The Immediacy of the Mystic's Knowledge. It is the *direct* and *immediate* quality of the mystical experience that best characterizes it and distinguishes this way of knowing from all ordinary sources of knowledge. Any other source—perception, reasoning, or authority—can give only knowledge that is mediated or indirect; in each case there is something that stands between us and the real. This barrier may be the sensory apparatus, or the successive steps in the chain of reasoning, or the minds and manuscripts by which authority has been transmitted; in each case we are at least once removed from reality. Only through intuition and mystical experience can we get *immediate* knowledge. It alone can eliminate all second-handedness from the knowing process, bringing the subject and the object face to face in a unique manner. In some mystical experiences subject and object become one, and here immediacy reaches its ultimate degree.

Two Contrasting Explanations of the Mystical Experience. It will be noticed that mysticism as we have described it thus far implies that sense and reason are inadequate to give us true knowledge. It also implies that speech is inadequate to describe the nature of that knowledge after it has been received. In short, reality cannot be apprehended except directly and individually; it is a strictly private experience, indescribable and unsharable.

There are two schools of thought concerning the source of this experience. The *naturalistic* explanation finds the origin of our intuitive experiences in that vast and vague mental underworld where instinct, memory, and the subconscious elbow one another, and into which psychology has as yet penetrated only a little way. Naturalists are impressed, for example, by psychological studies of subliminal perceptions. These studies have shown conclusively that what many persons consider "intuitions" are produced by perceptions that are too weak to enter consciousness, and yet are capable of motivating behavior. Thus when a person becomes "intuitively aware" that a room he thought unoccupied now contains some other person besides himself, although he has not heard or seen the other person enter behind his back, what has actually happened is this: the second person entering the room "silently" has actually made sounds too faint for the first person to hear consciously, but which have nevertheless been perceived subliminally. Or his genuinely silent movements have disturbed the air sufficiently for the first individual's skin to respond to the atmospheric motion—again without affecting consciousness directly. Scientific explanations of this type impress naturalists very much, and give them faith that all so-called mystical experiences will some day be provided with natural explanations.

It need hardly be said that those persons who hold mystical experience to be the ultimate source of knowledge reject any such explanation. Instead they believe these intuitions have a supernatural origin. They attribute the experience to a less mundane and subjective source—namely, to God or a cosmic Mind of some sort. It is therefore logical for any person who accepts such a supernatural explanation to place great faith in these experiences as a reliable source of knowledge. The naturalistic interpretation would put knowledge gained through this channel in the same class as behavior that is motivated by instinct, it holds that both may be reliable when controlled by reason and tested by experience, but that they are inadequate by themselves as a way of knowing or a guide for conduct. Most mystics, on the contrary, believe that mystical experiences cannot be compared with such natural things as biological instincts. Such an account would not only degrade the mystical experience, but would understate its importance. It comes from a higher source, and this supernatural origin is sufficient guarantee (to mystics) of its reliability.

The Sources of Knowledge: Rationalism

Those persons who refuse to accept intuition as the answer to the knowledge-problem usually endorse either *reason* or *experience* as better candidates for epistemological election. The supporters of these alternatives are known respectively as *rationalists* and *empiricists*. While the members of these two schools frequently quarrel among themselves, they agree that mysticism is out of the running. This is hardly surprising, since as we already have seen, the mystic is skeptical of both reason and experience—except of course mystical experience.

While rationalism, strictly speaking, represents an historical movement that reached its peak in the seventeenth and early eighteenth centuries, rather than a well-defined contemporary school, it also represents a recurring tendency of the mind, a tendency that can be found exemplified in the thought of any age. In general, rationalism holds that the ideal form of knowledge is that which is represented by mathematical demonstration. Such demonstrations start with axioms, or truths that are self-evident, and through a series of step-by-step deductions arrive at conclusions which are logical, inescapable, and incontrovertible. Euclidian geometry represents the classic example of such rationalistic methods in action. Beginning with a group of axioms that are taken as self-evident (for example, "equals added to equals give equals," "a straight line is the shortest distance between two points," and so forth), a series of theorems are proved by means of propositions that are derived deductively from these original axioms and their related postulates. The process is one of very strict reasoning, as every student who has been through high school geometry will remember.

Whence Come "a Priori" Truths? It immediately becomes evident that the validity of such a method depends upon two things: the soundness of our reasoning, and the character of our original axioms and postulates. Experience has revealed that the human mind can, with some training, achieve great precision in the use of deductive reasoning. As a result, nearly all attacks upon rationalism have centered around the problem of securing premises which will be adequate for the tremendous weight they must bear in a chain of deduction. As already suggested, in mathematics these initial axioms are usually derived from "common sense" or (according to the rationalist) from clear, distinct, and intuitively certain basic principles. These in turn are regarded as coming from the "natural light of reason," or the structure of thought itself, and they require no more guarantee than is afforded by their self-evidence. Very important for the rationalistic position is the supposed independence of these principles from any empirical origin. They are regarded as a priori or pre-experiential, and instead of their depending upon experience, the rationalist regards experience as dependent upon them. For (says the rationalist), what is true for mathematical knowledge holds for all our ultimate knowledge, which may likewise be derived deductively from first principles of purely rational origin. Therefore under proper conditions our ultimate knowledge can attain that degree of certainty found in the propositions of Euclid.

When we examine the list of a priori truths upon which the several systems of rationalistic philosophy have been built, we are almost certain to be struck by the absence of agreement among them. This may serve to recall a point made in an earlier chapter: "self-evidence" is a term that is easy to use, but a fact that is hard to prove. What is self-evident to you may or may not be so to me. Further, a priorism is also hard to prove; what the rationalist takes to be pre-experiential often impresses the empiricist as derived from experience, although indirectly and perhaps unconsciously. Among rationalists, however, there are at least a few of these general principles that are agreed upon, and these are held to be prerequisite to all thought and all existence. Further, these universal principles are regarded as not only *prior* to experience, but *outside* of experience. They can only be apprehended intuitively (here the method of rationalism parallels that of mysticism), and they therefore give us a knowledge of reality which no amount of sense perception could give. Rationalistic knowledge is thus qualitatively different from empirical knowledge.

The Principle of Noncontradiction. Probably the most important of these rationalistic a priori universal principles is the "law of noncontradiction." In brief, it states that of two contradictory propositions, both cannot be true. In the language of logic, a thing cannot at the same time exist and not exist, nor can a figure be both a square and a circle. Aristotle, and all formal logicians since his time, have regarded this principle of noncontradiction as the most fundamental of all the laws of thought. The newcomer to philosophy is rarely so much impressed; the usual student reaction is, "How silly—that's self-evident." "Exactly!" replies the rationalist. "And furthermore, it is not derived from experience by a process of generalization; it is an a priori principle, intuitively apprehended by all normal minds. As such, it offers more certain knowledge than any mere generalization from experience could possibly give."

Other Examples of Rationalistic Method. A less abstract example of the rationalistic method at work is the celebrated ontological proof of the existence of God. We shall have more to say regarding this proof when we consider the problem of God in our final chapters, so here we need only state the argument briefly. The concept of God is the concept of a perfect being—the most perfect conceivable. Such a being must, if it is to be perfect, lack no attribute of perfection. For instance, if it lacked existence, then other beings that had existence would be more perfect. Therefore, since by the laws of thought there can be only one "most perfect," God must exist. His existence is thus proved conceptually—that is, by the very definition of the term "God." One writer has defined rationalism as "the theory that knowledge is obtained by comparison of ideas with other ideas; or, briefly, that we know what we have thought out."[3] The ontological argument just given illustrates this process very well; for the rationalist, true knowledge comes from rubbing two or more ideas together —in this case, the ideas of "perfection" and "existence."

The Sources of Knowledge: Empiricism

Rationalism's usual opponent in the battle of the epistemologies is *empiricism*, which we have defined as the doctrine that the final source of all knowledge is experience or sensation. To quote again, empiricism holds "that we know what we have found out."[4] It must be emphasized that this school does not deny the validity or importance of our rational processes as means for *extending* our sense-given knowledge, but it insists again and again that the final proof of these rationalistic extensions must be a return to experience. Scientific methodology offers the classic example of this departure-and-return cycle. Starting with sensory data, the scientist formulates (through reason) an explanatory hypothesis. Next, still using reason, he deduces what results may be expected when he performs a crucial experiment (worked out by a combination of reason and sense perception) which will give a definite "yes or no" answer to his hypothesis. Then the experiment is performed, which means that the results of the rational processes that intervened between the original observation and the experiment are empirically determined. Hence in science we have a superb combination of the rational and empirical methods; each does what it is well qualified to do, and relinquishes to its rival what the alternate method can do better. In the last analysis, however, it is particularly the empiricist who comes into his own in scientific activity. For however rationalistic some of the steps in scientific method may be (if mathematics is employed, for example, we have pure rationalism), it is a process that must both begin and end in sensation. If sense data are lacking at either the beginning or the end of the process, we do not have science.

The Empiricist Critique of Rationalism. We have stated that the empiricist believes that supposed a priori self-evident principles (which

[3] George P. Conger, *A Course in Philosophy*, p. 205.
[4] *Ibid.*, p. 207.

the rationalist considers to be intuitively apprehended) are derived from sensory experience. Let us consider for a moment a favorite example of the rationalist, the principle of causation. He argues that we could never derive this universal principle empirically. Our experience cannot include all present events—not to mention those past and future—so there must be some other source for our confident belief that every event has a cause. The empiricist admits this limitation of the mind, but attacks the rationalistic position by challenging the original statement that causation represents *absolute* knowledge. In brief, empiricism argues thus: our belief in universal causation represents only an extension of our experience; every event we have observed has, on analysis, proved to depend upon an antecedent cause. We therefore extend these empirical facts into a universalization, *but this universalization represents only a probability and not a certainty*. We do not *know* that all events, past, present, and future, have causes; we assume that they do, on the basis of our experience to date with events of all kinds. However, this is only a belief, and not a fact of absolute knowledge. In short (concludes the empiricist) the only possible ground for argument here between rationalism and empiricism is whether or not the principle of causation represents *absolute* knowledge. If rationalism insists on taking it as such, then admittedly we cannot derive such universal absolutes from our limited experience. However, there is no need to regard the causal principle as anything more than a working hypothesis involving a very high degree of probability. Science manages very well by using causation in this manner, and there is no reason why rationalism should get itself out on an epistemological limb by regarding it as absolute knowledge.

Rationalism vs. *Empiricism in Ethics.* One of the most heated controversies between rationalism and empiricism has occurred in the ethical realm. The rationalist believes that he can uncover the same self-evident truths in the field of ethics as in those of logic, mathematics, and metaphysics. Here again, the list of a priori ethical principles which various rationalistic thinkers have drawn up reveals wide divergence; the principles run all the way from "*All* lying is absolutely wrong—even the doctor's lie to save his patient's life," to such lofty maxims as the Golden Rule. As might be expected, the empiricist challenges all claims to a priorism in ethics. Instead he believes that even the highest and most inclusive moral axiom is derived from our actual experience as to what advances or retards the welfare of the social group. Since our chapter on ethics will include considerable discussion of these rival claims, we need not discuss them further here.

Kant's Contribution to Epistemology

The work of Immanuel Kant, undoubtedly the most influential thinker in modern philosophy, represents an attempt to harmonize the opposing doctrines of rationalism and empiricism. As with most compromises, the extremists on either side have never been satisfied with Kant's solution of the problem. Many contemporary philosophers, however, feel that his system does an excellent job of harmonizing the rival claims of the two schools. It will therefore be well to consider the Kantian epistemology briefly.

Historically considered, Kant was attempting to effect a compromise between the subjectivism of Berkeley, with its doctrine that nothing exists except minds and their perceptions, and the empiricism of such thinkers as Locke. Locke held that there is a whole world of matter existing independent of our perceiving minds, although he was forced to admit that we have no way of discovering the character of this material substratum that underlies sense qualities. Kant begins by admitting that there must be a cause for all sense impressions, and that this cause must lie outside the mind itself. However, to admit its objective existence does not prove that we know anything concerning its nature. We can know *that* there is an external something, but we cannot know *what* it is. It remains, and always must remain, the unknowable "thing-in-itself." Our minds are equipped to deal only with the appearances of things, or *phenomena;* their *noumena,* or true reality, can only be guessed at. Even science, with all its methods and achievements, does not get behind phenomena to discover reality.

The Kantian Compromise. Thus, according to Kant, our minds make "nature" or "physical reality," but they do not make it out of nothing. Our senses supply the raw material by their reactions to the appearances of the "thing-in-itself." However, this contribution of the senses is really raw; it is a chaos, without structure or organization of any kind. Any form or order it acquires is imposed upon it by our minds, which provide the framework or mold into which the undigested manifold of perceptions must be poured before it can have logic or intelligibility. The mind is not a mere passive recipient of impressions, as earlier thinkers held, but an active instrument that never rests from its labor of turning the flux of sensation into order and meaning. And finally, it is the peculiar structure or constitution of the *mind* itself which is revealed in the finished product of the cognitive process. "Reality" as we know it is more *made* than *given;* it is a construct rather than a datum. All that makes the world coherent and meaningful comes from what Kant calls "the understanding." Even time and space, the chief modes under which we know our world, are a priori mental forms of the understanding, as also are all the basic categories or conditions of experience: quantity, quality, causality, and so forth. While the raw material may come exclusively from the outside via sensation, it is we who make our "world"—the ordered, intelligible universe in which we find it possible to live and think.

Thus Kant gives equal importance to the rationalistic "forms of the understanding," which are innate in thought and prerequisite to intelligible experience, and to empirical data. These perceptual data supply the whole content of the mind, while the conceptual "forms" do just what their name suggests: give form to this content. Kant sums up his inclusive compromise position in a famous phrase to which reference has already been made: "Concepts without percepts are empty, percepts without concepts are blind."

The Metaphysical Implications of Rationalism and Empiricism

It seems hardly necessary to point out the close relationship existing between rationalism and empiricism and our old friends, idealism and naturalism. It is not possible completely to identify idealism with rationalism, or naturalism with empiricism, but the relations between the respective pairs are very close. With one outstanding exception (Spinoza) the great rationalists have been either idealists (such as Leibniz and Wolff) or dualists with strong idealistic leanings (for example, Descartes). Empiricism, on the contrary, goes hand in hand with the naturalistic world-view; and the essence of the naturalistic attitude is to remain as close as possible to experience in the natural world of here and now. Unlike this view, idealism has tended to minimize the significance of the empirical world by emphasizing the superior reality of a transcendental (that is, extra-empirical) order which is accessible only through the rational, conceptualizing activities of the mind.

Thus it is evident that the fundamental opposition between our two great metaphysical schools extends into the field of epistemology. This is hardly surprising: when a thinker sets out to formulate (or defend) a total view of the nature of things, it is logical that he should favor that method of thought or mode of knowledge most favorable to his position. It should be understood, however, that it is the metaphysical consideration which stands paramount; the means of knowing are chosen to support the over-all position. The epistemology grows out of the metaphysics, and not vice versa. As always, the world-view is fundamental.

CHAPTER 9

METAPHYSICS:

What Is Reality?

IT IS PROBABLE THAT THE CHAPTERS NOW LYING BEHIND US APPEAR TO have covered the problems of *being, being known,* and *being communicated* rather thoroughly. It is almost certain that any original curiosity which the reader may have had concerning these speculative problems has been either satisfied or suffocated by the mass of possible answers. As far as many professional philosophers are concerned, however, we have thus far only hinted at *the* philosophical question. It is high time, therefore, that we come to grips with what has usually been regarded as the key problem of the whole speculative field, to which all that has been discussed up to this point may be considered introductory: What is the nature of ultimate reality? What is the world—what lies behind it all? What is the basic thing (or stuff, or idea, or substance, or principle) in the universe?

This question underlies all the lesser questions that have been asked in previous chapters, and many of the answers which we have suggested have implied answers to this great problem also. Our presentation of the opposing world-views, idealism and naturalism, clearly pointed towards equally opposed views as to the character of reality. But thus far we have not faced the problem in a direct manner. We may expect such an analysis to tie together all the other discussions and analyses thus far presented, so that the student will at last be able to see the kingdom of philosophy as a whole. That the result will be a cohesive whole we can only hope. In any case, we shall then be in a better position to tackle the remaining problems of the speculative field, which concern the nature of "the good life," the question of duty, the freedom of the will, the esthetic problem, and the existence of God and immortality. These are the more practical problems of philosophy, and it is advisable that we complete our metaphysical analysis before we turn to them. For as we have pointed out repeatedly, our answers to these practical problems will inevitably depend upon our solution of the metaphysical question.

The Complexity of the Problem. At first glance, the metaphysical problem appears to be a simple question of the *number* of entities involved in reality—that is, is the ultimate real single, dual, or plural? Basically, the situation is indeed this simple, but this original simplicity is soon considerably complicated by the fact that there are also *qualitative* issues involved. For example, if the real is single, what is the nature of this one stuff, principle, or entity? If it is dual, what are the natures of the two entities or essences involved, and what are their relations to one another? Further, are these two really ultimate? Or are they perhaps like some of the double stars known to astronomy, which appear to be revolving around an invisible common center that may be larger and more important than either of them? In other words, could it be that such metaphysical twins (usually called "mind and matter" or "spirit and body") are only the two opposing aspects of a single underlying real, so that our apparent dualism would turn out to be an actual monism? Or, if we conclude that the universe is pluralistic, what are these entities into which the apparent whole actually breaks down? How many of them are there, what are their qualities, and what are their interrelations?

Why So Many Answers? It is thus evident that there are complicating factors in our originally simple quantitative problem—that of finding monism, dualism, or pluralism. This fact should serve to make the reader sympathetic with the philosopher in his attempts to reach an answer, and also with his failure thus far to find one universally acceptable. It will be well to face the fact that there is no more unanimity on this issue than we have discovered in the case of the other problems of philosophy. If anything, there is even less agreement. In addition to the usual opposition between idealism and naturalism, there are conflicts between the three quantitative schools, so that we may find a pluralism which is essentially idealistic battling one that is definitely naturalistic, or an idealism that is categorically monistic opposing an idealism which is predominantly dualistic. "Must philosophers disagree?" is a question that is sometimes asked, but it should be noted that it is rarely posed by those who know much of philosophy and its problems. Certainly it would never be asked by anyone who is well acquainted with the complexity of the metaphysical search for ultimate reality. To the person who has been in the field a long time, the wonder is rather that philosophers agree as well as they do. It will be with the aim of reducing the number of conflicting metaphysical points of view as much as possible that we begin the present chapter.

The Essence of Monism

Historians of philosophy sometimes argue as to whether monism or dualism should be considered the "natural" human point of view. Such an argument usually reveals that the decision must depend upon whether we are speaking of the naïve, uncritical view of the so-called "plain man," or the intellectually sophisticated position of philosophy and systematic theology. To the uncritical mind, dualism appears to be virtually incontrovertible. The philosophically naïve person, be he civilized or primitive, falls naturally into the habit of regarding the world of his experience as composed of two separate realms: a physical, material world, above or behind which lies a separate domain of the mental or spiritual. This may be called "common-sense dualism," and it is so widespread as undoubtedly to constitute the most popular metaphysical view, both throughout history and in our own day. The philosopher, on the contrary, seems just as predisposed to gravitate towards a monistic position. This tendency is strong enough to warrant the statement that both dualism and pluralism represent a metaphysical second-best as far as philosophy is concerned. For those who give themselves to it seriously, the metaphysical search is usually a quest for a single ultimate of some kind. When the result turns out to be twins or worse, it is either because of a methodological reason[1] or because there is an implied acknowledgment that the searcher has failed to reduce the universe to a single underlying substance or principle. Since this book is an introduction to systematic philosophy rather than to popular thought, we therefore begin our analysis with consideration of the monistic position.

[1] As in the case of Descartes, who by settling on two independent ultimates was able to free the physical realm from "final causes" and other idealistic presuppositions. The point will be discussed further in the chapter on Determinism vs. Indeterminism (Chapter 14).

The Common Element in All Monisms.   While metaphysical monism takes a variety of forms, these all have a common central doctrine: the foundation of the world is single—all existence is grounded in one "stuff" or principle. Monism is therefore that world-view which seeks and finds *unity* in reality, thereby reducing the rich variety of human experience to multiple aspects of a single ultimate. This unification may be in terms of one matter or stuff, one spirit or self, one law or principle, or perhaps one activity or process. The several schools within monism have found their source of unity in various places. As a result, the completed systems of thought have been so dissimilar that "singleness" constitutes the only common denominator. When these systems are as opposed to one another as are some of the extreme forms of idealistic and materialistic monism, it becomes evident that other metaphysical positions within dualism or pluralism may stand closer to each other than some of the monistic schools do.

The Monist's Burden of Proof.   As we have indicated, monism is not the "common-sense" or man-in-the-street view of things. On the contrary, much of our daily experience runs directly counter to its basic postulate. In order to find sufficient cause to doubt the views of any kind of monism, we need only look at another human being—or at ourself in a mirror. For we definitely appear to be a combination of a body *and* a conscious something which we ordinarily call "mind" or "soul" or "consciousness." Nor can common sense conceive how either of these two elements could be reducible to the other; each seems to be an ultimate. Turning from ourselves to the external world, one does not need to be a mystic or a poet to experience the feeling of a Presence or Spirit abiding in nature. Even "common sense" has frequent intimations of something more in nature than organized matter. Thus, in view of both our inner and outer experience, the question naturally arises as to how the monist can establish the position he does—and, more important, how he can maintain it.

The monist himself, regardless of what type of unity he advocates, is usually the first to admit that his viewpoint is not easy to hold. He is fired on from all sides. Frequently "common sense," dualism, and pluralism seem to vie with one another to see which can set off the biggest bomb under his neat monistic structure. The attack of common sense is particularly critical, and if the philosopher seeks to maintain any contact with the world of daily human experience, he must come to some sort of terms with its objections. When our experience so definitely seems to point to the existence of two separate realms of being, the burden of proof is obviously on anyone who claims that this dichotomy is only an appearance.

Monism and Common Sense. This burden of proof is heavier for the monist than for the advocate of the opposite metaphysical extreme, the pluralist. Most men can be persuaded that the world is more complex than they thought, and that perhaps its basic constituents are innumerable. However, it is far more difficult to persuade them that its apparent diversity and complexity are only apparent, and that at bottom all things and all experiences—including even the contrasting realms of "matter" and "mind"—are reducible to one ultimate. Fortunately for the monist, this does not involve as great a stretch of the imagination as once it did, or at least we are more accustomed to such stretches today. Educated people are now adjusted to the fact that the physicist's view of the matter is well outside the range of common sense. We can accept the scientific statement that the table top in front of us is not the solid, static thing which our senses perceive, we are acclimated to the idea that it is a dynamic mass of millions of whirling protons and electrons. Thus we are probably less startled than our grandparents were when some philosopher announces quite earnestly that the surface diversity of the world is only a mask upon what is at heart single, or that all things within the ken of our experience are only manifestations of one matter or one spirit. This does not infer that the monist can now get by on weak analogies or careless reasoning more easily than he could in the past. It is only that we are less likely to cry "Inconceivable!" to such suggestions. We are more willing to hear the monist out, whether we agree with him or not.

The Schools of Monism: Materialism

There are two aspects of the doctrine of metaphysical unity which should be kept apart. These arise from the fact that the problem of ultimate reality is basically a twofold issue. First, what is the *nature* of being? and second, what is the *number* of being? While few philosophers actually maintain a separation between the quantitative and the qualitative problems, it is important to realize that logically they are distinct. Otherwise we may be puzzled to meet a thinker who holds that there is only one *kind* of being (that is, one stuff or substance or principle) but who is just as insistent that the *number* of actual beings is unlimited.[2]

It is difficult to say at first sight which of the several types of monism is more credible. For most of us, having grown up in some sort of dualism, there seems to be little choice. The philosophers themselves usually consider *materialism* the most convincing on first meeting, without implying that mere plausibility is any necessary evidence of truth. An extreme school of materialism holds that matter in its various forms constitutes all of existence; nothing exists except matter, all appearances to the contrary notwithstanding. Far more common today is a moderate type of materialism, holding that while matter is the fundamental reality, mind may be allowed a secondary or semi-reality, which derives from or is dependent upon matter. In this moderate view, mind is considered a development of matter, an organization of matter, or a flowering upon it, "just as the blossom flowers upon the tree."

Some Problems of Definition. It becomes apparent immediately that any such identification of matter with reality can have meaning only if the term is adequately defined. It is unfortunate that the materialist himself has often been careless in the use of his key terms. In general, he has been content to have "matter" mean whatever the scientist means by the word. We thus arrive at a view of reality which would make it identical with the physical world, spatially extended and operating according to the laws of motion. In fact, the older materialisms usually defined "matter" and "motion" as the two ultimates, and then tried to formulate systems in which everything was reduced to these two. Today the materialist usually defines reality as synonymous with the domain of physiochemical

---

[2] The distinction, avowed or only implied, between these separable aspects of the problem sometimes leads to a confusion in terminology. It will accordingly be helpful to define the terms as we shall be using them. *Monism* will be used to indicate the doctrine that the universe is *qualitatively* single—that is, that all the apparent diversity of objects, together with the contrasting realms of "mind" and "matter," can be reduced to (or derived from) a single substance or causal principle. For the doctrine that there is only one *being*—that is, that all things are only parts of fragments of an all-inclusive whole of some kind—the term *singularism* will be used. Hegel's system, with what James called its "block view of the universe," is a classic example of singularism: all things are parts of the one all-inclusive Absolute or Spirit. Both monism and singularism appeared in early Greek thought, but in general the latter has been peculiarly characteristic of much of the German philosophy of the nineteenth century and its British and American derivatives. Looking over the history of philosophy as a whole, however, monism has been more common than singularism.

events. Thus for materialism the physical world is primary. The mental, the spiritual, and the moral must therefore come to terms with this physical order, and be content to regard themselves as aspects of it.

It is often pointed out to the materialist that the concept of matter is undergoing constant change at the hands of science, with the implication that building a world-view upon such an unstable concept is a dubious metaphysical procedure. Materialism acknowledges this change, but its exponents are in no way abashed by the fact. As a philosophy it is quite willing to build upon science. It glories in a close affiliation with the sciences, and takes the description "a philosophy of science," which is sometimes disdainfully hurled its way, as a distinct compliment. Furthermore, it answers this charge that it builds upon a shifting concept by pointing out that mentalism, spiritualism, idealism, and all metaphysical systems that build upon mind or thought as ultimate, are in the same situation. For the concept of mind is also undergoing constant modification. Indeed, "mind" has gone through more change in the last half century than "matter." The development of modern psychology has profoundly altered our concepts of the origin, the nature, and the function of mind. Freud alone, with his theory of the subconscious, has probably brought a greater change in our ideas on the nature of mind than all the physicists of the last fifty years have wrought in our views concerning the nature of matter.

Classical vs. *Modern Materialism.* What may be called the older or classical materialism regarded matter as composed of tiny solid particles which reacted on each other in a purely mechanical manner—that is, by impinging on one another like billiard balls. Matter was considered inert or "dead," and all changes or events were the result of shifts in position among these particles. This older view, generally known as mechanical atomism, has given way before the advances of modern physics. Matter is no longer regarded as "dead," nor even as solid. Only its discrete composition, or general atomic character, has survived unchanged. Instead of inert solid particles, matter is now regarded as "organized energy arranged in patterns,"[3] so that today the material world is considered to possess many of the dynamic qualities formerly associated exclusively with the domain of mind or spirit. Today, instead of talking about "matter" as ultimate, materialism follows the lead of science and speaks of "energy." It is now frequently objected that the term "materialism" no

[3] R. W. Sellars, *The Principles and Problems of Philosophy*, p. 184.

longer has any relation to the doctrine it is supposed to describe, and the word "energism" has been suggested as a substitute. In general, however, the thinkers who hold that the physiochemical world is ultimate prefer to keep the traditional term—but with the understanding that "materialism" does not mean the interpretation of reality in terms of atoms in motion, but refers to the reduction of both experience and existence to whatever basic units are accepted by the physical sciences.[4]

Whether or not we make a change in terminology, it is imperative that we understand the distinction between earlier and contemporary materialistic systems. Otherwise our criticisms of this first great type of monism will consist of that futile intellectual activity known as "attacking a man of straw." In fact, many of the attacks against materialism that are heard today in idealistic circles are aimed at views which no longer are held by any representative of this school. Assaults against contemporary forms of materialistic monism should offer the idealist ample sport without the necessity of dusting off historical views in order to tilt a lance against their venerable hides.

A Broader View of Materialism. We shall gain a clearer picture of materialism, both past and present, if, instead of regarding it as a system that is built upon matter, we regard it as the doctrine which holds reality to be identical with the physical universe. There are distinct advantages in taking this interpretation of materialism. In the first place, we are spared any highly technical controversy regarding the nature of matter. Secondly, we have a view that can survive all sorts of changes in the scientific view of "matter." And third, we thereby put the emphasis where the materialist himself places it, upon the *natural* world as over against any kind of a *supernatural* realm. Seen in this light, materialism is revealed to be the ontological core of a far more inclusive world-view, naturalism. Thus we see the relation of materialistic monism to the whole field of philosophy, and we are again brought face to face with our original metaphysical poles, idealism and naturalism.

The Materialistic Views of Mind. It is evident that whichever of the great monisms we choose we immediately have a major problem: how to account for the contrasting aspect of our experience in terms of the doctrine we have selected. Thus materialism faces its toughest test when it tries to account for mind or consciousness in terms of the physical

---

[4] Cf. James Burnham and Philip Wheelwright, *Introduction to Philosophical Analysis*, p. 241.

realm, while spiritualistic monism is most likely to break down when it attempts to derive the physical world from mind or spirit. The task immediately before us is to see how materialism explains the existence of mind in the universe.

There are three ways of relating mind to matter within the framework of materialism, and all have had historical significance. First, we can regard mind as a mere *attribute* of the material world, standing in the usual relation of an attribute to its substance. Second, we can view mind as an *effect* of matter; the term used in this view, "causal materialism," indicates the relation between the two realms. And finally, there is "equative materialism," which holds that mental activity is really material in nature.[5] This last is clearly the most rigidly monistic of the three possible positions, since it attempts to identify the mental with the material. The first, "attributive materialism," is almost too vague to be enlightening, as the relation between a substance and its attributes is difficult to define. The second or causal position is the one most acceptable to modern psychology. This is what we would expect, for like any science, psychology is primarily interested in organizing its phenomena within a frame work of causal laws.

The Contemporary Position. As far as contemporary materialism is concerned, the relation between the physical and the mental may be described as follows. Mind or consciousness is dependent upon the motion of matter—that is, upon the material component of the brain and central nervous system. More precisely, it is dependent upon *motion within matter*, for mental processes are regarded as a form of neural energy, related to energy changes within the whole nervous system. The attempt is sometimes made to identify completely the mental and the neural processes, as we have already seen in our chapter on Mind. This "equative monism" says that the mental process or event in consciousness merely is the neural change. This is in contrast to the less extreme position of causal monism we are describing, which holds rather that the mental is *caused by* or *dependent upon* the energy change within the nervous system. The extreme equative viewpoint runs into immediate difficulties, at least in the eyes of most philosophers. For while there seems to be no doubt that consciousness is located in the brain and connected with neural changes within it, any identification of the two does violence to thought and language. To say that consciousness is the *same* as "motion" or "energy"

[5] On this threefold classification, cf. Kulpe, *Introduction to Philosophy*, p. 117.

is either to use these terms in something other than their accepted sense or to say nothing at all.

The objection here is that such a view implies that mental processes are merely a delusive appearance of certain properties of matter, while our common-sense experience forbids any such reduction of consciousness. We cannot even conceive, it is argued, how a sensation could be the result of a *movement* of some kind, be it mechanical or neural. However, the equative monist replies that, as we have already seen in an earlier chapter, "inconceivability" is no proof at all, as the history of science has abundantly shown. Further, he continues, since motion appears to be the universal accompaniment of all events in the universe, is it not logical to assume that it is also present in every mental event?

The Problem of Terminology. It is evident that the argument here soon breaks down into a matter of definitions and terminology. The central issue seems to be whether physical motion is a *cause* and *accompaniment,* or the *actual equivalent,* of mental process. A majority of modern materialists take refuge in the causal form of the doctrines, holding that all mental change is *caused* by a physical change of some sort—"no psychic event without a neural event," as the psychologist states it. Just how a neural change can bring about a mental change is a problem that is left to the neurologist and the psychologist. These scientists have numerous theories, some of which are logical and convincing, but in the last analysis the means whereby neural events cause psychical events remains something of a mystery. The materialist acknowledges that we know very little on this crucial point as yet, but with his great confidence in science as a technique for solving "mysteries," he does not feel defeated by this ignorance. He believes that it is more logical (and certainly more consistent with the rest of our scientific knowledge) to assume that mind is based upon a material foundation of some kind, than to follow the lead of some idealistic schools and postulate a "Mind" unrelated to physical origins and independent of physical changes.

It will be recalled from our chapter on Mind (Chapter 6) that such a causal dependence of mind upon body does not necessarily lead to a complete physical monism. One can hold, with the proponents of the emergence theory, that the mind has come into being as the result of a new level of neural organization, but argue that, once it has emerged, it constitutes a new reality in the universe which is qualitatively distinct from the material realm. While such a position is not ruled out logically, most advocates of emergence have been causal materialists of the type we are describing, because any causal dependence seems to point to a monistic metaphysics. Obviously, since the present view makes mind depend upon the body and bodily processes for its very existence, the over-all result would be a materialistic world-view. Under such a view, while the mental realm would possess a derived or dependent sort of reality, ultimate reality would be physical or material.

The Schools of Monism: Spiritualism

It will be noted that the monism we have just described is a true monism and not a singularism. Its unity is grounded in a single ultimate "stuff" rather than in a single being of some kind. While the materialistic monist may hold that everything that exists is included in the physical universe, he stresses the singleness of the "stuff" from which the universe is made rather than its inclusive, blocklike wholeness. When we turn to the spiritualistic monisms, however, we are far more likely to find *singularism*. This we have described as the doctrine that all things are only parts or fragments of an all-inclusive whole or totality. Absolute idealism was mentioned as a classic example. There have been advocates of pluralistic spiritualism (for example, Leibniz and Berkeley) who held that individual minds or "spirits" are more or less independent of one another, but in recent philosophy singularism and spiritualistic monism have become almost synonymous.

The Principal Arguments for Idealistic Monism. There are numerous arguments advanced in support of idealistic or spiritualistic monism, but these can be reduced to two basic contentions. The first is the by now familiar Berkeleian argument, which is the foundation of modern idealistic epistemology: all existence as we know it is dependent upon experience, therefore all existence is dependent upon the agent of that experience, which is mind or spirit or consciousness. Thus minds or spirits and their ideas are all that exist, and consequently mind or spirit is the ultimate reality. The second argument points out the undeniable fact that we sense or "perceive" ourselves to be nonmaterial or spiritual beings, whose existence cannot be identified with that of our physical bodies. This intuition has been accepted at its face value by many idealistic thinkers, and for them it naturally offers a strong argument for spiritualistic monism. It may be objected that the fact that we feel ourselves to be spiritual beings, even if it is a valid intuition, does not prove that the universe as a whole is spiritual in its ultimate nature. For idealists of all schools, however, who hold that man's nature reveals the character of universal nature, such an intuition is of utmost importance in metaphysical considerations. "As our minds are structured, so is the real"; we know ourselves to be spiritual beings, therefore we are warranted in holding the world to be spiritual in character.

The Spiritualistic Explanation of Matter. It is evident that, just as materialistic monism faces its greatest difficulty in explaining the source and nature of mind, so its opposite, idealistic monism, must struggle mightily with the converse problem. Why does matter exist—or, to reduce the question to its most human instance, why does the mind have a body? To common sense, many of the answers offered by idealism appear to be magnificent examples of putting the cart before the horse. Some, however, are soundly logical and, granted the original assumption of all idealistic thought, quite convincing. Probably the two strongest arguments are these. First, the mind needs a body as an instrument of effective action, for it is only as ideas are acted upon that they can become effective, and this requires a physical organism. Second, the mind needs the body as an instrument of communication. As spiritual beings we are like "island universes," isolated from other spiritual beings; we can make contact with one another only through our senses—"soul speaks through flesh to soul"—and sensory apparatus is necessarily physical. Hence the mind's need for a body.

The materialistic monist has answers for both these arguments, as might be expected. Or rather, he has one answer that covers both. He argues that the two contentions assume the very thing they are seeking to prove: the necessity for a physical or material realm. "Body" would be required for effective action *only in a pre-existing physical world.* In other words, we need bodies to execute ideas only because we live in a world of material objects, including other bodies. If the whole universe were spiritual or mental, there would be no need for physical bodies to serve as either instruments of action or channels of communication. Certainly it is conceivable that in a nonmaterial realm of existence minds would be able to contact and affect other minds directly, without having to utilize the inadequate means provided by sensory mechanisms.

The Battle of the Monisms. In the battle of the monisms, each side feels that its position requires fewer initial assumptions and leaves fewer loose ends dangling. Each is forced to admit that it has difficulty explaining the existence of the opposite realm, but each also feels that it can do this better than its opponent. For example, the idealist acknowledges that bodies and their sensory equipment appear to be inadequate channels of communication or instruments of action. He feels, however, that it is more credible to hold that physical means are inadequate to mental purposes than to hold that physical sources are sufficient to explain the existence of mind. In other words, granting that each position has its weak spots, the idealist feels that his shaky sections are less weak than those in materialistic system. And the materialist feels the same way; he grants that it is difficult to account for mind on the materialistic hypothesis, but contends that this difficulty is child's play compared to the problems idealism faces when it sets out from its mentalistic assumptions. And, concludes the materialist, one of the greatest of the idealist's problems is how to satisfy common sense. For surely it is more sensible to believe that mind could have evolved or emerged from the physical than to think that Mind had to generate the material realm as a theater of action for itself. This last view seems to the materialist as absurd as Fichte's doctrine that Mind (the Ego, in his terminology) creates an external physical world for itself because man is essentially a moral being who requires a recalcitrant material realm with which to struggle. The Ego deliberately sets up a limitation upon itself in order to overcome that limitation; the will creates matter as a foil for itself, in order that its moral nature may be exercised in striving. For the materialistic monist, this view of Fichte's, absurd as it is, is merely the logical outcome of the idealistic inversion of the metaphysical cart-and-horse: begin with the idealistic-spiritualistic premise, he warns, and you quite logically end up with Fichte's foolishness.

Neutral Monism

It is by now evident that both of these monistic systems represent an oversimplification of the fundamental issue. Both appear to be guilty of the reductive fallacy at times, and both appear to have congenital blind spots regarding the significance of certain aspects of human experience.

However, centuries of debate between the two schools have served many useful philosophical purposes. This debate has revealed the fundamental character of the issue involved; it has shown the futility of facile solutions to the problem of reality; it has, by forcing each side to dig deeper, revealed many new implications of experience that have become part of our permanent intellectual heritage; and finally, by revealing the inadequacy of both extreme positions (that is, revealing it to everyone except those who hold the point of view) it has forced thinkers to seek more inclusive and more satisfactory solutions. The sometimes bitter controversy has thus been as worth while as it was inevitable. Much has been learned from it, even if few persons have found completely satisfying answers by it.

One of the more inclusive solutions to this metaphysical problem, proposed early in the history of modern philosophy, was that of Spinoza. This is the ontological correlate of his double-aspect theory of mind-body relations, which was described in Chapter 6. The Spinozistic position is usually known as *neutral monism,* and its doctrine is indicated by the name: the ultimate Real is neither mental *nor* material, but is instead a neutral substance, of which mind and matter are only *attributes.* As we have seen, such a view treats man's mind and his body as only two aspects of the same underlying substance. Whether we call an event "physical" or "mental" thus depends upon how we view it. If seen under one aspect (that is, in certain relations) it appears as a mind event; if we look at it in terms of the physical, it naturally appears to be a body event. Actually, however, it is the same event, representing only a modification in the one single substance.

Spinoza's System. While neutral monism should not be regarded as identical with Spinoza's system, his thought represents the classical example of this viewpoint. We can therefore hardly do better than to examine a few of its details. In the first place, for Spinoza this underlying substance is the only real existent; all things else, physical and mental alike, are only attributes or modes of it. Substance is defined explicitly: it is "that which exists in itself, and is conceived by means of itself." Moreover, substance is identical with God. All that exists is also God, and since substance or God is single, eternal, and infinite, reality is also single, eternal, and infinite. This identification of God, substance, and reality is extended (in Spinoza's system) to include *nature.* Spinoza usually confines his terminology to the last two terms of this inclusive series, and speaks ordinarily of *Deus sive natura,* "God or Nature."

We shall have more to say in our final chapters regarding this identification of God and nature, a position known technically as *pantheism.* The varying reactions to Spinoza's system, both in his own lifetime and later, indicate how difficult it is to form a satisfactory evaluation. While alive he was execrated alike by Catholic, Protestant, and Jew (he was himself a Jew), and was known as "that hideous atheist." A century later he was described as "a God-intoxicated man," and since then he has been elevated into the nearest thing to a saint that modern philosophy can show. The fact of the matter seems to be that the reduction of mind and matter to one common substance does not necessarily imply any particular doctrine concerning the existence of God. However, if we begin with the postulate of neutral monism, any deity that appears in our system must necessarily be pantheistic in character.

A Final Evaluation. A general evaluation of the neutralistic position will be largely a repetition of our evaluation of the double-aspect theory of mind. We need to emphasize again that common sense finds little meaning in such a representation of reality. We must suggest, too, that any such view exists in a verificatory vacuum, since there is no conceivable way that it could be either proved or disproved. Even if the psychologist should some day verify the double-aspect theory of mind-body relations, this would not prove that the theory can be enlarged into an inclusive world-view. Therefore, for all practical purposes, such a system as Spinoza's remains scientifically sterile, however important it may be ethically.

But in fairness to this type of monism we should admit that, in the last analysis, all metaphysical systems exist in this same verificatory vacuum. All represent logical constructs rather than empirically derived edifices of thought. Not only do metaphysical systems constitute a considerable logical extension of man's experience but they also are frankly transempirical—that is, beyond the reach of experience. In the case of neutral monism this transcendental character of the system is particularly pronounced, for we cannot even imagine what a third substance, of which mind and matter are only attributes, would be like. It not only transcends our experience, but our imagination as well. Even if, as is questionable, we could *conceive* of such a neutral entity, certainly we cannot visualize it or imagine what its character might be. To call it "God" hardly aids our comprehension, since even the vague ideas of God which most of us hold do not coincide with this Spinozistic deity.

In sum, while neutral monism avoids the extremes and possible over-simplifications of both its monistic rivals, it appears to do even less justice to the richness and complexity of human experience than they do. Admittedly it fuses that experience, whereas between them the other two monisms bifurcate it hopelessly. However, as an account of reality or of our experience in the universe around us, either of their more extreme solutions seem more promising.

But now let us see what the other possible metaphysical positions have to offer.

CHAPTER 10

METAPHYSICS:

Dualism and Pluralism

I N THE PRECEDING CHAPTER WE EXAMINED THREE KINDS OF MONISM, and we have found all three to be encumbered with difficulties— possibly fatal difficulties. The failure of monism—real or supposed— has usually led to the formulation of some type of *dualism*. In its minimum essence, dualism holds that reality consists of two ultimate and irreducible entities or substances or principles. The division between these twin ultimates is established in various ways by various thinkers. Most often they are called "mind" and "matter," or "spirit" and "matter." With reference to human nature, dualism stresses the contrast between "body" and "soul," or between "flesh" and "spirit." Sometimes the dualist speaks of "physical existence" as against "mental existence"; Plato, for example, established the division between the sensible (meaning, the perceivable) world and the intelligible (that is, the conceptual) world. Dualists today are likely to speak of the material realm as against the spiritual realm. But, wherever the division comes, and whether it is in- dicated by nouns or adjectives, the general viewpoint remains the same: there are two kinds of existence, completely separate from one another. The term *dualism* is self-explanatory, provided we take it in its meta- physical connotation as indicating a basic split within existence.

It is essential to any genuine dualism that the twin ultimates involved be truly irreducible—that is, neither one should be reducible to the other, and neither one nor both should be reducible to a third something still more basic. In other words, a genuine dualism does not regard its two ultimates, whatever they are called, as merely different manifestations of something more fundamental. Further, dualism believes that this split within existence is permanent, and not just a temporary condition that will be eliminated in time by the progressive spiritualization or increasing materialization of reality. The division is assumed to be inherent in the very nature of existence, and not just a superficial aspect of things.

Dualism usually postulates the complete independence of these two realms of being, each with its own laws and own processes. Moreover they are generally regarded as opposed to one another. This is well exemplified by the classic dualism most of us have known all our lives through Christianity, which is dualistic in its metaphysics, its ethics, and its psychology. In early and medieval Christianity particularly, there was a tendency to regard human life as an unceasing war between "flesh" and "spirit," and the outcome of this lifelong warfare was supposed to determine the postmortal destiny of the individual's soul in either heaven or hell. If we permitted "the flesh" to win the war, then hell would be our eternal abode; but if "spirit" won the struggle, then heaven was our destiny. Early Christians often carried the warfare into the body's own territory by denying it adequate food and sleep, or even sufficient clothing to keep it warm. In this way the struggle between body and soul was intensified and dramatized. But these ascetic practices are only an exaggerated manifestation of the dualistic opposition between the two levels of ultimate reality which Christianity assumes in principle.

Dualism in the Moral Realm

However, Christianity has no monopoly on dualism of this kind, as proved by the fact that several oriental religious philosophies have placed an equal or even greater emphasis upon a basic duality in the moral realm. Furthermore, moral dualism is held by many westerners who believe they have left the Church and its influences far behind, which suggests that this is a view capable of standing on its own feet without theological underpinnings.

Moral dualism normally postulates two opposing forces operating in the universe; these are usually called "good" and "evil"—or less accurately, "right" and "wrong." Human experience thus involves a struggle, or at least a choice, between these conflicting powers. This is a struggle in which each individual necessarily participates, selecting the side he will fight on.

Dualism Opposed to Relativism.   While the moral dualist does not claim that every choice we make and every act we perform is a blow for either righteousness or evil, he is almost certain to hold that there are moral absolutes. In other words, while he does not regard every action as necessarily either "good" or "bad," he does insist that those actions which do fall within the moral field are definitely, clearly, and absolutely good or bad. Hence this type of dualism is strongly opposed to *ethical relativism*. To the relativist, things are seldom pure black or white, but only varying shades of gray. Obviously this relativistic view is incompatible with dualism, since the core of any dualistic viewpoint is a fundamental division between two irreducible (and usually absolute) entities of some kind.

Throughout history there have been world-views built up around moral dualism. Most of these systems teach that cosmic processes, the very operations of nature, are manifestations of a titanic struggle between the powers of evil and the powers of good. In our day, however, these moral dualisms are usually less interested in formulating an over-all world-view. They are instead satisfied with only a general ethical doctrine. Although the terminology may not be very precise, today one frequently hears someone called a moral dualist because he preaches (or practices) a life built around clear-cut moral judgments. In fact it is now popular to call anyone a moral dualist whose major evaluations are in terms of right and wrong, particularly if this individual is firm and uncompromising in his judgments and considers them absolute. Under this loose but common meaning of the term, millions of Americans—probably the majority—would fall within the class of moral dualists. Certainly any Christian sect which puts emphasis upon sin and repentance implies a dualism of this type. For it is difficult to build a religion stressing sin and its consequences without having clear-cut distinctions which separate acts that are sinful from acts that are not.

What Americans know as "puritanism" constitutes a famous instance of moral dualism. Seventeenth-century Puritanism (with a capital P) involved far more than this one doctrine, but the so-called "puritanical attitude," still widespread in our own day, is obviously a dualism of this type. It involves a rigidly held sense of right and wrong, which are regarded as absolute and unchanging. In popular speech the puritan is a person who is straight-laced and intolerant, opposed to most forms of pleasure including even those pleasures most of us consider innocent. Such individuals base their tight-lipped attitude upon a philosophy of some sort, and this philosophy is moral dualism. This dualism in turn is usually derived from a metaphysical dualism which regards the body and its desires as necessarily evil *simply because they are part of the material half of reality.*

Classic Dualism: Descartes

Among the many metaphysical dualisms which philosophy has produced, the most rigorous was given classical expression by the French thinker Descartes in the seventeenth century. In his (the Cartesian) terminology, the ultimates, "mind" and "matter," are described in terms of their most unique and essential characteristics. They are called "thought" and "extension"—or, more precisely, "substance thinking" and "substance extended" (that is, occupying space). For Descartes and his followers the division of reality was absolute: body and mind are each self-sustaining, and the properties or characteristics of each are completely different. In fact, they are mutually exclusive; whatever is a property of mind cannot be a property of matter, and vice versa.

Descartes was certainly not the inventor of dualism, but his formulation of the dualistic position is significant and outstanding because it utilized strict mechanical determinism to explain all events in the material world, while rejecting determinism in the mental-spiritual realm. Thus Descartes assumed not only two kinds of existence, but also two kinds of causation.

Physical World Determined, Spiritual World Undetermined. In the physical world, Descartes held that although God is the First Cause or Prime Mover who initiated all motion, ever since this initial push all motion has been strictly mechanical, hence subject to deterministic causation. So the physical world is not only real and independent of men (and here Descartes obviously parts company with idealists like Berkeley), but furthermore its behavior is controlled by the mechanical forces so much stressed by mechanists and determinists. Descartes regarded science's task as the discovery of those laws which operate in the physical order. He apparently regarded these laws as absolute and deterministic.

But when he came to consider the mental and spiritual order of existence, particularly in relation to its principal manifestation, the human soul, Descartes reversed himself completely. In this area he argued for freedom of the will, even going so far as to claim that a man can choose freely between alternatives in favor of one which his intellect tells him is less desirable. (This is in contrast to one school of free-will thought, which holds that we can choose what we will, but this choice is always in favor of the more desirable alternative—which clearly restricts freedom of choice quite a bit.) So for Descartes, however much a man's body may, as part of the physical world, be subject to deterministic influences, his mind or soul remains unaffected by either earlier choices or external forces.

Descartes's separation between the physical and mental worlds was clear-cut, and his determinism in the first was as complete as his indeterminism in the second. As a consequence of this dualism he fathered some strange theories. He held, for example, that among living creatures only man possesses free-will; the animals he regarded as automata, devoid of not only freedom but feelings also. He believed that a dog, for example, was nothing except a mechanism whose behavior is as unthinking and unfeeling as a machine's. The dog's barking and tail-wagging are mere reflexes, unaccompanied by emotion. Only man has awareness and freedom of action. Man is, he maintained, the union or meeting point of physical and spiritual forces. Only human beings, among all things existing in the universe, partake of both "substance extended" and "substance thinking," so only human beings can have free-will.

Extreme Dualism: Occasionalism. Having thus separated the twin realms of mind and matter as completely as possible, Descartes proceeded to play the scientist and seek out the laws of mechanical causation operating within the physical half of reality. Unfortunately, after so effectively splitting existence in this way, he largely left to his followers the problem of getting the two halves back together again, in order to account for the working relation which they obviously have. Dualists are usually more successful at splitting reality than at putting it back together, and Descartes's immediate followers were no exception to this generalization. Some members of this Cartesian school came up with the desperate solution called Occasionalism. This teaches that God produces a miracle whenever a body-event occurs which has a mental accompaniment (as when I sit on a tack and feel pain), or whenever a mental event brings about a physical result (as when I decide to move my leg and behold! it moves). In a completely dualistic world like the one Descartes pictured, some such extreme and fantastic explanation of the obvious interaction of mind and body is required. Hence once the Occasionalists had accepted the dualistic hypothesis, it is not too surprising that they came up with the explanation they did.

Dualism's Difficulties. All antidualists feel that any flirtation with this hypothesis of two separate realities necessarily produces insoluble intellectual problems. For example, if mind and matter (or mind and body) are as dissimilar as dualists claim, how is *any* interaction between them possible? How is it even conceivable that they should be able to interact? Furthermore if the twin realms of existence operate under two different systems of cause and effect—one deterministic and the other indeterministic—then how can they possibly integrate with one another? For example, let us return to our instance of sitting upon a tack. Dualism admits that the laws of nature determine that the experience shall have a physical effect—that is, that the point of the tack will penetrate the skin to a certain depth. But dualism cannot explain why, if our minds are completely free and our wills can operate arbitrarily, we should be forced to feel the pain, since perception is wholly in the mental sphere. (A Christian Scientist would not admit that we are forced to feel the pain, since this is only "an error of mortal mind"; few dualists are willing to maintain this, however.)

Or, if we approach the interaction problem from the material side of existence, why does our body normally obey our wishes? Let us assume with the dualist that our wills and minds are free, although our bodies are bound by mechanical determinism. At what point, then, in the cause-and-effect situation (for example, I will to move my leg and it moves) does an "undetermined" (uncaused) idea become a "determining" cause of physical motion? And if due to fatigue or illness the body refuses to obey my mind, how do we explain this breakdown: at what point in the causal series has the body ceased to obey a determining cause and instead acquired a will of its own? The dualistic answers to such problems as these are frequently as desperate as those offered by Occasionalism, at least in the eyes of nondualists.

Most philosophers consider dualism's greatest weakness to be its failure to relate its two basic realities to one another in any very convincing explanation. These critics would be willing to accept the existence of two differing ultimate stuffs in the universe, *provided* those thinkers who assume this basic division could formulate a convincing picture of how these dual elements within reality are linked together. Throughout the history of Western philosophy, however, this has proved an impossible task for dualists. At least, only other dualists seem to be satisfied with the answers offered.

Dualism in the Arts

Dualism is a philosophy that has always had particular appeal for artists, poets, and literary people generally. The reasons for this appeal are not hard to discover: of all the world-views which have secured large followings in the western world, dualism is by far the most dramatic and colorful. Consequently it has lent itself well to artistic purposes, so that much of western art and literature expresses (or at least implies) a dualistic world order.

As we all know, conflict is the life-blood of drama, and no situation is considered more clearly dramatic than one in which powerful opposing forces meet face to face. And, since the essence of the dualistic world-view assumes just such a titanic struggle, the dramatic values in this philosophy are obvious. The dramatic conflict here is doubly impressive from the fact that the opposing forces involved are the ultimate forces in the universe. This war is no puny local engagement, and certainly no summer's campaign; it is the basic contest between two worlds, the spiritual against the material, the higher against the lower. Furthermore it is a conflict that is assumed to involve every human being, since human nature is the focal point of these opposing forces. Strange mixture that he is of both flesh and spirit, man's whole existence appears to be inextricably linked with the eternal struggle between the two realms of being.

The Divided Man. It is this dual nature of man which, since it demands a divided allegiance to two different and even contradictory sets of laws, makes him the heroic but essentially tragic creature he is.

Many poets have described this harrowing divided allegiance which racks every man, but no one has expressed it better than Fulke Greville, a contemporary of Shakespeare's, in his famous "Chorus" from *Mustapha*:

> O wearisome condition of humanity!
> Born under one law, to another bound;
> Vainly begot, and yet forbidden vanity,
> Created sick, commanded to be sound.
> What meaneth Nature by these diverse laws?
> Passion and reason self-division cause.
> Is it the mark of majesty or Power
> To make offences that it may forgive?
> Nature herself doth her own self deflower
> To hate those errors she herself doth give.
> For how should man think that he may not do
> If Nature did not fail and punish too?
> Tyrant to others, to herself unjust,
> Only commands things difficult and hard,
> Forbids us all things which it knows we lust,
> Makes easy pains, impossible reward.
> If Nature did not take delight in blood,
> She would have made more easy ways to good.
> We that are bound by vows and by promotion,
> With pomp of holy sacrifice and rites,
> To preach belief in God and stir devotion,
> To preach of Heaven's wonders and delights;
> Yet when each of us in his own heart looks,
> He finds the God there far unlike his books.

In this poetic way Greville conveys some of the implications of a genuine dualism. And certainly the three and a half centuries since this poem was published (1609) have not resolved the basic dilemma he describes. But there is one striking difference between Greville and most philosophic dualists, both those of his own day and those of our time: obviously he was not happy with his dualistic philosophy. He found it forced upon him, as it were, but he protests strongly. Most avowed dualists appear more at peace with this world-view. In fact many of them appear happy in it, and find Greville's interpretation morbid and exaggerated. I do not suppose many would change his first line to read

O excellent condition of humanity!

but obviously most dualists find the human condition less wearing than this Elizabethan poet did.

A Third Metaphysical Possibility: Pluralism

Many thinkers have been convinced that both monism and dualism must be counted metaphysical failures. Consequently, unless these thinkers have been willing to abandon the metaphysical quest entirely, they have had to move on to the third of the great world-systems. *Pluralism*, strictly speaking, is any world-view which holds that there exist neither one nor two ultimate principles or entities, but many. Speaking even more precisely, it is any view which sets the number of irreducible metaphysical elements at more than two. Thus a view such as that of the Greek philosopher Empedocles, with its four primary substances (earth, air, fire, and water), would be no less pluralistic than a system postulating an infinite number of substances.

In order to have a pluralistic system it is not necessary that the number of ultimate entities be *qualitatively* separate. A spiritualistic atomism such as Leibniz's in which the common element of the innumerable monads is perceptual awareness, would be a *quantitative* pluralism: all the entities are similar in their nature, but distinct from one another and infinite in number. Empedocles, with his four elements combining to form the innumerable objects of our experience, offers a pluralism that is both quantitative and qualitative. Another Greek pluralist, Anaxagoras, believed there are as many elements as our senses can differentiate: redness, coldness, roughness, and so forth. In sum, while the term pluralism implies a number of ultimate entities, these may or may not be *qualitatively* numerous.

Pluralism is difficult to present to beginning students, both because there have been numerous types of pluralism and because these have sometimes had little in common except their rejection of both monism and dualism. Such being the case, it will be best to select a few of the most characteristic or most influential pluralistic systems and consider them briefly. As we study these, we shall find that (to quote an authoritative source) "we get a variety of theories that find philosophical solace in variety rather than in any knowable or unknowable one."[1]

We began our chapter by describing dualism as the common-sense view, with monism as a sort of philosopher's ideal. In general philosophers have been enamored of unity or oneness; as a consequence many have regarded anything other than monism as either a methodological convenience (for example, Descartes) or as a second-best position for those who could not achieve a monism of some sort. Naturally not all dualists have been willing to accept this patronizing attitude of monists towards dualistic systems, but probably a majority would acknowledge monism to be intellectually desirable *if* it can be achieved. Thus monism might be regarded as the ontological norm, with both dualism and pluralism as variations from the norm. Certainly pluralism has usually been regarded as a greater aberration from this norm than dualism, for however much monists and dualists may quarrel among themselves, they have always been able to organize a common front against pluralism. In fact, both have frequently proclaimed their doubts that pluralism can be considered a legitimate metaphysical position. There have even been suggestions that pluralism constitutes a betrayal of philosophy, or at least an abandonment of the metaphysical quest. If dualism is a second-best position, then pluralism (according to all nonpluralists) is an "I-give-up" doctrine. For, in the eyes of its opponents, it seems to make no effort to integrate our experience, or to cut through the admittedly pluralistic appearance of things in an attempt to find their underlying unity—or at least their underlying duality. But let us listen to the pluralist himself.

Early Greek Pluralism. The first pluralistic system in western philosophy was that of Empedocles (fifth century, B.C.) whom we have already mentioned. Previous to his time, Greek philosophy had been monistic; each thinker had sought to explain the world in terms of one single underlying "stuff," such as moisture, air, fire, and so forth. Empedocles, however, took the characteristically pluralistic step: he abandoned monism as an ideal, and postulated the famous tetrad of medieval science—earth, air, fire, and water. These four, activated by the opposing forces of love and hate ("attraction" and "repulsion" would be a better modern translation of the terms), are the constituents of all that exists, including the human mind or soul. Generation and decay are thus only a change of composition: "There is no coming into being of aught that

[1] "Pluralism," in Runes' *Dictionary of Philosophy.*

perishes, nor any end for it in baneful death, but only mingling, and separation of what has been mingled." Thus, while this first pluralism was simple, it was nonetheless thoroughgoing. Within its crude framework and its very restricted limits, it was a true pluralistic world-view.

Standing near Empedocles in time is the other Greek thinker whom we have mentioned, Anaxagoras. For him, such a simple tetrad of elements was inadequate to explain the infinite variety of sense impressions. As has been well said, where Empedocles shattered the monistic realm of being pictured by the earlier thinkers, Anaxagoras pulverized it. He postulated as many ultimate substances or elements as there are simple sensory qualities, such as heat and cold, moisture and dryness, hardness and softness. Further, these elements were regarded as all present in varying amounts in all things. They are diffused everywhere, so that no particle of matter is simple or pure in character. However, each has its predominant essence or characteristic which serves to distinguish it, and it is from this that we derive both the character and the name of a stuff— as, for example, when we call snow "white," although actually it is not pure whiteness.

Modern Pluralism

We have already outlined the spiritualistic pluralisms of both Leibniz and Berkeley, so it will not be necessary to describe these systems further. It should be understood, however, that both were of great importance in the history of pluralistic thought. Leibniz represented the high-water mark of the school in modern philosophy prior to the pluralists within our own century. After Berkeley's death in the mid-eighteenth century, pluralism was virtually driven underground by the rising tide of monistic German idealism. Its recent revival was due to in considerable part to William James, the famous American pragmatist.

James' philosophical enemy was the absolute idealism of the Hegelians with its singularistic or "block-view" of the universe. James felt that any system attempting such singularistic unity could not possibly do justice to the richness and variety of human life. He was, in short, arguing on the basis of our direct experience, as against the logical abstractionism of Hegel's Absolute. James believed that the degree of abstraction required to achieve this absolute synthesis, involving numerous logical steps intervening between concrete experience and the Absolute Mind, could only produce a view of reality that was utterly empty—"a night in which all cows are black."[2] James loved life, with all its multiplicity, complexity, and challenging possibilities, as few philosophers have loved it. He consequently held any such singularistic outcome to the metaphysical quest as Hegel proposed to be a blasphemy against life.

James' thought is typical of modern pluralism in that it is less concerned with the substance (or substances) that constitute reality than with its structure. Today's pluralist is not likely to ask "What is the world stuff or stuffs?" but rather, "How is ultimate existence organized?" More specifically, modern pluralists are concerned primarily with the *relations* between the various parts of our experience, instead of searching for whatever may be presumed to underlie that experience.

What Are Relations?   The term "relation," as used in philosophy, is usually difficult for students to understand. Since modern pluralism is largely a theory of relations, it is logical for us to clarify this important term before we go further. Let us take a simple situation common to every classroom, involving only two entities: a book and a desk. Consider all the possible relations that can exist between these two, starting with just the spatial relationships. The book can be *on* the desk, *in* the desk, *under* the desk, *above* the desk, *beside* the desk, *behind* the desk, and so on. Expanding the concept of relation slightly, but still staying in the realm of space, the book can be *smaller than* the desk, *lighter than* the desk, and so on. If we bring in time relationships, the book can be *older* or *newer than* the desk. Then, going still farther afield into the field of values (economic and otherwise), the book can be *cheaper than* the desk, *rarer than* the desk, even *more important than* the desk.

Now all of these phrases indicate relations, as does every preposition in a language. It will be helpful to remember that "relation" and "relative" are from the same root. Whenever we compare two or more things, or state the position (spatial, temporal, or evaluational) of one thing relative to the other(s), we are indicating relations. Obviously many of our most important judgments are of this relational kind, and there can be little significant human communication without prepositions. It may

---

[2] It is ironic that this phrase, so often used to describe the Hegelian Absolute, should have been coined by Hegel himself in criticizing one of his fellow singularists.

be helpful to the reader, in the paragraphs just ahead where we will be considering the pluralistic emphasis upon relations—admittedly a difficult part of modern philosophy—to keep a list of the common prepositions handy to refresh his mind as to the meaning of "relations": *in, on, under, of, from, beside, to,* and the rest.

The Doctrine of Internal Relations. As we have seen earlier, the absolute idealist regards the universe and the ultimate real as an organic whole, in which everything is part of everything else and an integral part of the whole. We will get a clearer understanding of this type of idealism if we emphasize "organic" rather than "whole." It is the unified, integrated, inter-related character of the universe, rather than any singularness, that constitutes its most essential feature.

In a system such as this one proposed by the absolute idealist, obviously relations would be not only *inter*-relations but *inner* relations as well. It is this doctrine of internal relations, basic to singularistic idealism, which most sharply separates it from pluralism, since a pluralist regards all relations as *external* to the entities involved. For singularism, a relation must be either between a part and the whole to which it belongs, or between parts within a whole—provided that these parts are regarded as belonging to the whole and not as standing independent of it. Thus for a singularistic system such as Hegel's the very concept of a relation would imply an organic whole—"relatedness" would presuppose "wholeness"— and relations would be grounded in the nature of the terms related.

But all this is pretty abstract and theoretical, so let us return to our example of the desk and the book. For the singularist, it is not enough to know that the book is on the desk. This is only the beginning: they are both *in* a room, and also *within* a building, which in turn is *in* a certain geographical location. It is also *on* the earth and *within* the solar system, which is *in* a certain galaxy *within* the total universe. The singularist believes that only as we are aware of both the book and the desk in this total context can we have genuine knowledge about them; things have meaning and significance—some singularists would say, have existence— only as parts of this organic whole. To see the book only in relation to the desk, even if we could attain a total knowledge of all actual and possible relations between book and desk, is to have only very fragmentary knowledge.

Obviously such a theory of knowledge necessarily makes all relations inner, or internal. Since everything is part of an organic whole, all relations between things are only relations between parts of this whole. And, since the parts are within the whole, the relations between these inner parts are also inner relations within the organic totality.

While we have drawn our example above from the field of spatial relations, it must be understood that singularism goes far beyond just the spatial realm in its theory of relations. Furthermore it includes more than just spatial and temporal relations ("before," "after," "earlier," "later," and so forth) combined. *All* types of relationship are subject to the inclusive sweep of a singularistic system such as that of absolute idealism, but all of them remain internal, since all are parts of the Absolute.

Pluralism's Theory of External Relations. For pluralism, on the contrary, relations are basically external. They are independent of the things related, which can pass in and out of relations without implying that they belong to an inclusive whole of any kind. Even when things are parts of wholes, it is still possible for these parts to be related to one another independently, without regard to any relationship they may have to the whole. For instance, the location of the book in relation to the desk— above it, below it, in it, and so on—holds regardless of where the desk may be in relation to anything else. A pluralist insists that regardless of whether the desk is in the classroom or in a moving van, in storage, in transit, or in hock, there can still be separate relations holding between it and the book.

Modern Realism

Some of the more important modern epistemological schools, classified as various types of *realism,* build largely upon this doctrine of external relations. The several statements of these schools are difficult and highly technical, but a simplified summary of them may be helpful toward an increased understanding of contemporary pluralism.

In general modern realism is a revolt against idealism, both subjective and objective. In particular it is a revolt against the central idealistic doctrine that the mind plays a basic role in bringing the objects of knowledge into existence. Realism thus reasserts what common sense has never doubted: the universe of nature or physical objects exists independently before it is experienced by us. However, modern realism is more sophisticated than common-sense naive realism since it acknowledges that objects are related to consciousness, but (unlike idealism) denies that they are *dependent* upon consciousness. This realistic doctrine of independence admits that when knowledge occurs there is obviously a knower inter-acting with objects, but it does not admit that this knowing relation is responsible for the character of the objects which are known. Being known (that is, becoming an object of experience) is something which happens to a thing that already exists. The characteristics of this pre-existent thing determine what happens when it is known. This reverses the idealistic viewpoint, which holds that the act of knowing not only affects the character of an object but is somehow responsible for its very existence.

Objects Not Affected by Being Known. Realism is particularly em-phatic in its denial that objects are changed in any way by becoming known; a thing is the same before it enters consciousness, while it is in consciousness, and after it passes out of our awareness. In the word of one prominent realist, "An object owes neither its qualities as known nor its existence to the mind that knows it."[3] In less technical language this means that objects freely enter our minds (and later leave them when we shift our attention to something else) without themselves being affected. Like a dust particle in the air, which drifts through a beam of sunlight and then drifts on out of the light without its dusty character being al-tered by this brief illumination, so with the objects in our environment: their own nature remains undisturbed by their occasional moments of epistemological glory when we become conscious of them. They both pre-exist and post-exist in relation to our minds, and their transit through our stream of consciousness is an event which in no way alters their in-dependent being. Hence the name "realism" for this theory that objects have a real (that is, actual or nonmental) existence which is wholly inde-pendent of us and all our cognitive activities. This clearly makes the knowing relation an external one, since the so-called objects of knowledge freely pass in and out of this relation without being thereby altered. And here again we have an obvious pluralism implied, since ultimate reality consists of a vast number of things possessing autonomous existence.

In contrast to this realistic-pluralistic position, the singularist holds that no object exists by itself and no fact is complete by itself; further-more no statement, standing by itself is completely true. For every fact

[3] Samuel Alexander, *Time, Space and Deity*, Vol. I, p. 16.

leads eventually to every other fact, so that ultimately all the facts of the universe are involved in any single statement or proposition. If we will recall for a moment our analysis of the problem of "truth" in Chapter 7, it will be clear immediately that this singularistic doctrine of internal relations is intimately bound up with the coherence theory of truth. We learned that this theory holds a proposition to be true if it coheres or is consistent with the rest of our knowledge or system of beliefs. We have seen that mathematics offers the perfect example of such a truth-system in operation, and we noted how strong a preference the idealist has for this coherence theory.

The Pluralistic Rejection of Coherence. Pluralism, on the other hand, rejects the coherence theory as a final test of truth, and prefers either the more empirical correspondence theory or the more practical pragmatic test. To the pluralist, propositions may supplement one another, but this *supplementation* does not necessarily involve a *modification.*[4] Thus, to the pluralist, facts can be independent of one another, the various parts of our experience need have no relation to each other, and the universe may be only an aggregate—a "universe of discourse," rather than an organic entity or being of some sort. This would make our environment infinitely challenging in its possibilities of genuinely new situations. Pluralism (at least in its pragmatic version) depicts a tychistic universe, in which there may be considerable loose play in the mechanism, and where chance may be a very real and very significant factor. The pluralist stresses what has been called the "each-form" of reality, rather than the "all-form" as represented in singularism; he views the real in terms of "the many" rather than in terms of "the one."

Pluralism and American Culture

It is not surprising that contemporary pluralism has had its greatest development in the United States. For this is a philosophy which makes a virtue out of change, unpredictability, and adventure. Instead of finding these elements in human experience something to be explained away or swept under the metaphysical rug, pluralistic thinkers find them not only basic within reality but also intriguing in the challenges and opportuni-

[4] Cf. Sellars, *op. cit.,* p. 159.

ties they offer. The formulation of the pluralistic systems coincided with the rapid development of American culture during the past three-quarters of a century, and it is difficult to believe that this coincidence was "purely coincidental." Even if, as many social observers today believe, Americans are becoming more interested in security and conformity than in adventure and opportunities that require taking risks, it appears certain that pluralism will still appeal to many Americans. Our whole civilization is pluralistic to a degree that is virtually unknown elsewhere.

In part this comes from the sheer physical size of the United States. In part, too, the diversity of racial stocks and old-country cultures which have gone into the melting pot has encouraged pluralism. Our relatively uncentralized system of government has helped: with federal, state, county, and municipal governments all competing for our devotion and our tax dollars, Americans are further forced into a plurality of loyalties and taxes. Then too, America still has much social mobility, which means that most of us can take up new residences and new jobs, and make a new circle of friends, almost any time we wish. This naturally encourages the changing of interests and loyalties. Our regional differences, although less important than a generation ago, still are very influential: the standards of one region are different from those of another, and while persons who have lived in the same region all their lives may regard its standards and attitudes as the only right ones, there are enough population shifts to keep these standards from becoming absolutes.

And finally, American civilization, like that of any modern industrial nation, is so complex and rich that no person can experience more than a small fraction of this complexity and this richness. Occupational specialization, combined with the brevity of human life and the finitude of human energies, means that even the most gifted and most energetic persons must confine their activities to a small part of the possible field. This necessarily means that people from different educational, occupational, and social levels, or from different parts of the country, speak the same language only in the literal sense that all speak English. But what they talk about, or what they understand by the words they speak and hear, may vary so widely that the use of a common tongue means little. Throughout American society, from the departments of federal government on down, the right hand all too frequently does not appear to know what the left hand is doing. We have pluralism in government, pluralism in our social classes, pluralism in our moral standards, pluralism in our occupational specialities, pluralism in the arts (different schools of painting, music, drama, and so on), and pluralism in our philosophies—schools of thought, as we usually call them. Thus metaphysical pluralism would seem the most logical system for Americans to hold—at least according to the pluralists themselves.

A Final Evaluation of Pluralism

The final evaluation of pluralism as a metaphysical position must, as usual, in this textbook, be left to each individual reader. In comparison with either monism or dualism, this world-view gives us a picture of reality that makes it stimulating, dynamic, and ever-changing. Pluralism finds the universe to be characterized primarily by *change;* to speak of the universe as "eternal" does not mean that it is static, or "blocked-out" as singularism holds. Change and variety can be as eternal as fixity: the universe need not be an organic totality, frozen into an absolute, in order to constitute the real. Change is even more fundamental in our experience than nonchange, and the innumerable things that make up our experience—"the many"—are far more significant than any imagined "one" could ever be.

The reader may believe, as many thinkers do, that however stimulating the pluralistic view may be, it is not intellectually satisfying. Its picture of reality may impress us as too "loose-jointed," perhaps too "hodgepodge," to be a permanently acceptable view of things as they are fundamentally. We may agree with those philosophers who hold that a worldview which cannot impose more order and unity upon our experience than pluralism does is not a genuine system of metaphysics. In short, the pluralistic view appears to many minds as "synthetic" (in the popular sense of the term), rather than "synoptic," as philosophical systems are supposed to be. Surely, one may argue, the human mind seeks and deserves something better than this agglomerate view of things.

But the pluralist has the last word. In our day, he is usually also a naturalist, so the pluralist and naturalist combine to answer. It is certainly true, they reply, that many minds seek a more integrated view of reality than pluralism offers. And, if all who seek diligently deserve to find, then such minds deserve a better solution to the ontological problem than any which pluralism can produce. *But,* to "seek" or even to "deserve" has nothing to do with hard, brute, realistic facts. For it is certainly conceivable that the universe may have precisely the aggregate character which the pluralist describes. In such a case, what would "seeking" or "deserving" have to do with the matter? Are they not likely to give us a distorted picture of reality which would be "satisfying," no doubt, but nonetheless untrue? Furthermore, to speak of "deserving" a certain type of answer to our metaphysical quest is to betray the very spirit of philosophy. In the search for generalized truth, the mind "deserves" to find only what actually exists. Nothing else can be called truth. Nothing else can be worthy of the philosopher and his quest.

Résumé of Metaphysics: Monism

It will be well to conclude our presentation of the metaphysical problem with a résumé of each of the schools we have covered in these two chapters. We shall concentrate on the implications of each view, particularly in relation to general human experience. Many of these implications have been stated or inferred as we presented the viewpoint in question, but a final summary should leave the student with a better understanding of both the metaphysical problem as a whole and the potentialities contained in each of the several suggested solutions. We shall summarize in the same order as our original presentation.

In the first place, all monisms (as distinct from singularism) have two characteristics which appear to be inevitable in such systems. Since, as is commonly admitted, the "common-sense" appearance of things suggests a basic metaphysical dualism, with "matter" and "mind" as the irreducible ultimates, any monistic formulation is almost certain to run counter to common sense and be guilty of oversimplification at some point or points within the system. Both of these tendencies must be considered weaknesses or disadvantages of monism as a metaphysical position, regardless of the kind of ultimate "stuff" which is postulated.

1. Materialistic. In physical or materialistic monism, for example, the challenge to common sense comes in denying the reality—or at least the efficacy—of mind or spirit in the scheme of things.[5] Since all our everyday experience seems to point to the existence of two categories of being, physical and mental, the materialist must assume a heavy burden of proof when he attempts to formulate a monistic position which denies the actuality of this apparent duality. The oversimplification of materialism comes when its exponents try to reduce all mental events to mere epiphenomenalistic accompaniments of physical events. To make these mental occurrences (whether they be sensations, perceptions, ideas, or concepts) "nothing but" events in the material world is to be guilty of the reductive fallacy, as was pointed out in previous chapters.

2. *Idealistic.* A spiritual or idealistic monism has the same two difficulties. Again, with common sense pointing towards a dual reality, the denial or extreme subordination of the physical world for the benefit of an all-inclusive (or at least strongly dominant) spiritual reality appears to fly in the face of our day-by-day experience. And if this type of monism is not so given to the reductive fallacy as materialism is, its oversimplifications are no less glaring—at least in the eyes of all philosophers who are not idealistic monists. To take a conspicuous example from a previous chapter, idealistic monism's explanation of why the mind has a body, or why the material world should exist in a universe where reality is ultimately mental, appears so simple as to seem absurd to many thinkers.

3. *Neutralistic.* Neutral monism has an even more difficult time when put to the test of common sense. By reducing all existence to a neutral "Substance" which has no relation to direct experience, this viewpoint cuts itself off completely from common sense. The other two monisms, while faced with serious difficulties in trying to reduce an experiential duality to a metaphysical unity, still have some relation to our experience in that the ultimate which they select has some meaning for ordinary thought and discourse. Neutralism, however, with its "Substance," of which "matter" and "mind" are only two "modes" (out of many possible ones), offers us no point of contact with experience by means of which we can understand the nature of this ultimate real. It is all very well, intellectually speaking, to define Substance as "that which receives modifications but is not itself a mode" (as the dictionary does),

[5] As we have seen in Chapter 6, this denial is particularly characteristic of older extreme forms of materialism. The more moderate contemporary position usually allows real existence and causal efficacy to the mental realm, although it makes this mental or spiritual category of being strictly dependent upon a physical foundation for its existence.

or as "that which exists in itself, and is conceived by means of itself" (as Spinoza, the most celebrated exponent of neutralism, does). But in relation to both everyday living and ordinary thinking, such statements tell us very little about either ultimate reality or the character of the universe in which we have to live. It is evident that this third neutralistic form of monism also involves even more drastic oversimplifications of experience than its rivals, although in this case such reductions could be more accurately called overabstractions. All attributes, qualities and modes are stripped off, until nothing remains but mere "existence" or "being," than which there is nothing more abstract. Obviously the reduction of the infinite variety and complexity of existence as revealed by our senses to such a thin conceptual ghost as "Substance" requires simplifications of the utmost drasticity.

The Advantages of Monism. It need hardly be said that monism as a metaphysical position has advantages which recommend it strongly, *if* it can be legitimately achieved and consistently maintained. It is paradoxical that the chief virtues of monism are closely related to the faults which we have just enumerated. First, a monistic system usually possesses a simplicity and unity which neither dualism nor pluralism can match. To achieve this unity may require some questionable diminutions and oversimplifications, but the result, once attained, generally has a simplicity that is impressive. This unified simplicity, in which all the variety and complexity of experience are reduced to a single ultimate of some kind, probably explains the large role which monism has played in the history of thought. For however much our common sense may suggest that reality is dual in nature, the human mind has persistently sought for a unity underlying the appearance of things. This predisposition to strive for a single explanation, reason, principle, source, law, stuff, formula or system to organize our experience is one of the mind's most habitual responses to its environment. Hence while monism may run counter to common sense, it has a powerful ally in what appears to be an innate tendency of the mind itself. To rest content with a "multiple factor" explanation of anything requires a considerable amount of intellectual sophistication.

So much for the advantages of monism in general. Glancing very briefly at the three types, we find that each has certain advantages that are peculiar to it. (1) Materialism, particularly in its more moderate contemporary form, has the great virtue of a close relation with science. This enables the mind to move freely from philosophy to science, or vice versa, with no sense of shifting gears, changing to a new language, or entering a different world. The result is a unification of *knowledge* (in contrast to a unity of *system*) which no other metaphysical position can equal. (2) Idealistic monism has an emotional advantage that is unique, analogous to the intellectual virtue just conceded to materialism. For a world-view in which the ultimate real is Mind or Spirit offers an environment that is at heart friendly to man and to his dreams, his aspirations, and his values. (3) Neutral monism can show no such practical advantages as its two rivals. Any virtue it possesses is best described as systematic. Granting its extreme simplifications of experience and its drastic abstraction of all experienceable qualities from "Substance," in the hands of an intellectual giant like Spinoza the doctrine attains a formulation which is systemically remarkable.

Singularism

Singularism, particularly as embodied in absolute idealism, has characteristics and implications somewhat different from those found in monism. Emphasizing as it does a tight organic unity in the *structure* of reality, with all parts (that is, individual objects, persons, and events) cohering in a Whole which gives them meaning, value, and even existence, such a world-view makes everything that occurs only the progressive revelation of this all-inclusive Whole or Absolute. While the doctrine does not deny change (Hegel for instance stressed history as the unfolding of the Absolute in time) it does eliminate the possibility of genuine novelty emerging from the flow of events. Thus the "block-view" of the universe conveys to most thinkers an impression of staticism: the future seems "blocked out" or "cut and dried" before it occurs. The challenging adventure of a malleable future, such as offered by more dynamic views of the cosmos, is lacking.

There are other weaknesses in any singularistic view of the world besides this mood of staticism. A second objection for many thinkers is the generally absolutistic character of such systems. For not only do they picture the real as an Absolute, but the logic and general quality of thinking which they exhibit also reveals an absolutism (that is, a nonrelativism) that is extreme. The general effect of absolute idealism, for example, upon persons who are not members of the school is one of exaggerated confidence and frequent dogmatism. As has been well said, Hegel was probably the most self-confident philosopher who ever lived,[6] and his followers for the last hundred years have generally displayed the same attitude. While Hegel's philosophy does not represent the whole of singularism, this statement is applicable generally to this school and its members.

The Advantages of Singularism. The advantages of such a worldview are numerous, as proved by the enormous following which absolute idealism enjoyed during most of the nineteenth century. Two of these have appeared pre-eminent. The first advantage is strictly and peculiarly intellectual: any singularistic metaphysics is almost certain to be tightknit and structurally organic to a degree impossible in most other systems.[7] Logical coherence is the foundation of absolute idealism, as it must be for any singularism. A "block-view" of the universe, in which the concept of the whole is all-important, naturally is a coherent view, and it is not surprising that absolutists should be the outstanding supporters of the coherence theory of truth. Hence to certain minds, in which the urge for logical consistency, systematic neatness, and tectonic cohesion amounts to a passion, singularism proves irresistible. It has a double attraction if these are minds which find a unified whole, however abstract, more significant than a concrete part, however rich or real.

Besides this intellectual satisfaction, singularism offers certain emotional advantages. Most of these are shared by all idealistic systems, as we saw in Chapter 3. The satisfaction offered by a view of things which leaves no loose ends dangling is more than merely intellectual. Certainly there is esthetic charm in such an elegant structure of rational architecture, but even more obvious is the emotional assurance that comes from a system in which the various parts are gathered up into a cosmic unity. For then all that occurs within human experience becomes a part of the grand scheme of things, where it has meaning and purpose. Hence no

[6] W. K. Wright, *A History of Modern Philosophy*, p. 317.

[7] Spinoza's system achieves much the same unity and structural elegance, but this resulted more from his method of presentation and the rigor of his thought than from any close similarity between neutralism and singularism. However, Hegel's Absolute impresses many minds as no less abstract than Spinoza's Substance. Hegel's famous description of the Spinozistic Substance, likening it to a lion's den which has many tracks leading in but none coming out, could be applied to his own Absolute.

life is wasted, no unrequited love is merely thrown away, no suffering is pointless, and no human experience is without significance. While many thinkers believe that such splendid virtues as these can be purchased in the philosophical market only at a very steep intellectual price, the history of thought shows that numerous persons have been willing to pay that price.

Résumé of Metaphysics: Dualism and Pluralism

Our résumé of dualism and pluralism can be somewhat briefer than that of monism, since the presentation of these two positions within the present chapter should make them fresher in the reader's mind. Then too, they have fewer different forms which require separate treatment.

Dualism. Dualism's major difficulty is intellectual. Having accepted at its face value the common-sense view of reality, with its fundamental bifurcation into the irreducible categories of "mind" and "matter," this world-view usually impresses the newcomer to philosophy as very promising. But there are tremendous barriers between that promise and its realization, barriers which few dualistic systems have been able to overcome. We have discussed these difficulties too recently for much repetition to be necessary, except to say in summary that these problems may be classified as follows: (1) the question of the exact nature of the two basic categories, together with their respective boundaries; (2) the relations between these categories; (3) the method or mechanics by which these relations are effected. Most dualistic systems are quite adequate in dealing with the first of these three, less satisfactory regarding the second, and usually very weak in explaining how the relations between the supposedly independent and irreducible realms are effected. Dualism generally seems to promise more than it can deliver, and if we approach it with large hopes, our disappointment is likely to be in proportion.

Besides the enormous advantage of building directly on common sense (and thus avoiding that abyss between daily experience and metaphysical speculation which has been all too frequent in the history of philosophy), dualism has the virtue of laying bare the whole problem of basic categories and ultimate existence as no other system does. It is consequently the beginner's system *par excellence*, for once we have thought through the implications of dualism and have the arguments for and against the view clearly in mind, we are ready to undertake the more difficult tasks of understanding monism, singularism, and pluralism.

Pluralism. Pluralism, emphasizing the "each" form of things instead of the "all" form (as monism does), or the "either-or" contrast of dualism, likewise builds closely upon experience. But this close contact with the empirical domain is different from that found in dualism. For pluralism, instead of taking as its starting point the *categories* into which the objects and events of our experience seem to fall, takes *the objects and events themselves as basic.* This school is not only less concerned with principles, categories, wholes, and abstractions than the other world-views are—the pluralist definitely regards these as less important than the individual concrete thing, person, or event—but pluralism concedes value to principles and categories only as means for either explaining or relating individual things and occurrences.

Perhaps the best evidence of pluralism's emphasis upon the reality and significance of the concrete individual entity is its doctrine of external relations, which was briefly described earlier in the present chapter. For the singularist, stressing the Whole or Absolute, relations between the parts of the whole are all-important: it is they which make the part, be it an object or an event, what it is. Modern pluralism, on the contrary, regards both the reality and the significance of relations as very secondary in comparison with the primary reality of concrete objects and events in themselves, which (according to the pluralist) can move in and out of relations without being altered, and without losing their basic independence.

Thus the great appeal of pluralism lies in its full recognition of the reality, the poignancy, the richness of our actual experiences. No other system of thought can compare with modern pluralism (for example, the philosophy of William James) in this regard. Just as singularism appeals to a certain type of rigorously logical mind, to whom unity and coherence are most important, so pluralism attracts those minds which revel in the richness and complexity of concrete human experience, and which find tremendous challenge in the numerous possibilities offered by this dynamic view of the world.

The weaknesses of pluralism are the obverse of its virtues. It is hardly to be expected that a world-view which places such emphasis upon the reality and importance of individual things would be remarkable for its structural logic or its organic cohesion. In fact very few pluralists since Leibniz and Berkeley (both idealists, it should be noted) have attempted to formulate a complete system of metaphysics. Instead, like James and the other pragmatic pluralists, they have generally been content to work on special problems within philosophy, such as those of methodology and the theory of truth. That a systematic metaphysic of pluralism is possible was proved by the work of two earlier members of the school whom we have just mentioned, but a complete modern formulation of the viewpoint has yet to establish itself in the philosophical world.

CHAPTER 11

LOGICAL EMPIRICISM

O UR SURVEY OF THE PRINCIPAL METAPHYSICAL THEORIES IN the two preceding chapters has undoubtedly affected various readers in various ways. One group of readers, however, will be certain to have reacted in a manner which is especially significant, for it will approximate the reaction that a powerful contemporary school of philosophy has to all metaphysical speculation. Known as *logical positivism* or *logical empiricism,* this school is probably the most radical and intellectually aggressive yet to arise within philosophy.[1] Its effect upon traditional systems has been devastating, and the conflict between it and the classical schools has produced more really basic controversy than any previous clash within philosophy. The implications of this empirical movement have cut deeply into metaphysics, epistemology, logic, and ethics. The consequence has been a self-analysis and soul-searching within philosophy that can best be compared with the upheaval in physics produced by relativity and modern atomic theory. This philosophical upheaval has been so recent that the dust is not yet settled, but the picture is clearer now than when the first positivistic-empiricist attacks of the 1920's and '30's threatened to subvert traditional philosophy completely. Because this movement has produced revolutionary changes in both the procedures and the pretensions of philosophy, it is imperative that even the beginning student understand something of its theories.

[1] The term *logical positivism* is more widely used, although *logical empiricism* is rapidly gaining in usage. Members of this school much prefer the latter term. They argue that "positivism" more accurately describes the early, crude, and extremist days of the movement, rather than its current emphases. After some hesitation I have settled on their choice of terminology, both because I believe that a school like a person has the right to name itself, and because "empiricism" better describes the central concept of this whole movement.

It is not easy to present a brief and necessarily simplified outline of logical empiricist thought. Part of the difficulty comes from the complex issues involved and part from the fact that there are splits and subdivisions within the movement. There are, for example, important differences between the Continental positivists (formerly centered in Vienna but now largely scattered, many to the United States) and the British school, particularly the group known as the Cambridge Analysts. We shall be forced to limit our exposition to some of the concepts which appear fundamental in all logical empiricist thought. This will give the student less than a total picture of this thought, but it should convey something of its astringent flavor and enable him to understand why the whole movement has produced such effect upon contemporary philosophy.

The Basic Mental Attitude. First, what is this attitude of mind, discoverable among some beginning students as well as among some professional philosophers, which impels one toward the extreme of logical empiricism? And why should it be produced particularly by a survey of metaphysical theories? It is perhaps best described as "toughmindedness," but a different type of toughmindedness from that we saw to be basic in naturalism. Whereas the naturalistic type of mental toughness involves an entire world-view or attitude toward the universe and man's prospects in it, the toughness of the logical empiricist is more limited. It is primarily epistemological rather than metaphysical. This puts logical empiricism closer to skepticism than to naturalism, since as we saw in earlier chapters the skeptic formulates a theory of knowledge rather than an inclusive world-view.

The general mental attitude of logical empiricism is most clearly revealed in its theory of meaning—or more precisely, meaningfulness. Known technically as the "verifiability theory of meaning" this view holds that the determination and communication of meaning is absolutely basic, not only in philosophical discourse but in all discourse whatsoever—and not only in discourse but in the acquisition of knowledge. The empiricist insists there can be no knowledge, other than direct sensory experience, until we are certain as to the meaning of all sentences cast in the form of factual statements—that is, all declarative sentences. Certainly there can be no communication of knowledge until meaning has been analyzed and clarified. Hence linguistic and logical analysis is central in logical empiricism. The movement could just as properly be called either "logical analysis" or "analytical empiricism"—in fact almost any combination of the three adjectives "logical," "analytical," and "empirical" would serve to indicate both the goal and the method of this school.

Why Are Metaphysical Problems Insoluble?   Like many other thinkers both inside and outside of philosophy the logical empiricists are disturbed and depressed by the apparent insolubility of most traditional philosophical problems. The metaphysical area has been particularly notorious as a hotbed of persistent problems and century-old controversies which seem as unsettled today as they ever were. During the long history of philosophy there have been skeptics who doubted that these problems could be solved in any real or final sense, but the glory is usually granted to David Hume, writing in the middle of the eighteenth century, for having given this skepticism a truly rigorous intellectual foundation. Hume thus became one of the real founders of today's logical empiricism, which might be described as an extension, refinement, and application of Hume's method.

Hume demanded that all general ideas or concepts be verified by tracing them back to the "impressions" (that is, perceptions) from which they came. If no "impression" could be discovered—if no perceptual experiences were available to establish or disestablish the concept—then he would have none of it. "Into the flames with it!" is his favorite prescription for any abstract idea lacking perceptual parentage, and during his analytical lifetime he consigned a good many of the philosophical and theological concepts then current to the flames of skepticism. Let us see how logical empiricism has taken Hume's test of meaningfulness and greatly elaborated it, particularly in the direction of linguistic analysis.

The Problem of Meaning

The Meaning of "Meaning."   The central problem for logical empiricism is this: What makes a cognitive statement (that is, a declarative sentence) meaningful? How is its meaning established; how is its factuality-claim verified? Any declarative sentence appears to be (and usually claims to be) a statement of fact, but a glance at several such sentences will indicate that there are different degrees or kinds of factuality. (1) "The book is on the table." (2) "I am in great pain." (3) "The universe is the creation of a Supreme Intelligence." (4) "The sum of the angles of a triangle equals 180 degrees." (5) "My love is like a red, red rose." (6) "A potsherd is a fragment of a broken earthen pot." (7) "We are obliged to love our fellowmen." (8) "A socialist is a traitor to his country."

Logical empiricism holds that all cognitive statements whose function is supposedly to convey information fall within one of two groups. Propositions are classifiable on the basis of whether their meaning is (a) formal and purely logical, or (b) factual—that is, strictly empirical. We must fully understand this classification if we are to comprehend logical empiricism, for otherwise the whole movement seems like a prolonged quibble.

(a) Formal Meaning. A statement with formal meaning is one whose truth or falsity is determined solely by its form—that is, either by (1) its relation to an already established logical or syntactical structure of some kind, or (2) by the internal relations of logic within the sentence itself. This second type of formal significance is probably easier to understand, so we will begin with it. Known as a tautology, a sentence of this type has a predicate that merely restates the subject. In framing definitions such restatement is valid; most dictionary definitions are of this kind—for example, sentence number (6) above: "A potsherd is a fragment of a broken earthen pot." Here it is obvious that the predicate says nothing more than is contained in the subject, although the statement may nevertheless be vastly helpful to anyone inquiring the meaning of "potsherd." Any person with much education has little difficulty spotting tautologous phrases ("audible to the ear," "funeral obsequies"), but a complete proposition containing a tautology may slip by undetected. Hence we may think the speaker or writer is saying something meaningful, whereas logical analysis will reveal that he is only making explicit what was implicit in his subject term.

The first class (1) of formal statements are those whose truth or meaning is derived solely from the consistency of the particular sentence with a logical system of some kind. The classical example of this can be found in any mathematical system, which sets up specific postulates or axioms and then derives the rest of the mathematical-logical structure from these. Hence "truth" or "validity" becomes a matter of internal systematic consistency. We discussed formal truth briefly in Chapter 7 under the heading of the coherence theory of truth. It will be recalled that we there pointed out that it is possible to erect intellectual structures, wholly self-consistent, upon postulates which have no basis in experience. This is a possibility which is of utmost concern to logical empiricism, as we shall see shortly.

(b) *Factual Meaning*. The logical empiricist holds that factual meaning is identical with empirical meaning: only statements which are verifiable by observation can be considered factual, and there are no "facts" which are not empirically determined. This central doctrine of logical empiricism constitutes the basis of its famous verifiability theory of meaning. The empiricist requires that for any cognitive statement to have meaning (that is, to escape being nonsensical—and we should remember that the term "nonsense" originally meant "without meaning") it must either express a formal truth as defined above, or else say something that is capable of being confirmed or disaffirmed by observation.

At this point there appears a very real ambiguity which has produced much analysis and controversy within the ranks of the logical empiricists and much misunderstanding on the part of their critics. When the empiricist says that the only factual statements are those that are verifiable through observation, he may mean one or more of three different things. (1) He may intend that the only factual statements are those already confirmed by observation; or (2) he may include those not yet verified but which can be at our convenience whenever confirmation is desired for any purpose; or (3) those which in principle are verifiable in that we know what would be required for verification. This third class includes statements for which we at present lack means, but which conceivably could be confirmed at a later date—for example, statements regarding geographical features on the other side of the moon, or life on other planets.

Some of the first logical empiricists, during the cruder, more positivistic youth of the movement, attempted to restrict the class of "factual" to those statements which had been verified (number 1 above). Even in this early period, however, there were more moderate members of the school who argued for an extension of "factual" to include those propositions for which verifying procedures are available, regardless of whether or not they have actually been employed. As the movement matured and refined its analysis it became apparent that even this limitation was too severe. It seemed particularly drastic because it was widely interpreted to be an unwarranted and presumptuous effort to legislate for science by drawing a sharp distinction between completely verified scientific theories and those only partially confirmed—thus seeming to deny the scientist flexibility and freedom which he needed for drawing tentative conclusions indispensable to his further progress.

In its present more mature state logical empiricism includes condition number 3 as a valid determination of "factual." Even though the practical difficulties to verification of a statement appear permanently insurmountable, it may yet qualify as meaningful if we at least know what would constitute verification. If a conceivable empirical situation exists, however undiscoverable it may still be as an actuality, then the sentence is not nonsensical. If on the contrary its character is such that no possible observation would have bearing upon its truth or falsity, then it is nonsense —however impressive it may be as rhetoric, metaphysics, or theology.

It must be emphasized that the empiricist restricts condition number 3 with some very explicit checks, lest much of what he has thrown out the epistemological door be smuggled back in through the metaphysical window. On paper the requirement that for a statement to be meaningful it need only be "in principle confirmable" or "theoretically verifiable" or "conceivable" appears to include nearly any declarative sentence that is not obvious nonsense by the rules of semantics and syntax (as would be a proposition like "Hard is the sum of red"). But logical empiricism would quickly have lost its reputation for epistemological toughmindedness if it had not imposed firm checks. The safeguards set up to control theoretical verifiability are such that logical empiricism in the mid-twentieth century, if less crude than earlier empiricism, is no less skeptical and no less destructive of metaphysical and theological pretensions.

Types of Verifiability

The Restrictions on Verifiability. The safeguards protecting the empirical criterion of verifiability are not difficult to understand, regardless of whether or not we think they are warranted. First, when we say a sentence must be "in principle verifiable" what we really mean (if we are logical empiricists) is that we must know the conditions under which it would be confirmed. There must be some reduction or transformation procedure available which will enable us to translate words into actions, concepts into concrete situations, and thus permit us to specify exactly what will constitute proof or disproof of any statement. If the statement cannot meet requirements number 1 or 2 (that is, either have been already verified or be capable of verification whenever need arises), then, if it is to be meaningful, some testing operation must be conceivable, even if we cannot now construct the actual test situation. The statement must, in short, be of such a character that testable differences would be discoverable if it were true, as against its being false.

Here the logical empiricist invokes a principle formulated in 1878 by the American mathematician-logician, C. S. Peirce. Peirce's epoch-making essay entitled "How to Make Our Ideas Clear" became the starting point of pragmatism and one of the foundations of both logical empiricism and its epistemological cousin, operationalism. Peirce insisted that for a statement to have meaning it must imply a difference: it must assert something that will *make* a difference. If the sentence is such that its assertion or denial contains an implied difference capable of being established observationally, then it is meaningful—and only then. If on the contrary no observed difference will follow regardless of whether it is true or false, then whatever else the statement may be (poetry, inspiration, exhortation, etc.) it is factually meaningless and hence cognitive nonsense.

A. G. Ramsperger gives an excellent example of this "difference must make a difference" test applied to one type of metaphysical utterance.

> If a Hegel tells us that "The eternal Idea, in full fruition of its essence, eternally sets itself to work, engenders and enjoys itself as absolute mind," he apparently intends to assert a fact. He should be able, then, to say what this means by translating it into sentences which refer to some observable state of affairs which would be evidence for its truth. Perhaps the defender of Hegel will claim that this statement can be given an interpretation that will meet this demand, but more likely he will argue that there are metaphysical existences which are not to be known by any empirical means. The only answer to this is to ask him what he means by saying that his metaphysical propositions are true rather than false.[2]

The prime question which a logical empiricist asks regarding any statement, before he considers whether it may be true or false, is simply

2 A. G. Ramsperger, *Philosophies of Sciences*, p. 108.

"What does it mean?" And to this question he requires an answer which tells how the truth or falsity of the statement can be determined. Logical empiricism is unique among the philosophical schools in that its members do not spend their time trying to show members of rival schools that they are wrong; instead they mostly are content to show their rivals that their statements are meaningless because they are untestable by any conceivable procedure of observation or experimentation. This constant demand for verifiable meanings in metaphysical propositions has not made logical empiricists popular with their philosophical fellows. It is irritating enough to be told by a philosophical opponent that your statements are erroneous, but to be told that they are meaningless and really nonsense is worse than irritating!

Direct and Indirect Evidence. At this point the thoughtful student may raise a significant question: Does all scientific knowledge meet this stiff test of meaningfulness which the empiricist tries to set up? Or is this an impossible epistemological ideal, too rigorous for even science's exacting requirements? What about some of the remote and extremely indirect testing processes utilized by science to verify its explanatory hypotheses? For example, what can observation, in the ordinary sense of that term, tell us about atomic structure? Has not scientific knowledge become too complicated and its research techniques too refined to be regarded as based upon strictly empirical foundations? And what about the ever-increasing use of mathematics in science: are not scientific proofs now largely cast in the form of equations, often enormously complex and involving hundreds of steps in mathematico-logical reasoning?

Logical empiricism is quite aware that a large proportion of scientific research, particularly in the physical sciences, is carried on at a desk or blackboard rather than amid the array of apparatus we usually find in a laboratory. The empiricist is also aware that the percentage of paper work in scientific experiment (in which paper work means mostly mathematical calculation) seems to rise steadily as a science becomes more advanced and its procedures more refined. But the empiricist knows that *all* scientific research and experimentation, however involved its mathematical processes may be and however indirect and devious its experimental techniques, *must both begin and end with observation.* Starting with observed facts, the researcher may wander for months, perhaps even years, through a wilderness of formulas and mathematical reasoning-chains. But, no matter how prolonged and roundabout his intellectual nonobservational journey may be, he must come back home at last to the realm of nature *as observable*, in contradistinction to nature as reasoned about. Unless this return trip back to the home base of observation is made (often in the form of a crucial experiment) we do not have science.

Logical empiricism points out the glaring contrast in this regard between science on one hand and metaphysics and theology on the other. Metaphysicians and theologians likewise begin their intellectual activities with observation. This is of course more generalized observation than science employs, since it is usually the whole cosmos and man's experience in the cosmos that provides the basis for their search for inclusive explanatory world-hypotheses. Unlike the scientist, however, these other intellectual explanation-seekers are not able to make a satisfactory return trip to the realm of empirical data. In short, the metaphysician or theologian cannot construct experiments which will test his explanatory hypothesis regarding the character of nature, Reality, human destiny, and so on. His hypothesis (say a pluralistic one) may be contradictory to some opponent's (for example, a monist's). Hence both cannot be true: there is clearly a difference here of the kind Peirce had in mind. But how does —in fact, how can—this seeming difference *make* a real difference? What in our experience will be changed if one view is correct and the other false? What will occur differently, what will be changed? Admittedly our feelings may be altered if we accept one view or the other, but what in the common objective world which we all share will be affected in any manner? Would things behave any differently in a proved pluralistic universe than in a verified monistic one? Would the cosmos and human history be altered if we could finally establish beyond doubt either theism or atheism? Clearly not, as proved by the fact that these competing metaphysical-theological views have been produced by the same set of historical facts and the same body of cumulative human knowledge; if it is possible to have contradictory intellectual systems explaining the same observed facts, then (argues logical empiricism) obviously the explanations are meaningless. Since they *make* no difference, any apparent difference between them is purely verbal or illusory.

The Crucial Experiment and Its Significance. The crucial experiments of science are expressly designed to prove one hypothesis and disprove its rival or rivals. This definitive situation is attained by a deductive step in the total chain of scientific reasoning. In this step, anticipated consequences are prescribed in advance; the consequences are ones which can occur only if the hypothesis in question is true and the alternative hypothesis false. As he sets up his experiment the scientist is saying (at least by implication) essentially this: "Our cumulative knowledge of this field makes us certain that the properties of the phenomena in question are such that only one thing can happen when we take our final step, if our hypothesis is true. We (or our scientific predecessors) have eliminated all the remaining possibilities, so our last experimental step must show a difference one way or the other and thus give us a clear-cut yes-or-no answer."

The logical empiricist points to such experimental situations as perfect examples of how to satisfy Peirce's requirement that a difference must make a difference. Furthermore he cites these as ideal instances of what makes a statement true or false, for a crucial test leaves no doubt, and one of the rival hypotheses is eliminated. In metaphysics and theology, however, it is impossible to discover which of the several views is true or false because none of them makes any real difference. Each provides its supporters with emotional satisfaction, peace of mind, intellectual assurance and orientation, but this subjective difference does not make it true or meaningful in any universal or objective sense. In view of this lack of difference in actual observable consequences, the logical empiricist asks what we mean when we claim that one metaphysical-theological statement is true and the other false. Since both are equally unconfirmable, any proposition deriving from them is likewise unverifiable, and hence in the final analysis meaningless.

This then is the outcome of the logical empiricist's analysis of metaphysical truth claims. Starting with his verifiability theory of meaning, he is logically compelled to reject both metaphysics and theology as meaningless. If the only significant cognitive statements are those which are either formally valid or factual, the propositions of the metaphysician and theologian lack significance. A brief quotation from one of the best-known British empiricists summarizes this point of view.

> We may accordingly define a metaphysical sentence as a sentence which purports to express a genuine proposition, but does, in fact, express neither a tautology nor an empirical hypothesis. And as tautologies and empirical hypotheses form the entire class of significant propo-

sitions, we are justified in concluding that all metaphysical propositions are nonsensical.[3]

The Implications of Logical Empiricism

Does this celebrated rejection of metaphysics by logical empiricists mean that they advocate the abandonment of all philosophical activity and the relegation of existent philosophical systems to museums as historical curiosities? Would they close the schools of philosophy as the Emperor Justinian did those of ancient Greece in 529 A.D., putting the philosophers to more practical and presumably more useful tasks? What would be the future of philosophy under a logical-empiricist dictator?

The Future of Philosophy. In drawing up a program for the future of philosophy the logical empiricist makes a distinction between what he considers its valid and invalid functions. The former he of course believes can and should continue, but he sternly eliminates the remainder. These invalid functions he opposes are deductive and synoptic. Those which are deductive constitute an effort to deduce a system of Reality from "first principles" or "a priori postulates," as rationalistic metaphysicians (for example, Descartes, Hegel) have done. The inductive functions involve the attempt to put together an inclusive world-view by synthesizing human experience in the jigsaw-puzzle manner we have often mentioned in preceding chapters. The empiricist naturally has more sympathy with such inductive efforts (since they at least start with empirical data) than he has with the deductive-rationalistic attempts of thinkers like Hegel. But, since even the inductive world-view necessarily requires us to go well beyond empirical limits and formulate generalizations which cannot possibly be put to observational test, induced metaphysical propositions are in the final analysis as devoid of verifiable meaning as the rationalist's. In sum, logical empiricism would purge philosophy of all metaphysical activity whatever, both deductive and inductive.

This means that philosophy, as defined and defended by the logical empiricist, is exclusively analytic and logical in character. It is not a theory or a system but an activity—namely, the clarification of thought. This clarification is carried on by the logical, semantical, and syntactical

[3] A. J. Ayer, *Language, Truth and Logic*, p. 41.

analysis of propositions, and the formulation of rules for the transformation (that is, translation) of meaningful statements into other meaningful statements. This theoretically requires the creation of an ideal language, so logical empiricists have been extremely active in the development of modern systems of logic which have this ideal as their goal.

But what do we mean when we speak of "the syntactical analysis of propositions" or "the formulation of transformation rules"? This is best answered by examining the empiricist's view concerning the proper relation which should exist between philosophy and science, so let us turn to this. According to logical empiricism, philosophy should be the theory or logic of science—that is, the logical analysis of the concepts, propositions, proofs, and theories of science. The basic task of the scientist is the formulation and verification of hypotheses; the complementary and no less productive task of philosophy is to reveal the logical relationships of these hypotheses to one another and to define the symbols which they employ. This recalls our discussion in Chapter 2, where we described philosophy's chief contribution to science as an analysis of its concepts and terminologies.

The nature of this complementary activity makes it impossible for the philosopher (as licensed by logical empiricism) to compete with the scientist, much less to contradict him. For science is occupied with the behavior of things, and its statements concerning this behavior are empirical propositions which refer directly or indirectly to observations of the physical world. The statements of philosophy, on the contrary, are not empirical: they are linguistic and logical. A. J. Ayer summarizes the difference thus:

> In other words, the propositions of philosophy are not factual, but linguistic in character—that is, they do not describe the behavior of physical, or even mental, objects; they express definitions, or the formal consequences of definitions. Accordingly, we may say that philosophy is a department of logic. For we shall see that the characteristic mark of a purely logical enquiry is that it is concerned with the formal consequences of our definitions and not with questions of empirical fact.[4]

Does Logical Empiricism Imply Materialism? There is a second major implication of logical empiricism which must be considered, although members of the school and their critics are not in agreement

---

[4] *Op. cit.,* p. 57.

regarding it. Briefly it is this: if the empiricist requires that all meaningful statements be capable of observational verification, is he not, despite all his disclaimers of metaphysical doctrine, implying a metaphysical theory, that of materialism? While he rarely says so, there can be no doubt that his requirement of empirical verification means sensory confirmation. And since our senses respond only to physical phenomena, does this not necessarily make empiricism's criterion of reality (or "significance" or "meaningfulness") material in character? In short, does not logical empiricism by implication postulate a world-view which, however refined, analytical, and epistemologically sophisticated it may be, is still at bottom the same materialism that was so popular among scientists and radical philosophers during the nineteenth century?

While it is almost impossible to catch an empiricist sufficiently off guard for him to admit there are metaphysical implications in the verifiability theory of meaning, some leading members of the school have been willing to espouse a viewpoint they call *physicalism*. However, this too they much prefer to present only as a theory of linguistics and communication, which makes it appear epistemological rather than metaphysical. Unfortunately the concept of physicalism is tied closely to logical empiricism's great goal, the unity of science, so we must complicate our exposition by considering both at once.

Physicalism and the Unity of Science. The logical empiricists early announced that their major aim was to secure a firm intellectual foundation for science. Furthermore they expected this secure foundation (to be achieved through the logical analysis of all propositions and concepts, both those of the sciences and those of everyday speech) to produce the outline of a unified science. By unified science, the empiricist means primarily an inclusive system of concepts and terms which are common to all the various sciences but not specific to only one or two of them. This would in effect be a universal language of science that would permit us to combine statements from the different fields into meaningful propositions. Otto Neurath, one of the founders of contemporary empiricism, gives an example of what he considers the obvious need for such a system, which will enable us to move freely over the whole domain of scientific knowledge.

> The universal language of science becomes a self-evident demand,
> if it is asked, how can certain singular predictions be derived; e.g.,

"the forest fire will soon subside." In order to do this we need meteorological and botanical sentences and in addition sentences which contain the terms "man" and "human behavior." We must speak of how people react to fire, which social institutions will come into play. Thus, we need sentences from psychology and sociology. They must be able to be placed together with others in a deduction at whose end is the sentence: "Therefore, the forest fire will soon subside."[5]

This means that logical empiricism is trying to formulate a system of communication which will actually make "science" out of what are now only the many "sciences." It is true that we now freely use the term "science" as though we already had a unified system of thought and knowledge. But as every scientist (i.e., every worker in a particular scientific field) is well aware, there is as yet no such integrated structure. The contemporary empiricist feels that there can be no inclusive science until an adequate means of intercommunication between the particular fields has been formulated. We must have a common linguistic—which means a common logic and set of symbols—that will enable us whenever necessary to connect all types of laws with one another as components of one single system.

But what would be the character of such a universal language for a unified science? The logical empiricist believes it cannot be purely mathematical, regardless of how useful mathematics may be as a scientific tool. Instead he believes ,it must be a refinement of the language we already have which we all use in everyday situations. This is the thing-language we employ in physics, engineering and daily life whenever we discuss physical things. Starting with this ready-made but often carelessly-used language, the task then is to work out the rules of formation and transformation of this language in order that all propositions and concepts can be expressed in it. The aim here as always in the unification of science is to reduce the number of deductive systems to the minimum—ideally to a single system. Rudolph Carnap, perhaps the best-known member of the movement, writes as follows concerning this point:

> In our discussions . . . we have arrived at the opinion that this physical language is the basic language of all science, that it is the universal language comprehending the contents of all other scientific languages. In other words, every sentence of any branch of scientific

[5] Quoted by Joergen Joergensen in *International Encyclopedia of Unified Science*, Vol. II, No. 9, pp. 76-77.

language is equipollent to some sentence of the physical language, and can therefore be translated into the physical language without changing its content.[6]

Logical empiricism holds that this thing-language has three characteristics, each of which is required for an adequate means of communication in unified science. It will be necessary to limit ourselves to a brief statement of these qualities, but even if we do little more than define them, the nature of the empiricist's aim becomes clear. We will also be able to understand why only a physicalistic language can fulfil these requirements.

The language of unified science as formulated by logical empiricism is (a) intersensual, (b) intersubjective, and (c) universal. *Intersensual* means that statements in this language can be tested by more than one of our senses. This is important, because in science we find it necessary to coordinate qualities from different sensory spheres. Perhaps most often it is visual and tactile data that require coordination, although the visual-auditory combination is scarcely less important to the attainment of knowledge. Hence the ideal scientific language must be capable of expressing such coordination by translating one sense quality into another in the same way that an oscilloscope converts sound waves into an image on a screen. When we use the oscilloscope we are seeking (in terms of an intersensual language) to coordinate the phrase "a tone of such and such pitch, timbre and loudness" with a phrase in the physical language: "material oscillation of such and such basic frequency with such and such harmonic frequencies with such and such amplitudes."[7] We then verify this linguistic coordination empirically by converting sound to sight via the oscilloscope.

Intersubjective, in the language of logical empiricism, means objective—that is, the statement in question can be tested by several subjects (persons). In science this requirement is so basic that it hardly needs comment. Indeed it is usually agreed that objectivity is the essence of scientific knowledge. Unless the data and the conclusions drawn from this data are shareable, and unless the experiment can be repeated by all competent workers in the field with the same results, we do not have science. Hence obviously any language that does not provide complete

[6] Rudolph Carnap, *Philosophy and Logical Syntax,* p. 89.
[7] Cf. Joergensen, *op. cit.,* p. 78.

intersubjective communication cannot qualify as an adequate language of science.

Universal means simply that the language is such that every factual (that is, empirically testable) statement can be translated into it. This includes both scientific propositions and factual statements from everyday experience, as well as any combination of the two. Here again logical empiricism maintains that only the thing-language of the physical world can qualify as truly universal.

Logical Behaviorism. It is plain that considerable ingenuity is necessary if all the concepts of psychology and the social sciences are to be translated into this physical language. So far as mental phenomena of all kinds are concerned, the empiricist is fortunate to have the path broken by behavioristic psychology. Behaviorism is that psychological school which attempts to bypass consciousness and other purely mental phenomena by studying the behavior of subjects, rather than their thinking, feeling, dreaming, or remembering. More precisely, behaviorism holds that the only way psychology can be scientific is to limit its subject-matter to what can be intersubjectively observed. This of course means overt behavior or action, including speech and other symbol-using activity. Therefore the behaviorist studies his human subjects by the same method the animal psychologist does his animal subjects—namely, by putting them in observable behavior situations and recording their reactions.

The logical empiricist argues (as does the behaviorist) that the only significant thing about any subject, human or animal, is in the last analysis its actual behavior. Thinking, feeling, and the like have significance only as they lead to action of some kind. And, since this action is all that can be observed, and therefore all that can be treated scientifically, we must abandon efforts to probe the psyche or study the "mind" as an entity separate from the body and its reactions.

Empiricism would extend this same behavioristic approach to all the so-called "nonphysical" sciences. Under the suggested name of *logical behaviorism* this extension would constitute an important part of the unification of science. In fact it is difficult to see how an integration of physical, biological, psychological, and social sciences can be attained except by a broad extension of the behavioristic method.

The logical empiricist has no rosy hope that such unification will come soon or easily, but he is confident that it will be possible to reduce the total number of separate concepts now required by the various sciences. There has been considerable progress in this direction, particularly by what used to be the hyphenated sciences: psychophysics, biochemistry, biophysics, social psychology, and the rest. The empiricist feels that while scientist search out the data which will give significance to this integration, he meantime is doing an important preparatory job by developing a unified language and a common logic which will be the indispensable tools of any genuinely inclusive and unified science.

Metaphysics vs. Empiricism: Is a Solution Possible?

It will be remarkable if, as we reach the end of these three chapters on matters metaphysical, the student is not somewhat confused. Our survey of the controversies that separate monists, dualists, and pluralists from one another was undoubtedly confusing enough; but then to be told in the present chapter that all such controversies, as well as the concepts around which they center, are meaningless must seem to the student to add insult to injury! The student may wish we had considered logical empiricism first, since this would perhaps have rendered the other chapters on metaphysics unnecessary.

At first glance it may appear that we are faced with a choice: either we agree with the empiricist and reject metaphysics, or we reject logical empiricism. There are thinkers among both the empiricists and their opponents who insist that the alternatives are this simple and clear-cut. Many men from both camps have been willing to take one step or the other, insisting that no compromise is possible.

The present author does not believe that the alternatives are so stark and mutually exclusive as they have been pictured, and he consequently finds no necessity in making an all-or-none choice between them. While it is true that no one who values his intellectual self-respect can ignore logical empiricism and the whole positivistic movement it sums up, this does not require us to go to the other extreme and accept uncritically the empiricist's total rejection of metaphysics.

When logical empiricism first began to establish itself as a movement during the 1920's, it was possible to dismiss it as a philosophical flash in the pan, perhaps as a by-product of the skepticism and disillusionment following World War I, or as an excessive intoxication with the achievements of modern science. Such easy dismissal is no longer possible; the movement is now in its second generation, and its hold upon younger thinkers in both Europe and America is tremendous. A roll call of the empiricists among philosophers now active or just recently deceased would include perhaps a third of the significant contemporary philosophers, whereas an extension of the roll call into the past would include such giants as Hume and (in some of his thinking) Kant. Although there have been schools of skepticism and rigorous analysis in the past that seemed subversive to established philosophies, the situation with logical empiricism is quite different from that of earlier movements with which it might be compared. The contemporary movement is far more closely reasoned than were its predecessors, and has far closer affiliations with science. Then too the development of semantics, the newer logics, and changes in mathematics have provided it with analytical tools far sharper than any formerly available.

One thing which has given logical empiricism growing strength has been its skill at self-correction. This has permitted it to avoid the death-trap of so many extreme movements: a tendency to become increasingly extreme—to crawl farther and farther out on an intellectual limb, as it were—until only fanatics and blind partisans could remain affiliated with the movement in question. Contemporary empiricism has moved in the opposite direction, eliminating early reductive excesses and crudities and constantly broadening its base. This has enabled it to enlarge its membership and its influence, thus making it increasingly more imperative for other schools to come to some sort of terms with it. As a trend rather than as a body of completed thought, this positivistic empiricism now appears to be a permanent addition to the philosophical family which other members have got to live with whether they might want to or not.

Must Metaphysics Be Eliminated? And what about the other alternative, involving the rejection of all metaphysical speculation as meaningless? Frequently metaphysical activity is defended on the grounds that it is traditional—that it has always been a central part of philosophical thought. From this it is usually argued that it would be more honest intellectually to abandon the term "philosophy" entirely if metaphysics is to be outlawed.

The traditionalistic argument is not usually one that appeals to Americans, particularly young Americans, most of whom would probably argue that if a venerable institution like philosophy and a traditional activity like metaphysical speculation have lost their value they should be junked. But even if we agree with this common American attitude that a valueless thing should be discarded (and the present author does agree) this hardly solves the problem. I would argue that metaphysics is here to stay, despite all the brilliance of the empirical attack, for the Aristotelian reason we have quoted frequently in earlier chapters: whether we will meta-physicize (to slightly alter Aristotle's original) or whether we won't, we must all be metaphysicians of a sort. We may be able to avoid some of the subtleties and involvements of traditional metaphysical thinking, but we cannot avoid having a view of the character of the world we inhabit. We may be able to avoid using the term "Reality" (with a capital letter or without) and refuse to spend time discussing its theoretical character; but we cannot escape acting as though certain things—that is, certain aspects of our world—are more real to us (and certainly more significant) than others. To do this, however, is to imply a metaphysical position of some kind, "whether we will or not." The most consistent logical empiricist has never persuaded anyone except perhaps his fellow empiricists that he succeeds completely in avoiding a metaphysical viewpoint.

A Possible Solution. The solution to this issue would seem to be to acknowledge the inevitability of metaphysical activity but to cut systematic metaphysics down to size, so to speak. This can be done by refusing to honor any claims a presumptuous metaphysician may make that he establishes truth or asserts fact in the sense that science does. We must also sternly reject any pretension metaphysics may parade regarding the certainty of its statements, together with any demand that we judge its propositions by a transempirical "higher" logic that differs from the logic we employ for other areas of discourse. We must, in short, persuade a thinker whose interests are synoptic rather than analytic to accept the same epistemological status for his world-view that we allow to the poet's or novelist's or artist's view of reality. We are warranted in regarding a metaphysical system as essentially a work of art—more intellectual, of course, than most art creations, and certainly more dependent on logic and close reasoning, but still at bottom a personal interpretation of human experience which is no less subjective than the artist's. Like a major art work, such a system may have universal significance and carry great conviction. We thus can honor the metaphysician for his insights, his creative power, and his skill as an intellectual architect. But we need not (and the study of logical empiricism seems to me to prove we cannot) accept his truth-claims as we accept those of the scientist.

Does this make metaphysical statements meaningless? It obviously does if we limit meaningfulness to that which can be empirically verified. But it also puts the metaphysician in some rather distinguished company, since the writings of literary artists and religious thinkers are similarly meaningless. However, since the majority of the population continue to find these nonverifiable statements very meaningful, the logical empiricist seems to be in the position of a man trying to drink the sea dry. He is of course quite within his linguistic rights when he chooses to define meaning exclusively in terms of empirical verification, but he is certainly in a minority.

In conclusion it seems clear that we should be grateful to the logical empiricist for having forged us a potent weapon to free ourselves from the frequently excessive truth-claims of both metaphysicians and theologians. We should also, I believe, be grateful for his healthy reminder that scientific knowledge is the most reliable knowledge we can attain—in fact, that it is in a class apart so far as concerns allowable knowledge-claims. But since metaphysical speculation is an apparently permanent aspect of human nature, it would seem wiser to acknowledge the tendency and keep it disciplined by criticism and analysis (particularly linguistic analysis, which the logical empiricist performs magnificently), rather than trying to eradicate the ineradicable. I for one see no more reason why metaphysics should be banned from the good society than why poetry and art should be banned. But I also see no reason why the formulators of metaphysical and theological systems should be allowed to pretend that, because they deal in generalities and make declarative statements that are linguistically identical with those of science, they should be accorded the same epistemological honor we pay the scientist. From this delusion, and the dogmatism it has frequently produced, the empiricist has helped to deliver us, and this is no small contribution.

CHAPTER 12

ETHICS:

What Shall We Do Meanwhile?

T HERE ARE TWO POSSIBLE WAYS TO REGARD PHILOSOPHY: AS
detached intellectual activity or as a guide to life. The former
attitude has many advantages to recommend it. If we approach
the subject in this manner we are less likely to take our search,
our answers, or ourselves too seriously; we can be more impersonal and
disinterested in our intellectual analyses and regard them more as the
scientist views his problems in the laboratory. Carrying on our quest in
this more disinterested manner, we are more likely to reach conclusions
that conform to the actual nature of things than if we make philosophy
a substitute for religion and look at it as a guide for life. If we approach
philosophy from the second point of view, there is always the possibility
that our hopes and fears will color our picture of the reality. Our hearts
are likely to interfere with our heads, and when we have completed our
world-view the result may be nothing but a projection of our human
nature, with its characteristic strengths and weaknesses, upon the screen
of the universe.

Without attempting to judge these two approaches, we must point
out that their contrasting attitudes leads each approach to choose a different subdivision within philosophy as the focal point of its intellectual
efforts. If we view philosophy primarily as a theoretical activity, we will
probably direct our thinking to the epistemological-metaphysical problem.
On the other hand, the guide-for-life school focuses its thought largely
upon the ethical problem: What is the Good Life? This school considers
the metaphysical search of little value unless it results in a "philosophy

of life"—that is, a definite ethical system of some sort. In contrast, those who are playing the intellectual game for the satisfaction it offers in itself regard ethics as subordinate to epistemology and metaphysics. They are thus likely to hold that the significance of any ethical system depends upon the validity of the metaphysical position which underlies it.

We have already presented enough elements of metaphysics and epistemology in earlier chapters to give the student who prefers to regard philosophy as an intellectual pastime ample materials for his theoretical activity. In this chapter and the next two we shall side with the ethical-minded group and hold with them that the chief purpose of philosophy is to shed light on our road as we search for the Good Life.

The Problem of the Good

The complexities within the field of ethics are notable. Not only are there many opposing points of view, but we also find many different categories, divergent lines of cleavage, and seemingly unrelated frames of reference. Thus it is often difficult to classify the various positions, or to compare them with one another. We may meet views that have no apparent relation to each other, in that they neither oppose nor supplement one another. Even our old landmarks, idealism and naturalism, offer less guidance through this territory than we have come to expect from them.

In part this confusion arises from a division within ethics that is fundamental, but difficult either to describe or to maintain. On the one hand ethics can be regarded as a subdivision of the systematic study of *value*. In this case our basic problem is, What is the nature of the Good? On the other hand, we can consider ethics to be the study of *obligation*, which would make our fundamental issue the nature and the source of "duty." The two chapters we are now beginning will constitute an analysis of these two questions, together with the principal answers to each. As a preliminary to this analysis, it will be necessary for us to see the major implications of each of these questions.

The Two Main Problems Within Ethics. It seems evident that the first of these alternate approaches to ethics, which begins with the idea of *value*, will be concerned with discovering what is to be *sought*—that is, what is *good* or what has *value*. It will study the goals or ideal ends of conduct. In contrast, an approach to ethics through the theory of *obligation* will be concerned with the problem of what is to be *done*— that is, how should we go about realizing this "good" or "value"? While this second problem appears more immediately practical than the first, and consequently usually impresses the layman as far more important, the philosopher is likely to have a strong preference for the first, the search for the Good. For, he argues, how can we know what should be done until we have determined what it is that we are seeking? Are not *ends* more important than *means*? Since in ethics the ends under discussion are the ultimate goals of human life, what problem could be more practical than the one which concerns the theory of values? In the last analysis, the ethical thinker asks two questions: *What* are we living for? and, *How* should we live? Naturally these overlap, but the sharper the demarcation between them, the clearer our analysis will be.

When we make value judgments, we are engaging in one of mankind's most regular and most important intellectual activities. While we may not consciously hold any of the several theories of value which will be described shortly, there is hardly a waking moment of our lives that does not find us engaged in either making such a judgment or doing something to realize one that we have already made. Most of the decisions in our lives, including the trivial decisions, represent either expressed or implied judgments of value; most decisions are based upon our judgments that certain things are good or bad, desirable or undesirable. Even when we use the principal term of evaluation, "good," in such divergent ways as "Justice is good" and "I was at a good party last night," its normative or evaluative implications are still present. Hence, why the philosopher should be so much occupied with the problem of the Good is not a mystery.

The Nature of Obligation: Two Views. We have described the problem of obligation as appearing to be more immediately practical than the question of the Good, but the whole concept of obligation is more difficult than the newcomer to philosophy would suspect. If by "obligation" or "ought" we mean only a conditional situation, there is no particular difficulty involved. That is, if we mean only that *if* you want to achieve certain ends, then you *ought* to do such-and-such, we have a simple practical problem of ends and means. Often, however, we use the word "ought" in an unconditional sense: we say, "You ought to do your duty!"—not just because you want social approval, or an easy conscience, or a raise in pay, but solely as a matter of ethical obligation. Further, you ought to do it regardless of any personal advantages or disadvantages that may be expected to result.

When obligation is asserted in this unconditional, absolute sense, we immediately involve some of the thorniest issues in philosophy. The skeptic can always ask, "*Why* should I do my duty, particularly when it is not convenient for me to do so?" For the philosopher, it is not enough to answer, "You just *ought*, that is all." Eventually a thinking person must face the most difficult of all ethical problems: whence comes the force of moral obligation—or, as it is sometimes phrased, whence comes the "oughtness" of ought? Any obligation involves the necessity of someone doing something. What is the source of this necessity?

In this chapter and the next we shall be concerned with these various aspects of the ethical problem. As we proceed, we must try to remember that, regardless of how complex the issues or how theoretical the discussion, we shall be attempting to answer the most important, most fundamental, and most inclusive practical human problem: What is the Good Life? It is unfortunate that the significance of the question cannot be matched by a simplicity of answer. But as the issue involved is nothing less than the problem of what we should do with our lives, it is hardly to be expected that a single easy answer will be found.

What Status Does "Good" Have in the Universe?

The first great controversy involving the problem of "good" or "value" concerns its status: does "good" have an objective, absolute existence? Is there Good with a capital "G" so to speak, or is it always relative to the preference or satisfaction of some individual? Are there value judgments which are universal, valid for all men everywhere? Is there anything which all human beings regardless of time, place, race, or culture unite to call "good"? Or does each person, in the final analysis, have an individual and perhaps unique system of values? Each person appears to decide, consciously or unconsciously, what he considers of value in the world and what he will spend his life trying to attain. Are there any objective standards by which we can judge this system of values that his actions imply? Or is his bald statement, "I find X to be good," the last word that can be said on the matter?

The Traditional View.   The belief that values are objective, existing outside our minds as part of the universe, has been the dominant view in Western thought. We shall therefore consider it first. The advocates of this position begin the argument by pointing out that some values do appear to exist for all persons; however much these values may vary at first, as training and critical reflection increase they are brought nearer and nearer to a common norm. Persons of a comparable level of culture or civilization are in substantial agreement as to what actions are good and what things are valuable, even though they may live on opposite sides of the earth or in different centuries. Second, there is frequently more implied agreement underlying the surface differences than many persons realize. As an illustration of this,[1] the headhunters of Borneo would seem to have a moral code that completely contradicts that of a Quaker. But if the savage reflected as to why the slaying of his enemy is "good," he would almost certainly come to realize that its value depends upon the fact that this act helps to maintain a strong tribal unity, which primitive conditions of life usually demand. Such an act is thus a contribution to the common good of the group, since it realizes some such ethical principle as "Tribal welfare is good." The Quaker would judge the same specific act to be bad, but the ground or principle of his judgment would be the same—namely, the welfare of the community. The difference clearly lies in the extent or scope of the concept "community." For the savage it means a small tribe, while for the Quaker or internationalist it may be the whole race. Thus the two judgments imply a single common *ethical* ground, however different the *sociological* ground may be. Both locate value in the common welfare, and both strive to advance it.

The defender of the objective theory of value believes that sufficient analysis will reveal a similar identity of ethical principles underlying all divergencies of conduct. Josiah Royce, probably the most eminent idealist America has produced, advocates a "philosophy of loyalty," in which supreme tribute is paid to all loyalty, regardless of the object of this devotion. "Be loyal to loyalty" was for Royce a supreme ethical command. Such a view represents one attempt to lay bare the universal or objective standard of evaluation.

[1] Borrowed from Urban, *Fundamentals of Ethics,* who in turn borrows it from Sorley, *Moral Values and the Idea of God.*

The objective theory of value holds that "good" is inherent in certain objects or situations, and that we esteem or desire these because of the appeal they have for us.[2] Such a doctrine would make all judgments of value primarily a description of what we discover in objects or situations, and value itself becomes a quality which attracts our preference or demands our appreciation. Thus a value judgment is fundamentally a description of the nature of things—that is, of reality itself. In this way the objective theory ties ethics (and esthetics) very closely to metaphysics: the good is intimately related to the real. In such a view the good and the real may even be identical.

The Subjective View. The *subjective* view of value, which is closely related to the doctrine of relativism, holds that variations in value judgment from person to person and from age to age are profound and greatly significant. For, psychologically speaking, all value appears to come from *satisfaction:* we call "good" or "valuable" or "desirable" whatever satisfies a need or promotes an interest. Those things which best satisfy a need, or which satisfy one of our strongest needs, possess the most value. As a corollary to this, whenever an object or a situation loses its ability to satisfy us, it also ceases to have value. Our day-by-day experience is constant proof of this shift of "value" from one object to another, from an old love to a new. William James speaks of "the expulsive power of a new affection," and one of America's first important poets, Philip Freneau (1752-1832) has described the universal human experience thus:

> The object of our fancied joys
> With eager eyes we keep in view:
> Possession, when acquired, destroys
> The object, and the passion too.
>
> The hat that hid Belinda's hair
> Was once the darling of her eye;
> 'Tis now dismiss'd, she knows not where;
> Is laid aside, she knows not why.

All this the subjectivist takes as evidence that values have existence only in our minds; a value judgment is not a description of inherent

[2] This would also be true of esthetic values, as we shall see in a later chapter. In this case beauty is held to inhere in the object itself, and as a consequence we can formulate objective standards of beauty in the same way that we can establish objective norms of the good.

qualities of goodness or desirability in objects (and certainly not a description of the objective Real), but only a statement of *preference*. And, in the last analysis, this preference is always a personal one. It is a declaration of what *I* like, what *I* find good, what satisfies *my* desire or interest. And even in this realm of personal preference our judgments are changing constantly. One does not need to be a cynic to hold that all our value judgments not only express a personal preference, but represent a preference strictly of the moment, subject to change without notice. Any "good" is necessarily an experience for some individual, and when a group of persons agree concerning the value of any experience, we still have only a group of *individual* experiences which are judged to be good. Thus, instead of defining value as something inherent in objects or situations, the subjectivist would define it as whatever satisfies a desire, a need or an interest.

Is There an Absolute Good?

Closely related to this argument between the objective and the subjective theories of value is the conflict between absolute and relativistic standards of the good. Historically this second controversy has been more important than the first, since it is closely related to legal and political theory, as well as to religious thought. Since absolutism has been the "official" view of Western civilization throughout most of its history, and since the growing relativism of our own day is plainly a revolt against this traditional view, we shall consider it first. Although the battle between absolutism and relativism extends to all types of value judgments, we shall here limit our discussion to the ethical realm.

The Absolutistic Argument. Stated briefly, the absolutist holds that there exists only one standard (in the case of morality, one single "code") that is eternally true, and that is valid for all mankind. Not only is this single standard universal in validity, but it is also independent of epoch, geographical location, ordinary social conventions, legal practices, or anything else. What is an obligation for me here and now is likewise an obligation for a Chinese, a Spaniard, or a Polynesian. Further, it was also an obligation for the ancient Greek and the man of medieval Europe, regardless of whether he knew it or not. And it will be an obligation for all those races and those civilizations that succeed ours, whether they are aware of it or not. What is good now was good then, and will be good in the distant future; what was evil in the past is still evil, and ever shall be. There is not one ethical law for the past and another for the present, nor one standard for the Oriental and another for the Occidental. The Good or the Right is universal, absolute, ubiquitous, and eternal.

The absolutist is of course aware that moral standards appear to vary tremendously from age to age and from place to place. It did not require modern anthropology to teach him this, since Herodotus, the earliest Greek historian, took considerable delight in describing the divergent standards of his day. The scientific study of man has only emphasized what educated persons have always known—namely, that there is hardly an act which we consider abominable which has not at sometime and somewhere been regarded as virtuous and even sacred. But the absolutist finds no disproof of his position in this vast array of anthropological data now available. He believes that these variations in ethical standards and practices merely prove that men are often ignorant of the one true and valid standard. The fact that the cannibal sees nothing wrong in his dietary habits proves only that he is unenlightened. It in no way makes his action right, even for him. His conduct remains, despite the innocence of his ignorance, as contrary to his *true* moral code as enemy-eating would be for us; for this true code is absolute and unvarying, independent of knowledge or ignorance just as it is independent of time or place.

Absolutism does not imply that we today are necessarily any nearer to realizing or practising the true standard than the cannibal is or than our ancestors were. The absolutist is consistent, for he admits that we too may be ignorant or inadequate in our morality. Furthermore, the absolute standard is independent of all actual moral practices, including our own; nor will our descendants necessarily be nearer to it than we are. In brief, this doctrine holds that the concept of moral evolution or "progress" is irrelevant: neither the antiquity nor the novelty of a moral practice means anything. The sole criterion for evaluating ethical concepts and practices is their relation to this timeless, unchanging (that is, non-progressing) absolute. However, this does not necessarily imply moral conservatism. It is quite possible that we are steadily coming nearer to a realization of the single true norm, and the absolutist can with equal logic be a moral radical or a moral conservative. In short, his position does not require that he praise or condemn any specific moral act. It commits him only to the belief that *whatever* is right or wrong holds true for all men, everywhere and always.

The Close Relation Between Absolutism and Objectivism. The absolutist is logically an objectivist—even an extreme objectivist. He normally regards the moral law as not only absolute, but also basic in the world-structure. It is universal in a double sense: it not only extends everywhere and holds for all rational beings, but forms an integral part of reality. This clearly removes it from the realm of the subjective. The absolutist himself likes to compare the moral law with the law of gravitational attraction. He regards the two as equally binding, equally universal, and equally unvarying in their action; it would be absurd to believe that gravitational force has only a mental or subjective status, and it is equally absurd to hold that men each create their own "good" or "right" out of their preferences. The analogy can be carried ever farther: just as gravitation existed before Newton discovered its laws, and just as there would still be mutual attraction between all objects in the universe if the human race were eliminated from the scene, so the moral law existed before we knew it and remains independent of our knowledge. Many absolutists would say that humanity could disappear, or never have come into existence, without the status of the Good being affected in any way.

The Sources of Ethical Absolutism

1. Historical. The chief source of ethical absolutism is not difficult to discover.[3] The background and foundation of our Western civilization are Christian, and to say "Christian" is (as far as concerns philosophy) to say "monotheistic." The belief in a single God, who rules over the universe which He created, is fundamental in our religious thought. Further, this is a rational God, whose thoughts and commands are self-consistent throughout.[4] These commands are universal, applying to all men everywhere. And as the moral law is the edict of this rational, self-consistent God, it is logically a universal unvarying law. An absolute Deity could hardly be the author of anything except an absolute moral

[3] I am indebted to Stace, *The Concept of Morals,* for these suggestions as to the sources of ethical absolutism. The contrast between relativism and absolutism, given in the first two chapters of his book, is about as lucid as can be imagined.

[4] Cf. Stace, *op. cit.,* p. 6.

law. Therefore the divergence of moral standards which we observe from place to place and age to age can only be due to ignorance regarding God's will. If all men knew His will, all would have the same moral code; all would call the same things "good" and the same actions "right."

It is significant that just as men in Western civilization have until recently taken for granted the existence of a monotheistic God, so also they have regarded as self-evident the existence of an absolute moral standard. All the traditional philosophical arguments concerning ethical standards, even those of a profound thinker like Immanuel Kant, started with the assumption that such an absolute standard exists. As long as Christian monotheism was an unchallenged belief, it was inevitable that ethical thought should be absolutistic.

2. *Logical.* The logical foundation of absolutism is not as apparent as the historical basis, but it has much greater importance for contemporary thought. For more than a century, ethical absolutists have been trying to supply a rational or logical underpinning to provide the foundation which monotheism formerly gave. Kant is probably the most important of these ethical rationalists; he believed that analysis would always be able to demonstrate that a violation of the moral law is also a violation of the laws of logic: immorality always implies a logical contradiction. To quote his most famous example, when we make a promise with no intention of keeping it, we are acting wrongly because we are acting upon two contradictory principles at once. The first of these principles is that people ought to believe in promises. But if I break my promise, this means that everyone has a right to break promises, since the moral law must be universal. And, if everyone were to break them, then promises would no longer be believed and we would have another principle—namely, it is right that no promise should be believed—which contradicts the first principle. Kant maintained that all instances of wrongdoing can similarly be reduced to instances of logical inconsistency. Thus the law of noncontradiction becomes the basic principle of ethics, just as it has always been for logic.

3. *Qualitative.* Among the more recent attempts to give a rational basis to absolutism stands a doctrine which we have already mentioned: "Good" is an irreducible and indefinable *quality* of certain objects, actions or situations, comparable to a color quality such as yellow. While the physicist can define yellow in quantitative terms (so many vibrations per

second in a presumed ether), as far as our direct experience is concerned any color constitutes an irreducible sense-datum that can be known only by experience. Value (in this case, moral value) is likewise an irreducible and indefinable quality which certain objects or situations possess in the same way that a ripe lemon possesses yellowness.

Arguments Against the Qualitative View. While it is not our purpose here to criticize absolutism, but rather to present it as the position which relativism has revolted against, it is nonetheless pertinent to point out one or two arguments against this quality theory of "good." In the first place, one can argue that the color analogy is completely invalid. For even if we grant that color is objective and inheres in the object (which very few psychologists would concede), "good" and "yellow" are hardly comparable qualities. For every person with normal vision will presumably have the same experience when he looks at a yellow object. In other words, "yellow" as an experience has a universal status. Can "good" claim any such comparable status? While there may be a few experiences or objects that are universally regarded as "good," their number is very small in comparison with the countless things about which there is no hint of agreement. Hence the invalidity of the color analogy.

There is a second and probably more serious objection to this view that goodness is an inherent quality. For even if we should admit that goodness inheres in certain objects and situations, this admission would not provide a sufficient basis for moral obligation. To quote Stace's forceful argument on this point,

> The fact that something has a quality does impose upon me the purely intellectual, or theoretical, obligation to admit that it has that quality. But how can it impose upon me any obligation to *act?* Why should I *do* anything about it? If it is pointed out to me that a certain flower is yellow, and if I see this with my own eyes, then I can understand that I am obliged to admit the truth of the proposition. "This flower is yellow." I cannot indeed do otherwise. . . . I *have* to accept it. But this cannot possibly oblige me to any kind of action. It cannot oblige me, for example, to pick the flower. I shall only do this if I like yellow flowers, or have some other inclination which prompts me to pick it. So too, if it is pointed out to me that a thing or an action has the quality of being good, and if I myself perceive this, I can see that this will compel me to admit the truth of the proposition "This is good." But it cannot impose on me any *practical* obligation whatsoever. I shall still

not do anything, unless it happens that I like good things. And in that case it is my inclination which obliges me, not the theoretical truth which has been pointed out to me.[5]

The Revolt Against Absolutism

The relativistic position is, as already indicated, primarily a revolt against absolutism. It is also an integral part of the general intellectual temper of our time; to most of us, relativism in all fields seems as "self-evident" as absolutism did to the medieval mind. The relativistic temper is so pervasive throughout modern thought that all forms of absolutism—scientific, political, moral or religious—are on the defensive.[6] After giving so much time to our presentation of the absolutistic view, relativism will fortunately be easy to describe.

In brief, relativism is diametrically opposed to everything that is essential in absolutism. Where absolutism is monistic, relativism is strongly pluralistic. Instead of one universal, unvarying moral law, we have a large number of such laws. Instead of one "Good," there are only innumerable "goods." In place of "Value," we have only "values." In sum, this school holds that all good is relative either to what the group says is right, or to what the individual feels to be right. All value is relative to the time, the place, and the civilization; it is dependent upon the nature of the human species, and the needs of the individual organism within that species. To speak of "good" as something independent of these is meaningless. The relativist feels that it is particularly absurd to ignore the nature of the species and the unique interests which characterize humanity. Any absolutistic talk of a "cosmic good" which supposedly would hold for any conceivable type of rational creature, including a Martian or an angel, is sheer nonsense.

The Historical Bases of Relativism. Perhaps the best way to secure a clear picture of relativism is to examine both its historical roots and its present-day arguments. While the viewpoint was well established in

[5] Stace, *op. cit.*, pp. 41-42.
[6] It should be pointed out, however, that World War II was at least in part a conflict between political relativism (i.e., democracy) and a resurgent political absolutism (i.e., totalitarianism).

ancient Greece—the Sophists were probably the most thoroughgoing relativists philosophy has yet seen—its modern development began with the Renaissance. The Renaissance has sometimes been described as a revolt against medieval absolutism in all fields. This description is undoubtedly an oversimplification, but, as far as it goes, contains much truth. Strangely, however, while both political and religious relativism were important movements during the Renaissance period, there was not much development of ethical relativism until after the doctrine had established itself in other fields. As we have seen, late in the eighteenth century Kant could still take for granted that there was a categorically binding moral law. We have also indicated why true ethical relativism appeared so late: the fracture of Christendom which began with Luther did not mean any less emphasis upon monotheism; so long as an absolute God with an absolute will was assumed without question, belief in an absolute moral standard, pervasive throughout the entire universe, was inevitable.

During the last century and a half, however, several things have made the extension of relativism into ethics no less inevitable. First, there has been the tremendous development of science. The over-all effect of this development has been to make belief in either a monotheistic deity or an absolute system of values more difficult than in Kant's day. The second influence towards the rise of ethical relativism was the beginning of one social science and the refinement of another: the scientific study of man which we call *anthropology* came into being, and *history* was put upon a secure foundation of research and scholarship. Both of these studies have piled up such imposing collections of data concerning the variability of human customs and moral standards that one has to be very keen-minded not to read relativism into these masses of evidence. In the third place, the theory of evolution has relativistic implications, since it suggests that moral standards have evolved along with society and human institutions. Such a moral evolution in turn implies that change is as basic to ethics as to biology, and change logically suggests the absence of any absolute standard.

The Logical Arguments. In addition to these scientific and historical arguments for relativism, there are several which are purely logical in nature. First is the fact that all morality appears to be based upon emotional reaction—or, more strictly, emotional preference. This viewpoint constitutes a pointed attack upon the rationalistic absolutism of such thinkers as Kant. While not all relativists accept this emotion thesis, it has played an important part in putting absolutism on the defensive, and thus deserves a brief examination. In short, it holds that whatever men regard with approval, or whatever excites a pleasant emotional reaction, is called "good." Whatever arouses resentment, jealousy, or disgust is disapproved as "wrong" or "bad." However, since emotions are variable, both from individual to individual and from moment to moment in the same individual, it follows that ethical evaluations will also be variable and personal. What will disgust one person will leave another unmoved; hence what will impress the first individual as immoral or "bad" will not impress the second as a moral matter at all. If by chance it should impress the second spectator as amusing rather than disgusting, it will call forth a "good" reaction, since being amused is definitely a pleasant experience.

The second logical argument of the relativist is probably accepted by all advocates of the doctrine. It points out that any absolute moral law implies a categorical obligation that the law be obeyed. In any form of ethical absolutism there is always an implied command. As we have seen, there is nothing hypothetical in the absolutistic doctrine: it is not a matter of "You ought to do your duty *if* you want to be happy," but a categorical imperative, "You ought to do your duty." This has the effect of a command: "Do your duty!" But all commands imply a source of authority; an obligation requires someone who obliges.[7] Thus we are soon deep in the difficult problem concerning the source or basis of moral obligation. For the present it will be sufficient to indicate that the relativist denies the existence of any such authority or commander. He never tires of pointing out that historically no one has been able to discover an objective basis for ethical obligation. Certainly it is true that since the breakdown of religious authority the absolutist has had a difficult time trying to establish a source of categorical command. As long as all men accepted the authority of the Church and believed in an omnipotent God whose will was absolute, there was no difficulty in pointing to the commanding agent. Is it possible to establish a comparable secular basis to take the place of this religious foundation? This is the question which the absolutist tries to answer affirmatively, but which the relativist insists can only be answered in the negative.

[7] Cf. Stace, *op. cit.*, pp. 27-28.

The Implications of Relativism

It is probable that everything we have said up to this point regarding relativism will be acceptable to most readers. So far, however, we have shown only the more positive side of this viewpoint. Unfortunately there are certain implications of the relativistic position which prevent many thinkers from accepting it even after they have found absolutism unsatisfactory.[8] Some of these implications must be understood before we attempt to choose between the two positions, or before we undertake to formulate a compromise viewpoint of some sort.

All persons are aware of the relativity of moral *practice*, and many make an extension from this fact and consider all moral *standards* to be relative. The absolutist is certain, however, that no rational person will accept the logical consequences of such an extension. In the first place (according to absolutism) it would mean that there can be no standard for judging one moral code better or worse, higher or lower, than another. There would be no valid grounds for evaluating conduct, other than its conformity with local or national custom. Consider the full implications of this: if all "good" or "right" is relative to time, place, and circumstance; if the Oriental's conduct is "right" as long as it conforms to oriental standards and occidental behavior is "right" if occidental moral sensibilities are satisfied, then the use of torture in medieval justice was right, and the British were wrong when they outlawed the Hindu practice of burning widows alive on their husband's funeral pyre. In the second place (the absolutist continues) under a relative standard there can be no moral progress. How can we say that the abolition of slavery was a "good" thing, or that the elimination of war would be "good," or that the ethics of Christ were "higher" than those presented in the Old Testament? Third, why should anyone strive to realize a better moral life than the one he is now living—in fact, how can we even speak of a "better" moral life? "Better" than what? We can say that a person's moral conduct has been brought into closer conformity with the standards of his age or

[8] There have been several attempts to work out middle-of-the-road viewpoints of one sort or another. Limitations of space do not permit us to go into these compromise positions, especially since many are extremely difficult to understand. Since the historical battle has been (and very largely still is) between the two more extreme positions, it will be sufficient if the student gets a clear understanding of these.

community, or we can say that he is now acting in a manner that will bring him more happiness or more social approval. But unless there is some common, universal (that is, nonrelativistic) standard, any talk of "better" or "worse," "higher" or "lower" is meaningless. Indeed, what can terms like "right" and "wrong" mean in a strictly relativistic system? Certainly they can have no meaning that bears any relation to what these terms have signified in the past.

Is There Any Alternative Besides Absolutism? There are some ethical thinkers who are willing to accept these anarchistic implications of a complete ethical relativism. Usually, however, it has been sociologists and anthropologists, concerned with the mere observation and classification of behavior patterns, who have been the most aggressive advocates of such a view. Other thinkers have tried to find a middle ground between the extremes of relativism and absolutism. Sometimes this is achieved by disclaiming any cosmic foundation for "the good." In this case ethics would be separated from metaphysics, and we would limit ourselves to a purely humanistic type of ethical theory. A second and perhaps more fruitful line of speculation has come from separating universality and absolutism. This is done by giving a psychological or biological foundation to ethics: we attempt to formulate a code which will be universal for all men because, as members of the same species, they have a common biological (and to a large extent, psychological) nature. Such a point of view would necessarily hold that the similarities among men are more significant than the differences between them. Thus the African savage and the modern European or American have enough in common as far as concerns desires, interests, and potential satisfactions for us to describe a "good life" for all mankind. Once we have determined these common needs and this general welfare, then all evaluations of "good" or "right" can be—indeed, *must* be—within this framework. That object or situation will be "good" which satisfies one of these universal human needs; that conduct will be "right" which promotes the common welfare in which all men share because of their common humanity.

The Classifications of Value

More or less independent of this fundamental problem concerning the status of the good, numerous attempts have been made to classify values in relation to various criteria or frames of reference. These classifications have usually assumed the form of a series of contrasting pairs, such as intrinsic *vs.* instrumental values, higher *vs.* lower, permanent *vs.* transient, and so on. However, not all these pairs are equally significant, so we shall mention only those which are widely accepted as fundamental.

1. *Intrinsic and Instrumental.* The one contrast that is universally regarded as basic in any classification of values is that between those which are intrinsic and those which are instrumental. We have had occasion to refer to this division in previous chapters. In brief, an intrinsic value is one that does not serve some end—that is, which does not derive its significance from being a means to some further end. It is good in, by, and for itself, without reference to some more inclusive value. "Happiness" is perhaps the most satisfactory example of intrinsic good. It is obvious that we do not pursue happiness for the sake of anything except happiness; we do not seek to be happy in order to secure something else. It is not a means to anything beyond itself, but has value without reference to anything external.

In contrast to such an intrinsic value stand most of the things which we ordinarily call "good." Analysis will reveal that most of the objects we seek, or the situations we strive to realize, have value for us only because they are a means for attaining something that has inherent or intrinsic value. The classic example of such an instrumental good is money. Obviously money has value only as a means to many of the desirable things in life. Nobody except the miser regards it as an intrinsic good, as something to be gained and hoarded without regard to need or potential satisfactions.

The Problem of Intrinsic Values. The ethical thinker soon becomes keenly aware of three things that are involved in any relation between intrinsic and instrumental values. The first is the very small number of values that are truly intrinsic. Some authorities have concluded that there may be only one, and it has even been denied that there are *any* that can be classified as incontrovertibly intrinsic. Second, it is necessary to develop a sharp sense of the difference between the two classes of values if we hope to order our lives and our activities with ethical intelligence. And finally, like any thoughtful person, the philosopher is painfully aware of how difficult it is for most persons, including himself, to keep this distinction clearly in mind. For all men tend to confuse the two classes of goods, and we frequently act as though our immediate goal (which is almost always only an instrumental value) possessed the supreme importance of a truly intrinsic value. We easily forget that most of the things we do have meaning only because they serve some larger end, such as "happiness" or "contentment" or "peace of mind."

Some thinkers have made the distinction between intrinsic and instrumental goods the major division within ethics. Certainly as far as the psychology of satisfaction is concerned, there can hardly be a more important distinction. Speaking in these terms, "the good life" is one which yields the maximum of intrinsic good, and at the same time organizes the instrumental values as servants of those that are intrinsic. The primary problem of intelligent living is to decide what has intrinsic value and then organize our lives around the realization of this and this alone, refusing to be seduced into pouring our time and energy into the pursuit of mere means as though they were the ends or goals of life.

2. *Higher and Lower Values.* In comparison with this division of values into intrinsic and instrumental, the other possible classifications within ethics appear less significant. A brief mention of them will suffice for our purpose, which is to give the reader the general lay of the land within the ethical field rather than to map out the domain in detail. One well-known writer on ethics, W. M. Urban, classifies values as *organic* (that is, bodily, economic, and recreational) and *hyper-organic* (that is, character, intellectual, esthetic, and religious)[9] A similar and somewhat better-known classification divides values on the basis of *higher* and *lower*. Unfortunately there is not always agreement about just where the division should come, nor is it possible to give a satisfactory statement as to exactly what should be the basis for the dichotomy. It is generally agreed, however, that higher values are more delicate, subtle, fragile, and precious, and that these presuppose the lower values, without which the higher cannot come into existence.[10] The lower, however, do not depend upon the higher. For example, intellectual values presuppose bodily and even economic values, but health and sufficient income do not depend upon a love of knowledge or a passion for truth.

While this distinction between *higher* and *lower* values was a commonplace of nineteenth-century ethical discussion, today the terms seem far from satisfactory to ethical thinkers. These two classes of values could

[9] *Fundamentals of Ethics*, pp. 164 ff. Urban's classification is a refinement of the standard categories of value; a list of these appears in W. G. Everett's *Moral Values*, Chapter VII.

[10] Cf. W. H. Roberts, *The Problem of Choice*, pp. 230-231.

probably be defined in a way that would make them more acceptable now, but even in precise usage they inevitably seem to imply an ethical dualism. This dualism is often so extreme that puritanism or asceticism results. The lower values easily become identified with physical satisfactions of all kinds, while higher values become those which are strictly nonphysical. This separation implies that no physical satisfaction can be anything but "low," whereas all values associated with man's mental and spiritual activities are guaranteed a "high" status.

The major objection to this classification is probably the terms themselves. "Higher" and "lower" are of course neutral, nonevaluative terms when used in their original meaning to indicate spatial relations. But, as used in ethics, "lower" is always disparaging, since it suggests a value which is less worthy, noble or pure than "higher" values are supposed to be. If the terms were not associated with the body on one hand as against the spirit on the other, there could be little objection to their use. As commonly employed, however, they indicate a dualistic contrast—even a warfare—of flesh against spirit which contemporary thought no longer takes for granted.

3. *Inclusive and Exclusive Values.* Clearer and less controversial is the distinction between *inclusive* and *exclusive* values. As an example, economic goods are usually exclusive; my possession of them prevents you and everyone else from having these same goods. In contrast, such a value as humor is not only shareable but may be increased if some other person or persons can participate in the humorous situation. In a theatre audience, for example, one frequently sees strangers glance at one another when laughing at something on the stage or screen, obviously finding their own hilarity increased when they catch the eye of a neighbor. Another example of inclusive value is found in the enjoyment of beauty. Most of us find this pleasure far greater when we can share the esthetic experience. For some strange reason, the person or persons by whose presence beauty is enhanced must be individuals we like—in contrast to humor or laughter, to which (as we have just stated) the presence of even casual strangers may contribute greatly. Moreover the value of beauty seems to increase directly in proportion to the degree of affection we have for our partners in the shared experience: the effect of beauty upon lovers is notorious. No less celebrated is the blight which can be cast upon an esthetic situation by the presence of persons whom we dislike.

4. Permanent and Transient Values. Still another classification of values distinguishes the *permanent* from the *transient*. Contrary to what we might expect, it is not true that permanent values are always to be chosen over transient. In the case of physical pleasure, for example, intensity joined with brevity may be preferable to mildness joined with duration. A drink of water to a man dying of thirst for the time being certainly outweighs all the enduring values of art and religion combined. In other words, we are wise to choose a permanent value over a transitory one only if the two are equal in all other respects. *All else being equal,* a permanent value is obviously to be preferred. Unfortunately it is often difficult to set up a situation where all else is equal, particularly as far as our desires are concerned. A bird in the hand is all too often worth half a dozen in the bush, and it takes all our ethical intelligence to make decisions in favor of a permanent value in the future as against an admittedly transient good directly before us, waiting to be enjoyed right now.

The Hierarchy of Values: the "Summum Bonum"

This analysis of the various kinds of values suggests that it might be possible and profitable to arrange our "goods" in some sort of a scale or hierarchy. We would probably make the less inclusive subordinate to the more inclusive, the higher dominant over the lower, the permanent over the transient, and (most important of all) put the intrinsic ahead of the instrumental. As we have already observed, there are very few really intrinsic values. Instead, most of the things we call "good" prove to have value only as a means to some other more inclusive good, and this in turn is usually discovered to be only instrumental to some still more ultimate good. Thus we inevitably get a hierarchy of values. Any such hierarchy will logically have a crown of some kind, and we thus necessarily arrive at the concept of a supreme value or ultimate good. This is usually given the traditional Latin name of *summum bonum*—literally, the "highest good." The problem of the "good" (as distinguished from the problem of "obligation") thus ultimately leads to a search for the *summum bonum*, and the achievement of the good life becomes in large part the organization of all other values in relation to this ethical ultimate.

The Requirements for a True "Summum Bonum." What must be the characteristics of the *summum bonum* if it is to be the highest good and the goal of life? First and decidedly foremost, it must be an indubitable intrinsic good. It must be of such character that, after the most thoroughgoing analysis, we can still say, "*This* is good, not for X or as a means to Y, but just for itself." A second characteristic which any possible *summum bonum* must have is an all-inclusive scope—that is, it must be inclusive enough so that all our activities fall into place as means to its realization. The importance of this is obvious: if there were activities aiming to achieve other, unrelated goals—goals which did not in turn become means to our supposed *summum bonum*—then clearly we would not be dealing with an ultimate inclusive good, but only with an instrumental good of some kind.[11]

A third characteristic which any highest good should possess is the possibility of at least a partial realization. An ideal of value which is so lofty as to make even a partial attainment impossible would have little practical relation to human life. But note: there is no requirement that our *summum bonum* must be *completely* attainable. It is enough if men can feel that there is the possibility of sufficient realization to justify devoting life to the pursuit of this goal. Again, practical considerations suggest that any candidate for the office of highest good must be such that a design for living can be built around it. If the ideal is too vague or too abstract, if it demands the sacrifice of the little day-by-day satisfactions which seem indispensable to our sense of well-being, or if it is so long-range that we can see no immediate results of our effort, then it becomes valueless as an ethical ideal. This is the criticism that has often been leveled at some of the ideals proposed by both philosophers and theologians. The Good (or, in the case of theology, Heaven) perhaps can wait, but some modicum of satisfaction man must have meanwhile.

Now that we have established the requirements for a *summum bonum* and have outlined the general relation of any such ethical ultimate to our total experience, let us turn to an examination of the various candidates for this high office.

[11] The only escape from such a conclusion would be the possibility that there is more than one highest good. This possibility has frequently been suggested, and there is no logical reason for ruling it out. However, since historically the concept of a single *summum bonum* has dominated ethical thought, we shall not be guilty of oversimplification if we limit our discussion to the various monistic views.

CHAPTER 13

ETHICS:

But What Is the Highest Good?

N OW THAT WE HAVE SEEN THE IMPORTANCE OF THE *summum bonum* in ethical thought and also some of the qualifications which any legitimate contender for that position must have, we turn to an examination of the possible candidates. The first of these is probably the oldest—and certainly the most popular—contestant for ethical election: pleasure.[1] The school which regards pleasure as the highest good and the ground of all value is known as *hedonism,* from the Greek *"hedone,"* "pleasure." The viewpoint of this school constitutes a pole in ethics comparable in importance to naturalism or idealism in metaphysics; and, just as much philosophic activity can best be understood as a conflict between these two poles, so a large part of ethical thought reveals a constant warfare between hedonism and the various schools of antihedonism.

The Essence of Hedonism. In essence the hedonistic position appears very simple. "Good" is identified with "pleasant," and "evil" is identical with "unpleasant." For the hedonist pleasure alone has ultimate value. One of the greatest attractions of this viewpoint has been its apparent simplicity. However, the doctrine is more complex than at first appears, for it includes perhaps half a dozen separable ideas. First, both pleasure and pain are regarded as simple feelings—that is, they are unanalyzable, incapable of being reduced to more ultimate psychological terms. They can neither be defined nor described. Fortunately this in-

---

[1] In modern ethical thought the term "pleasant consciousness" or "pleasant feeling" is often preferred.

definable character is not fatal to the theory, since we all know by direct experience what pleasure and pain are. Second, hedonism considers every feeling of pleasure good, and every feeling of pain bad, to the individual who experiences it.[2] These are absolute experiences whose goodness or badness is independent of everything else. Third, in pure hedonism all pleasures are considered identical in *quality*. Pleasure is pleasure, and pain is pain, regardless of the source. This necessarily reduces the difference between any two pleasures to a *qualitative* basis. The two pleasurable experiences will probably differ in intensity and duration, and one may be purer (that is, less mixed with pain) than the other, but aside from these quantitative differences, they are the same. Such a reduction of quality to quantity implies that the final evaluation of any experience will be determined by the amount of pleasure or pain it yields, and this amount will be discovered by multiplying the intensity of the feeling by its duration. This in turn suggests what is called the *hedonic calculus*, in which we weigh experiences against one another in terms of their pleasure-pain yield and then evaluate the object or situation in terms of this mathematical result. If the algebraic addition comes out with a plus of pleasure, we have a "good" object or situation; if we end up with a negative answer—that is, with more pain than pleasure—it is "bad."[3]

Two Types of Hedonism

1. Psychological

Before we proceed further it is necessary to establish a fundamental distinction between *psychological hedonism* and *ethical hedonism*. The first is, as the name suggests, more of a psychological theory than a philosophical doctrine. Instead of being concerned, as we expect any ethical theory to be, with the question of what men ought to do (that is, what *ought*

[2] On this and the remaining points in this paragraph, cf. De Laguna, *Introduction to the Science of Ethics*, pp. 248-249.

[3] Most of these points are characteristic of pure hedonism, which must be regarded as an historical position rather than a present-day school. As we shall see shortly, a majority of modern hedonists have accepted modifications in these ideas. In general, however, the various antihedonistic viewpoints we shall consider are largely reactions against the doctrine as we have given it here.

to be desired), psychological hedonism limits itself to a consideration of what men actually do (that is, what *is* desired). The psychological school does not acknowledge that any question of obligation is involved. All animals, including man, are so constituted that they automatically seek pleasure and avoid pain. This is the universal law of nature, admitting no exceptions. Pleasure is the only thing that is desired as an end in itself and its pursuit is the prime motivation of life activities. Since we cannot desire anything else, it clearly becomes a waste of time to ask whether or not we should have other goals. In fact, as far as the psychological hedonist can see, the only legitimate concern of ethics is the question of how we can secure the most pleasure, or most successfully avoid pain.

Arguments Against Psychological Hedonism: 1. Pleasure a By-product. Psychological hedonism is so plausible and offers such a simple explanation of human behavior that it has always had a large following. However, this following has not usually been drawn from the ranks of the philosophers, but from the general public. Ethical thinkers have long since come to realize that this surface plausibility masks a multitude of objections. The most significant objection is the observation, made long ago by Aristotle and confirmed by much evidence since, that men rarely pursue pleasure directly. Furthermore they rarely pursue it consciously. Instead we ordinarily desire specific objects or concrete situations, and pleasure or satisfaction is merely a by-product of their pursuit or their realization. Thus when we are hungry we seek food, not the pleasure of eating (which is incidental); when we are in love we seek the object of our love, rather than the pleasure of making love. As Aristotle pointed out, pleasure is a state of feeling that arises when the organism is functioning smoothly in any of the various activities to which it is suited. The pleasure, however, is incidental to the activity. We do not engage in the activity for the sake of the resultant pleasure, but in order to attain certain objects or realize certain situations. "The man who desires food desires food; the man who desires a game of billiards desires a game of billiards; a man who desires the conversion of the heathen desires the conversion of the heathen—not pleasure. The thought of pleasure may not enter his mind at all."[4]

The hedonist feels he can easily answer this argument. He admits that the idea of pleasure as a conscious purpose may not be present, but insists that the ultimate goal is nevertheless pleasure or satisfaction of

[4] De Laguna, *op. cit.*, p. 254.

some sort. The fact that we are unconscious of our goal, or that we have not articulated it, does not prove that we would perform the act whether or not it gave us pleasure.

Now such a controversy as this is futile, since it is evident that it cannot, from its very nature, ever be settled. The antihedonist is correct when he points out that ordinarily we are not consciously aiming at pleasure when we act. On the other hand, we cannot prove that the hedonist is wrong when he argues that the expectation of pleasure is the ultimate, if unconscious, motivation of all behavior. For hedonism appears to be on firm ground when it claims that many actions would not be repeated if they did not either yield pleasure or eliminate pain. Thus the real issue seems to be whether this fact proves that the pleasure-pain principle is the basis of all motivation. But as any decisive answer on this point is impossible, each side is free to form its own speculative hypothesis.

2. *The Hedonistic Paradox.* The second objection to psychological hedonism involves what is known as the hedonistic paradox, which points out that to aim at pleasure directly is usually to miss it. The notorious unhappiness of the professional pleasure-seeker is cited as evidence. It is argued that if we would see someone who is having a good time we will not find him among the pleasure-seekers, but will instead discover him to be someone who is erecting a house, or making a dress, or carving out a career, or raising a family, or reading a book. Always our happy person will be engaged in an activity which has the accomplishment of some specific task as its goal. In short, as moralists—and more recently, psychologists—have often pointed out, to find supreme happiness we must forget our pursuit of it and lose ourself in some activity, throw ourself into some cause, or enter into some personal relationship which will absorb us and provide both a channel for our energies and a focus for our dreams.

2. Ethical

When the hedonistic theory of value is transferred to the moral sphere we have *ethical hedonism.* This viewpoint is concerned not only with what *is* (as in psychological hedonism), but even more with what *ought to be.* For philosophy as a whole, ethical hedonism is much more important than its psychological counterpart, since ethics is concerned primarily with the establishment of norms for conduct.

Egoistic vs. *Social Hedonism.* The several schools within ethical hedonism can be divided into two classes, "egoistic" hedonism and "universalistic" hedonism or "utilitarianism." In general, the egoistic doctrine is characteristic of ancient thought, while utilitarianism represents the modern viewpoint. The egoistic view holds that all evaluation of conduct as good or bad, right or wrong, must be in reference to the agent—that is, in terms of how much pleasure or pain the act brings the doer personally. The universalistic school, on the contrary, has a less selfish norm. It holds that any action must be viewed in terms of its value *to all persons who are affected by it*—that is, how much pleasure or pain it will bring to each member of the entire group involved. It is possible to argue that in the last analysis the good of the individual is identical with the good of the group, and modern ethical hedonists have expended much energy attempting to prove this identity of interests. Historically, however, the distinction between the personal and social points of view has been important. This will become clear if we analyze the views of four men, two of whom are "egoists" and two "universalists."

The Extreme View of Aristippus. The first and probably most extreme hedonist was Aristippus, who lived in Cyrene, on the African coast of the Mediterranean, in the fifth century B.C. He also resided for a while in Athens, where he became a disciple of Socrates. It was apparently the well-known conviviality of his master that impressed Aristippus, for when he returned to Cyrene and started his own school of philosophy, certain aspects of the Socratic doctrine were taken as the basis for a viewpoint which perfectly suited his pleasure-loving nature. In brief, Aristippus held that all good is determined by pleasure, and more explicitly, by the pleasure of the moment. There is no "higher" or "lower" pleasure, and the element of duration can be ignored. Intensity and immediacy are the only criteria for evaluating pleasures, and thus the Good Life is that which yields the greatest amount of the most intense pleasurable sensation.

Epicurus's Moderate Position. We need not pause to discuss the failure of this extreme Aristippean hedonism, since the three other positions we shall consider were all intended to eliminate its defects, which will be laid bare as we go along. The first important modification of this starkly simple doctrine was the system of Epicurus, who taught in Athens a century after Aristippus had lived there as a pupil of Socrates. The founder of Epicureanism emphasized that, while "pleasure is pleasure," some forms last much longer than others and some are purchased at a higher cost in effort or hang-over. Epicurus further modified the extreme doctrine of Aristippus by making the hedonic criterion negative rather than positive; the greatest good is the absence of pain, and the best life is one which is most free from want, suffering, and the agitation of strong passion. This last point, the avoidance of strong passions, was peculiarly characteristic of Epicurean doctrine. Where the Cyrenaics had sought violent pleasures, the Epicureans shunned them as disturbing and short-lived, with a high cost in unpleasant reaction. The followers of Epicurus were taught to cultivate the tamer but more lasting—and certainly less disturbing—joys of philosophy and friendship. The true goal is *ataraxia,* "serenity." Anything that disturbs this serenity should be shunned, regardless of how intense may be the immediate pleasure it offers.

Social Hedonism: Bentham's "Utilitarianism." It is evident that ethical thought moved a long way during the century that separated Aristippus and Epicurus. No comparable step in the development of hedonism was taken until Jeremy Bentham began his work late in the eighteenth century. This common-sense British thinker was largely responsible for the shift from egoistic to universalistic hedonism. He was much interested in social amelioration and legal reform, hence it is not surprising that his ethical thinking should have been social and practical to an unusual degree. Furthermore he managed to combine psychological and ethical hedonism, as is evident from the frequently quoted passage in his *Principles of Morals and Legislation.*

> Nature has placed mankind under the governance of two sovereign masters, *pain* and *pleasure.* . . . They govern us in all we can do, in all we can say, and in all we think; every effort we can make to throw off our subjection will but serve to demonstrate and confirm it. . . . The principle of utility recognizes this subjection and assumes it for a foundation of that system, the object of which is to rear the fabric of felicity by the hands of reason and law. Systems which attempt to question it deal in sounds instead of sense, in caprice instead of reason, in darkness instead of light.

Bentham goes on to define his principle of utility as "that principle which approves or disapproves of every action whatsoever, according to the tendency which it appears to have to augment or diminish the happiness of the party whose interest is in question." He was convinced that this principle is the means by which men both make and ought to make their choices. What he desired was to make this the *acknowledged* standard of morality and legislation, in order that society might be ruled by it instead of by some abstract standard of duty unrelated to human welfare.[5] For he saw that any such abstract, nonutilitarian principle was "one of the most convenient and effective weapons of tyranny. It served to persuade the victims that not only must they obey their oppressors but really ought to."[6]

The Hedonic Calculus. Bentham was persuaded that the best bulwark against social oppression is a frank avowal of each person's primary concern with his own good, but this left him with the problem of avoiding social anarchy. In other words, how can we make the individual realize that his own good is identified with the common good? As the first step toward establishing the identification of private and public good Bentham offered the most explicit statement of the hedonic calculus that had been formulated. He argued that the value of any action must be judged by reference to the following seven "circumstances": (1) the *intensity* of the pleasure or pain which results; (2) the *duration* of either; (3) their *certainty* or *uncertainty*—that is, the degree of probability that they will occur as anticipated; (4) the *promptness* of their occurrence; (5) their *fecundity,* or likelihood of being followed by sensations of the same kind; (6) their *purity,* or freedom from either present or future sensations of the opposite kind; and finally, (7) their extent, or the number of persons affected by the sensation in question. Bentham himself summed up these points in a bit of verse that is often quoted:

> Intense, long, certain, speedy, fruitful, pure—
> Such marks in pleasure and in pain endure.
> Such pleasures seek if private be thy end;
> If it be public, let them wide extend.
> Such pains avoid whatever be thy view;
> If pains must come, let them extend to few.

By the use of this calculus, its author held that we can readily determine the goodness or badness of any act.

Even the most hasty consideration of Bentham's seven points will reveal that the last one introduces something altogether new into hedonistic thought. The first six can be regarded as merely refinements of the

[5] Cf. Roberts, *op. cit.,* pp. 147-148.
[6] *Ibid.*

Epicurean calculation of pleasures *vs.* pains. If Bentham had stopped with these, his system would have been no less egoistic than that of Epicurus. However, as soon as we begin to evaluate actions in terms of the number of persons affected, or the total amount of pleasure or pain experienced by all these persons, we enter a different ethical sphere. Bentham did not believe that this addition of a social factor required the introduction of any *qualitatively* new concept; it would still be theoretically possible merely to total up all the pleasure that would result, everybody considered, and weigh this against the total pain. However, even if this could be a strictly quantitative calculation, the addition of social considerations complicates the issue so greatly that it constitutes a fundamental change in the history of hedonism.

The Heresy of Mill. Bentham's utilitarianism would have seemed absurd to Aristippus and questionable to Epicurus. When we come to John Stuart Mill, who was born two generations later than Bentham, we meet a hedonism so altered in character that it is doubtful if even Bentham would have accepted it as a valid position. One recent writer[7] has described the modifications introduced by Mill as "Mill's heresy," and the description is not an exaggeration. When Mill's *Utilitarianism* appeared in 1863 it was evident that much of old-line hedonism was probably gone forever.

Despite the differences between Aristippus, Epicurus, and Bentham, they had agreed on one basic doctrine: pleasure is pleasure, whatever the source, the intensity, or the duration. The three thinkers might argue among themselves as to whether some pleasures were worth the cost, or whether anyone except the agent himself should be considerd in determining the hedonic value of an action, but there would certainly have been complete agreement among them concerning the *qualitative* sameness of all pleasure. Mill's "heresy" lay in the fact that he introduced a new and logically subversive concept into the evaluation of pleasure and pain. One of the oldest and most persistent criticisms of hedonism had come from its refusal to acknowledge qualitative differentiations between pleasures. Bentham particularly had been explicit in denying any difference within this category. By Mill's time many thinkers, such as Carlyle, had renewed the old charge that hedonism is a "pig-philosophy": a life devoted to the pursuit of pleasure is not worthy of a man, but only of swine.

[7] Philip Wheelwright, *A Critical Introduction to Ethics.*

Mill replied to this charge just as Epicurus had two thousand years earlier. It is not the hedonists who imply a mean and degraded view of human nature, but their opponents; for to suggest that a life evaluated solely in terms of pleasure and pain is fit only for animals is to imply that man is capable of only animal pleasures. Epicurus explicitly admonished his followers to seek the pleasures of philosophy and social intercourse—a point which both the anti-Epicureans and antiutilitarians always overlooked. Mill goes on to acknowledge a difference between pleasures, and insists that we must differentiate between the "higher" and "lower." In one famous passage he declares that "it is better to be a human being dissatisfied than a pig satisfied; better to be a Socrates dissatisfied than a fool satisfied." Especially important in the determination of truly satisfying and man-worthy pleasures is that sense of human dignity which Mill believed all men possess in some degree.

The Vitality of Hedonism

Probably no position within philosophy has been attacked so persistently as hedonism, nor is there any viewpoint that has more regularly survived attack. While the hedonistic doctrines have been much modified and refined during the long history of the school, the basic emphasis upon the "feeling" roots of value has remained unchanged. Contemporary hedonists insist that all ethical principles must be based upon the results of an act as measured in terms of human welfare, which in turn means human pleasure or happiness. Like Bentham, the hedonist today regards as thoroughly vicious any moral standard which ignores the *consequences* of conduct by trying to judge human behavior in terms of its conformity with some abstract ideal of duty or obligation.

The Principal Objections to Hedonism. The various objections to ethical hedonism center in either its supposed unworthiness as a human ideal, or its inadequacy as an inclusive ethical system. The charge of unworthiness need not detain us long, since we have heard Mill's answer to this accusation. We should also note that this objection implies a preconceived criterion of what is and what is not worthy of humanity—that is, it begins our analysis of the "good" with a preconceived notion of what the "good" shall be. We are thus invited to hoist ourselves by our own ethical bootstraps, attempting to determine what is "good" by what we already hold to be such. It hardly need be said that this is not a sound way to reason, and arguments against hedonism formulated along this line need not be taken seriously. The charge of inadequacy is much more serious, however, and we must consider it fully.

To begin with, we must recall that ethical hedonism can stand on its own feet, quite independent of the truth or falsity of the psychological type of hedonistic doctrine. We need not believe that all of man's behavior is inexorably motivated by the pleasure-pain principle in order to hold that ethical evaluations should be in terms of human happiness and welfare. Thus when it is charged that hedonism is inadequate as an explanation of our behavior, or that the doctrine has been discarded by modern psychology, we must find out whether or not the critic is including the ethical form of the doctrine in his indictment. If ethical hedonism should prove to be an inadequate theory, this will be the result of its own internal weakness; it will not be due to any possible invalidity of the psychological doctrine. As we study the alternatives to hedonism, its intellectual inadequacies may become more apparent. The sharpest conflict within the field is between formalism and hedonism, so we shall consider this most aggressive antihedonistic doctrine first.

Hedonism's Sharpest Critic: Formalism

Ethical formalism has close relations with the absolutistic view described in our last chapter. In essence, it holds that the rightness or wrongness of an act is an inherent quality which is independent of everything—time, place, circumstance, and so forth. Furthermore, this inherent or absolute quality of an act is independent *of any results which follow from it*. The consequences of an act have no relation to its goodness or morality. Where the hedonist holds that all standards of right and wrong must ultimately be based upon the consequences of each act, the formalist believes that ethical standards have only one authority: their own intrinsic nature, which has no relation to the consequences of any action.

We must be fair to the formalist and point out that he does not pretend that the results of an act have no practical importance or relation to human welfare. The formalist is just as aware as the hedonist that most of our behavior has implications of eventual happiness or unhappiness for either ourselves or other persons, *but he denies any relation between these practical implications and the rightness or wrongness of the act.* Thus as far as consequences are concerned, formalism regards human behavior as taking place in a sort of moral vacuum. It may be of great importance to me if someone steals my automobile, but this has nothing to do with determining whether theft is right or wrong. It happens to be wrong, says the formalist, because of an inherent quality in acts of theft which no circumstances—even what a court might consider "extenuating circumstance"—can alter. The formalist believes that, in general, good consequences follow from right actions and bad results from wrong ones. But despite this assurance, there is no *necessary* connection between the two: "Right" actions would still be right even though virtue always led to unhappiness for the agent and suffering for everyone around him. And conversely, even though a "wrong" action resulted in added happiness for everybody concerned, it would still be wrong.

The prince of ethical formalists is Immanuel Kant. Unfortunately his thought is not easy to comprehend, and its austere and rigorous conclusions do not appeal to most students today. However, his commanding position in the history of ethics makes it imperative that we understand his basic ideas. Because Kant's system culminates in the most celebrated theory of "duty" (the type of theory formalistic systems in general reach), it will be helpful to introduce his thought by sketching briefly the history of the concept of "duty."

The History of "Duty"

The classical Greeks, so modern in much of their thought, had little sense of duty as we now understand the term. For a Greek, the moral life and the good life were the same thing—that is, the good life was one in which certain virtues or excellences were necessary because in no other way could men find happiness. "Temperance," the most frequently praised Greek virtue, is a good example. For a Greek it was not a *duty* to be temperate—temperance was not an obligation imposed by some law or authority—but rather a matter of simple cause and effect. Intemperance produces unhappiness, so therefore we ought to be temperate. But the "ought" involved here is only a conditional obligation: *if* we want to be happy, then we ought (that is, it is necessary) to be temperate in our habits. To live well is to be temperate and courageous and just and magnanimous. But this is a matter of common-sense cause and effect, not a categorical or abstract obligation such as is usually involved in moral commands.

The Stoic Theory of Duty. Toward the end of the Greek period, with the coming of Stoicism, a new idea was introduced into ethical thought which eventually shifted ethics from a "good-centered" to a "duty-centered" study, and hence paved the way for both Christian morality and, later, puritanism. This was the idea of "virtue" or "right living" as obedience to a law, rather than as merely an observance of the rules of cause and effect. The Stoic held the good life, which every wise man should seek to lead, to be the life in which a man's duty was determined by the law of nature or the rational order of the universe—the World Reason, in Stoic terminology. His cosmic law of the World Reason prescribed for each individual his place in the scheme of things, and established the duties and obligations which went with this assigned status. The essence of Stoic wisdom consisted in acknowledging this place prescribed for oneself and the duties accompanying it, and thus consciously living in harmony with Nature—that is, with the World Reason. Furthermore, according to Stoicism, everything which happens in the universe occurs by logical necessity. Hence accepting what life brings us is both obligatory and wise.

It can be readily seen that this Stoic doctrine represents a real shift from earlier Greek ethical thought, although it was still a long way from the Christian concept of "duty." The Stoics, by making morality or "right living" a matter of conformity to law, necessarily emphasized the idea of duty more strongly than it had been stressed before, at least in the Western world. But by identifying the law of Nature with the law of Reason, and then identifying this World Reason with the finite reason each man possesses, they managed to keep the obligations which duty commands from being arbitrary or purely authoritarian in character. Our individual reason permits us to recognize the justice and wisdom of the World Reason and its necessary commands. Hence the duties laid upon us by this World Reason are freely accepted (by every wise and virtuous man) because they square with the pronouncements of our own private reason. Thus private and cosmic judgment agree, and there is no feeling of external compulsion or arbitrary commandment.

Christianity and Duty. Christianity brought still another important change in the basic concept of morality, and also brought the idea upon which official Western ethics has been built for the last seventeen hundred years. This is again the doctrine that moral living consists in obedience to law, but this is a very different law from the one acknowledged by Stoicism. This new law is not one which human reason discovers, and which therefore seems "reasonable"; it is instead a law given us by divine revelation which simply has to be obeyed, regardless of whether it appears reasonable or unreasonable, logical or arbitrary, just or unjust. It has to be obeyed solely because it is the will of God, and not because we can see in it the means to our own immediate happiness. Of course we naturally assume that because this divine law is promulgated by a good deity, it will be a good law expressing ultimate wisdom. But, since our salvation directly depends upon obedience to this law, we obviously are required to perform whatever duties it specifies regardless of our human opinion of these edicts. It should be further noted that in Christianity this connection (between man's obedience and his salvation) is also established by God's ordinance, rather than by human reason. Consequently the Stoic relation between the World Reason and our finite individual reason is weakened still more. Right down to the present day, the performance of one's Christian duty has remained a matter of *obedience,* rather than of *insight.* As has been well said, the question of why this obedience is good, or even why it is required, is not our concern. All that really matters is that it is required.[8]

Deism and Duty. In the eighteenth century, as a by-product of the controversy between theists and deists, more thoughtful theologians attempted to modify the arbitrariness of this divine ordination by showing the close relation between moral duty as indicated by revelation and moral duty as proclaimed by our individual conscience. They argued that God has not only established the moral law in the universe, but has also implanted in each soul an echo or instrument of this same moral law. Thus by listening to our conscience, or by utilizing "the clear light of natural reason" (a favorite eighteenth-century phrase), we will discover

[8] Cf. article on "Duty" in Hastings, *Encyclopedia of Religion and Ethics* (1924). Part of the material for this section on the history of "duty" has been drawn from this source.

the same commands that revelation has given us through Scripture and the writings of the church fathers. So revelation supports conscience, and in return conscience proves the authority of revelation. Hence our duty is indicated by more than just the authority of Scripture or ecclesiastical law. It is also indicated by internal perception, although this perception is really a *recognition.* We both hear our duty from without, *via* the pulpit and other conventional moral authorities, and we also hear it from within, *via* the still small voice of conscience. We thus have here at least a partial return to the Stoic view of duty and its sources.

Popular Doctrines of Duty. There was another development within eighteenth-century ethics which undoubtedly had more popular influence than the view just outlined. As is usually the case with popular ideas, it was easy to understand. It also had an emotional appeal lacking in the more intellectual theological and philosophical theories of that day. This popular view argued that while our duties can be *known* by the light of natural reason, their *sanction* (that is, the authority or "teeth" enforcing obedience to them) is strictly the rewards and punishments that will follow our obedience or disobedience. These rewards and punishments may occur in either this world or the next, but those in the next world are most certain and most significant. So in this view "heaven" and "hell" become all-important as stimuli for ethical conduct. The advocates of this view could easily have rephrased the well-known argument for the existence of God: "If God did not exist it would be necessary to invent him," and said instead, "If heaven and hell did not exist it would be necessary to invent them"—in order to make people perform their Christian duties promptly.

This doctrine seems to imply that ethics is essentially a matter of expediency, and morality nothing more than "good policy." If we wish God's blessing, or if we wish to stay out of trouble, both in this world and in the next, then we must obey the commands of morality, particularly Christian morality. However, this attitude is not confined to popular Christianity. On the contrary it has been widespread ever since men had gods to obey, to appease, or to supplicate. Simple minds have always tended to make religious worship a system of barter, in which the worshipper promises to do something for the deity—obey, sacrifice to, or merely acknowledge—in return for which some favor is expected from the deity. Greek popular religion reveals many evidences of this bartering spirit, and there is ample indication it has been an important part of naïve religious worship from times beyond memory. So it is not surprising that the eighteenth century, for all its "enlightenment" and rationality, could not stamp out this age-old tendency to regard religion as a bargain between two parties. Obviously this would make our "duty" consist simply of carrying out our half of the bargain. Duty thus becomes contractual, rather than arbitrary or rational or intuitive.

Kant's Philosophy of Duty

Certainly the most famous and most imposing advocate of a duty-centered system of ethics is Immanuel Kant. Much of his ethical thought is a revolt against doctrines of moral expediency and "good policy" maintained by moralists in his day, and some of the apparent austerity of his thought would be softened if we had space to show how low a level some of this purely expedient morality had reached. However we must plunge directly into Kant's system, for it is from this that much of nineteenth-century thinking regarding duty was derived.

No Relation Between Inclination and Morality. Kant held that there is no relation whatever between inclination and morality. That is, whether we want to do something or not has no bearing on the rightness or morality of that act. For one reason, inclination is notoriously changeable. What I am inclined to do today I may be disinclined to do tomorrow. Furthermore inclination is always a personal matter, strictly subjective. But, argues Kant, the basis of morality must be truly objective and universal. It must be free not only from personal bias or whim, but from the accidents of time, place, and cultural environment. Genuine morality must be the same in every culture and in every historical period; it must hold true regardless of "race, creed, or religion." Because—and here we come to the heart of Kant—unless "right" is right, whether we like it or not, and unless this "right" remains objective and compelling regardless of any private inclination, *the concept of duty is meaningless.*

Kant is very explicit on this point. Not only is inclination totally irrelevant to morality or "rightness": *only those actions performed from a sense of duty are truly moral.* Now this is admittedly a harsh saying. Undoubtedly this one statement has done most to give Kant his reputation for ethical austerity. He not only means that actions must be performed in accord with the commands of duty, but also that they must be done for the sake of fulfilling our duty, and for no other reason, if they are to be genuinely moral. A brief quotation from Kant makes this explicit.

> To help others where one can is a duty, and besides this there are many spirits of so sympathetic a disposition that, without any further motive of vanity or self-interest, they find an inner pleasure in spreading happiness around them and can take delight in the contentment of others as their own work. Yet I maintain that an action of this kind, however right and amiable it may be, has still no genuinely moral worth. It stands on the same footing as other inclinations—for example, the inclination to honor, which if fortunate enough to hit on something beneficial and right and thus honorable, deserves praise and encouragement but not esteem; for its maxim lacks moral content, namely, the performance of such actions, not from inclination, but from duty.[9]

In other words, we get no credit in heaven or in any moral scorebook for good acts performed on the basis of their helpfulness, or because motives of kindness, sympathy, or love prompt them. But if these same acts, or even ones less helpful and less productive of happiness, are performed from a sense of duty pure and simple, then they automatically become moral actions worthy of all possible esteem.

As might be expected, Kant's ethical doctrine has been criticized and caricatured for more than a century and a half. And certainly at first sight it invites caricature. But within the framework of Kantian thought it follows logically. Even Kant's opponents have been forced to admit that he honestly stated a hard truth which all too many ethical thinkers have tried to evade or soften in some way—namely, if "duty" means anything, it does not mean "inclination" or "pleasure." In other words, duty does not offer to bargain with us. It commands, and either we obey or disobey, but it is useless to seek compromise or halfway evasion of the full command.

Criticisms of Kant's Views. It is much easier to attack Kant on the obvious grounds that he ignored the social factors which establish and transmit the actual content of duty. He was, in short, too much concerned with proving that the commands of duty are absolute. He failed to realize (or at least to acknowledge) that, however absolute the demands of duty may be, the actual content of these demands is socially determined and transmitted. Children may be born with a "conscience,"

---

[9] *Fundamental Principles of the Metaphysics of Morals,* Section I, p. 14.

in the sense of a latent capacity for making moral judgments, but no psychologist or sociologist today would acknowledge that this capacity is anything more than latent. The conscience is a blank sheet of paper, as it were, upon which society (largely in the persons of our parents and teachers) proceeds to write moral commandments from the hour of our birth.

It can also be charged that Kant put excessive emphasis upon the supreme value of a *good will*. He made the famous statement, for example. "There is nothing either in the world or out of it which is good without qualification except a good will." He seems to have been oblivious to the fact that a well-meaning fool can often do as much harm as an intentional scoundrel. Kant's emphasis is a necessary part of his whole doctrine that morality has no relation to the consequences of our actions. He does not deny that the results of our actions are important for human happiness, but he specifically denies that these results, happy or otherwise, are relevant to the rightness or wrongness of our actions. This plainly puts Kant at the opposite ethical pole from all hedonists, who of course judge actions entirely in terms of their bearing upon happiness or pleasure. But since Kant was consciously attacking hedonism, he was quite willing to end up at the opposite pole from it.

And now let us briefly summarize the Kantian ethics up to this point. In them, the sole criterion of morality is the motive of the performer. If an act is performed with a good will and from a sense of duty, it is automatically a moral action. Those acts performed from any other motive are either nonmoral or immoral. We must note that Kant does not say that all human actions whatsoever should be done from a sense of duty. Even so rigorous a moralist as he was knew that many things we do have no relation to morality, such as deciding which shoe to put on first, or whether to water the lawn in the forenoon or the afternoon. But he does insist categorically that only those acts which *are* performed in obedience to the commands of duty constitute moral actions.

Who Issues the Commands of Duty?

At this point we are approaching another issue which is involved in all philosophies of duty—namely, who issues the so-called "commands of duty"? Does not any command always imply a commander of some sort? Does not the whole concept of duty imply the existence of an authoritative agency to determine what is and what is not a duty?

The Theistic Answer.   All persons who acknowledge "duty" as the principal component of the good life also acknowledge this implication. But, as might be expected, they do not agree regarding the source of these commands. Many duty-oriented individuals are fortunate in that they are also theists, since this fully solves the problem. To any theist, God is the commander; doing one's duty is equivalent to doing the will of God. We are obligated to such performance by the very nature of our relation to God: we are his creatures and his children, and it is axiomatic that creatures obey their creator and children their parent.

Various religious sects of course have their individual doctrines as to how God's will is communicated to men. Among Christians, for example, Protestants acknowledge either Scripture or private conscience (or a combination of both), while Catholics accept the authority of the Church (that is, of its clergy and hierarchy). But for any theist, the means by which God communicates to us are far less important than the fact that He does communicate. So duty-bound theists are seldom bothered by the variety of views, often contradictory, regarding the channels through which God's commands reach us.

But Who Issues Commands for the Nontheist?   Now this belief in God as source of duty-commands may work very well for theists. But how does "doing God's will" solve the problem for a conscientious person, prepared to perform whatever duty requires, who does not believe in God —or at least not in a God who issues moral imperatives? Such persons are not unknown in our culture, and their number appears to be increasing. Even Kant, who believed in God, was aware of this problem. He attempted to produce a theory of duty which would be independent of theism and free from the sanction of supernatural rewards and punishments. Thus his ethical theory was intended to be secular as well as Christian—or, as Kant himself preferred to describe it, universal.

Kant does this by putting ethics and morality upon a purely rational foundation—that is, he tries to build ethical obligation entirely upon *logic*. In typically rationalistic fashion he attempts to prove that whenever we violate a moral law, or fail to perform a duty, we are also being logically inconsistent. By one single act we violate the laws of both logic and morality, thereby putting ourselves in a kind of double jeopardy. Kant obviously feels that if he can establish this necessary relation between immorality and mental inconsistency, he will have the firmest possible foundation for obligation. Since any rationalist considers logical inconsistency nearly as great an evil as immorality, Kant naturally felt that a system which eliminated both these evils at the same time was worth striving for.

The Formalistic Element in Kant's System. Let us see how Kant accomplishes this dual feat, at least to his own satisfaction and that of his fellow-rationalists. His view is the best example of an ethical formalism, which evaluates actions solely in terms of their consistency (that is, their formal agreement) with certain axioms or postulates. If an act harmonizes with, or can be derived from, one of these general principles, then it is moral, regardless of its consequences. In other words, the formal consistency which members of this school prize so highly is worked out by first discovering or assuming certain general ethical principles, and then deducing a system of morality from these. This is comparable with a mathematical system like Euclid's geometry, which begins with a handful of axioms ("A straight line is the shortest distance between two points," "A whole is equal to the sum of its parts") and then derives numerous theorems from these initial postulates.

Kant's most important axiom (in fact the only one relative to our purpose here) is this: *Always act in such a way that you would be willing to have your action become the universal law of mankind.* This of course has some relation to the Golden Rule of doing unto others as you would have them do unto you, but the emphasis upon universality gives the Kantian axiom a different flavor. Here the supreme test of any action is rather the implied question, "Would I be willing to have everyone do as I am doing?" If we can sincerely answer "yes" to this question, then the act may be safely regarded as moral. If not, then it is immoral.

An Example of Inconsistency. To cite an example, lying is immoral because the liar is imposing on society by making an exception of himself. He expects others to tell the truth, for how else would his lie be believed? Unless truth-telling were general, so that we normally take people's statements as true without requiring proof, how could the liar gain advantage by his lie? His situation is similar to that of a counterfeiter, who is able to ply his trade and put false money into circulation because most money is good and circulates freely without question. But it takes only a small amount of counterfeiting to ruin a system of currency, since bad money tends to drive out good. So no counterfeiter wants his peculiar craft to become widely practiced. The worst thing that could happen to him, aside from getting caught, would be for enough other individuals to start printing money to drive the accepted currency under a cloud of suspicion. A currency must be good, for counterfeiting to work even temporarily. And so with lying: if it became general, no man's statement would be believed, and the liar could not get by on the basis of his word.

But this is clearly inconsistent. The liar wants truth-telling to be general and dependable, but he wants to be an exception to this generality. In short, he would not be willing to have his own conduct generalized; if it became "the general law of mankind" he would be out of luck. So, basically he is advocating one standard for himself and a second standard for everyone else. Thus any man who tells a lie is involved in a contradiction. By making an exception of himself—by violating the rule that in all social situations each person is to count for only one, and each one is to have the same value—our lying friend acts out a basic inconsistency. Or, as we usually say of such individuals, they pay only lip-service to standards, but do not practice them.

Same Inconsistency Present in all Unethical Conduct. Now Kant believes that all unethical conduct involves this same inconsistency, since it always involves behavior we would not be willing to have become universal. Hence unethical conduct is at bottom illogical or irrational conduct, because it necessarily means logical contradictions on the part of its practitioners. Thus there exists a rational or logical basis for ethics, independent of divine command, ecclesiastical edict, or social convention. In fact this basis is independent of *all* authority, either human or divine. It is strictly autonomous. Perhaps it would be clearer to call it self-contained: there is no need for support from any outside agent or agency. The a priori laws of valid reasoning provide all the justification it needs. So even skeptics and atheists have a basis for ethical judgment, while the theist is offered an additional foundation to reinforce his God-given ethics.

The critical reader may discover flaws in this Kantian scheme insofar as it claims to be the basis for a universal, binding ethics. For example, suppose a person whose conduct is unethical does not care whether he is consistent or not. If we accuse this individual of illogical, contradictory behavior and he merely shrugs his shoulders and says, "So what?" then what do we do? On what basis can we appeal to him? If he is not a rationalist, and has no concern for mental consistency, then where are we? Obviously Kant, by putting all his ethical eggs in this one rationalistic basket, took a major risk. There is always the chance that some unethical person, by ignoring logical consistency, may steal the eggs and the basket too!

Kant's Permanent Contribution. But whatever flaws may be found in Kant's ethical system, they are not logical flaws. Certainly he practices his ideal of consistency most consistently. And certainly his system remains the most thorough-going attempt yet made to establish ethical obligation upon a strictly rational basis, independent of supernatural support in the will of God. As such it merits respect, even if we cannot feel warm affection for it. Kant may not have succeeded in making a life lived according to duty sound attractive, but he definitely made it challenging. And he provided a foundation for a philosophy of duty which has influenced many persons in succeeding generations. His requirement that we do some things *simply because they are our duty and for no other reason* may be an austere philosophy, but there have been a surprising number of persons who have risen to the challenge of its lofty austerity.

"Self-Realization" as the Highest Good

It is probable that those readers who had hoped to find in formalism an adequate antidote to hedonism have been disappointed. Regardless of how much one may dislike an ethical theory that acknowledges no obligation to anything except human happiness, most modern minds find the idea of a morality which completely ignores that happiness even more impossible.[10] Thus we are naturally moved to ask if there cannot be a position somewhere in between these extremes of hedonism and formalism. The general viewpoint which attempts to effect this compromise is known by several names: *Self-realizationism, perfectionism, energism, eudæmonism,* and *humanism* have been the most common. There appears to be a growing tendency to adopt *self-realizationism* as the most satisfactory term, so we shall follow this usage.

[10] Kant was forced to acknowledge that man is a sensuous creature as well as a rational being, and that consequently the man who combines obedience of the categorical imperative with pleasures lives a "happier" life than one who finds only unhappiness and frustration in that obedience.

The doctrine of self-realization holds that the highest good consists in the realization of the self or personality. This means the complete realizing or energizing (hence "energism") of all the potentialities and capacities within the individual. Furthermore, it means that these must be developed into a unified, integrated whole; the goal is *wholeness* as well as *completeness*. It is the emphasis upon these coequal aims which serves to separate the doctrine of self-realization from formalism on one hand and hedonism on the other. Formalism stresses man's rational nature, but sacrifices his feelings, sensations, and general emotional life. Hedonism tends to the other extreme, viewing man solely as a creature of feeling. Thus, in comparison with self-realization, the goals of both its rivals appear incomplete. It alone (claims the self-realizationist) seeks to include *all* man's energies and capacities within an integrated whole. The only proper *summum bonum* must be the harmonious development of all aspects of man's nature.

So much for a simple statement of the doctrine of self-realization. However it is largely the implications of the position which make it such a potent force in contemporary ethical thought, so we must analyze these more fully.

Self-Realization and "Higher Values." The advocates of self-realization speak much of "hyperorganic values," and place their primary emphasis upon the attainment of these. By this term is generally meant all goods or values other than the purely physical or biological satisfactions of the organism. While man shares virtually all his organic values with the animals, he is the only creature that is capable of realizing those values which are hyperorganic—that is, above or beyond the organism as a physical being. For man has needs and capacities that are far beyond the range of even the higher animals. It is these capacities which this ethical school particularly emphasizes. Proponents of self-realization point out that organic satisfactions can never make up more than a part of the Good Life, for these have only an instrumental status; they are merely the physical foundations of the fully realized human life. The body must be fed, sheltered, and given sexual satisfaction, but these are only necessary preliminaries to the chief end of man. It is the realization of the higher values that constitutes true *self*-realization, and it is usually these which the members of this school have in mind when they argue in support of their position.

Several subschools within the self-realization movement carry this emphasis upon higher values so far as to imply a dualism of some kind. The hyperorganic satisfactions are given such stress that we may find a tendency to minimize the importance of man's physical welfare. The name "idealistic perfectionism" is usually applied to this extreme spiritual-minded wing. At the other extreme are those exponents of self-realization who view man's capacities largely in physical terms. Here the stress is placed upon adjustment to the environment, or biological adaptation. The term "naturalistic perfectionism" describes the general temper of this left wing within the school of realizationists.

An Inclusive Position. It is a moderate group, standing between these two wings, which constitutes a majority of the self-realizationist school. This middle viewpoint makes a definite effort to bridge the gap that separates the opposing extremes. It is careful not to stress either organic or hyperorganic values at the expense of the other kind; instead the goal is a complete realization of *all* human capacities, with no single one or single kind selected for special emphasis. The chief aim is inclusiveness, and no hierarchy of values is set up which subordinates the physical to the spiritual, or vice versa. On first thought this appears to be a happy compromise, and as such it makes a strong appeal to many persons as the best ethical goal. Unfortunately, like so many compromises, it proves unsatisfactory as soon as we attempt to apply it in practice. For life is nothing if not an unbroken series of choices that must be made; we must choose *which* capacities we will realize, and *which* we will reluctantly decide to let remain only potential. Probably no man can in a single lifetime develop all the capacities that are latent within him. And as choice always implies some standard by which we choose, we are soon back where we started with our original problem unsolved. *Which* values shall we realize, *which* capacities shall we develop, *which* criterion of perfection shall we accept?

Other Objections to Self-Realization. Other objections to self-realization as an ethical ideal have been voiced from time to time, and while none of these appears to be fatal to the doctrine, they must be mentioned at least briefly. Probably the criticism most often heard involves the charge that the goal of self-realization is essentially a selfish ideal. For, it is argued, to focus the attention upon the self in such a manner is to risk developing egoism and self-centeredness of the worst kind. It is only as we lose ourselves in some cause, or in the service of our loved ones, that we reach our maximum development. On this point one of the most profound sayings of Christ is often quoted as an argument against the gospel of self-realization: "He that saveth his life shall lose it, but he that loseth his life shall save it."

A second objection to the doctrine is the claim that men may "realize" themselves in ways which are antisocial quite as readily as in ways that are socially approved. All of us have potentialities for evil that are as real a part of our "inner capacity" as our more desirable aptitudes are. To urge that we develop *all* the capacities latent within us gives no hint as to which we should put first, or which we should favor when they prove to be mutually exclusive of one another. Here again the problem of choice is all important, and the doctrine of complete self-realization is useless as a guide in making such choices.

The Self-Realizationist Replies. The advocates of self-realization have ready answers for both of these objections. The charge of egoism is met by pointing out that man is a social being who can realize his maximum potentialities only in social relationships. Since there can be no true development of the individual in a social vacuum, the realization of personal values necessarily also involves the development of other selves as well. To be selfish is to stunt the development of the total self. Thus while it is possible that a misunderstanding of the doctrine—or, more likely, a false concept of the self—would lead to selfishness, this would be a perversion of the realizationist viewpoint and not its logical fruit. It is true that absorption in a cause or in some labor of love is probably the best way to achieve a maximum development of the self, but this only proves that the self is primarily a social product.

This same answer is used to meet the charge that an individual may realize himself in ways that are socially undesirable. For, if man is a social creature, it is difficult to see how he can achieve his highest personal development in ways that run counter to social development. The idealistic perfectionist has an additional argument here, since he stresses the development of all that is *highest* in man. By setting up this hierarchy of values, the perfectionist can argue that we must inevitably subordinate some of our potentialities if an integrated self or personality is to be realized; and, since man is a social being, it must be the antisocial potentialities which are subordinated.

It is evident that we cannot carry the discussion much farther without becoming involved in what is perhaps the most abysmal part of philosophy's domain, the problem of the Self. However, by walking carefully we can merely skirt the edge of that problem and conclude our discussion of self-realization with a brief statement of the views of its greatest exponent, Aristotle.

The Ethics of Aristotle

It is always refreshing relief to turn to the ethical thought of Aristotle. While his views have not been immune from attack, and the expansion of democracy has made some of them appear a bit snobbish, his ethical thinking has a clarity, a balance, and above all a common sense that makes it a delight no matter how often we review it. His *Nicomachean Ethics* is not only one of the greatest source books in this field but also one of the most unfailing fountains of philosophical refreshment.

In contrast to both his immediate predecessor Plato and a majority of the ethical thinkers who followed him, Aristotle held that the one single realm of reality is the visible natural world. The existent and the ideal, the natural and the spiritual, are one and inseparable. Such a rejection of dualism means that the Good Life must be described in terms of here and now, without reference to the transcendental or the supernatural. As one recent writer states it, for Aristotle "the moral idea is found in the structure of man's own nature."[11] Therefore to discover the character of the Good Life or the form of the *summum bonum* we must examine man's nature. To find the Good we must first answer one great preliminary question: What is it to be a man?

What Is It to Be a Man?   To be a man, answers Aristotle, is to perform certain functions. Some of these we perform in common with all living creatures, some in common with only the animals, while still others are peculiar to our species. Thus we share with all things that have life the purely "vegetable" functions of metabolism, and share with the animals the processes of sensation and impulse. Our capacity for reasoning, however, is unique, and it is the exercise of this function which most clearly defines what it means to be human.

But this uniquely human rational capacity is exercised in a variety of ways by different individuals. For men seek many things; nothing is more characteristic of our species than the number of interests men follow and

[11] Harold H. Titus, *Ethics for Today*, p. 83.

the variety of goals they pursue. On this point Aristotle gives some of his famous common-sense examples: the bridle-maker seeks to make good bridle equipment, the soldier seeks victory or skill in military exercises, those engaged in medical activities seek health, and so on. But in the last analysis all these activities are only means to ends, so we are again brought to the concept of human activities as constituting a hierarchy or "goods" or "values." This implies a final end which shall be truly intrinsic, the *summum bonum*—or, as Aristotle puts it, "the good at which all things aim." This highest good he calls *eudaemonia*, which is usually translated as "well-being" or "vital well-being."

Eudaemonia as the Highest Good. The *eudaemonia* for each species will naturally be different. In each case, however, it will consist of the complete development of those functions which are particularly characteristic of that species. In Aristotle's thought this will normally be a single function, since he holds that each form of life has its unique typical activity. Thus our problem is to discover what it is that man does best and most characteristically, since human well-being will consist in the maximum development of this function or activity. We have seen that this cannot be found in man's metabolic processes, since all living things have this same function. Nor can it be in his sensuous, impulsive nature, since the animals share this nature with man. Therefore it must be in man's unique rational activities that the *summum bonum* of humanity is to be found.

Thus we have in Aristotelian ethics the first systematic presentation of the doctrine that the realization of hyperorganic values constitutes the ultimate good. To state Aristotle's view more precisely, man's *summum bonum* is found in the development of all his functions, but particularly those which make him a rational creature and a social being. Just as the excellence of the flute-player consists in the skill with which he plays the flute, and the excellence of the sculptor in the skill with which he practices his craft, so the excellence of man lies in the skill with which he practices the art of being human. And this, we have seen, consists in living so far as possible in terms of our rational nature. Our Good Life is an expression of reason.

The Twin Functions of Reason. Now man's rational nature may be exercised in two directions. For the great mass of mankind its chief use is to control the sensuous and impulsive in us—our irrational nature. Aristotle emphasizes moderation or the "Golden Mean" as the chief guide for organizing our life according to virtue. That conduct is truly virtuous which follows the middle path between the extremes of either excess or deficiency, as when we are "courageous," rather than either "rash" on one hand or "cowardly" on the other. Furthermore a virtuous life is one in which right conduct has become a habit—that is, in which reason has become the automatic determiner of the mean between extremes and the dependable judge of what is proper to the time, place, and circumstance. In realizing all our capacities through a balanced control and integration, we will find not only our highest realization but also our happiness. For, concludes Aristotle, happiness is essentially an accompaniment of proper functioning. It is, to use a term we have employed before, a byproduct; happiness follows upon normal functioning as "the bloom of youth does on those in the flower of their age."

However, the highest standard of human good is neither pleasure nor virtue attained through rational control of our irrational natures. It lies rather in *theoria,* or the activity of reflective contemplation. The highest felicity of which man is capable lies in the enjoyment of reason as an end in itself—thinking for the sake of thinking. Such activity represents the fullest development of man's unique function. Furthermore the disinterestedness of this activity renders it almost foolproof as far as satisfaction is concerned, even as its nature makes it largely independent of circumstance. Aristotle is a blood-brother of Epicurus in his enthusiasm for the pleasures of philosophy. He calls these the purest of pleasures, since there is no mixture of pain from a high cost or depressing hangover. In speaking of the glories of *theoria* Aristotle departs from his normally calm scientific mode of presentation and soars to lyrical heights. Describing the supreme felicity of a life of contemplative reflection, he remarks,

> But such a life would be too high for man [i.e., if lived all the time]; for it is not in so far as he is man that he will live so, but in so far as something divine is present in him; and by so much as this is superior to our composite nature is its activity superior to that which is the exercise of the other kind of virtue. If reason is divine, then in comparison with man, the life according to it is divine in comparison with human life.[12]

Criticisms. Aristotle's devotion to *theoria* has been criticized on two counts. One of these is the result of a misunderstanding, while the other

[12] From Scribner's *Selections,* p. 281.

charge is of doubtful validity. Sometimes he is misinterpreted as meaning that the highest life is that of a speculative spinner of empty metaphysical theories—the stock caricature of the philosopher. A careful reading of the *Ethics*, however, reveals that Aristotle is not thinking of any such ivory-tower activity. The scientist would appear to come nearer to his ideal than the traditional philosopher, although the latter will qualify if his thinking grows out of life and represents a contemplation of human experience in general terms. In some ways the mathematician comes nearer to the Aristotelian ideal than either the philosopher or the scientist, for here if anywhere may be found a thinker who appears to enjoy thinking for its own sake. However, the philosopher has one advantage over all who engage in *theoria*: his breadth of knowledge and experience which we call "wisdom." For, says Aristotle, "the philosopher can contemplate truth . . . the better the wiser he is."

The second objection that is sometimes raised against the life of contemplation accuses Aristotle of advocating an aristocratic, snobbish standard that can be attained only by the intellectual person of ample economic means. There is some validity in this charge, for certainly Aristotle would admit that only the person with some capacity for abstract and disinterested thinking can attain this felicity. He states frankly that, for most men, "the life lived according to reason" means an existence in which reason is used primarily to control the appetitive sides of our nature. He would admit, in other words, that he is concerned with what is highest in man as a species, rather than with what is highest in each individual man. If this is aristocratic, it is an aristocracy of brains only.

A Possible Realization. The charge that an independent income is required for such a mode of life would have been largely true in Aristotle's own day. He explicitly denies, however, that anything more than a modest income is required—merely enough to give us a reasonable amount of leisure. In our day, technology has brought such leisure to a large part of the population, and promises eventually to make it available to all men. Thus, although Aristotle's ideal of human happiness may have been a "class-conscious" standard when it was formulated, that stigma is rapidly fading. Persons now alive may see the day when all men, in so far as their ability permits and their interest beckons, will be able to realize this pattern of the Good Life.

Summary. It will be well to summarize the chapter briefly, for the many names and viewpoints we have mentioned make confusion not only easy but likely.

We began by distinguishing between two types of hedonism, psychological and ethical. The arguments for and against the psychological position were given and we concluded that the doctrine is probably too simple to be adequate, which explains why modern psychology has rejected it. Ethical hedonism, however, we saw to be very much alive, and its various exponents constitute one of the dominant schools of ethical thought. We discussed four examples of hedonism, two from ancient philosophy and two from modern. The doctrines of Aristippus and Epicurus both represent individual or "egoistic" hedonism; both hold pleasure to be the sole good, but whereas Aristippus maintains a crude theory which values only the *intensity* of pleasure, Epicurus refines the doctrine to emphasize *duration* and *cost* (in energy expended and resultant pain or undesirable reaction). Thus he is led to recommend social and intellectual pleasures over those of the body, and he particularly extols the satisfactions of friendship and philosophy. We noted too that while Aristippus holds a strongly positive attitude toward pleasure, Epicurus's doctrine is essentially negative in that he considers the *summum bonum* to be freedom from pain or distress.

Bentham's utilitarianism represents a major change within hedonism, for it involves social happiness or universal good rather than merely personal pleasure. However, this change constitutes only an addition to the earlier doctrine, which Bentham tries to render more precise by the formulation of an hedonic calculus, whereby the positive elements (intensity, duration, certainty, social spread, etc.) are weighed against the negative to determine the value of any action or situation. Perhaps Bentham's greatest service, however, was his insistence that things are to be evaluated in terms of human welfare rather than in conformity with some theoretical, transcendental, or religious ideal.

Mill introduced a wholly new and even heretical factor into hedonism by allowing the *quality* of a satisfaction to constitute an element in its value, whereas all previous members of the school had maintained a strictly *quantitative* standard for the evaluation of human satisfactions.

The various criticism of (and reactions against) hedonism occupied the second half of the chapter. First we considered the basic objections to the doctrine in generalized form. Two have been particularly prominent: the arguments that the theory is (a) unworthy of man's highest nature and (*b*) that it is inadequate as an ethical standard. The first of these two criticisms was easily disposed of, since it begins its search for "good" with a preconceived idea of what that good shall be. The charge of inadequacy is much more serious, and we considered it indirectly by analyzing fully the two principal antihedonistic philosophies, formalism and perfectionism (or "self-realization").

Formalism was presented largely through a study of Kant's ethics, since he is indubitably the most prominent representative of this school. We noted the formalists' search for some moral authority to replace the waning force of Christian belief in the supreme will of a single God as the source of such authority. We noted the a priori maxims and categorical imperative Kant set up as successors to a binding religious authority, and considered both the strength and the limitations of any ethical system built upon these formalistic foundations.

The doctrine of perfectionism or "self-realization" as the *summum bonum* holds up an ideal of wholeness or completeness of personality. This is to be achieved by realizing to the maximum degree all the potentialities or capacities within each individual. However, as this can be only a theoretical ideal (due to the shortness of human life), the several subschools of perfectionism select particular classes or levels of human capacity as most significant, with the remainder subordinated. Thus the most influential of these subschools, "idealistic perfectionism," stresses the hyperorganic values, sometimes even to the extent of disparaging the realization of physical potentialities. "Naturalistic perfectionism," on the contrary, emphasizes environmental or biological adaptation as the goal.

Aristotle's ethical thought offers an early but still influential example of the self-realization theory. Here the *summum bonum* consists in the free functioning of that activity most characteristic of any particular species—in the case of man, of his intelligence, since it is our intellectual life that most clearly separates humanity from the rest of the animal order. While this intellect can be exercised in a variety of ways, Aristotle holds that it realizes its highest potentiality in *theoria*, the activity of reflective contemplation most fully exemplified in philosophy.

CHAPTER 14

DETERMINISM *vs.* INDETERMINISM

How Free Is Man?

W E HAVE SEEN THAT A LARGE PART OF ETHICAL SPECULA-tion consists of an analysis of the concept of obligation. Whence comes the "oughtness" of ought? What is our duty? Why is it our duty? And why should I do my duty anyway? These questions, added to those that center in the problems of the *summum bonum* and the Good Life, indicate that ethics is a *normative* study, concerned with the definition of certain norms or standards.

Among the basic assumptions which any normative study must make is what has been called the "postulate of possibility." This postulate holds that the norms we establish for any field must be to some extent achievable. Thus far in our ethical discussion we have made this assumption; we have taken for granted that man can determine the nature of ideal conduct, and then realize this ideal—at least in part. It is now time that we admit that this is a very large assumption, one which may be quite unwarranted by the facts in the case. In making this admission, we are acknowledging that we have also taken for granted something even more fundamental to ethics. We have throughout the last two chapters assumed that man is a free agent—the master of his will, the sole determiner of his conduct, and the maker of his own moral destiny. We have, in short, assumed the *freedom of the will*, ignoring the possibility that man's actions may be as strictly determined by the laws of cause and effect as are the movements of a falling rock. We have throughout avoided one of the most controversial issues within philosophy, that of *determinism vs. indeterminism*. Most of the present chapter will therefore be devoted to compensating for this neglect.

The History of the Free-Will Controversy

In our preliminary discussion of the problems of philosophy (Chapter 1) we traced the background of the deterministic controversy. We pointed out how the principle of causality had gradually been extended to include one field after another. From its first formulation in the simplest laws of mechanics, the scope of the causal principle was broadened until eventually even the mechanics of heredity were brought within its framework. First material objects, then later supermundane things such as stars and planets, had their behavior subjugated by the extension of scientific law and order. When finally the behavior of animals was shown to be at least partly predictable, and Darwin's theory had revealed the working of a vast orderly process that determined the very forms of life, it looked as though the steady march of determinism had reached its farthest limits. All events in the natural order were now seen to be direct consequences of antecedent events, and almost every phenomena within our experience was explicable (or promised eventually to be) in terms of the iron-clad laws of cause and effect. More and more it became evident that the major work of science was the formulation of these causal laws. Scientists themselves were convinced that they would achieve everything which the mind demanded as explanation when they could announce a complete integration of the various aspects of our experience in one great system of cause and effect relations. Meanwhile, philosophers became increasingly involved in the problem of causality, and they too had come to feel that "cause" is a central concept of human experience. Thus, by the end of the nineteenth century, the domain of determinism had attained almost universal extent.

There remained, however, one last bit of unconquered territory. Still outside the all-inclusive causal law stood man. "Human nature" was still something apart from "nature," for it was independent of the deterministic principle. Man was, in sum, an exception. However rigorously causal chains might bind the rest of the universe, man's actions and motives were somehow free. He could, at any time, make a decision or perform an act which had no relation to his previous decisions and actions. The behavior of the animals appears to be only a reaction to physical forces (called stimuli) and therefore each act they perform is a caused event. Men, however, apparently can cause their own events, either by interrupting a causal series already in progress or by beginning a new series *ab initio*.

The Early Determinists. Long before the end of the nineteenth century there had been strong protests against this view of man as an exception to the universal deterministic principle, but the protesters were a small minority. In ancient Greece the universality of the principle was taught by materialistic thinkers such as Democritus. The first modern system of philosophic determinism was that of the Englishman Thomas Hobbes, formulated in the middle of the seventeenth century. The greatest of the precontemporary determinists, however, was Spinoza, who died in 1677. We have already described this great Jewish thinker as an outcast from both his own people and orthodox Christians, and it should be pointed out that it was probably his determinism even more than his supposed atheism which led to this excommunication. While Spinoza's concept of causality has subsequently been criticized by Hume and others, his general deterministic principle, particularly in its application to man, still sounds amazingly modern. It is no exaggeration to describe this aspect of his thought as more than two centuries ahead of its time.

The Ambiguous Position of Descartes. We shall describe Spinoza's position more fully in a moment, but first we must understand what he was reacting against. Descartes, born a generation earlier, had formulated a daring but still orthodox position. As a part of his famous dualism, he had established a basic separation between "nature" and "human nature." Everything except man was pictured as bound completely by deterministic laws. Even the animals were to Descartes mere automata, reacting to stimuli in purely mechanical fashion. Indeed, the Cartesian system went to the extreme of denying consciousness to animals; they are merely organized matter, existing entirely in the realm of "extension" and moved only by the laws of mechanics. It is in man alone that the realm of "thought" has existence or influence. Men's bodies are merely parts of the realm of extended matter, with the same status as animal bodies, but in addition man possesses consciousness and an immortal soul. These clearly belong to the higher realm of "thought," so that man represents a union of "substance extended" and "substance thinking."

It has sometimes been suggested that Descartes was made cautious by the Inquisition's persecution of Galileo and other advanced thinkers, and that he consequently formulated this dualism to keep within the graces of the still-powerful Church. Certainly the result of his bifurcation of reality was to free the natural order, both physical and animal, from the scientifically sterile concepts of "final cause" and "ultimate purpose." As a consequence, science was able to start its career on a strictly deterministic basis. Henceforward, as long as science kept out of the domain of theology—that is, man's origin, nature, and destiny—it was free to go its own way. It is probable that Descartes was sincere in his dualistic belief, but the result of his dichotomy was all that he could have wished had he been consciously trying to separate physical science from theology. Unfortunately, in thus freeing physical science from the domination of the Church, he unknowingly gave psychology over into intellectual bondage; for this particular science, with mind or consciousness as its subject matter, appeared to fall within the theological sphere. As a result, the old concepts of teleology and final purpose, discarded by all the other sciences, were retained in this particular area.

It was this reaffirmed bondage that moved Spinoza to revolt, for he believed that man's actions are as strictly determined as anything in nature. Acknowledging man's ability to conceive a goal and act in the direction of that goal, Spinoza nonetheless established a causal law for human behavior that links us directly with the rest of the natural order. Our feeling of freedom is, in sum, only an illusion. But more on Spinoza's thought in a moment.

The Status of the Controversy Today

Nearly two hundred years elapsed before philosophy caught up with the full implications of Spinoza's determinism. During that period, science grew from diffident adolescence into almost its present maturity, and this development was always in the direction of a more inclusive determinism.

Each discovery made in the laboratory, each hypothesis verified, meant that one more part of the natural order had been brought under the laws of cause and effect. The deterministic frontier was extended steadily, and steadily it became more inevitable that man's unique position outside the causal boundaries should be challenged by science. Finally, during the middle of the last century this challenge was forthcoming, and by the opening of the twentieth century it was so aggressive as to put the orthodox view on the defensive.

Unfortunately the attempts to extend determinism to the human sphere have caused an increase in tension and a decrease in objectivity. Men can discuss the movements of the stars with a high degree of impersonality, but they find the analysis of their own actions a very different matter. Another difficulty has been that the extension of strictly causal concepts into human affairs has involved subtle modifications in the terminology of the subject. In many instances these modifications have been unrealized, and as a result mechanistic concepts have sometimes been stretched almost to the breaking point. We must take care, therefore, to define and employ our key terms as carefully as possible.

The Confusion Between Determinism and Fatalism. The involved controversy over determinism has been further confused by an original failure to distinguish between this view and *fatalism.* The opponents of determinism have rarely been able to see (or at least to admit) a difference between the two positions, while the determinist himself feels that the difference is profound. Speaking precisely, fatalism is the doctrine of *pre*determinism; the popular term "predestination" is a good synonym, provided we do not have in mind a specific tenet of Calvinistic theology. The fatalist holds that every event in the universe is fixed or destined from the beginning, both as to the time and the manner of its occurrence. There is no means of altering this predetermined course of events; when the time comes, "what will happen will happen." This iron law of fate is sometimes expressed poetically by saying that one's destiny is written in the stars.

Fatalism is traditionally associated with an attitude more oriental than Western. In Islamic thought the term "Kismet" is used to express a comparable doctrine, and the term is frequently (though not very accurately) translated as "it is written." Omar Khayyám has given classic expression to the same mood:

The Moving Finger writes, and having writ
Moves on: nor all thy Piety nor Wit
Shall lure it back to cancel half a Line,
Nor all thy Tears wash out a word of it.

It must be emphasized that fatalism views destiny or "cause" as something wholly external to the organism. It is the universe—or more precisely, the vast forces of the universe—that rule our lives. We move through our days in the grip of forces over which we have no control. Our only possible reaction must be the traditional oriental attitude of resignation (with perhaps Omar's cup as a handy helper) or the Stoic's apathy and inner indifference. Against the cosmic powers and predestining stars of fatalism, however, there is nothing that man can summon from within himself that will have any real effect.

Mechanistic Predeterminism. In modern times, parallel with the rise of nineteenth-century science, there has grown up what may be called a scientific or mechanistic predeterminism. Few scientists, even among the extreme mechanists, formally advocated such a doctrine, but popular writers have often felt that it necessarily followed from developments within the laboratory. Many facts are supposed to point in this pessimistic direction, and their cumulative effect has sometimes been extended into the outline of a complete world-view. The principal foundations, both factual and extrapolated, upon which this scientific predeterminism claims to rest are the following:[1]

(1) The conservation of energy principle, which seems to imply that mental energy is only a particular form of physical energy, and consequently is subject to the same laws of cause and effect that rule the physical world. (2) The mechanistic and semimechanistic concepts of both chemistry and biology, which reduce living matter to a complex combination of physiochemical elements completely subject to the laws of physics and chemistry; these same concepts make all animal behavior little more than the interplay of physical forces which remain blind and mechanical even when organized in complex human patterns of ethical conduct. (3) Our increased knowledge of various tropisms—that is, innate tendencies to react in a definite manner to stimuli, as for example the movement of certain plants and insects and animals in reaction to stimuli such as light or chemical agents. (4) The laws of heredity, which make

---

[1] Several of these points are borrowed from Conger, *op. cit.*, pp. 333-4.

any organism the product of inheritable factors in the selection of which it had no say, but which nevertheless operate throughout its lifetime to exercise constant influence in determining choices and shaping behavior patterns. (5) Our increasing awareness of the influence of geographical and climatic factors in human life, which means that the physical environment into which a person is born or moves may affect his behavior (and hence his character or personality) in inescapable ways. (6) The overwhelming evidence from modern psychology, particularly the psychoanalytic schools, that much of human behavior is subconsciously motivated, and that most of this motivation is irrational and even illogical in character. Compulsive actions of all sorts, such as those produced by phobias, manias, and obsessions, are perhaps the most striking instances of subconscious motivation dominating certain behavioral situations. (7) And finally, from the social sciences, the enormously influential theory of economic determinism in which history is viewed as the competitive struggle of social groups or "classes" for economic goods. This theory considers all cultural standards—religious values, ethical norms, moral aspirations, and even esthetic ideals—as an expression of this class struggle and an indication of which side (that is, which class) the person who professes these standards is fighting for. Added to all these is our astronomical and our geological knowledge, which makes man an infinitely small creature in an infinitely large universe, and all human history only the briefest of episodes on an incredibly old planet. Such an aggregation of facts and implications serves to render many individuals today as fatalistic in their attitude toward life as any Oriental with his doctrine of "Kismet."

Determinism vs. Indeterminism

Two alternative points of view stand in opposition to both the moral fatalism of oriental thought and the quasi-scientific mood just described. At the opposite extreme from fatalism is *indeterminism* (or *libertarianism*), and somewhere in between the extremes, *determinism*. As far as concerns philosophy in general—and ethics in particular—the chief controversy has raged around these last two points of view. Despite the importance of fatalism in Eastern thought, and its occasional poignant expression in occidental literature, the doctrine has had little significance in the philosophical systems of the West. We shall therefore limit the remainder of our discussion to the opposition between determinism and indeterminism.

Indeterminism. As we have just indicated, indeterminism is directly contradictory to fatalism. The indeterminist holds that, however completely physical objects and perhaps animal organisms are subject to the laws of cause and effect, man remains free from those laws in his will or capacity for making decisions. Like all objects in the space-time order, our bodies are necessarily subject to such mechanical laws as gravitation, inertia, resistance, and so forth. Furthermore our bodily functions are largely physiochemical in nature, subject to all the laws of physics and chemistry. But, argues the indeterminist, neither mechanical nor physiochemical laws extend to—or account for—man's moral and volitional nature. These are free and undetermined in the fullest sense of the words. Even if we possessed an omniscient knowledge of an individual's past, his character, and all the factors involved in the present situation (as for example all the stimuli he is reacting to) it would still be impossible to predict what choice he will make in any given situation. In other words, it is not just our ignorance which makes us call a person's behavior "unpredictable." Human behavior is genuinely immune from any forecast for the simple reason that only those events can be predicted which have a causal foundation. If we are ignorant of causes, or if (as in this case) there are no causes in the ordinary sense of the term, then, obviously, forecasting is a futile pastime. Indeterminism holds that the individual not only can make uncaused choices—that is, can make decisions which have no relation to his previous decisions or to any factor in his past experience—but also can initiate courses of action that represent genuine novelty in his life pattern. The indeterminist position thus involves two central ideas, unpredictability and genuine novelty.

Determinism. The indeterminist position is synonymous with what we have already described as the majority view in Western civilization. It was this doctrine of "freedom of the will," accepted by most philosophers and virtually all theologians, which led to the revolt of such deterministic pioneers as Hobbes and Spinoza. In our own day, the philosophical opponent to indeterminism has been a position somewhat more moderate than the views of these seventeenth-century path-breakers. This modern form of determinism represents an attempt to integrate our view of man with the scientific system of nature, but seeks to do this without denying the obvious facts of our inner experience. This compromise position (which henceforth we shall simply call "determinism") holds that fatalism is right when it insists that all behavior originates in stimuli, and therefore has an immediate "cause." But on the other hand it agrees with indeterminism when it maintains that the self is something more than merely a complex of stimuli and responses. Determinism even acknowledges that the self may represent a new creative synthesis, whose actions are determined by its own nature rather than by external forces. This middle-of-the-road school speaks much of "self-determinism," and by this term indicates that our actions are the result of our character and habits, which in turn are the product of all our previous decisions and experiences. For these moderate determinists, man has *moral* freedom, and consequently *moral* responsibility. His decisions are truly his own, for they originate in the total self. In sum, our decisions come from within, but the inner self has been modified—and to a large extent formed—by previous reactions to, and decisions about, the external world.

To state the deterministic position in still another way, the "external forces" that discourage the fatalist are accepted by the modern determinist as genuinely influential in forming the self or character. However, once they have wielded this influence, it is absorbed into a new and constantly changing synthesis or "personality," which thenceforth will react in a unique way to further stimuli or external forces. Our actions are thus in a peculiar sense our own; no other self would react in the same way, for no other self has undergone all the same previous experiences and made all the same previous decisions. As Tennyson once wrote, "I am a part of all that I have met." The self is the sum of all previous reactions and decisions regarding "all that I have met." Thus, while our actions are determined, it is by the nature or character of the self, and not by external forces. And it is in this self-determination that our moral and ethical freedom consists.

The Arguments for Each Side

So far we have merely stated, in somewhat dogmatic fashion, the respective positions of determinism and indeterminism. We must now examine the chief arguments advanced by each party, for obviously it is only by evaluating the supporting evidence that we can make an intelligent choice between the two viewpoints. Since indeterminism has been the "official" view of Western thought we shall begin with its arguments. As we shall see, most of the deterministic arguments are really counter-arguments, so we will do well to hear the originals first.

The Indeterminist Arguments. The indeterminist has four principal arguments, all probably of equal importance.

1. One of the most evident facts of our volitional life is a feeling of freedom. No matter what decision we are trying to make, and regardless of how difficult it may be to reach, when we finally do decide, we have a feeling that the choice is undetermined by anything other than our own will. External forces or personal inadequacy may limit our choice to only two alternatives, both perhaps undesirable, but we feel that the final decision is always an arbitrary act of choice on our part. We are certain that the other alternative could have been selected just as easily—and just as "freely." As a correlate to this sense of an undetermined choice, there is usually an intuitive sense of "ought." To many indeterminists, such as Kant, this feeling of obligation is even more convincing proof of freedom than the intuition of an uncaused decision. For, they argue, such a sense of obligation would be quite meaningless if there were no genuine choice possible. The "I ought" must have as prerequisite "I can."

2. The second argument in support of indeterminism is related to this sense of obligation. Any concept of moral (or even legal) responsibility requires freedom of the will to give it significance. It would be illogical to hold a person responsible for an act unless it is his own—that is, unless he has the genuine capacity to choose between alternatives and make moral decisions. All judgments that we ordinarily make regarding the "rightness" or "wrongness" of conduct not only presuppose an undetermined will, but would be unjust and unreasonable under any conditions except those postulated by the indeterminist.

3. The next argument in turn grows out of the preceding one. Indeterminism is the only *intelligible* view, for not only would the deterministic position make evaluations such as praise and blame meaningless, but all values, and even thinking itself, would be equally pointless. For if everything that happens is the necessary result of not only what has gone before but of the very nature of things, which could not be otherwise than they are, then it is futile to talk of "ideas" or "ideals" or "purposes." Reason itself would be inexplicable, since its chief function is to

evaluate and to discriminate; if "all things happen of necessity," as Spinoza and other determinists have taught, rational activity would be both futile and incomprehensible.

4. Finally, argues the indeterminist, there is no middle ground between complete freedom and fatalism. The compromise position of determinism is impossible because it is unstable: in spite of all efforts, it inevitably breaks down into the fatalistic alternative. When thought out to its logical conclusion, the deterministic view denies the freedom which it claims to make possible. For if the self is primarily the product of its experiences—that is, of the external forces which act upon it—then clearly at the moment of actual decision the choice will be the result of these forces and not of an undetermined will such as the postulate of freedom requires. Furthermore, if the determinist is right, would not the question as to what forces will shape our character depend in part upon the nature of the organism which we inherit? Thus our choice would be limited and influenced in a double sense: we would partly be what our environment has made us, and partly what raw material we came into the world with. Anyone who insists that we are free despite these facts is simply not using language as it is ordinarily used. For (concludes the indeterminist) unless the self is transcendent, in the sense of being able to rise above the cause and effect relation that binds the rest of the universe, it is not free. Unless our will is independent of stimuli, heredity, and previous experiences— unless it can at any moment make a choice which always *could* have been otherwise—human freedom is an illusion.

The Arguments of Determinism. The determinist feels that he can meet all these arguments and offer some cogent ones for his own case.

1. To begin with, the deterministic hypothesis is in agreement with one of the most fundamental assumptions of science. As far as all the sciences are concerned, this assumption is absolutely necessary. Indeed it is usually held that the whole structure of modern science is built upon the concept of causality. And, argues the determinist, any principle as fundamental and widespread in application as this one may be presumed to hold for *all* phenomena—not only those which science studies, but all events in the universe. In short, determinism cannot accept the claim that the human will exists in a causeless vacuum; the causality principle is universal in scope, and man is in no way an exception to it. Scientific discovery is possible only because the scientist can postulate an orderly

and intelligible universe, in which every event exists as an element in a causal relation.[2]

2. Further, the science which deals most directly with problems of human behavior, psychology, has made all its advances by building upon the causality postulate. What is even more convincing, psychology has been able to analyze the act of choice, and this analysis has revealed that choice or decision always occurs as the result of certain conditions. When these conditions are present, a choice results; when they are absent, there is none. In sum, all decisions are the result of motivation, and the strongest motive always wins.[3] And, concludes the determinist, since psychological analysis cannot discover any instance of unmotivated (i.e., uncaused) choice, it may be presumed that there is none.

3. The determinist also believes that his position is the basis of all intelligent behavior. The better we know a person, the more we discover that his conduct is both dependable and predictable. Moreover, the behavior of men is in general characterized by a reasonable amount of dependability, as proved by the fact that every society is built upon a mutual trust of its members for one another. We expect people to act in certain ways, because we have discovered that certain stimuli (causes) lead to specific responses (effects); when people disappoint us it is always an exception to the generality of their behavior. Without this overwhelming margin of safe predictability, not only would ordinary social intercourse be hopelessly haphazard, but such sciences as sociology and psychology could not exist.

4. And finally, the indeterminist is wrong when he argues that moral responsibility requires complete freedom of the will. For how could we legitimately hold a person responsible for his actions if they are the result of an arbitrary decision made at the moment of choice—a decision that has no relation to his character, his habits, or his previous experiences?

[2] The degree to which the "principle of indeterminacy" (Heisenberg Principle), important in the study of nuclear physics, challenges the universality of causation is still a controversial issue among both scientists and philosophers. However, the indeterminacy principle has no effect upon nonnuclear physics, since the behavior of matter outside the atom seems to be as rigidly deterministic as ever. Again, the question of what the indeterminacy principle means in the free-will controversy is still a warm issue among physicists and psychologists—and philosophers, of course.

[3] Cf. Cunningham, op. cit., p. 379. Cunningham's treatment of the opposing arguments may be recommended as concise and well organized.

It is only as his choices are truly *his*, inseparably linked with his whole self, that he can properly be praised or blamed, rewarded or punished for them. From the practical standpoint, both morality and social legislation presuppose determinism. For example, all social legislation is based upon the assumption that human conduct can be controlled by proper means; why would we pass laws if we did not assume that they will influence men's behavior? As another example, what is formal education but a long and expensive process of training (or "conditioning," to use the psychologist's favorite term) the individual so that he will react in desirable ways to many of the stimuli which day-by-day experience is sure to bring him? Why should we devote so much time and energy to education unless we are reasonably confident that this conditioning process will be successful— that is, unless we are sure that we can establish a behavior pattern which will be relatively permanent and reliable? If after years of schooling the individual were able to turn his back on the pattern established and act arbitrarily in complete independence of his learned responses, what justification would education have?

The Problem of Legal Responsibility. There is one further point of debate between determinism and indeterminism which grows out of the several arguments we have just given. This is the issue of legal responsibility and legal punishment. The argument of the indeterminist usually runs something as follows: If the will is determined, then legal punishment cannot be justified; because the criminal, motivated by external forces over which he has no control, or by hereditary factors which were set before his birth, cannot do other than he does. Therefore, what justice can there be in punishment under the deterministic view?

The determinist has little difficulty in answering. In the first place, he points out that this indeterministic argument is based upon an outmoded and discredited concept of legal punishment. It assumes that fines, imprisonments, and so forth, are *vindictive* in intention—that is, that society uses these to take revenge on the criminal. This barbaric idea plays no part in enlightened modern penology, which has two purposes behind its punishments: (1) to protect society by restraining the wrongdoer, particularly if he is an habitual criminal; this usually means imprisonment of some kind; (2) to reclaim the wrongdoer by giving him a new set of motives, which may be either more worthy social ideals, or (if he is impervious to these) fears resulting from his current experience with the law. It is this second or "reconditioning" aim of punishment that looms larger and larger in modern penology. And such an aim clearly assumes the deterministic postulate: human conduct is caused by certain motivating factors, and the law intervenes to change the criminal's motivations. If this were a complete waste of time—that is, if the indeterminist is right and the criminal can act arbitrarily without regard to conditioning factors—then how are we to explain the high percentage of ex-criminals who make good by "going straight"?

The Choice Between the Two Positions

As always, the reader must weigh the arguments of both parties in this great controversy and then make his own decisions regarding their claims. A choice between the two is unavoidable, unless we are willing to go to the extreme of embracing fatalism. Such a way out of the difficulty is not likely to appeal to many, however, so we shall consider the real issue to be between determinism and indeterminism.

We may conclude our presentation of the whole problem by suggesting several points which any impartial survey of the situation reveals. Some of these considerations will appear favorable to one side and some to the other. Our purpose in presenting these is not to influence the reader toward one side or the other, but rather to make it more probable that his choice between the two will be an intelligent one.

1. *Is Causality Necessarily Universal?* The first consideration appears to favor indeterminism. The deterministic argument that all science is built upon the principle of causality can hardly be conclusive, for several reasons. It is quite possible that man is a unique species in the organic realm, and that his intelligence and capacity for rational choice do indeed make him an exception in nature. As he is admittedly unique in many ways, we can hardly exclude a priori the possibility that man may be able to initiate new courses of action by making genuinely undetermined decisions. In the second place, the fact that the deterministic principle has proved fruitful in science does not mean that it should be extended to all phenomena, and certainly the fact in no way guarantees that the principle can be so extended. Again, man's volitional life, par-

ticularly where moral choices are involved, may be a separate group of phenomena requiring other concepts than causality to explain them. And third, the idealist may be right when he insists that the law of causation is mind-made—not in the obvious sense that it represents a mental formulation, but in the metaphysical sense that causality represents a demand made by the mind upon the universe. As articulated by Kant, for example, this view holds that causality is one of the forms or categories of thought; it is one of the molds or frames into which sensory phenomena must be poured if they are to constitute an intelligible "world." "Cause" thus becomes subjective rather than objective. And, *if* cause is mind-made, then it is possible that our mental and volitional processes are outside its laws. The mind could impose causation on everything else without necessarily imposing it upon itself. We must therefore conclude that, however indispensable the principle of causality may be to the scientist in his efforts to understand the natural order, its applicability to the mental and moral realm remains unproved.

2. *How Valid Is the Feeling of Freedom?* The second consideration we must note before making any decision between determinism and indeterminism favors the deterministic hypothesis. The indeterminist makes much of our undeniable feeling of freedom; at the moment of actual choice we are usually certain that we could, if we wanted, select the other alternative instead. However, the determinist believes that this intuition of arbitrarily selectable alternatives is an illusion. At least, it is no proof that we really possess an uncaused will. It is more probable that this sense of freedom only indicates our ignorance concerning the causes which actually operate to determine the choice.

It was Spinoza who gave the classical statement of this libertarian fallacy:

Men are born ignorant of the causes of things and yet have a desire of which they are conscious to seek for their own utility. From this it follows, firstly, that they think themselves free, because they are conscious of their wishes and appetites but, because of their ignorance, never even dream of thinking about the causes by which they are led to them; ... Thus the infant believes that it is by free will that it seeks the breast; the angry boy believes that it is by free will that he wishes vengeance; the timid man thinks that it is with free will that he seeks flight; the drunkard believes that by a free command of his mind he speaks the things which when sober he wishes he had left unsaid. Thus the madman, the chatterer, the boy, and others of the same kind, all believe that they speak by a free command of the mind, whilst, in truth, they have no power to restrain the impulse which they have to speak, so that experience itself, no less than reason, clearly teaches that men believe themselves to be free simply because they are conscious of their own action, knowing nothing of the causes by which they are determined. It teaches, too, that the decrees of the mind are nothing but the appetites themselves, which differ, therefore, according to the different temper of the body.[4]

Elsewhere Spinoza uses the analogy of a stone flying through the air, which, if it had consciousness, would undoubtedly be certain that it moved by its own will, being ignorant of the forces which set it in motion.

While Spinoza's statement could hardly be improved, we can give it added emphasis by pointing out how abundantly modern psychology has proved his point. The theory of the subconscious has been an unlimited source of supply for deterministic ammunition. Psychoanalysis is in large part a technique for uncovering hidden causes and suppressed motives which have potent effect upon the conduct of the individual even when he is completely unaware of them. Thanks also to psychology, today even the layman realizes the subtle and insidious influence that rationalization may have upon our thinking and acting. Rationalization is sometimes defined as finding good reasons for bad actions—usually selfish actions of which we are really ashamed. In this self-justifying mental process we try to make our conduct acceptable to ourselves by finding defensible reasons for it which we can persuade our minds are the real reasons. We may be genuinely ignorant of our motives, or merely self-deceiving, but psychology has been able to expose the true cause of our behavior in so many instances that Spinoza's statement, shocking as it was to his century, now seems like a psychological commonplace. Because of unwillingness to be honest with ourselves where unpleasant things are concerned, we call actions that are fundamentally selfish "justifiable." And because of our ignorance as to why we do as we do, we call ourselves "free."

The Changing Concept of "Will." There remains one final consideration which, although an historical fact rather than an argument, lends indirect support to the deterministic position. This is the fact that

[4] *Ethics,* Book I, Appendix, and Book III, Proposition II, *scholia.*

there are two different meanings of the term "will." First there is the traditional meaning, based upon the faculty view of the mind. Since modern psychology no longer regards the mind as a collection of separate agents or "faculties," such as reason, will, imagination, etc., this older meaning of "will" must be ruled out for purposes of precise intellectual discourse.

The current meaning of the term reflects the functional theory of mind held by contemporary psychology. The will is no longer regarded as an entity or separate agent: instead the psychologist prefers to speak of the "act of willing," which he considers a function of the total organism. Through a process of insight and deliberation, the individual coordinates his desires and integrates his impulses; the result of this coordination—often a compromise between opposing desires—is an action, or at least a decision that will eventuate in action. This action can be called an "act of will," but we must keep before our eyes the functional and organismic view of mind when we describe such an act as volitional in character.

It is evident that the outmoded faculty view of the will has close affiliations with the indeterministic position. It is easy to argue that an independent "faculty" or "agent" is free from causal laws, but it would be difficult to claim that the total organism functions in a vacuum of indeterminacy. The very definition of will under the old view as an "independent entity" prejudiced the case before the argument began. Since it was not specified in what way the will is independent, we can hardly blame the indeterminist for interpreting this as a *causal* independence. Today the shoe is on the other foot: since volitional activity is now regarded as an integral part of our total response to the environment, we cannot blame the determinist for using this as support for *his* case. Thus the whole history of the free-will controversy presents an excellent example of the interrelations between philosophy and the current scientific concepts at any date. Science appears to have greater influence on philosophy today than at any time in the past, but this is only a reflection of the enormous influence of science over all fields of human thought. Philosophy has always been responsive to new ideas and ideologies circulating around it; even when the philosopher has seemed most withdrawn into his ivory tower, the "winds of doctrine" blowing outside have inevitably influenced his thinking. There could hardly be a better instance of this than the controversy we have been discussing.

The Permanent Contributions of Each View

The Inspiration of Indeterminism. Whichever party in the argument between determinism and indeterminism finally wins our vote, it should be apparent that each view has played an important role in the history of thought by keeping in circulation certain significant ideas. The greatest contribution of indeterminism, for example, has undoubtedly been its unshakable conviction that we are at least in part the creators of our own destiny—that

> I am the master of my fate,
> I am the captain of my soul.

The fatalist may call this pure illusion, and the determinist would certainly call it only a half-truth. Nonetheless it is a belief that has saved innumerable persons from despair and possible suicide. If as an indeterminist I can believe that the otherwise universal sway of mechanistic cause-effect laws stops abruptly when it reaches the area of human judgment and ethical decision, I am well fortified against some of life's worst blows. Such a belief can provide me with an inner fortress where my soul or personal integrity ("the inner me," as one school of inspirational thought calls it) can remain intact and serene no matter what comes. The indeterminist belief permits me to retain the rock-bottom confidence that even if I cannot control external circumstances, I can still refuse to let these circumstances have ultimate power over me. For I can refuse to let them break me; even when things are at their worst, I can still oppose my will to all their destructive force, defying them to do their utmost.

Few indeterminists would be willing to acknowledge that this basic belief in the power of the individual to triumph inwardly over external circumstances is all that this school has to offer, but probably all would agree it is indeterminism's greatest contribution. For it obviously offers an assault-proof retreat to which we can always retire when life seems to come crashing down upon us, and where we can regather our strength for facing life again. Hence on pragmatic grounds indeterminism has much to offer. If we were to rate the various ethical viewpoints in terms of what they can contribute to human happiness, indeterminism would certainly stand high on the list. For those who can hold this belief it is a permanent source of inspiration. Even those who oppose the belief are forced to acknowledge that few other doctrines can do more to keep morale on a high level.

The Promise of Determinism. The determinist has also made contributions of great value, and he promises even greater benefits in the future when the full implications of the deterministic position have been realized. In the first place, he has done much to link human nature with the rest of the natural world. This has helped toward the realization of a dream long cherished by both philosophy and science: a completely unified knowledge that will include and explain all of man's experience. A second contribution of determinism has been the formulation of a more scientific and more realistic picture of man. In part this picture has been sobering and even discouraging, since it has proved that man is dependent upon his environment in not only his physical but also his mental life. In larger part, however, this picture has been challenging and inspiring, for it suggests enormous possibilities for human happiness if we can learn better to control our environment. It is here that the great promise of determinism lies. If, as the deterministic hypothesis holds, our self or character is the result of all that we have met acting upon the physical organism with which we were born, then it follows that we can (through eugenics and education) produce something approximating first-class human beings. For if we can condition an individual to react to certain things and make certain choices, then obviously we can achieve much greater social control and social efficiency—and thus greater human welfare than has yet been dreamed of.

On the other hand, if the indeterminist is right and man can make completely uncaused choices, then, as we have seen, both education and effort to control the social environment are largely a waste of time. This is the reason why the determinist often accuses his opponent of being more fatalistic than the avowed fatalist. If we can at any moment disavow our entire individual history and arbitrarily act as if we were suddenly new-born into a causeless world, then obviously we have almost no control over human conduct. A society composed of genuinely undetermined wills could only be a moral anarchy. Even the world as pictured by fatalism appears to contain more order than the indeterminist's scheme of things.

The Issue in Relation to Idealism and Naturalism

Indeterminism and Idealism. The relations of the free-will controversy to the larger opposition between idealism and naturalism appears almost too obvious to require articulation. Idealism and indeterminism have been so closely associated throughout the history of Western philosophy that to name one has usually been to imply the other. For most idealists, even such a moderate position as contemporary determinism represents is unthinkable; either man is free in his mental and volitional life, or he is a slave bound by the chains of fatalism to the workings of a blind, mechanical universe. The idealistic mind finds this alternative inescapable; either man is truly free, or he is completely enslaved. To the naturalist, on the contrary, because nature is more ultimate than mind and human nature is an integral part of the natural order, it logically follows that the laws of the natural order must also apply to man. And, among the laws and principles which govern nature, none is more basic than the principle of causality.

The contrasting attitudes of the two great metaphysical schools toward determinism follow logically from their own assumptions and postulates. For idealism, holding that reality is spiritual, it is logical to believe that our mental and volitional activities may be above or outside the laws which govern the non-mental realm. Furthermore, if the real is regarded as a Creative Force of some kind, then such laws (for example, those of cause and effect) may be regarded as specifically created to govern the material world. This would imply that these laws were not intended to govern the mind and its activities. The situation would be comparable to a legislator who formulates laws that do not apply to himself.

Determinism and Naturalism. As usual, the naturalist accuses the idealist of two intellectual crimes: putting the cart before the horse, and indulging in wishful thinking. Surely it is more logical (the naturalist argues) to believe that the mental has emerged from the physical, and that the general laws which govern the source also govern the emergent. The idealist here reveals his habitual tendency to make the world safe for values at *any* cost, even though this means shutting his eyes to facts and ignoring the principal implications of science. Obviously, continues the naturalist, the indeterministic doctrine which is so dear to the idealist is not primarily concerned with facts; it is concerned rather with picturing the world as a well-designed hothouse in which man's tenderest values can thrive and be guaranteed their full flowering. We should notice, for example, that the only actual fact which the indeterminist offers in support of his case is the feeling of freedom which we possess when we make a decision. When this one intuition is weighed against the innumerable facts of science, particularly the discoveries of psychology, this single indeterministic "fact" appears rather lonely and not too impressive. Is it any wonder (concludes the naturalist) that the indeterminist-idealist has to argue his case primarily on grounds of what *ought* to be the situation in a moral and value-centered universe—that is, what would be good for man?

A Word of Summary. Thus inevitably the problem of human freedom ends as nearly all the problems of philosophy end: we have alternative answers, each impressive and logical, and each with much to recommend it, between which we must choose. In making this choice we shall inevitably be influenced by whatever general view of the world we hold. And what determines which world-view we shall hold? To answer this we have to move in a circle: the indeterminist would say that our choice of world-views is arbitrary since it can be made on moral and intellectual grounds in a causeless vacuum. The determinist, on the contrary, would say that our choice of world-views is determined for us. He would name numerous factors that contribute to this basic determination: mental factors (such as education, general intellectual environment, etc.), physical factors (such as health and glandular balance), and social or economic factors (the economic group into which we were born, the amount of security we have been able to attain, and so on). For the determinist, our world-view is controlled by these combined internal and external factors just as surely as the trajectory of a meteor is determined by the forces involved.

In our final chapter we shall again consider this fascinating practical question of the origin of such divergent attitudes toward the world and human experience as idealism and naturalism represent. Before we attempt a final analysis, however, we must meet several more of philosophy's great problems, including some specifically related to contemporary ethics.

CHAPTER 15

CONTEMPORARY ETHICS AND ITS PROBLEMS

I N THE THREE CHAPTERS ON ETHICS JUST CONCLUDED WE HAVE BEEN
thinking largely within the framework of traditional or classical
ethics. The terms, the concepts, and the arguments have all been
well established by long use. They are the tools or counters which
ethical thinkers have used for generations, and many of the concepts
and controversies date back to the time of Socrates, Plato, and Aristotle.
In a general introduction to philosophy it has been impossible to avoid
this traditionalism in ethical thought. Until recently it could be said that
no subdivision of philosophy was so well explored and mapped out as
ethics, and certainly none promised fewer new developments in the
future. It was almost as if the various schools within ethics had fought
one another to a standstill—or at least had all run out of ammunition,
with no new sources of supply in sight. Although axiology, or general
value theory, had developed considerably during modern times, thus
providing more strictly theoretical foundations for ethical speculation,
conditions within ethics proper appeared quite stable. All that could be
said for each viewpoint had been said many times over by successive generations of adherents to that position. Surveying ethics as a whole during
the first decade or two of the present century, an observer would have
gained the impression of a relatively static area of thought.

During the past quarter century or so, however, there has been a marked revitalizing of ethics. The former complacent jogging around in the well-worn ruts of ethical thought has largely ceased, and today this subdivision of philosophy is again as dynamic as any part of the field. It is not obvious exactly what has awakened ethics from its static state. Probably a variety of factors are responsible. As one surveys the literature of the subject published during the past three or four decades, two influences seem to have been particularly stimulating. One of these has been slow and cumulative in its effect, whereas the other has been more sudden and unsettling. Between them thinkers concerned with moral theory have had a lively time of late, and fresh controversies erupt upon the ethical landscape with stimulating frequency.

These two major influences upon contemporary ethics are (1) the growing social sciences, particularly psychology, sociology, and anthropology; and (2) logical empiricism. Looking back over several decades the first of these two influences has been more important; in terms of the last few years, logical empiricism has been more significant. Their combined impact has been so great as largely to transform the whole field of ethics. Unfortunately the controversy stirred up by logical empiricism is now raging violently, and the dust is still so thick that we cannot even tell how the battle is going. Consequently any presentation we might attempt would perhaps be seriously out of date within a few years, giving students a false picture of an important event in the history of ethics. For this reason it seems best to concentrate upon the much clearer influence of social science upon contemporary ethics. While many issues produced by social science still remain to be settled, ethically speaking, the issues are at least now well exposed and cataloged so that a balanced presentation is possible. We shall therefore devote our limited space to these.

Ethics and the Social Sciences

As soon as the social sciences attained intellectual status it was inevitable that they should have an effect upon ethical thought. For, contrary to the popular idea that philosophers (including ethicists) inhabit ivory towers which have no channels of communication with the outside world of daily human living, ethical speculation has always been closely bound to the social theory and practice going on around it. In fact it has usually been closely bound to its immediate social setting: if ethical theory has one general weakness it is a tendency to be nothing but a subtle rationalization or intellectual subflooring fitted under the official or approved morality of some particular society at some particular date. In short, ethics has by and large been provincial. Far from being "universal" or "eternal" or "absolute" or "ideal" as usually claimed, most ethical systems have been relative to both the culture and the historic period that produced them. In addition many have been clearly relative to the social class to which the philosopher belonged, or with which he unconsciously affiliated himself.

If we had to summarize the over-all effect of social science upon ethics, it would be fair to describe it as increased sophistication and (conversely) decreased provincialism. This sophistication is really self-awareness and objectivity—a growing realization that there is always the danger we have just described, whereby ethics becomes merely a theoretical foundation for the accepted morality of the day. This means that ethicists are making steady effort to cut through the atmospheres of cultural climate and bypass the boundaries of local moralities to get to the real foundations of ethical judgment. We are more aware than ever before of the need (and the difficulty) of determining the basis for a truly universal system of ethics, rather than one applicable only to occidental civilization or suitable only to Christians.

Social Anthropology and Ethics. It is probably social anthropology that has been the major influence here. We pointed out in a previous chapter that the anthropologist was not the first to discover that human customs and ethical norms vary widely over the world. However, he was the first to lay bare many of the ideological foundations which justified these variations. Anthropology has revealed to us how drastically different some of these ideologies are, so that it is no exaggeration to say that members of some particular cultural group do not live in the same world with members of another group. If, for example, we contrast the animistic view of nature, which endows physical objects and forces with intelligence and will, with the scientific view that specifically excludes these spirits from the physical world, we can see that an animist and a scientist do not speak the same language in any real sense of the term. Anthropologists are likely to conclude that it is equally vain to expect the two parties to speak the same ethical language. For is it not possible, even probable, that the realms of value which animist and scientist inhabit have as little in common as their respective views of the natural world?

Throughout the latter half of the nineteenth century the apparent relativistic implications of anthropology's findings became more and more difficult for traditional ethics—which has usually been committed to the search for a single, timeless system of values—to cope with. As the anthropological data increased, the job of explaining the tumultuous variety of ethical norms in terms of a single concept of the Good appeared increasingly hopeless. Early in the present century it became apparent that a new approach to the whole problem was urgent. The question which had to be resolved was essentially this: Can ethics, or in fact any value theory, be based upon science—particularly social science? Or is the field of values an area which the scientific method can neither invade nor contribute to with any profit? In sum, do man's evaluations and normative judgments constitute a wholly distinct realm, unrelated to the rest of his experience?

The situation facing ethical thinkers was analogous to the one which religion has faced since the rise of science, particularly since the tremendous growth of scientific knowledge during the last hundred years. Religious thinkers, particularly those responsible for doctrinal decisions, have been forced to choose: should they continue to absorb this new knowledge as it is announced and somehow square it with religious belief, even at the cost of diluting this belief until it had little resemblance to Christian doctrine of previous generations? Or should they on the contrary hold the religious line by ignoring, even repudiating, scientific discovery? This has indeed proved a difficult choice. In America the liberal Protestant groups have followed the first course, the fundamentalists the second, but each choice has been made at such a high price that it is sometimes difficult for the outside observer to decide which has been more costly in terms of intellectual prestige and integrity.

And so with ethical thought in the present century: should ethics and value theory make constant effort to utilize scientific knowledge, particularly from anthropology and psychology? Or should it ignore science as irrelevant to the problems of the Good and the Right? The most basic split within contemporary ethics follows from opposing answers to this all-important question. While there are of course many schools within ethics now as in the past, in general they cluster around these two poles of ethical thought. If we can get a clear picture of this basic polarity, much of the confusion and controversy apparent in the field will be clarified.

The "Naturalistic Fallacy"

G. E. Moore, the British philosopher who has contributed much to several branches of contemporary philosophy, is the thinker most responsible for bringing the issue into sharp focus. In his *Principa Ethica,* which is undoubtedly the most controversial book in modern ethics, Moore set forth the view that intrinsic values are (1) absolutely unique, (2) indefinable, and (3) intuited. He furthermore charged those ethical thinkers who do not accept these values as unique, indefinable, and intuitively known with the "naturalistic fallacy." For several decades now the assertion and denial of this "fallacy" has been the focal point of ethical controversy, so an understanding of it will give us the key for a comprehending entrance into contemporary ethics.

The Nature of Intrinsic Value. At various points in preceding chapters we have employed the logical term *sui generis* to indicate something that is in a class by itself—that is, something which is not a subform of this or that, and which cannot in any way be classified under some other heading. The ethical view we are now considering, as exemplified by Moore, holds that the clearest instance of the *sui generis* lies in the realm of values. To come to the heart of this doctrine, it holds that "value" or "goodness" is strictly unique; it is not merely another name for something else such as "pleasure" or "happiness." The Good (even if spelled without a capital) is wholly distinct from all else that we can know. We do not call things "good" because they possess certain qualities which can also be found in things lacking goodness—that is, goodness is not a sum of natural or descriptive qualities, and there is no way goodness can be derived from natural qualities by either abstraction or summation. Thus, we come to the first formal statement of the naturalistic fallacy, which we will define in Moore's own words: "The naturalistic fallacy consists in the contention that good *means* nothing but some simple or complex notion that can be defined in terms of natural qualities."[1]

[1] *Principia Ethica,* p. 73.

The concept of the naturalistic fallacy has usually been associated with the belief that there is a permanent dichotomy between the "is" and the "ought," between fact and value, between the normative and the descriptive.[2] Moore and his non-naturalistic allies hold that the fallacy arises whenever we attempt to bridge the gap between the "is" and the "ought," particularly when we try to derive the latter from the former. The usual example of this attempt is to argue that pleasure is good *because* it is sought by all men, thus deriving value from fact. The anti-naturalist or intuitionist always asks, whenever he hears such reasoning, "What has *that* to do with the case? Does a thing become good just because men desire it—if so, then how many men? What percentage of the race must agree in their desires before these become good—or can any single man's desire, however antisocial, be considered good?"

We have already quoted Spinoza's famous question on this point: Do we desire things because they are good in themselves, or do we merely honor and justify our desires by calling their object "good"? Spinoza answered in the second alternative, as did his British contemporary Thomas Hobbes, who wrote, "Whatsoever is the object of any man's appetite or desire; that is it, which he for his part calleth *good*." Most forms of ethical naturalism have agreed with these two seventeenth-century thinkers. But the intuitionists such as Moore are categorical in choosing the first alternative: Goodness is inherent in some objects and situations as yellowness may be in particular things. And the comparison may be carried still further: in the same way that color as an experience is indefinable, and can be known only by direct confrontation with colored objects, so value or goodness can be known only intuitively by discovering it in objects and situations. It cannot be reasoned about nor argued over. Goodness is intrinsic, and if some individual cannot perceive it we must assume there is a moral blindness analogous to color blindness.

David Hume was probably the first to realize how often ethical thinkers have converted from fact to value—from "is" to "ought"—at some stage in their argument, and how readily most of their followers have accepted this switch uncritically. Hume's comment is worth quoting in full.

[2] Cf. W. K. Frankena's excellent paper, "The Naturalistic Fallacy," originally published in *Mind*, Vol. 48 (1939), and now available in Sellars and Hospers, *Readings in Ethical Theory*. This paper is both the best statement and the best refutation of the naturalistic fallacy I have found.

I cannot forbear adding to these reasonings an observation, which may, perhaps, be found of some importance. In every system of morality which I have hitherto met with, I have always remarked, that the author proceeds for some time in the ordinary way of reasoning, and establishes the being of a God, or makes observations concerning human affairs; when of a sudden I am surprised to find, that instead of the usual copulations of propositions, *is* and *is not*, I meet with no proposition that is not connected with an *ought*, or an *ought not*. This change is imperceptible; but is, however, of the last consequence. For as this *ought*, or *ought not*, expresses some new relation or affirmation, it is necessary that it should be observed and explained; and at the same time that a reason should be given, for what seems altogether inconceivable, how this new relation can be a deduction from others, which are entirely different from it. But as authors do not commonly use this precaution, I shall presume to recommend it to the readers; and am persuaded, that this small attention would subvert all the vulgar systems of morality, and let us see that the distinction of vice and virtue is not founded merely on the relations of objects, nor is perceived by reason.[3]

In more concise terminology, Hume is saying that we cannot draw ethical conclusions from nonethical premises. The intuitionists go much farther and insist that we cannot define ethical concepts in terms of nonethical ones. For the ethical or value realm is wholly separate from the nonethical and can in no way be reduced to it, since ethical qualities are completely different in kind from nonethical ones.

The list of things which the intuitionists specifically deny that value can be reduced to is long, but it will be instructive to mention a few of these since it is probable the reader has himself unconsciously made some such reduction, and it will be well for him to become aware of the fact. To list these rejected reductions will be to call the roll of many of the rival schools of ethical thought, but since we have already discussed several of these, our roll-call can be brief.

Value Not a Natural Process. As is obvious, intuitionism denies that value can be reduced to a natural process or its outcome. It consequently rejects evolutionary ethics, which holds that in ultimate analysis value is whatever aids survival or promotes the welfare of the species. Even such lofty human characteristics as cooperation and sympathy (which some evolutionists, including Darwin, believe to be products of natural selection) are denied entrance into the intuitionist's hall of

[3] *A Treatise of Human Nature*, Book III, part ii, section i.

values *if* they are proposed for admission because they aid human beings. This does not mean that a thinker like Moore denies that sympathy and cooperation are values; he rather would deny that they are good *because* they have survival value, or *because* they ease the difficulties of human life, or *because* good results flow from them. To repeat: they are intrinsic —they are good because they are good, and for no instrumental reason.

The intuitionist position also forcefully rejects the view that value is determined in any way by social processes, as distinguished from a biological process such as evolution. The two most widely held social-process theories, Marxism and pragmatism, are specifically attacked. The Marxist doctrine, for example, holds that the major values in any society are largely an expression of the interests of the dominant socio-economic class within that society. Hence there can be no universal values, particularly in the ethical realm. There can be only "bourgeois morality" (a favorite Marxist term), or "capitalist ethics" or "proletarian group values." This makes value strictly relative, and the intuitionist theory of intrinsic value perceived by all minds becomes absurd. At most, values can be common only to members of the same class who also share the same economic and political interests.

Value Not Dependent upon Approval. The intuitionist view is no less opposed to the many value theories which attempt to identify evaluation with approval or approbation. These rejected views agree with Spinoza and Hobbes: to call anything "good" means nothing except that we (as individuals or as a society) approve of it, finding it "pleasant," "desirable," "satisfying" and the like. Such approbative views impress the intuitionist as revealing the very essence of the "naturalistic fallacy," since they plainly equate the "is" which is desired with the "ought" that any ethical system commands us to seek.

Perhaps the most telling criticism that the intuitionist levels against approbation theories of value is the fact that, in the last analysis, they make value purely subjective and personal, thus permitting something that approaches ethical anarchy. For clearly such theories make it possible for me to approve something which you disapprove; but if "good" means nothing except approval, we obviously can have situations in which "good" and "bad" are applied to the same object—which makes the terms meaningless as far as any inclusive system of values is concerned. What is needed (says the intuitionist) is some general or universal standard of value, but the notorious disagreement of men regarding what is to be approved makes approbation theories impossible. Even if we require social or group approval, we would still have disagreements between social groups, so we are little nearer to a general standard than when we accept individual approval as our norm.

Value Not Dependent upon God or Reality. By this time the reader probably feels that ethical intuitionism is closely related to Kant's system of categorical ethics, as well as to idealistic (and possibly theistic) systems generally. It may therefore be something of a surprise to learn that the intuitionist, besides rejecting any attempt to base values upon either nature or human nature, also repudiates efforts to ground values in a metaphysical order of some sort (as idealism does) or even in a theological setting (as the religionist does). Specifically repudiated is the typical theistic doctrine that "good" or "right" is determined by God's will or approval. While the intuitionist usually does not enlarge upon this point, most members of the school would say that God approves of certain things because they are good in themselves, independent of the divine nature. Their goodness is antecedent to deity; God honors and seeks to realize values for the same reason we do: because they are intrinsic and irreducible to anything more fundamental. God does not make these intrinsic values, but only reacts favorably to them, even as you and I, and no act of the divine will could alter their goodness.

The same situation holds in the relation between the Good and the Real as conceived in metaphysical terms. Far from being "good" because they are integrated with the Absolute or the World Reason, values are for the intuitionist autonomous and real in their own right. If anything, they help to determine the character of Reality, and not vice versa as most metaphysicians believe.

How Are Values Known? This constant reiteration of the irreducibility of intrinsic values to anything, either natural or supernatural, other than their own unique selves logically leads us to the epistemological issue: How can such values be known? For that matter, how can anything be known which is wholly *sui generis,* so that the terms which are relative to the rest of our experience do not apply? If values are so unique that the descriptive terms ordinarily employed to classify our experiences do not fit, what can we say about these values that is not mystical gibberish? How can we communicate information regarding them, and how can we relate them to the rest of our own personal experience? Epistemologically speaking, does not a view such as Moore's parallel the mystic's experience of God, which is indescribable and unutterable?

Those thinkers who hold this position do not refer to it as a mystical doctrine, but neither do they evade the epistemological facts. They admit that whatever is unique cannot be known except by direct, intuitive apprehension. This knowledge is necessarily immediate, not discursive. We have already used Moore's favorite analogy of color experience: "yellow" is not something that can be described or known by a process of reasoning; it is known directly by presentation, or it is not known at all. And so with "goodness"; unless we apprehend it immediately whenever we are confronted with certain situations and objects, we do not apprehend it at all. We cannot be reasoned or argued into acknowledging goodness; if we perceive it we require no reasoning, while if we don't the reasoning is futile.[4]

Intuitionism and Obligation

We recall that there are two great problems which are central in ethical theory, equal in importance and complexity. These concern the nature of goodness and the source of obligation. It was probably inevitable that, once the intuitionist theory of goodness had been recognized, there should appear a comparable theory of obligation. Its most renown exponent has been another British thinker, H. A. Prichard. As early as 1912 he published one of the most discussed papers in modern ethics under the arresting title, "Does Moral Philosophy Rest on a Mistake?"[5] Prichard begins by acknowledging the uniqueness of the good quite as categorically as Moore does, but he goes on to deny that goodness is the only independent factor in ethics, and to deny that duty or obligation can be derived from goodness. Just as intuitionists deny that "the good" can be derived from "the existent," so Prichard in turn denies that duty can be derived

[4] Earlier intuitionists emphasized a "moral sense" that was supposed to be as specialized and as reliable as the sense of smell. However, since modern psychology knows nothing of any such specialized sense, present-day intuitionists seldom claim its existence. Hence their frequent use of the term "moral sense" should not be taken too technically.

[5] Originally published in *Mind*, New Series, Vol. XXI, but now widely reprinted—e.g., in Sellars and Hospers, *op. cit.*

from goodness. Nor can obligation be derived from anything else: it too is irreducible, autonomous, *sui generis.*

When we stop and consider how regularly we indoctrinate the youthful members of our society with the idea that they ought or ought not to do certain things because they (1) help or harm other people, (2) make other people happy or unhappy, (3) make themselves happy or unhappy, (4) invited social approval or disapproval, (5) obey or disobey God's commands, we begin to see how radical Prichard's position is. Even Kant's categorical imperative, although quite similar, seems less extreme because Kant went on to show that a violation of the command, "Do your duty because it is your duty," involves a logical contradiction, as we saw in Chapter 13. Prichard breaks with tradition even further when he denies that the obligation to perform an act depends upon the goodness of something involved in the act—for example, obeying the law. An act is good *because* it is done as a duty; it is the reason for doing an action which may make it good, not its consequences.

This theory of obligation also depends upon an immediate, unreasoned sense of obligation to reveal our duty to us. Provided that we are aware of all the facts in a situation, then we perceive the obligation directly and fully. Prichard compares this apprehension with that of mathematical relations, and he holds that both situations involve the perception of self-evident truths. In his own example, if we are uncertain that we have performed a mathematical operation correctly we can only do it over again: there is no appeal to some extramathematical source for confirmation. And so in ethical situations involving duty: if we are unsure that an obligation is present we can only do the moral problem over again—which means looking at the moral facts again.

Prichard would not deny that there are persons who have difficulty perceiving obligations, just as there are those who find it hard to apprehend mathematical relations. But, just as when we finally do see a relation in mathematics we wonder how we were so blind before, so when we ultimately do recognize an obligation we may wonder how we missed it before—and why others perhaps still cannot see it. In both cases, the truth becomes absolute and self-evident; it also becomes self-sufficient in that nothing from outside the situation is required to make it true.

Intuitionism and Social Science. It is evident that these intuitionist positions represent a reaction against social science, at least as concerns any possible ethical implications this science may have. It is also evident that they represent a reaction similar to the religious fundamentalist's against geological and biological science—namely, repudiation. Intuitionism in ethics is essentially a refusal to deal with social science, by denying that psychology, sociology, anthropology, economics, political science, and history have any ethical implications. By refusing to allow ethics to be contaminated by such influences, the intuitionist keeps "the good" and "the ought" pure. The question of whether or not he renders them sterile is still being discussed in ethical circles. The intuitionist position is clearly nonrelativistic, and although its adherents usually avoid classifying themselves as absolutists, their opponents find it easy to pin this label on them.

The Opponents of Intuitionism. While ethical intuitionism has been criticized on a variety of grounds, undoubtedly the most implacable opposition has come from those schools which *do* attempt to come to terms with the ever-expanding social sciences by absorbing their findings and facing their implications. Clearly such schools work in a very different intellectual atmosphere from that breathed by intuitionists. In brief, this group opposing intuitionism is unified by one fact: they all deny that the so-called "naturalistic fallacy" *is* a fallacy, and instead insist that ethical propositions not only can be derived from the factual world of nature and human nature, but must be so derived if ethics is to have any real meaning and validity. In short, they deny that ethical thought can be produced in a vacuum and then transferred to the world of human affairs. This means that these naturalistic schools expressly repudiate intuitionism's central doctrine regarding the autonomy, uniqueness, and irreducibility of values.

Unfortunately, once these schools have united in opposition to intuitionism, they largely go their divergent ways. This makes the task of presenting them to the reader very difficult, and within the limits of this book, frankly impossible. Many pages would be required to give a fair treatment of even the principal schools of naturalistic ethics, while an inclusive coverage would run to chapters. Each makes its own particular attempt to derive value from fact, "the good" from "the existent." Many of these attempts are ingenious and some are impressive. Nearly all are complex and difficult, and it must be acknowledged that none (and not even all combined) have converted many antinaturalists to ethical naturalism.

Rather than confuse the reader with necessarily brief and inadequate summaries of these naturalistic schools it will be better to outline some of the difficulties which plague any conscientious thinker who tries to integrate ethics with social science. These are of course the same difficulties which persuade most intuitionists that ethics cannot be derived from science or even related to it, and drive them to the extreme position they take. These are likewise the problems that produce a third possible reaction, which in its way is quite as extreme as intuitionism. This third attitude is *ethical skepticism,* which denies that *any* valid theory of values is possible, or that *any* logical ground for obligation can be found. The skeptic holds that all values whatsoever are not only relative but strictly individual and personal; in the last analysis they are also arbitrary in that they reduce to a judgment or choice which is irrational and probably unconscious.

The Three Possible Positions.   We thus find that if we examine contemporary ethics and social science as a whole there are three principal reactions to these sciences and their accumulating knowledge. At polar opposites are intuitionism and skepticism: both deny that we can derive value and obligation from social, anthropological, or psychological fact; but where one turns back to the intuitive perception of unique self-evident ethical truths, the other continues to insist that this is a desperate, mystical, and basically obscurantist doctrine which is even less justified than the naturalist's effort to escape subjectivism and arbitrariness by somehow distilling "value" from "fact" and "obligation" from "social custom." So the skeptic regards both naturalism and intuitionism as invalid, and denies that any ethical knowledge can be discovered. The naturalist meanwhile, rejecting what he considers the desperation of one position and the defeatism of the other, continues his hard and often discouraging task of trying to derive values from the world of nature and human nature, confident that we will eventually be able to erect value systems upon the foundations of science comparable to the knowledge systems we can now erect thereon.

The Difficulties Facing Contemporary Ethics

But now to the difficulties with which social science cannot avoid burdening contemporary ethics—difficulties which produce mystical retreat in one party, skeptical defeat in another, and dogged determination in a third. We have so often referred to the relativistic implications that seem to arise inevitably from the vast accumulation of anthropological data we now possess that we need say little more on this point. The variations in human standards and value systems appear infinite in number to anthropologists, and certainly it is rare to find a worker in this field who believes that moral or value absolutes exist independent of their cultural matrix. Anthropologists usually feel that at most we can do no more than discover a limited community of values that grow from the irreducible common core of human nature which cultural variations cannot eradicate. Consequently these social scientists are sometimes willing to make a cautious acknowledgment that there *may* be enough common social sentiments in all men to permit the formulation of a vague general ethical framework. It should be noted, however, that anthropologists think of this framework as something which, if it can be established at all, can only be derived from human nature. They thus give aid to ethical naturalists, rather than intuitionists, since this possible derivation clearly involves the naturalistic "fallacy."

Today the chief skeptic-producing difficulties come from sociology and psychology, rather than from anthropology. The latter gave nineteenth-century ethicists a bad time, but in our century the psychologist and sociologist give ethical theorists an even worse time. At bottom, these two particular social sciences unite to create one gigantic obstacle to systematic ethics and rational morality. This obstacle is the joint conviction of all psychologists and most sociologists, supported by an ever-growing mass of evidence, that man is an irrational animal whose behavior—even when apparently most ethical and value-conscious—is anything but logical or rational. To this conviction the sociologist adds his evidence that man is largely a product of social conditioning, which is often so effective as to distort ethical judgments to the point where any claim of objectivity or validity becomes farcical.[6] But let us hear from three outstanding pioneers in social science, whose combined influence has done much to give their science its contemporary character.

Sociology and Ethical Skepticism. There are two sociologists who have been particularly famous as spokesmen of ethical skepticism, and

---

[6] I am indebted to T. E. Hill, *Contemporary Ethical Theory*, for some of these ideas on the sources of ethical skepticism. Hill's opening chapters are an excellent summary of these influences.

while some fellow workers consider their viewpoint extreme, there can be no doubt it has been influential. Early in this century the American William Graham Sumner formulated his theory of *folkways*, which reduced ethical judgments to basically irrational manifestations of social forces that are themselves nonrational. By "folkways" Sumner means the customary usages of any social group; these may range all the way from putting useless buttons on men's coat sleeves to outlawing incest. These usages are independent of our ideas of them, follow no rational rules, and conform only to the general temper or attitude of their particular time and place.[7] They have what amounts to a life of their own: Sumner holds that they are born, grow old, and die, and few forces (including education) exert much influence upon them.

When members of a society think these usages contribute toward social welfare they may be called *mores* (from which comes our word "moral"), but even these are not ethical in the sense of being rational and objective. For they are not produced by ideals, but by external social forces. What we regard as ethical evaluations are only expressions or rationalizations of pervasive social customs, to which we are so habituated that they seem more than just customs to us and readily take on the status of absolute moral codes, "divine commands," and the like. As a final blow to pretensions of rationality, objectivity, and universality on the part of ethical systems, Sumner insists that philosophy and speculative ethics are both derived from folkways. They can no more escape the limitations of their origin than a man can lift himself by his own bootstraps. Nor is the social scientist any freer from this limitation; he too is strictly confined to the frames of reference established by the folkways of his period and culture.

In sum, the ethical thinker, even when he tries to build upon the foundations of science (and still more when he ignores this foundation as intuitionism does) is only expressing a wish when he formulates a positive theory of value. It is far more probable that he is merely rationalizing the prevailing or approved morality of his period. And since this morality, however lofty, is only an expression of the *mores* or socially oriented folkways, the noblest and most rational system of universal ethics is basically a pious fraud in that it pretends to be what by the very nature of social facts no intellectual system can ever be.

[7] Cf. Hill, *op. cit.*, p. 50.

Better known in international sociological circles is the contemporary Italian Vilfredo Pareto, whose four-volume *The Mind and Society* is probably the most influential work published in this field during the present century. Philosophers and logicians are particularly interested in the fact that Pareto has been much influenced by logical empiricism—his work is probably the best example of the thinking of a social scientist operating within the framework of this epistemological position as we outlined it in Chapter 11. He demands that all theories and statements be capable of verification in experience, and in his discussion of classical ethical theories he often says, "It is impossible to imagine how a proposition of that kind could be verified by experience." Thus much of his skepticism regarding ethics and social theory is logico-empirical rather than strictly sociological as with Sumner.

Some of Pareto's main ideas can be condensed into a paragraph or two. He holds that the structure of society involves two principal elements, both nonlogical and nonrational. First there are the more basic *residues:* these are the pervasive purposes, many of them instinctive, which underlie all our actions; these remain relatively stable in an individual, although they may change gradually over a period of time. Less basic but more conscious are the *derivations:* these are the expressions of residues, and are in large part the arguments we use to defend or rationalize these underlying residues. Like all rationalizations, which are the reasons we find to justify what we want to do (or have already done), the derivations have little or no logical value. Pareto describes most of them as only verbal proofs, if not sheer sophistries.

The majority of our ethical judgments ("this is good"; "that is wrong") are derivations—that is, more or less subtle rationalizations of desires. As derivations they have little effect upon the residues they decorate or justify; moral ideals have slight influence upon either a society or an individual, although they may force him to use considerable ingenuity giving his conduct the appearance of conforming with approved morality. Pareto does not hesitate to call most ethical theories and judgments a species of hypocrisy, although he would not claim that this is usually conscious hypocrisy.

Finally, Pareto sounds like a first cousin of Karl Marx in his description of the manner in which ethical theories easily lend themselves to the interests of a ruling class seeking to hold and exploit power. He holds that a large proportion of traditional ethical theories have been framed for precisely this purpose. Since ethical judgments are an expression of our basic desires and interests, it is not surprising that these judgments should often reveal more emotion than logic, more rationalization than reason. And since the ethical standards of a group or class are similarly an expression of its group interests and desires, it is inevitable that these standards should likewise be anything but logical or objective, regardless of how pseudo-logical a form they may assume.

It is not astonishing that Pareto should praise Machiavelli, who always sought to portray the actions of men as they actually were, rather than as they pretended they were or thought they were. And it is not astonishing that Pareto should seem cynical to some people, particularly if they themselves have any trace of tendermindedness. But, cynical or merely realistic, this Italian sociologist has been a genuine source of contemporary ethical skepticism.

Psychology and Ethical Skepticism. Many psychologists and psychological schools can be cited as contributors to the serious doubt that any valid ethical system can be established, but certainly Freud and the psychoanalytic movement he fathered have contributed most. In fact it is not too much to say that even if there had been no other psychological sources of this skepticism, Freud's influence by itself would have produced much the same result, making the most confident ethical theorist wonder if he were wasting his time attempting to put ethics upon a rational basis.

Freud's theory of man's mental life is so well known by now that it will be sufficient to give just a summary. He holds that what we call "consciousness" or the conscious mind is only a minor part of the total psyche possessed by each individual. Far greater in content, and far more important in determining our conduct, is the subconscious mind. This teeming, moiling basement of our mental structure is the home of instincts, desires of all kinds, and memories which are too deeply repressed to enter consciousness. The subconscious contains three components or powers whose commands the conscious mind merely executes. In fact, consciousness is an automaton with no will of its own; it serves only as a front or mouthpiece for the Big Three operating behind the scene.[8]

---

[8] Cf. J. Hospers' paper, "Free-Will and Psychoanalysis," as reprinted in Sellars and Hospers, *op. cit.* I have borrowed the term "Big Three" from Hospers; his examples of compulsive behavior are particularly good and make his paper fascinating reading.

These all-powerful three are the *id,* the *ego* and the *superego.* The id is insatiably demanding, completely selfish, and nonmoral; the only vocabulary it has are the words "I want," and it is the embodiment of all our blind desires and forbidden lusts. Over against this stands the superego, whose conscious manifestation we call "conscience." Freud regards it as the generalized voice of society, particularly as embodied in the remembered forms of parents and teachers who during our early years strove mightily to civilize us. This superego is tyrannical, puritanical, and in its own austere way just as demanding as the id. It automatically opposes the demands of the id, particularly its most powerful and persistent demands such as those for unlimited sexual satisfaction. The ego is the great compromiser; it seeks to reconcile the opposing demands of the twin tyrants, desire and conscience. To call this a difficult task would be a major understatement. Sometimes enough of this warfare and enforced compromise may get into consciousness for us to realize its intensity; in general, however, the battle is fought behind doors kept tightly locked by what Freud calls the *censor,* a fourth factor in our turbulent psychical life. The censor permits only those desires (and their repressing counterforces) to enter consciousness which do not outrage our moral standards, but this is a well-scrubbed, select cluster of wishes. The far greater body of desires are too obscene, immoral, selfish, and cruel to pass the censor, but they remain operative nonetheless.

Freud's great point as concerns ethical skepticism is this: our conscious, rational, and ethical conduct is determined by the subconscious and its battling Big Three. And, since these forces are wholly irrational and unethical, what can our conduct be except irrational and unaffected by ethical judgments? For even the moral-appearing superego is just as blind as the id, since it must reflect its accumulated content of taboos, parental threats and punishments, social embarrassments and ostracisms, religious warnings, and the like—most of which are irrational and arbitrary. Furthermore the superego can be incredibly cruel and vindictive, torturing the person who has disobeyed its commands by a lifelong "guilt complex," "anxiety neurosis," and other punishments well calculated to make happiness impossible.

Psychologists hold that our "rational" deliberations which lead to an "objective" ethical judgment, or which produce an ethical system, are only a front for the real forces motivating us—namely, unconscious wishes, defenses, and compromises. We are deceived because the ego appears rational, but this is because the ever-watchful censor permits only the nicer aspects of the psyche to appear above the threshold of awareness. Even the most rational and moral of men remain at bottom mere puppets moved by blind forces whose existence we are barely beginning to acknowledge.

While psychoanalysis as a form of therapy has achieved its most impressive results in cases where obviously irrational forces are operating—compulsions, phobias, manias—analysts are convinced that normal or well-adjusted individuals are as much motivated by unconscious impulses as are neurotic personalities. The so-called normal person is fortunate that the promptings of his particular Big Three are nearer the average or the socially approved or the efficient pattern of conduct than the neurotic's may be. But this is a lucky accident, rather than an indication of greater rationality or morality on his part.

Freud's conclusions regarding our avowed value judgments are the same as Pareto's: The judgments are nothing but expressions of our conscience, which is as unreliable a guide to human happiness as desire, for the simple reason that the roots of conscience are as emotional and irrational as our desires themselves. Hence, in Freud's words, men's value judgments are at best only "attempts to prop up their illusions with arguments."[9] He admits that ethics constitutes civilization's defense against aggression, but he insists that ethics "can cause as much misery as aggression itself."[10] In sum, as a source of human happiness ethics "has nothing to offer here beyond the narcissistic satisfaction of thinking oneself better than others."[11] In sum, man's idea that human conduct can be guided and controlled by rational ethics is one of his great illusions.

So Where Are We? Even if we discount the ideas of Sumner, Pareto, and Freud as exaggerated half-truths, the remaining half still constitutes a formidable mass standing squarely across the path of contemporary ethical thought. We can now begin to see why some thinkers, uttering the cry "Naturalistic fallacy!" as though it were a curse, have retreated into intuitionism. We can also see why others, crying "Hopeless! Hopeless!" have retired into skepticism. But it may be hard to see what makes the ethical naturalist willing to tackle the vast pile of socio-

---

[9] *Civilization and Its Discontents,* p. 143.
[10] *Ibid.,* p. 140.
[11] *Idem.*

psychological data in an effort to make it yield a valid foundation for value judgments.

If we question these determined ethical naturalists on this point they will reply, "Where else can we find a secure foundation for our value theory? After rejecting the supernaturalistic doctrine that values have a divine basis, and the intuitive view that they are *sui generis,* self-evident, and irrelevant to both nature and all human experience, where else can we hope to locate them? Obviously nature (including man himself) is the only remaining source. And, since our knowledge of nature comes from science and our best knowledge of human nature from social science, we must make these sources our allies."

It would be pleasant if we could leave the student with the assurance that ethical naturalists are making great strides in their self-appointed task of erecting a structure of value upon the foundation of fact. Unfortunately any such satisfying impression would be misleading. The persevering naturalists themselves claim only that some progress has been made in this direction; at least the ground has been cleared and the measure of the problem has been taken. Considering how recently pioneer social thinkers like Sumner, Pareto, and Freud revealed the magnitude of the problem, it is something just to have cleared the ground around it.

Does all this imply that systematic ethical thought in our day is confused and split? It obviously does. Does it also imply that the outlook in ethics is discouraging, even hopeless? When we look back over the long history of ethical speculation to see how many crises it has survived, we can hardly call the present situation hopeless; and it would be more honest to call it sobering and challenging, rather than discouraging. Meanwhile, until ethical thinkers have had time enough to pick up the pieces and start their work afresh on new foundations, it may well be our job, as sons and daughters of the turbulent twentieth century, to learn to live with uncertainties and build our lives upon probabilities instead of upon the value absolutes that our grandfathers claimed. As far as ethics is concerned, unless we accept either supernaturalism or intuitionism, there appears to be no other alternative.

CHAPTER 16

ESTHETICS:

Philosophy's Stepchild

N EWCOMERS TO PHILOSOPHY SOMETIMES FIND IT DIFFICULT TO understand exactly how esthetics and the philosophy of art fit into the over-all philosophical picture. In part this difficulty arises from the fact that most students have less interest in, and probably less knowledge of, the problems of art and esthetics than they have of some of the other problems within philosophy, such as those relating to ethics and morality. It must be admitted that this subdivision of the subject we are about to study requires more specialized experience than some readers will be able to bring to the undertaking. We have already indicated the inescapable character of ethical problems, since all human beings, during almost every hour of the day, must make choices which have ethical implications. While the field of esthetics is, no less than ethics, a realm of evaluation, with just as many possible occasions for choice, few people's lives are so organized that they find these esthetic choices compulsive. It is possible for an individual to live a whole lifetime without making more than a handful of esthetic judgments, and certainly many people do exist quite contentedly in what might be called an esthetic vacuum.

However, as we have stated in an earlier chapter, it is impossible to think deeply in any field without running first into general intellectual problems, and then eventually into issues which are definitely philosophical in character. The field of art and beauty is no exception. Although it is easier to stay out of this territory than to avoid the domain of ethics, once we set foot in the realm of the artistic or the esthetic, we are liable to step on a highly explosive philosophical mine at any moment.

There is probably no other subject in which there have been such persistent attempts to avoid not only ultimate philosophical issues (which may be a defensible attitude for anyone except the metaphysician) but even the most obvious esthetic problems. These attempts at evasion have ranged all the way from the banal, "I don't know anything about art, but I know what I like," to the avowed esthetic anarchy of impressionistic critics like Anatole France, who well describes his own critical activity as "relating the adventures of his soul among masterpieces." In such a critical creed as this, however, we have less intellectual candor than in the "I know what I like" attitude. For by referring to "masterpieces," the critic has implied some standard of evaluation outside his own personal preference. His adventures are undoubtedly personal enough, but he does not claim that the evaluation "masterpiece" is equally personal. Thus some critical criterion is implied, which logically entails the whole field of esthetic speculation. While there may be less practical necessity for most people to consider the problems of art and esthetics, there is no less logical compulsion than in the other subdivisions of philosophy for those who wish to gain insight into the life of the mind and the world of intellectual activity.

The Youth of Esthetics

Esthetics is the youngest of philosophy's children, having just celebrated its two-hundredth anniversary as a recognized member of the philosophical family. Prior to the middle of the eighteenth century, many thinkers had made reference to the problem of art and the nature of beauty, but very few had really come to grips with the basic issues. Plato had raised questions concerning the nature of art and its relation to morality, and Aristotle's *Poetics* contains one of the most influential theories of tragic art. But the esthetic consciousness, as we understand the term today, hardly existed at that time, as every word of Plato's theory proves.[1] Even much of the first modern thinking on the subject by such philosophers

---

[1] By "esthetic consciousness" I mean an awareness of esthetic values *as such*, independent of morality, economics, religion, politics, didacticism, or ordinary association. As Chambers has shown in his *History of Taste*, awareness of the value

as Baumgartner (who gave esthetics its name) was limited and largely preliminary. Hence esthetics, in the rich modern meaning of the term, is still a very young study.

In view of this youthfulness of esthetics, it is not surprising that we should find the field less ordered and well laid out than the other subdivisions of philosophy. Nor should we be surprised to find disagreement in the use of terms and occasional confusion regarding basic issues. Part of this confusion has a cause other than the youth of the subject. Since the time of Kant any complete, well-equipped philosophical system has traditionally included a treatment of art and esthetics. This has sometimes been unfortunate, for it has produced some rather casual speculation and some exceptionally muddy writing. Sometimes the philosopher had little real interest in esthetics and even less appreciation of art. There was an additional danger from this ideal of completeness. In some instances it meant that the esthetic ideas had little to stand on by themselves, but were forced into the framework of metaphysical systems already formulated. Thus esthetics has often been the stepchild of philosophy; it has sometimes been included in the family circle more from a sense of duty than from any genuine feeling of parental love.

Some Signs of Increasing Maturity.   Happily, increasing wisdom has been evidenced in this matter during the last half century. Two things appear to be responsible for this improvement in the status of esthetics. The first of these is negative: most philosophers today are less ambitious to achieve a total system of thought than were their predecessors, and are willing to omit those parts of philosophy which do not hold a genuine interest for the thinker, or in which he does not feel adequately prepared. A more notable reason for the increased significance of current esthetic speculation is the altered temper of philosophy in recent times. Until lately, say the latter part of the nineteenth century, philosophy was predominantly rationalistic in character. It was to a large extent based upon logic—not in the sense of using logic as an intellectual tool, but of growing directly out of logical processes and of taking on the character of these ratiocinations. "Reason" was the chief instrument of philosophical activity. Excepting only Schopenhauer and a few other lesser volun-

---

of beauty (either natural or artistic), separate from its didactic and other practical values, did not come into existence until late in the classical period. This esthetic consciousness disappeared in the Middle Ages and was absent even during most of the Renaissance, when, despite all the artistic activity, both art and beauty were prized almost exclusively for their social, moral, historical, or archeological value.

taristic thinkers, philosophers had not given the feelings or emotions much place in their systems. Indeed the tendency of most thinkers from Plato on had been to disparage the feelings and to discount their value as revealers of the real. The senses, feelings, and emotions (the three terms have been virtually synonymous in most philosophical literature) were regarded either as inadequate to reveal reality or as positive hindrances to its discovery. Many idealists, particularly those who were predominantly rationalistic, have appeared to begrudge the senses and the emotions *any* significance, even for the apprehension of beauty.

The rise of voluntaristic philosophies, particularly pragmatism, coupled with the general empirical mood of contemporary thought, has forced a reconsideration of the role of emotion in our cognitive processes. This in turn has encouraged the formulation of philosophical theories which acknowledge the enormous importance of man's feelings and volitions, even in our logical processes and rational activities. Thus, the coldly rationalistic and often artistically impoverished esthetics of the late eighteenth and early nineteenth centuries (with Schopenhauer again as a notable exception) has been displaced by speculations which frequently reveal a very wide background in the arts, plus a wealth of personal esthetic experience rich and intense beyond anything that such a thinker as Kant could conceive of.[2]

It may be difficult to persuade students of limited background in the arts, or of a limited response to beauty in any form, that esthetic speculation is important enough to warrant its inclusion in a general introduction to philosophy. However, any reader who has already come to realize the existence and vast possibilities of esthetic experience will find in the pages just ahead at least some concepts and distinctions which may cast light on that experience, both for its own sake and in its relations to the rest of man's intellectual and spiritual activities.

The Problems of Esthetics

Perhaps more than any single cause, the failure to clarify concepts has been responsible for the confusion that is so frequent in esthetic thought.

---

[2] As, for example, in the esthetic writings of John Dewey and Samuel Alexander.

There are only a few key terms in the field, but this very fact seems to encourage ambiguity and vagueness in the way they are used. Traditionally there have been three principal terms in esthetics, to which a fourth has been added in recent times. The traditional terms are simple and familiar to the point of banality: *beauty, art,* and *nature.* Yet it is around the character and status of these three, both in themselves and in relation to each other, that most esthetic argument has centered. The modern introduction of *expression* has greatly enriched—and vastly complicated—the problem, so that this newer concept is now the focal point of controversy. Although the whole field of esthetics is in a fluid state at present, certain possible islands are beginning to appear in the flux, and there is reason to believe that the subject may soon attain a greater clarity and an increased significance in the intellectual world.

What Is Beauty? To plunge boldly into the swirling flood, the greatest confusion has usually appeared around the terms "art" and "beauty." There are plenty of reasons for this confusion. Taking beauty by itself, regardless of whether it appears in nature or in art, there is first the difficulty of defining the term satisfactorily. Then, closely linked with this problem of the nature of beauty is the question of its status. Is beauty subjective or objective? Does it reside in the object, or does it exist only in the mind of the beholder? Or, if we effect a compromise and decide that beauty arises from some combination of the objective and subjective factors, under *what* combination does it appear? If we decide that beauty is objective, what is its relation to reality as a whole? What is the status of beauty in the universe? If, on the other hand, we regard beauty as subjective, does it reveal anything of the nature of external reality, or is it significant only as a revelation of human nature?

If we consider beauty more specifically in relation to nature and art separately, we face even more complex problems. Is the beauty created by the artist the same quality of beauty as that found in nature—does the element of purpose, the fact that artistic beauty is planned and calculatedly brought into existence, introduce a difference which places the two kinds of beauty in separate categories? Virtually all critics, artists, and estheticians have agreed that artistic beauty is expressive to a degree impossible in its natural counterpart, and there can hardly be any question that the artistic variety is more complex. And what is the exact role of beauty in art? Until recently it has been assumed almost without question that any work of art should above all be a thing of beauty. Most esthetic thinkers in the past have held that the creation of beauty was the primary purpose of the artist. The general public still believes this, as proved by the fact that the criticism of contemporary art most frequently voiced by laymen is that its creations are not beautiful in comparison with the works of the "old masters"—usually meaning, in this case, any artist whose work was done before 1890.

The Problems of Art

If we look at art itself with the esthetician's analytical eye, we soon find ourselves face to face with such issues as these: What is the purpose of art? Should it imitate nature; if so, then what aspects of nature—since any complete imitation is obviously impossible? Should art idealize nature, or at least confine its representation to the more ideal aspects of the natural order? Or, abandoning the copy theory altogether, should art be an expression of our *reactions* to nature? If so, then whose reactions—those of the supersensitive artist, or those experienced by all men regardless of their training, experience, intelligence, or sensitivity?

What of the relation between art and morality? Viewpoints on this issue have been extremely divergent, and even today, when morality is generally more liberal than it has been for several generations, we still find attitudes which are so far apart as to suggest that any consensus is impossible. Should the subject of any art work be judged by the same moral standards which we would use to judge that action or situation if it occurred in real life? Or is the artist free to handle any subject in any manner he sees fit? Does the work of art stand in a moral vacuum, or is there a kind of "higher morality," admittedly more liberal and perhaps more profound than any ordinary social morality, to which creative art must conform?

Art and Education. Standing adjacent to this warm issue is the problem of art in relation to education. Where this includes moral training, we are back in the same problem, but it is usual to extend the question to include the relations of art to all education. Plato, the first important esthetic thinker, discussed the topic at length, and his conclusions are still accepted by many conservative or idealistically minded persons. Can plastic young minds safely be exposed to the passionate and sometimes immoral actions portrayed in many works of art, particularly before they are mature enough to sense the difference that separates such actions in real life from their artistic representation? This question leads to the issue of censorship in art—a problem that is perhaps more acute today than ever before because of such mediums of mass expression as radio, television, and motion pictures.

How Important Is the Subject Matter in Art? And what about the use of art for purposes of propaganda, even supposedly good propaganda such as that found in religion or in works which aim to arouse our sympathy for the socially oppressed or the economically underprivileged? If art of this type may attain greatness (and nearly all critics have agreed that it often does), is this greatness achieved *because* of such propaganda content, *in spite* of it, or *independently* of the content? If we decide that such ideational content has little or no bearing on the excellence or mediocrity of a work of art, then we are led logically to a problem that is peculiarly characteristic of contemporary esthetic thought: What importance does the *subject* of any work of art have in our evaluation of it as an esthetic experience? Should the artist primarily seek to tell a story, recall our associations, point a moral, or move us to piety or social action? Or, to take the view at the other extreme, should he be primarily interested in creating beauty for its own sake—is he merely attempting to create a complex organization of surface textures and fully-realized formal relationships which will have no "meaning" and express little except esthetic pattern and the richness of formal values?

Other Problems of the Field. These difficult problems, controversial and numerous as they are, by no means constitute the whole of esthetics. We have not mentioned the technical problems that arise in connection with each of the separate arts, nor have we hinted at the distinction (actual or presumed) between the "fine" and "applied" arts. Then, too, any complete list of the major issues within esthetics would have to include the contrast between the space arts (painting, sculpture, architecture, etc.) and those which involve time in their presentation (music, poetry, drama, and the dance). Perhaps our most serious omission has been those problems which psychology attempts to solve by the scientific analysis of esthetic experience and the observation of the creative mind in action. However, as this study constitutes only one chapter in a general introduction to philosophy, we must be content to devote the rest of our allotted space to a presentation of some ideas regarding two of the problems which we have raised. Perhaps all we can hope to accomplish in such a brief introduction as this is a clarification of key terms and a statement of some basic distinctions within the esthetic field.

The Status of Esthetic Values

Let us turn first to the problem of esthetic objectivity—or, more precisely, the existential status of esthetic values. Until fairly recently it was generally assumed without much question that the satisfactions which an esthetic object yields are universal. All beholders were supposed to find much the same amount and kind of satisfaction in the contemplation of a work of art or a beautiful natural object. More recently, however, with the increasing critical acumen and relativistic temper of modern thought, this assumption has been challenged repeatedly, until today the thinker who believes that esthetic values have an objective status has been placed on the defensive.[3] But the objectivist can present powerful arguments to support his contention that at least some types of esthetic experience are common to all human beings, and that the satisfactions arising from these consequently represent values which are objective.

Three Types of Esthetic Value. The objectivist usually builds his case upon certain distinctions which he feels are ignored or minimized by the subjective school of thought. These distinctions divide the field of esthetic value into three types or kinds. These types are independent of one another, and each produces its own kind of response in the beholder. The values which result from these different responses may be classified as *sensuous, formal,* and *associative.*

1. Sensuous. Sensuous values are those which arise from the perception of certain colors, textures, or tones, independent of the formal organization in which these are embodied and the idea or "meaning" which the work of art is supposed to express. Thus the polished surface of marble, granite, certain woods, and many metals makes a direct appeal to both

[3] It will be noted that I am identifying objectivity with "universality within human experience." This necessarily bypasses the profound problem of the cosmic status and metaphysical significance of beauty, which will disappoint those who hold that there is a peculiar affinity between the Real and the Beautiful. Limitations of space preclude a consideration of this great problem, even if it were advisable in a first introduction to esthetics.

our visual and tactile senses. Many colors produce pleasure even if they appear as isolated splotches. The timbre of certain musical instruments, and also a number of sounds heard in nature, give an auditory pleasure that is quite independent of the melody, harmony, or rhythm in which the sounds are embodied.

2. *Formal.* Formal values are generally less obvious than their sensuous counterparts, and are almost certain to be more complex. They arise from the satisfaction which the mind finds in the perception of all types of relations. These relations may be those of identity, resemblance, similarity, contrast, and so forth. They may occur between the whole work and its parts, between the parts themselves, or between certain artistic wholes of various types. Thus in architecture, a building façade embodies numerous formal relations, such as the proportion of the building's height to its width, the comparative size and shape of the doors and windows, and the contrast between strongly illuminated areas and those in shadow. In painting, there are the obvious relations of similarity, contrast, and antiphonal response between curves and angles, or between various geometrical figures in the composition. In addition we have all the relational possibilities latent in color: these include not only the contrast of hues and intensities, but the opposition of cool receding colors (for example, blue and green) to warm aggressive colors (for example, red and orange). In music we have available for exploitation the relations of key, tonality, timbre, pitch, rhythm, and volume, not to mention the broader relationships between subject and countersubject in a fugue, or between the two principal themes in the sonata form. Each of the other arts has a similar wealth of relational potentialities, those of poetry being particularly notable. Formal values arise whenever the mind perceives these relations, if only dimly, and finds satisfaction or significance in them.

3. *Associative.* Associative values (also called "verbal," "ideational," "literary," "content," or "symbolic" values) are those which give esthetic objects a meaning that can be expressed in words, and which become attached to the objects because they remind the spectator or listener of things, ideas, or events which exist (or have existed) outside the esthetic domain. Thus a picture of a laughing man expresses jollity or good humor, since this is the meaning associated with laughter in everyday life; while a certain piece of music may please us because it is closely associated with some happy occasion in our past.

We must indicate a further distinction within the class of associative values, which divides them into *primary* and *secondary*.[4] The primary associations are those which are presumed to be universal among all men, as for example that relation just mentioned between laughter and good humor. Secondary associations are strictly individual and personal, such as happy memories linked with some musical composition.

How Objective Are These Three Types of Value? These various types of esthetic value differ considerably in their objectivity. Sensuous satisfactions appear to be definitely species-wide in their appeal, assuming only that the individual is not deficient in intelligence or sensory equipment (for example, color-blind or tone-deaf). Thus those esthetic values which arise from the exploitation of the material itself must be conceded an objective status. The situation regarding formal values is more complicated. Admittedly many formal relations are delicate and subtle, so that experience and even systematic training may be required for their perception. However, since practice does lead to their perception by normal observers, it is difficult to see how they can be considered any less universal (and therefore less objective) than those arising from sensuous satisfaction.[5]

When we reach the group of associate values, however, the situation changes. While there are certain associations which are undoubtedly common to the entire species, their number is smaller than most persons suppose, probably too small to be of importance in esthetics. Many of the responses which were formerly regarded as "instinctive" or "natural" have proved to be acquired, and many previously thought to be universal have been revealed as only "culture patterns," widespread within a cultural group, but by no means universal. Two instances of supposed uni-

---

[4] Some authorities deny that secondary associations have any esthetic value. Cf. Sully, in his outstanding article "Aesthetics" in the eleventh edition of the *Encyclopaedia Britannica*. Incidentally, this article has often been called "the best statement on esthetics in the English language," and certainly the student who wishes a better over-all picture of the subject than our chapter affords could do no better than to give this article a thoughtful reading. It should be noted that this is in the eleventh edition, published 1910-11.

[5] There is a widespread tendency to regard perceptions which result from training as somehow less real or valid—and certainly less significant—than those which result from an untrained response. The psychologist, however, who has discovered that all perception (as distinguished from sensation) is the fruit of experience, can acknowledge no distinction between trained and untrained perceptions as concerns their "reality." This issue raises the fascinating problem of the validity and value of acquired tastes, but we must postpone any discussion of the problem for another time and another book.

versal associations will indicate the dangers of dogmatism concerning the universality of any such response. For example, we regard the minor mode in music as naturally expressive of serious, somber, or introspective moods, particularly in contrast with the major. The ancient Greeks, however, held just the reverse of this opinion: to them our major mode sounded languid, self-pitying, even effeminate, while the one identical with our principal minor mode was to them virile, aggressive, cheerful, and confident. For a second example, what are we to make of the well-known fact that in large areas of the Orient mourning is symbolized by *white?*

Consequently we must conclude that even primary associations are frequently unreliable as a source of esthetic value, although within cultural groups or "civilizations" certain symbols may be practically universal in associative effect. The cross, within the confines of Christendom, is an obvious example, and in our day the hammer-and-sickle might also be cited. Concerning secondary associations, it hardly need be said that they are in general entirely personal and hence subjective.

The Personal Element. Any person's individual esthetic experiences each represent a blend of the three types of satisfaction. The average untrained spectator, as we have already suggested, will give most weight to the associative content, less to the sensuous, and least to formal value. An artist, in contemplating the same work, will be almost sure to reverse these weights, as will most art critics; either sensuous or formal elements will be considered far more important than the associative, and a combination of these two may—at least in the contemporary art world—constitute the entire value of the work. However, the main point for our discussion is not which mixture of the three types of esthetic value is "best" or "most legitimate." We are concerned with the bare fact that most esthetic experience represents such a fusion. And since the proportions of each kind of value will vary with every spectator—and even from one moment to the next in the same spectator—the over-all value of such experience must be variable, personal, and consequently subjective.

Individuals may be reasonably consistent in the relative weights they accord each of the three types of value, and they may learn to make allowance for their varying moods and strictly personal idiosyncrasies, as the critic must learn to do. It is also possible that, through a combination of similar training, similar experience, and similar temperament, two or more persons may come to hold an almost identical blend of these values as their personal criterion of esthetic significance or artistic excellence. In the last analysis, however, the relative proportion of each type of value will represent a choice which is not only personal but unique. It therefore seems logical to conclude that the realm of esthetic experience is not the most fruitful place to search for objective value.[6]

Much more is to be said, of course, on the subjective-objective controversy, but this is not the place to say it. It will be sufficient to our present purpose if the distinctions just established have given the reader some understanding of both the complexity of esthetic problems and the analytical methods which are used to attack them.

Esthetic Values in Art and Nature: A Comparison

These same distinctions separating the several types of esthetic value will prove helpful as we survey our other major problem of the field, which concerns the relation between "art" and "nature." Earlier esthetic thought formulated the problem in terms of a contrast between "beauty in nature" and "beauty in art," but with the modern tendency to broaden both art and esthetics far beyond the traditional concept of "beauty," we are compelled to consider the relationship between art and nature in over-all terms.

Art as the Imitation of Nature. Probably the most widespread and most persistent view of the function and purpose of art has been the so-called "imitation" theory. This doctrine has two forms. The first, characteristic of both classical and medieval esthetic thought, held that art is nothing more nor less than a copy of nature. Plato's views constitute a famous instance of this doctrine, and like most early opinions on the subject, had little to say concerning what aspects of nature were to be copied. Esthetic speculation during the Renaissance and neoclassic seventeenth century somewhat refined this naïve position. This refinement gave us the second form of the imitation theory, which is still supported by many laymen and idealistic thinkers today. This modified view also

---

[6] It is worth pointing out that contemporary artists and critics judge art almost entirely in terms of sensuous and formal values. Since we have decided that these two types of value are objective, judgments of artistic excellence based upon them are likely to embody a considerable degree of objectivity.

holds that the function of art is to copy the natural world, but only certain aspects of it—namely, the more ideal aspects. Art theory during the sixteenth and seventeenth centuries is full of advice to the artist about imitating both nature and the ancient artists, always with the implication that these two were (for all practical purposes) so similar as to be almost identical. But the men of the Renaissance realized that most classical art is distinctly idealistic. To secure consistency in their dual standard of "nature" and "ancient art" it was necessary to hold that only the beautiful, noble, heroic, and ideal aspects of nature should be imitated. It was this Renaissance viewpoint which we inherited, and both the general public and the conservative critic still hold that the primary purpose of art is the creation of beautiful copies of beautiful nature.

Beauty vs. Expression. Beginning in the eighteenth century, however, esthetic thought became increasingly aware of the *expressive* element of art.[7] In part, this change of attitude was the result of an increased knowledge of Greek originals, which are generally more "expressive" (and certainly less austere and coldly "beautiful") than their Roman copies. This increased awareness of expression brought many new intellectual problems, chief of which was how to reconcile the requirement of beauty-as-supreme with the new demand for expressiveness. The speculative solutions of this problem constitute a large part of esthetic literature from about 1760 to 1830, particularly in Germany. Even today the controversy regarding the primacy of beauty or expression is still heard in some esthetic circles. The formal intellectual fruit of the first battles over the issue was the development of the esthetic "categories": *the beautiful, the sublime, the tragic, the comic, the characteristic* and *the grotesque.* These were formulated in an attempt to describe more precisely just what the relations between beauty and the more expressive elements in art should be. Hence it was usually taken for granted that the last five categories mentioned were more or less opposed to the first, although they could be harmonized with "the beautiful" in varying degrees—for example, the sublime combines with the beautiful more naturally than does the comic.

As long as the general imitation theory dominated both artistic production and esthetic thought, the only real question regarding the relation of art to nature was: What aspects of nature should be imitated? But with the steady increase of emphasis upon expression—even if it meant

[7] Cf. Bosanquet, *History of Aesthetic,* particularly Chapter IX, Section 3, vi.

sacrificing beauty—some new relational formula was required, and a large part of recent esthetic thought has been devoted to such a formulation.

The Esthetic Values in Nature. The implications of this increased stress upon expression were probably more revolutionary than any eighteenth- or even nineteenth-century thinker realized. Because the change involved, at least by implication, a profound and far-reaching question: Is nature really expressive? If so, what does nature express? In terms of our tripartite division of esthetic satisfactions established in the preceding section, this question becomes: What esthetic values are to be found in nature, and how do these compare with their parallels in art?

1. *Sensuous.* On the first level, that of sensuous satisfaction derived from the perception of material textures, colors, tones, and so forth, there is no doubt that nature provides an abundance of instances. The texture of a flower petal, a mossy bank or a piece of glacially polished granite; the color of innumerable objects in nature; the quality of some bird notes and other natural sounds, such as the soughing of wind through pine trees— all compare favorably with their artistic analogues in sensuous values. Admittedly, the variety of such sensuous satisfactions offered by nature is smaller than that offered by art (for example, many types of polished surfaces are used in art, whereas few are found in a natural state) but those instances that exist in the natural world may be quite as affective sources of esthetic satisfaction.

2. *Formal.* On the level of formal values, which we have described as those arising from the perception of relations of all kinds, we find nature limited in comparison with art. There are, however, plenty of genuine natural instances, particularly in the visual field: The patterns in snowflakes, crystals, flowers, and shells; the ripples in sand caused by wind and water; the symmetrical structure of some trees and virtually all forms of animal life—all these constitute obvious examples of formal values. However, a little analysis reveals how comparatively simple and largely repetitive these natural formal relations usually are. For example, the symmetry found so widely in nature is almost exclusively a perfect symmetry, in which the two halves of the object are exact counterparts. Of the subtle, rich, and repeatedly satisfying types of equilibrium offered by art, nature can show very little. Equilibrium in natural forms nearly always means simple symmetry only, which we immediately grasp and quickly tire of, whereas the equilibriums embodied in each of the arts can be a source of recurrent delight and almost inexhaustible discovery. At

most, the formal values perceivable in nature never rise above a level comparable to arabesques and simple abstract designs like those found in wall paper and architectural moldings, while most natural forms are well below the level of even such simple artistic forms as these. Certainly nature can offer nothing comparable in complexity to the formal integrations achieved in painting, poetry, architecture, and music.

This formal limitation of nature is often summed up by saying that, esthetically speaking, nature lacks organization and unity. Natural beauty rarely has "a beginning, a middle, and an end," while what we call "climax" is virtually unknown in the natural realm. Any centrality that occurs is usually happenstantial, as when a landscape has to be viewed from just one location in order to be pleasing. Nature seems particularly poor in esthetic values when compared with the temporal arts. Only rare natural phenomena, such as storms, reveal any suggestion of the preparation-development-culmination-completion sequence found in a symphony or a drama. The blooming and fading of a flower, like any organic process which is developmental in character, has a vague parallel to the presentation of a work of art in time; but even the most analogous case in nature, the development of an individual human life, while it may be more complex than anything in art, is almost certain to be less unified, organized, and integrated than great creative works.

3. *Associative.* And finally, what of associative values in nature? Of what is nature symbolic—what does nature "mean"? At this point we come close to the core of the problem of expression in nature, and we are forced to consider the relative significance of natural and artistic beauty.

It does not require much thought to discover that our decision as to what nature "means" or symbolizes must ultimately depend upon our over-all world-view. Both the idealist and the religionist, for example, will find nature expressive of Mind, the Absolute, or God, so in terms of our esthetic problem natural beauty represents the creative production of the Divine Artist. The whole natural order represents a manifestation of the Idea in material form. Idealistic thinkers have been particularly fond of describing beauty as the presentation of the Idea in sensuous terms, while less intellectual types of religious thought have been content to call beautiful nature "God's handiwork" or "the art of God," which supposedly He creates for the delight and instruction of His favorite earthly creatures.

For the philosophical naturalist, on the other hand, there can be no such symbolic content in natural beauty. Naturalistic esthetics is almost certain to hold that all meaning and expressiveness—that is, all associative values—which we find in nature represent instances of the *pathetic fallacy*. This is the universal tendency of men to animate or humanize the natural world by projecting their feelings into its objects and occurrences, as when we speak of an "angry" sky, a "threatening" sea, or a "caressing" breeze. Man's long intimacy with nature easily leads him into these vague survivals of primitive animism, which once endowed every rock, hill, and tree with a spirit and a will of its own. It is sometimes difficult to realize that, if the naturalistic world-view is valid, *any* expressive meaning found in nature—even supremely beautiful nature—can only be what we ourselves "read into" our environment.

There are of course some symbolic associations in nature which are universal, regardless of our metaphysical orientation. In the experience of all men everywhere, sunlight warms, shade cools, rain wets, and fire burns. Such basic human responses to our natural environment represent true associations, and it is almost certain that these possess a greater degree of objectivity than any imitations of them in art. Hence we must conclude that nature does embody some objective associative values that are esthetic, although even these are probably subtly modified by our individual metaphysical predilections.[8] These associations are of course primary; any secondary associations we have with natural objects (such as the smell of one particular species of flower or the song of some bird are clearly as personal and subjective as their artistic counterparts.

Is the Personal Element Important in Nature Also? One last question remains to be answered in our comparison of the esthetic potentialities of art and nature. Does the observer of natural beauty make the same personal mixture of the three types of value as we noted in the case of the art observer? It is evident that he does, and it is no less evident that this mixture will vary with the experience, training, and temperament of the individual, as well as with his fluctuating moods. In the case of nature, however, there is still another possibility that may be significant, particularly over a long period of time. For as an individual matures, his metaphysical orientation may change, as from idealism to naturalism, or vice versa. The result of this shift in metaphysical polarity will almost certainly be a change in the "meaning" which he will find in nature, par-

---

[8] For example, sun warms and rain wets, regardless of our philosophy, but our reaction to these familiar experiences may be influenced by our idealism or naturalism, our theism or atheism.

ticularly (for our immediate purpose) beautiful nature. With this added variable to be included among the elements that constitute our personal blend of esthetic values, the final fusion in the case of natural beauty is necessarily even more definitely subjective than in art.

To summarize our comparison of the two fields of esthetic experience, we have seen that both nature and art offer the beholder the same three types of esthetic value. Further, we have noted that two of the types, the sensuous and the formal, appear to be objective in both fields, whereas associative values are mixed or doubtful in their existential status. Hence the principal difference between the two fields, as concerns their esthetic significance, lies in the far greater variety, complexity, and richness of values to be found in art, particularly in its formal relations and expressive capacity.

A Final Difference. There is one final way in which art differs from nature as a source of esthetic value, and this is the matter of expressive intention. For, as we have seen, all art is produced with the intention that it shall be expressive, even if, as in much contemporary art, it expresses only sensuous and formal values. Most casual observers and listeners are likely to mistake the exact intention of the artist, since they usually presume that he is largely interested in communicating associative values and verbal meanings, but we are not mistaken when we assume that *some* expressive significance is intended. Although we may mistake the *character* of the intention, the *fact* of an intention can always be presumed in the case of a work of art. In natural objects or scenes, however, we cannot take an intention for granted. Our philosophical or theological loyalty may lead us to postulate much expressive content in natural beauty; and even if we avoid this, there is always the danger that the pathetic fallacy will overtake us when we are in the presence of nature. Hence it seems reasonable to conclude that the arts can offer us not only richer and more subtle esthetic values than can nature, but also a realm where metaphysical prejudices and epistemological fallacies are less likely to stand between us and esthetic reality.

It cannot be denied that many persons, by temperament or lack of artistic experience, find greater esthetic satisfaction in nature than they do in art. Nor can we argue that a third-rate art-object embodies more esthetic value than a first-rate instance of natural beauty, particularly if the mediocre art-work happens to be an imitation of an outstanding example of beauty in nature. It is significant, however, that those persons whose experience in both fields of esthetic phenomena has been wide, and who have given much time and thought to criticism and evaluation, usually hold that the domain of art offers satisfactions which cannot be found in nature, however beautiful or sublime nature may be at times. Thus the popular confusion of "esthetics" with the "philosophy of art," albeit intellectually unfortunate, has a certain justification, for art constitutes the principal locale of esthetic value.

Some Other Philosophies of Art

In this brief comparison of the esthetic values created in art with those discoverable in nature, we have seemed to be thinking in terms of the imitation theory of art referred to earlier in the chapter. This has been unavoidable, for any comparison of nature and art appears to imply that the latter somehow represents or copies the former. It is difficult for most laymen to think of art, particularly in the media of painting and sculpture, as other than representative or imitative. This difficulty largely explains the wide gap separating professional art criticism from popular evaluations of art. Artists and critics usually hold a philosophy of art—that is, a theory concerning the purpose or function of art—which differs from the layman's favorite imitation theory. Consequently the professional approaches the work with different expectations and demands as to what the artist should do with his materials.

To conclude this brief introduction to esthetics let us glance at the principal nonimitative philosophies of art, for it will almost certainly be one or more of these which the critic uses as a frame of intellectual reference when he does his job of evaluation. As a professional judge of art he will probably differ significantly from laymen in another respect: he will be aware that there are several art theories, and he will almost certainly know which he accepts and judges by. The layman, on the contrary, will probably be unaware that there are many artistic philosophies, and he will almost certainly be unaware that he holds a particular one of these.

In our day the critic and artist are most likely to evaluate or create within the framework of a formalistic theory, which emphasizes the formal esthetic values described above. This emphasis is almost certain to be at the expense of associative values, particularly those of the literary or story-telling type.[9] In fact most contemporary critics make their judgments largely in terms of formal and sensuous values alone. Whereas the layman, generally oblivious to formal values and only temporarily touched by the sensuous aspects of any art, reacts in terms of either its imitational or its story-telling functions. Looking or listening for different things in the arts, it is not surprising that the professional and the layman discover different things there.

Art as Emotional Expression. A third major philosophy of art (after the imitative and the formalistic) is more popular with laymen than with contemporary professionals, although a century ago artists and critics also favored it. Indeed, the nineteenth-century art theorists did such a good job of persuading both themselves and the public that art should be primarily an *expression of emotion* (rather than an obvious copy of nature or the embodiment of formal values) that a large part of the general public is today still inclined to think of the various arts as media for communicating emotion. Music in particular is popularly regarded in this way, and in the visual arts the layman's philosophy of art is ordinarily a vague combination of the imitative and emotionally expressive theories—always with a tendency to ignore formal values to the converse degree that the professional emphasizes them.

Art as Social Influence. The last of the major philosophies of art is difficult to label and describe, since it includes a variety of views which are related but not identical. It could be called the social influence theory, the didactic theory, the propaganda theory, possibly even the moralistic theory. We referred to this view earlier in the chapter when discussing art and education, mentioning Plato as one of its principal spokesmen. Without defining this philosophy explicitly, we can be certain it is held by persons who advocate or practice any of the following: (1) censorship of art; (2) elimination of certain art as "socially degrading" or "degenerate"—for example, Hitler's purge of "degenerate" art and artists from the Nazi state; (3) evaluation of the arts in terms of their religious content or their political ideology; (4) utilization of art to inculcate young people, not with an appreciation of art or a general esthetic sensitivity, but with moral standards and social conventions.

This social utility philosophy of art usually enrolls both the imitative

[9] I am referring only to the visual and musical arts; in literary media even the most puristic critic has difficulty ignoring story values.

and the expressive theories as part-time partners. The reasons are obvious: if you are using art to control or influence, its imitative potentialities must be exploited fully. You must picture the joys of the redeemed or the socialized, or the greed and callousness of the opposition. You must, in short, picture certain human situations (real or imagined) in a manner sufficiently realistic or representational to incite social action. Just as obviously you must utilize art's tremendous potentialities for communicating emotion, since nothing can produce action like aroused emotion, and few things can arouse emotion in masses of people as readily as well-calculated books, plays, films, songs, and pictures. Only the formalistic theory of art stubbornly resists being drafted to assist the social influence philosophy; if social influence is your chief goal, the values arising from the perception of formal relations are negligible. In fact they may be an intrusion, since they might conceivably distract the spectator or listener from the central influencing purpose of the work.

It is therefore no surprise that those who hold the social influence view and those who are formalists should be antagonists and sometimes avowed enemies.[10] The other principal theories are not so mutually exclusive, although they could easily become so in certain cases. The advocates of non-objective (that is, abstract) painting, for instance, if they go to the extreme of insisting that only such art has significance for modern minds, are clearly holding the formalistic position to the exclusion of all others. This type of exclusiveness is rare; most critics, as well as the majority of creative workers in the arts, temper their formalistic focus with some acknowledgment of the values in both representation of nature and emotional expression. So long as formal values remain primary, they are willing to enrich these values with a judicious and subordinate complement of the other types of esthetic values.[11]

A Word of Caution. As we conclude our brief study of esthetics it will be advisable to caution the reader lest he believe that the perusal of this one chapter has given him an idea of "what esthetics is all about." In a book of this type, where we are attempting to give a first introduction to philosophy as a whole, it is necessary to limit the presentation of any single subdivision within philosophy to one or two chapters. Such drastic

---

[10] As an example of this enmity, see the pamphlet *Marxism and Modern Art* by F. J. Klingender (New York: International Publishers, Inc., 1945).

[11] All the issues discussed in this brief chapter are treated more fully in the author's *An Introduction to Aesthetics* (1952).

limitations mean that each subdivision must be given extremely sketchy treatment. However, since metaphysics, epistemology, logic, and ethics have existed as organized units within philosophy much longer than has esthetics, it has been possible for us to present them in more adequate fashion. The youth and present unsettled condition of esthetics precludes agreement as to just what constitute the chief problems of the field. Consequently it is almost certain that the two which we have selected as important—the objectivity of values and the comparative esthetic potentialities of art and nature—would impress many thinkers as less significant than certain other issues. As stated earlier in the chapter, it will be enough if the reader has gained some added insight concerning both the nature of esthetics and the methods whereby the problems of the field are attacked. If in addition those readers who began this section frankly skeptical of the value or validity of esthetic speculation have been rendered less skeptical, then both the writing and the reading of the chapter will have been well worth while.

CHAPTER 17

GOD:

What Then Can J Believe?

W HAT THEN CAN I BELIEVE?" AS WE CONCLUDE OUR IN-
troduction to philosophy it is almost certain this question
will loom larger and larger in the reader's mind. Many
problems have been raised, only to be answered with a
variety of solutions, most of which appear equally logical, equally well-
grounded, and sometimes equally popular. Those readers who have undertaken the study of philosophy with the great expectations which most
newcomers bring to the subject have probably been disappointed. For
doubtless many began this study with the feeling that philosophy was a
source of possible answers to all those persistent and perplexing problems
for which no answers have been found in science, religion, history, or any
other field of study. Instead of a single answer to each of the great questions, you have probably been irritated to discover a plurality of possible
answers. Instead of learning that philosophy holds this or that as the
answer to some ultimate problem, you have instead learned that almost
every individual philosopher seems to hold a different answer. As a net
result you have come out of philosophy's shop with a far larger load than
you took in. You have probably discovered more problems than you ever
suspected to exist, and for each of these there appear to be more solutions
than you can even remember. Thus you have gained both many more
questions and very many more answers; so far as attaining ultimate truth
or a satisfactory philosophy of life is concerned, the result of your study
may well appear to be a net loss.

The Inevitable Choice. It should be recalled that fair warning of such a possible outcome was given in our opening chapter. There we pointed out that choice is as inescapable in philosophy as in life. We suggested that all the keeper of any "thought-shop" can do is to lay his goods out on the counter in a neat and organized array, and then invite your selection. Of course, once that selection has been made, the philosopher-proprietor can usually be of great assistance in seeing that the answers the customer selects to all the various problems in which philosophy deals form a harmonious ensemble. It must be the customer's taste, however, which determines the choosing. You can be sure that the shopkeeper has his own favorites among the display laid out before you, and if you are too confused or too lazy to make your own selection he is usually quite willing to relieve you of the responsibility. However, there are always risks when we allow others to make such choices for us, be it in clothes or in ideas.

The possibility that the reader has been disappointed in his expectations from philosophy may also mean that he has been made skeptical, perhaps too skeptical to believe that any significant choice of philosophical answers can be made. Since all the answers are of the same logical grade and appear to be of the same metaphysical quality, what difference does it make which is selected? Why not just shut our eyes and point? The most obvious answer to this suggestion is that there is little likelihood that such a blind choice will be suited to our thinking, our temperament, or our needs. If the chief contention of Chapter 1 still holds, and some sort of philosophy we must have whether we will or not, then the only intelligent course of action is to make sure that we choose our philosophy as wisely as possible.

God: Some Preliminary Considerations

Of all the questions with which philosophy deals, there are two that stand pre-eminent as being peculiarly matters of belief rather than matters of fact. These are the problems of God and human immortality. While all members of philosophy's family of problems at times appear obstreperous and difficult to keep under control, these two are notoriously so. There are two principal reasons: first, no other questions affect our lives more deeply; and second, there are no other subjects of universal interest regarding which there is so little conclusive factual evidence. We are therefore face to face with ultimate issues that can be decided only as matters of belief. On the surface this lack of evidence would appear to mean that one man's opinion on the matter is as good as another's. Thus whenever discussion turns to these great issues, every man feels free to raise his voice as confidently as does his neighbor.

The Philosopher's Task. The philosopher makes no claim that his own personal belief on these issues carries more authority than does the belief of anyone else, but he does claim to be more aware of the complexity of the problem and the difficulty of forming judgments that are not merely thinly disguised instances of wishful thinking. As an example of the philosopher's task, let us consider the subject of this chapter, God. Does such a Being exist? If so, what is His nature, His relation to the universe, and His significance for mankind? Everyone has heard arguments regarding the existence of God, and we all know how difficult it is to maintain an attitude of calm, dispassionate objectivity where this subject is concerned. Probably no subject, including even politics, develops so much heat and so little light when under discussion. The philosopher, seeking to bring more light into the discussion, suggests that we analyze the idea of God into its various components in order that we may at least agree regarding the *possibilities* of belief. But the philosopher is not very hopeful that such a preliminary analysis will lead to any greater unanimity on the subject; all that he dares to hope is that it may organize our thinking by eliminating contradictions and establishing clear boundaries between the separate realms of *fact* and *belief.*

It is a truism that men attach innumerable meanings to the term "God." Indeed, it is almost a foregone certainty that any argument concerning the existence of God will be complicated by the fact that the disputants seldom are speaking of the same kind of Being. Historically, however, the great philosophical controversies have raged round questions concerning the *nature* of God rather than the question of His existence, which was usually taken for granted. Therefore it will be better to begin with this problem of God's nature; once the possible character of Deity's is clear, the problem of His existence should be less controversial.

The Problem of God's Nature

Transcendence vs. Immanence. The first fundamental cleavage on the subject of the nature of Deity concerns the transcendence or immanence of God: Is He (1) outside of and apart from the universe, or (2) an indwelling God, identical with the universe and existing as its inner soul, a Being

> Whose dwelling is the light of setting suns,
> And the round ocean and the living air,
> And the blue sky, and the mind of man.

The first view, that of a transcendent God, was for a long time the traditional Christian view. Any other view, particularly if it points toward the doctrine of immanence, has usually been considered heresy by the Church. The common arguments against immanence have been that the identification of God with the universe belittles His majesty and renders Him too impersonal for us to communicate with Him through prayer. Furthermore, it is evident that the fusion of God and nature would invalidate the doctrine of creation; the book of Genesis and the theology built around it would be rendered meaningless and even absurd. More serious theologically is the consideration that any such identification of God with His universe would make the evil in the world a part of His being; God would thus no longer be exclusively good, but would instead become morally neutral, or at best morally mixed.

Pantheism. The doctrine of an immanent or indwelling Deity is usually called pantheism, from Greek roots meaning *all* and *god*. In such a doctrine, all is God, and God is the sum total of existence. This view has persistently recurred in the history of philosophy, despite the strenuous opposition of the Church.[1] Sometimes pantheism has been idealistic,

[1] The theistic view of Deity, which is held by most theologians today, attempts to combine transcendence and immanence. God is a being who permeates and motivates the universe which He created, and is thus immanent as concerns His presence and activity. On the other hand, God's being is not identifiable with that of the universe, and thus in His essence He is transcendent—as proved by the fact that the universe is His creation. In other words, God existed before there was a natural order of any sort, and consequently can hardly be synonymous with that order.

While the modern theist claims to have reconciled the hithertofore opposed

as among several German absolute idealists; at other times it has been materialistic or naturalistic as in Spinoza's system, where God, nature, and Reality are all made synonymous. Or it has been moral, as in Stoicism; or mystical, as in the doctrines of its most famous martyr, Giordano Bruno. Always, however, pantheism has been monistic in its influence, leading to a heightened sense of the oneness of all things and of man's union with the world about him. The modern nature worshipper, who finds his God in the out-of-doors, is a close relative of the great philosophical pantheists. Many scientists in our own day can also be classified under this heading; certainly it is a tendency of scientific thought to find God—if any God there be—in nature itself, with its processes, activities, and forces. It is usually difficult for the scientific mind to conceive of Deity as a superpersonality of some kind who exists outside the universe; minds that have been trained to regard nature and nature's laws as the ultimate reality usually feel that if God cannot be identified with this reality, then He Himself is not real. God equals nature, and nature equals God.

God as Infinite

The second fundamental issue which must be faced in any discussion concerning the nature of God grows out of this problem of immanence versus transcendence. Is God *finite* or *infinite?* Either answer brings many problems. For example, if God is finite or limited, what are the exact limits of His power? On the other hand, if we accept belief in an infinite Deity, the problem of evil immediately confronts us in its most acute form: if God is omnipotent, omniscient, and omnibenevolent (all-powerful, all-knowing, and all-good), whence comes the evil in the world?

Belief in an infinite God has been so fundamental a part of Christian thought that many persons are startled and even shocked by the suggestion that God may not possess unlimited power, wisdom and goodness. The traditional position of Western theology has been that any limitation

---

concepts of transcendence and immanence, his great care to avoid any suggestion of an identification of God and nature appears to warrant our suspicion that this position is fundamentally transcendent. Other aspects of theism will be discussed later in the chapter.

of these essential attributes of Deity would be derogatory. Popular thought has agreed with formal theology on this point, holding that if God is not the Almighty, then He is not truly God. Furthermore, His infinity has generally been taken to include more than merely power, knowledge, and goodness. For example, "omnipresence" seems inseparable from these three attributes. In fact most Christians have held a concept of God's nature that can best be described as "all-everything." In other words, the popular idea of God conceives Him as a perfect being, and the inclusive attribute of perfection has seemed necessarily to imply the coexistence of all other attributes.[2]

Infinitude and the Problem of Evil. However, if we regard perfection as equal to an infinity of attributes, an exceedingly difficult question arises: Does such inclusiveness include evil? Obviously, if God is "all-everything," this must mean that He is not only omnibenevolent but also omnimalevolent—that is, both all-good *and* all-bad. If we admit such a possibility, what happens to our usual basic distinctions between good and evil, right and wrong? In short, if God is truly infinite and all-inclusive in His divine attributes, can He be anything but a neutral conglomerate of conflicting (or at least counteracting) qualities? And if this be granted as a possibility, what happens to our traditional view of Him as the source of all goodness and all moral value? Can the result be anything other than a pantheistic Deity who, being merely the totality of existence, is identical with the universe?

The Concept of a Finite Deity. Religious and philosophical thinkers have wrestled with these tangled questions for centuries. In an effort to short-circuit them the concept of a finite or limited God has sometimes been proposed. According to those who advocate this alternative doctrine, it is impossible to believe in an unlimited Deity without running into logical or moral contradictions, as we have just seen. If God is all-powerful and all-wise, then He is not all-good; the existence of evil in the world would imply that if He has the power and the wisdom to eliminate evil but fails to do so, He can have no concern for the good. On the other hand, if He is omnibenevolent, then either He lacks the power to effect the triumph of the good or He lacks the knowledge of how to employ His power, or both—and hence He cannot be also omnipotent and omniscient.

The doctrine of a limited Deity has been formulated in an honest

---

[2] We shall see the importance of this concept of perfection later in the chapter when we discuss the ontological proof of God's existence.

effort to relieve God of responsibility for the world's evil. For, argue the advocates of this doctrine, unless we deny the reality of evil, or postulate a God who is beyond good and evil, or accept the anomaly of a Divine Being who somehow reconciles and harmonizes the two, such a concept is inescapable. As for diminishing God's majesty by denying His infinity, is it not far more degrading to His Divine Nature to hold that He could eliminate evil but doesn't care enough for the good to do so? In other words, better a limited God than one who is morally neutral.

There are some religious thinkers bold enough to attempt the difficult job of arguing that God is beyond good and evil as man conceives these terms; hence there is no logical contradiction in holding that He some- how reconciles and harmonizes these opposites. This bold effort usually begins by claiming that we have no warrant for assuming that God's standards of evil are the same as ours; much of what seems evil to us may seem so in consequence of our limited, finite human understanding. If we could see the whole cosmic process as God does, much if not all that we consider evil would be seen as good—if not good in itself, then as a necessary adjunct to the good.

The immediate objection to this line of argument seems obvious, even to many theists; what the logical empiricist does to it can easily be imagined. In the last analysis, is this anything more than double-talk on a high level? For all it really says is that the term "evil" does not mean evil but something else, perhaps "good." But, contends the empiricist, is it not wholly meaningless to pretend that the significance of any term, *which has been and can be derived only from human experience,* is some- thing else in an experience (God's) which we cannot even conceive, much less undergo? To most philosophers and many theologians this solution to the problem seems as desperate as the effort to eliminate evil by crooning endlessly, "There is no evil, there is no evil, no evil, no evil . . ."

The argument that God, although a transcendent deity, reconciles good and evil (rather than merely transcending our limited human stand- ards of good and evil) is a difficult one for most minds to grasp because it seems to be self-contradictory. A God who includes such opposites is hard to distinguish from the deity of pantheism who is frankly all-inclusive, but one of the principal orthodox arguments against pantheism has al- ways been the fact that a deity who was identical with all existence must include the evil part of existence. How can God reconcile good and evil without becoming partly evil Himself? Thus any Christian theologian who embarks on this subtle line of reasoning usually finds he has jumped from the frying-pan into the fire: he has solved the problem of evil by embracing the heresy of pantheism.

Dualistic Implications of the Finite View of God. The concept of God as a being of limited powers usually leads to a dualistic metaphysics which pictures the world-process as a ceaseless struggle between good and evil. In the history of religion there has been a tendency to personify the opposing forces, as in the Zoroastrianism of Persia, where Ormazd represented the principle of good or light, and Ahriman the principle of evil or darkness.[3] Thus the individual human being becomes a warrior in the cosmic conflict between the two powers; he is forced to choose which he shall serve.

Many thinkers hold that this concept of limited Deity has several advantages over the more orthodox doctrine of an infinite God. In the first place, it acknowledges evil to be real, which has popular appeal because it agrees with our actual moral experience. Thus we feel that we are not merely tilting at windmills when we enter the battle against evil. This feeling gives us a sense of the individual importance of every human personality, and a sense of comradeship with our Leader in the cause of Right. Often the doctrine of an Almighty fails to attract us because there is no challenge to spend ourselves fighting for a Being who has the power and knowledge to end the struggle at any time in the complete triumph of the good. We naturally like to feel that it is no sham battle which engages our energies, and this view of God as limited, implying as it does that He needs our help, gives men just such a feeling of significance in the moral struggle. An old recruiting slogan of the Crusades conveys this appeal with brief poignancy: "Man, have pity on God!"

There is no better spokesman for this melioristic view than William James. He believed there is a Power at the heart of things working toward order and goodness, but this Power is limited. It does not do more because It cannot. Great as God's power may be, the task of erecting a moral order within an indifferent universe is greater yet. Consequently God may fail unless He has our individual help—and this means the help of all of us.

James here suggests what has since become a commonplace of liberal

---

[3] Even orthodox Christianity has its anti-Christ or Satan, whose supposed existence implies some sort of basic moral dualism.

religious thought: values are not something which are given and guaranteed by a friendly universe or an omnipotent God. They are rather something that must be achieved within the setting of an unconcerned cosmos. Fortunately we are not alone in this titanic effort; God is working toward the same great goal, so a pooling of divine and human energies appears logical—even imperative. There is a hope that the world may be saved, but it will not be by God (as orthodox theism holds) nor by man's efforts (as naturalistic humanism holds). Neither alone is sufficient, but God *and* man in partnership can impose a moral order on things and erect a structure of values, regardless of nature's indifference to those values.

God as a Personal Deity

The next important issue concerning the nature of Deity has a wider popular interest. It may be conveniently phrased thus: Assuming the existence of God, is He a personal or an impersonal Being? This question is involved at least indirectly in almost every "man-in-the-street" argument on the subject of Deity, for nearly always the person who initiates the discussion by asking, "Do you believe in God?" means belief in the existence of a *personal* Deity. In fact, such people usually refuse to admit that any other conception of God is legitimate. Unless He is a personal Being with whom we can communicate, He just is not God.

Theism. As might be expected, there are divergent doctrines concerning the exact nature of a personal Deity, although all these views are usually classified under the single term *theism*. The theistic view is almost synonymous with the popular or traditional God of Christendom. In its essence, the concept includes the following ideas: God is primarily a personality, with attributes similar to the mental and spiritual aspects of the human personality. Although He may be "without body, passions, or parts," He is nonetheless a personal Being who possesses reason, will, and (of course) consciousness. Indeed He *is* these very qualities, the source whence they come. Also basic in His nature, according to this doctrine, is a personal interest in His universe, including every creature and its welfare. He "marks the sparrow's fall," and "numbers the hairs of thy head." In His omniscience all things are known to Him, in His omnipotence all things are possible to Him, and in His omnibenevolence all that He wills is directed towards the good. As the Power and the Presence behind the universe, He can be reached through prayer and worship. Furthermore, not only does He hear prayer: He answers it—at least when it is sincere, worthy, and harmonious with His knowledge and intention of the good.

Jewish and Christian thought alike have been largely theistic in their views of God. To early Judaism, Jehovah was little more than a tribal deity, as jealous, vindictive, and capricious as a petty chief or local sheik. Gradually this primitive concept of a God in whom will was far more conspicuous than reason gave way to a loftier, more ethical, and certainly more intellectual view, such as that presented in the utterances of Isaiah and Hosea. Instead of a God of wrath, He became the God of love. Still later, in the writings of the New Testament, He becomes the Heavenly Father, with Christ as His son and chief revealer of His divine nature.

This doctrine of God as Heavenly Father represents the most popular form of theism. Indeed, this concept of Deity is so general in contemporary religious thought that most persons are surprised to discover that any other tenable view exists. To many people, if God is not the Universal Father—loving, all-understanding, and ever-approachable—He is for all practical purposes nonexistent. To such persons, who certainly constitute a majority in Christendom, the only alternative to theism appears to be its logical opposite, atheism.

Deism. There is a second form of the doctrine of personal Deity that has been important historically, particularly in the eighteenth century. Known as *deism*, this view represented a halfway position between the theism of popular religious thought and its more impersonal alternative, pantheism. Deism maintains belief in the creation of the world by an omniscient and omnipotent Deity, but, apart from this original act of creation, acknowledges no intimate relation between God and the universe. He is only a creator and legislator, not a providential caretaker and personal father. In deism we can speak of "divine providence" only if we understand the term to imply merely that God foresaw and foreordained all the parts and processes of nature. The eighteenth century liked the analogy of a clock, which, once it had been constructed and wound up, would continue to run indefinitely without further attention from its maker. And so with the universe: God, the master clockmaker, created the cosmos and set it going, with the intention that it should henceforth be capable of running by itself. Therefore He does not interfere in its operation, and has no responsibility for its moral defects. In fact, for the deist, God is not a moral being; He is neither the source of good nor the leader in the fight against evil. With no concern for the good, nor for the individual creatures who inhabit the world He long ago established, He remains aloof and independent—a cosmic constitutional monarch who "reigns but does not rule," and who is above any genuine participation in the affairs of the universe.

This deistic concept of God seems to have particular appeal to people who feel that science has made it impossible to believe in a deity who intervenes in natural processes; the aloofness and impersonality of such a God somehow appears to make Him more "scientific." However, this type of deity clearly has little relation to the traditional God of Christianity. Orthodox theologians sometimes caustically describe the deistic concept as the "absentee landlord" or "deity emeritus" theory of God. Certainly this deity seems as distant and indifferent to human affairs as absentee landlords frequently are.

It is not surprising that deism should have been popular largely with philosophers and scientists. This viewpoint supplies its adherents with none of the emotional warmth expected from religious faith by most believers. Today, even more than in its eighteenth-century heyday, deism attracts followers almost exclusively from among the ranks of intellectuals and those who consider themselves emancipated from orthodoxy and superstition, but who are still not able to move on to the extremes of agnosticism or atheism.

God as a Personal Experience. It is possible that the reader will feel that our philosophical discussion of the concept of God has somehow missed its goal of portraying His essential nature. This complaint is a common one—so common, in fact, that the philosopher usually expects to hear it immediately following any intellectual analysis of Deity. The religious-minded person generally formulates his objection as follows: "Your analysis of the concept of God may be intellectually adequate, but it remains only that; it is an analysis of the *idea* of God, not a description of the God-experience as most men know it. For most of us do not meet God as an intellectual concept, but as a presence and a direct emotional experience. Even if we agree with the deist that God is best understood as the rational Lawgiver, this is only a concept; this is not the meaning of God in human lives. We sense Him," continues the religionist, "as a 'power that makes for righteousness,' as 'an ideal tendency in things,' or as an indwelling spirit. We experience Him even more intimately as an abiding presence, a comforter, protector, guide, and constant companion. This is what God means to men, and philosophical analysis misses most of it. Like all the ultimate realities of life, He can be truly known only through direct experience."

The Proofs of God's Existence

This same difficulty of attempting to treat a direct experience adequately in conceptual terms appears again when we consider our other great problem relative to the God-idea. What are the *proofs* or *evidences* that He exists as anything more than merely a human idea, or a convenient name for a hypothetical ideal? As we have already suggested, it might appear more logical to have considered this question before going into the involved analysis of His nature which we have just concluded. Actually, however, the opposite is the case; we can now deal better with the problem of God's existence because we have gained some insight into what the idea of God involves. "Is there a God?" can be answered only after we have decided what we mean by the term. And, with such a diversity of meanings as we have already discovered, it is clear that any effort to reach a decision regarding His existence or nonexistence is going to be heavy, uphill work. There are, however, certain paths up the hill which offer little easier going than others and we shall make every effort to follow these.

No Proof Possible for a Pantheistic Deity. To begin with, we will probably get nowhere if we try to satisfy both the transcendence and immanence schools of thought. We will do well to eliminate the doctrine of an immanent Deity from our discussion altogether. This does not imply that pantheism constitutes an invalid or insignificant point of view, but only acknowledges there are no suggested evidences or proposed proofs for the existence of a pantheistic God. This view of immanence is essentially a mystical doctrine which relies on the affirmation of an intuition, or on the description of a mystical experience of some kind, rather than upon reasoned argument or logical proof. The pantheist can only proclaim his belief or relate his experience, leaving others to accept, deny, or suspend judgment as they will. For him, God is nature and nature is God; obviously little can be done to prove such a statement logically. If we accept this postulate of identity, the manifest existence of the natural world constitutes all the proof for the existence of God that is required.

Classification of the Various Proofs. Not so with the transcendence theory of Deity. Numerous arguments and evidences for the existence of a God of this type have been proposed from time to time, and unless this existence is taken as a matter of mere faith or blind authority, one of these proofs must be taken as the basis for any theology. There appear to be five possible sources of belief in the existence of God: (1) direct sense experience—real or imagined; (2) intuition or mystical insight; (3) "faith"; (4) authority of an institution (the Church), a book (the Bible), or some individual (a prophet or religious leader); (5) a logical or rational proof, based upon either a priori grounds, deduction from "self-evident" truths, or examination of the natural world. When we speak of the proofs of God's existence, it is usually these rational proofs which are meant. Many of them have been proposed from time to time, but all can be reduced to variations of three main types. Kant classified these as the *cosmological, telelogical,* and *ontological* arguments, and most philosophers since his time have accepted this classification. Fortunately these proofs are less difficult to understand than their long names might suggest, except perhaps the ontological argument.

1. The Cosmological Argument. The cosmological argument has enjoyed wide popularity among both philosophers and theologians for almost as long as there have been such speculative thinkers. It is based upon the principle of causality, holding that everything requires a cause to account for its existence. But causes are never absolute or final; each leads back to an earlier or more basic cause, which in turn refers to a cause still more primary. At length, however, we must end our regress with a "first cause" of some kind; this represents the final ground or reason for the existence of the universe—in short, God.

At first sight the argument appears convincing, but a brief consideration will reveal that it offers no real proof. For the same problem of cause now attaches to our supposed "first" cause: what brought *it* into being? The situation is given almost classic illustration by the story of the child who asked his mother who made the stars; on receiving the conventional answer that God was their creator, he then demanded, "But who made God?" If *everything* that exists must have a cause—that is, if *existence as such* logically requires cause to account for it, then how have we solved our problem by postulating an uncaused First Cause? For obviously if nothing brought this First Cause into being, it has always existed. But if we have to assume the eternality of something, why not simplify the issue by assuming that the universe itself is eternal? If the law of parsimony is sound, and explanatory factors are not to be multiplied beyond necessity, what warrant can there be for introducing a useless First Cause when we can just as logically take the universe itself as the uncaused entity?

Probably only the professional teacher of philosophy knows how difficult it is to convince some persons of the weakness of the cosmological argument. Their protests usually run like this: "But things had to come into existence at *some* time; they couldn't just always *be*. To say that the universe is eternal doesn't seem satisfactory: *some*thing had to bring it into being at *some*time! It couldn't just have existed always." When a person who argues thus is asked what brought God into being, the reply is almost inevitably a surprised, "God? Oh, *He's* eternal." Such minds have difficulty seeing that eternality can be postulated of a *thing* (the universe) just as logically as it can be postulated of a *being* (God), and that consequently the cosmological argument is worthless.

2. *The Teleological Argument.* The teleological argument is usually easier to rebut, thanks to the theory of evolution and the increased sophistication and critical acumen of the modern mind. Its general thesis is this: As we look at the world around us, we everywhere observe an order and a design which is so striking as to make the assumption of a planning intelligence not only logical but unavoidable. The marvelous adaptation of each species to its environment, and of each part to the whole, rules out the possibility of explanation in terms of mere chance. The elaborate and intricate structure of living organisms particularly bespeaks a cosmic architect; the wonderful mechanism of the human eye should by itself prove the existence of a creative intelligence in the universe. Further (argues the teleologist), not only is there abundant indication of purpose in nature, but this reveals itself as *benevolent* purpose; how else are we to explain the adaptation of species to environment, and the integration of the various parts of the environment with one another?

Man especially seems favored by a benevolent creator, as proved by our capacity for controlling and exploiting nature, and by our lordship over the animals.

The teleological view lies open to such easy attack that it is seldom taken seriously by modern thinkers. In the first place, whatever evidence there may be for purpose in the world, there is very little that is conclusive for a *benevolent* purpose. The evil in the world is so conspicuous that any God who can be held directly responsible for it can logically be regarded as an evil Deity. As Tennyson was reluctantly forced to admit, the law of nature is "red in fang and claw." Any mind that contemplates the world without prejudice must acknowledge that the primary law of nature appears to be "dog eat dog"—or, perhaps more accurately, "big fish eat little fish." Man does indeed enjoy a favored position in the world: he can exploit many of the animals to his advantage, and consequently has reason to believe in a friendly purpose—just as a shark doubtless finds the ordering of marine life clearly providential and intelligent. But even man's status in the natural order is hardly adequate evidence of teleology when we consider the evil that he too must face. As is frequently pointed out in this connection, it is possible to make out as good a case for diabolism as for benevolence. At most the unprejudiced mind can only allow that the universe appears indifferent to the life that swarms over the surface of the earth. In short, if the existence of God is to be proved, it must be by some other evidence than that offered by "the obvious benevolence of nature."

The teleological view, or "argument from design," was already on the defensive when Darwin published his *The Origin of Species* in 1859. As men absorbed the full implications of the new theory, and evidence accumulated to verify it, the teleological proof quickly lost most of its force. For here was a logical and convincing explanation of the marvelous adaptation of species to their environment that completely ignored "purpose" and "design." As will be recalled from Chapter 5, the evolutionary hypothesis holds that this adaptation comes about solely from the fact that only those members of a species survive and propagate who possess variations that are advantageous in the struggle for existence. Thus the adaptation which we observe around us becomes explicable without assuming a designing intelligence in the universe. Even the amazing ability of the human mind to analyze, understand, and exploit nature—for the teleologist the supreme evidence of a divine purpose and plan—loses much of its mystery. For if our minds are the result of a long process of evolution that has been strictly conditioned by the natural environment in which it has taken place, then what mystery is there in a close affinity between our minds and the order of nature? Is it surprising that a product should have close affiliations with the process that brought it into being? In sum, the work of Darwin and his successors has made the argument from design seem as naive as the attitude of the pious person who exclaimed, "Isn't it wonderful the way God has caused a navigable river to flow through almost every large city! Surely, here is evidence of His benevolence and omniscient foresight!" The evolutionist finds it easier to believe that the location of the river was a prime factor in the development of the city.[4]

3. *The Ontological Proof.* If neither the cosmological nor the teleological arguments for the existence of God can stand analysis, it is evident that the chief hope of those who would prove that existence rationally remains the ontological proof. We shall find less agreement among philosophers regarding the validity of this argument than in the case of the other two rational proofs. A majority of modern thinkers feel that Kant disposed of it permanently a century and a half ago, but it is still defended by a hardy minority of rationalists, so we must give it more serious attention than we have accorded the others.

In essence, the ontological proof holds that the existence of God is implied by His very nature.[5] The concept of God is the concept of a perfect Being—indeed, the most perfect of all beings. But if He is to be perfect He must lack none of the attributes which constitute perfection. Therefore He must exist, else some other being would possess an attribute (existence) which He lacks; but this would make the other being more perfect, which is contrary to the definition. Thus the existence of God is implied by the idea of God as a perfect Being. Again, if we define God as the most real of all things—the *ens realissimum* of medieval philosophy —we imply His existence in our definition itself; for how could "the most real" be nonexistent without being "unreal"?

When the student first runs head on into the ontological argument he is likely to be puzzled and perhaps exasperated. Usually he believes that the argument is invalid, but feels uncertain how to attack it. How,

---

[4] The example is from Dotterer, *op. cit.*, p. 166.
[5] We have already discussed this ontological proof as an example of rationalis' tic method in Chapter 8.

he asks, can we prove the existence of anything by a mere logical analysis of the term itself? How can any definition *by itself* prove the existence of the thing defined?

According to Kant and most philosophers since his time, it is impossible to prove existence merely by the process of definition. It is quite true that the concept of a nonexistent God may be logically self-contradictory, and that we may not be able to *conceive* of such a Being except as existing. But there is all the difference in the world between declaring that God cannot be *conceived* except as existing, and declaring that because we must think of Him in terms of existence, He must therefore exist independent of our conception. In other words, "the logical necessities of a self-consistent idea cannot be translated into the 'ontological' necessity of the existence of an object corresponding to that idea."[6] For example, if we define a circle as "a closed plane curve, all points of which are equidistant from a point within called the center," it necessarily follows that the radii of a circle must be of equal length. It does *not* follow that therefore circles must exist independent of our conception of them.

It is significant that Kant, who firmly believed in God, should have concluded an analysis of the traditional proofs for His existence by declaring that the greatest illusion held by pure reason is that the existence of God can be demonstrated *rationally*. As already suggested, nearly all philosophers since Kant's day have agreed with him in this matter. Theology sometimes continues to build upon the ontological proof, but in general it has been relegated to the past history of philosophy.

The Moral Argument

The inadequacy of the intellectual proofs for God's existence should not lead us to conclude that belief in that existence necessarily constitutes an act of blind faith. There may be other evidences beyond those contained in a purely rational demonstration. Kant himself, after demolishing all the intellectual proofs, put forward what he considered a conclusive argument for the existence of Deity. Furthermore he regarded it as the only valid proof that can be framed by the human mind. Although his sponsorship of the thesis has made it known generally as the Kantian argument,

[6] B. A. G. Fuller, *A History of Philosophy* (1955), Vol. II, p. 239.

the term "moral argument" is more indicative of its character. In brief it runs as follows: Moral values have an objective reality in that they are a part of human nature, which in turn has an undeniable reality in that it is a part of the world-order. Man cannot escape the conviction that both he and his values are as real as anything in this world-order, so consequently it must be in some sense a moral order. How else can we account for the existence of man with his ideas of value? But how can the universe be moral even in part unless it is ruled by a conscious, rational Being who has an interest in the Good and desires its ultimate realization? God must therefore exist as a necessary implication of the objective reality of moral values.[7] Good presupposes God.

The Strength of This Moral Argument. It is generally held that the moral argument remains the strongest of all those which claim to prove God's existential reality. As a consequence many modern theologians have abandoned the other intellectual arguments, not only because they are of dubious validity but also because they seem unnecessary. The moral argument by itself impresses some thinkers as sufficient foundation upon which to build an edifice of religious thought. Contemporary theology is closely allied with popular belief in this feeling that God is nothing if He is not the Power that works for and guarantees the Good. Modern science has made it more and more difficult to believe in a miracle-working Providence which has little to do except serve as a *deus ex machina* for untangling human affairs. Scientific knowledge has also rendered it difficult to believe in a creator, at least in the sense of a transcendent agent who at some moment in time agitated the ether or shook down chaos and thereby brought the universe into being. However, there is nothing in the scientific view of the universe which precludes belief in a God who is the source of goodness. Today we are not much concerned with the absolute attributes of God, such as His supposed omnipotence, omniscience, and all-round infinity. Instead we build our concept of Deity around the primary meaning which the term "God" has in our moral experience.

For whatever He may be to the philosopher or the theologian, God to most men stands for what James called "the ideal tendency in things," and "the divine More." Whether or not we dispute concerning the other aspects of Deity, there seems to be almost complete agreement regarding God as the source of righteousness. He represents in our experience the

[7] Cf. Cunningham, *op. cit.,* p. 418.

idealization (and perhaps personification) of those values which have always ranked highest in human life: goodness, justice, truth, love, wisdom. It is as the source, the embodiment and the guarantor of these values that He exists in the hearts and lives of most men. In short, the relation between God and Good remains even more intimate and basic than in the past. It is as the God of love and justice that we worship Him today. The role of Creator, Lawgiver, Ruler, or Omnipotent Providence seems less important than once it did. It is primarily as the moral center of the universe that the idea of God continues to have meaning in human experience. In comparison with this moral aspect of Deity, all the honorific terms indicating His infinitude seem as formal and empty as does the philosopher's intellectual analysis of His nature. Infinity we cannot imagine, but a God whose essence is goodness, loving-kindness, and mercy speaks directly to many hearts. Such a Being they can love, serve, and worship.

The Semantic Problem

It is almost certain that few readers will be satisfied with our treatment of God in this chapter. The religious person will find it too cold and skeptical, the out-and-out atheist will find it evasive, the mystic will feel that it ignores the most definite proof of God's existence: a direct experience of His presence. Probably the most dissatisfied of all will be the student of semantics and his philosophical fellow traveler, the logical positivist. For it must be admitted that, semantically speaking, the concept of God is extremely difficult to handle. If the meaning of any word must ultimately be tested by some experienceable referent, then it is hardly surprising that "God," for most persons, has such vague connotations. Few of us have had a direct experience of God such as the mystic claims, and the overwhelming majority know Him only as a logical concept, an article of faith, or a diffused emotional attitude.

It is a banal commonplace of linguistics that communication through symbols, verbal or otherwise, is possible only when both the person who uses the word and the person who sees or hears it have the same referent. In the present case, since any empirical indication of what "God" means is impossible, we are reduced to verbal descriptions of what we understand by the word. But since descriptions are satisfactory only when they are in terms of some sort of experience, we find ourselves trying to describe an abstraction in terms of other abstractions. Nowhere in the process is there an anchor in experience, and the net result must necessarily impress the critical student of language as confusion worse confounded.

God: Intellectual Concept or Emotional Experience? Perhaps we shall have to make a permanent dichotomy between God as a logical concept and God as an emotional experience. Those who know Him in the first role rarely have much in common with those who know Him emotionally. It is for this reason that the God of the philosopher and theologian ordinarily has little relation to "The One" of the mystic or the "Heavenly Father" of most believers. For intellectuals naturally think in intellectual terms, and emotional persons just as naturally react emotionally. It is thus not surprising that the philosopher finds the mystic's description of God so vague as to be meaningless, or that the mystic should find the intellectual concept of God futile because it lacks experiential content. It would be ideal if the logical and the emotional views of Deity could be combined, but it must be admitted that few individuals have been able to achieve such a fusion. Historically, it has usually been necessary to choose whether we will regard God as the crown of a logical system, or as the most inclusive and perhaps most intense emotional experience of which man is capable.

The implications of this dichotomy are clear as far as our present analysis is concerned. As students of philosophy, we have been analyzing "God" primarily as a logical concept, and our various criticisms of the God-idea have been directed chiefly toward the attempts to prove the existence of Deity, or to describe His nature, in conceptualistic terms. We thus find ourselves very sympathetic with the objections of the semanticist, for the rationalistic God has little if any relation to direct experience. This does not prove, however, that the semantic criticism of "God" can be extended to include the emotional denotation. It may be a waste of time to try to *describe* God as an emotional experience, but the term nonetheless has tremendous meaning for those persons who have undergone such an experience. To them, God is real in a peculiar and overpowering sense; indeed, He is probably the most real thing they have ever known or expect to know. In short, the inadequacy of our language must not lead us to conclude the unreality of the experience.

The Pragmatic Argument

The last few decades have seen the development of a somewhat different approach to the problem. In an attempt to combine all the various meanings of God into a significant unity a pragmatic argument has been developed. This argument builds its analysis of the God-idea entirely around the meaning of God in human experience, with particular emphasis upon the *utility* of belief. At first sight this would appear to be only a reassertion of the mystical or intuitionist argument. However, the pragmatic concept is much broader, since no appeal to direct experience is involved. Instead we have what may be described as an indirect proof of the reality of God. The pragmatist asks, Does the belief in God work out in practice? Is the over-all effect of such a belief individually satisfying and socially beneficial? Has the welfare of the race been advanced or retarded by faith in a Supreme Being?

The exponents of the view always assume that the belief in God can meet this pragmatic test—that is, they assume anyone will be forced to acknowledge that such faith has functional value in the lives of men. However, much is to be said on the other side, as Cunningham points out:

> The general line of argument is that the existence of God is proved by the fact that belief in God performs a useful function in human experience, that is, gives rise to valuable consequences in the business of living.
>
> If this line of argument is understood to mean that belief in God brings satisfaction to human beings and induces to high moral endeavor and that consequently the belief must be held to be true, it is open to two objections. The first concerns the question of fact at issue: undoubtedly many people do find great comfort in the belief and in many instances it does lead to high moral endeavor, but the other side of the account must not be overlooked; it lies in what evidence there is in support of the atheistic propaganda of Soviet Russia, where belief in God is held to be worse than useless, and in the tragedies of the "holy wars" and brutal persecutions which have sprung so fruitfully, and apparently so fatefully, from the belief. The second objection is that the mere utility of a belief, whether in God or in any other object, is no guarantee that the belief is true. Cannot one make a good case for

the utility of the belief in Santa Claus, for instance, and does such utility prove that there is a Santa Claus? How does the belief in God differ from this sort of belief in respect to its "utility"?[8]

It should also be pointed out that the argument from utility may be accused of that fallacy known in logic as *post hoc, ergo propter hoc*—"after this, therefore because of this." While it is true that many noble lives have been built upon a belief in God, and countless generations of human beings have found assurance and strength in such a belief, the existential reality of Deity is in no way proved by this fact. Many noble lives also have been lived without such faith, and the mere fact that a belief works for a certain individual proves only the influence of subjective experience in the life of the individual concerned. Once again, our problem is to convert a subjective certainty into an objective reality, and the *post hoc* argument is not sufficient to achieve this conversion.

The Last Word. However, in the last analysis the pragmatic test is implied in any argument that supports the existence of God. For even if we argue the issue in cold logic, those who achieve a logical proof have something that possesses intellectual utility—no matter how useless it may be to warm a doubting heart. And those who know Him as an emotional experience are likewise applying the test of utility; such an experience yields a satisfaction which no amount of intellectual analysis can either increase or diminish, and there is undeniable benefit to the individual concerned. Whether or not the same person could have found equal value in some other experience is another matter. And when we ask whether or not such an experience proves the actuality of God's existence, we seem to come to the inescapable last word: For those who have the experience, the proof is absolute; for those who do not, the proof is worthless. Those who have known God can hardly doubt His existence; those who have neither sensed His presence nor felt any validity in the various intellectual proofs can legitimately continue to doubt. At the risk of sounding absurdly redundant, we must conclude that we can believe what we can believe. For ultimately we each hold as true those ideas which work for us individually by providing satisfaction of some kind. Among such ideas, for many persons the belief in God stands foremost.

[8] Cunningham, *op. cit.*, p. 416.

CHAPTER 18

IMMORTALITY:

What Then Can I Hope?

THE SECOND ULTIMATE ISSUE, STANDING INSEPARABLY LINKED with the problem of God, is the question of immortality. Here is a problem that cuts even more deeply into our personal lives and intimate beliefs. Of all the issues with which philosophy deals, this is probably the one concerning which we expect most in the way of an answer. In the minds of many people, any system of philosophy must stand or fall upon the answer that it gives to this most ultimate of human concerns. Such an attitude represents a misleading confusion of philosophy with religion; but, whether or not it is legitimate to make this demand on the philosopher, it is inevitable that it should be made. And, consequently, it is also inevitable that the various systems of philosophy will attempt to formulate answers.

Here again, as in our study of the problem of God, we must begin with an analysis of the issues involved in the apparently simple question, "Does the human personality survive after death?" We must realize that the single term "immortality" has had several different meanings in the history of human thought, and obviously any answer to the question, "Is there an immortality?" will depend upon the meaning that we give to the term. We must also realize that no philosophical answer to the issue can come out of wishful thinking on the matter. An answer influenced by such thinking may be legitimate in some circles, but it can hardly have a place in serious metaphysical discourse. If as philosophers we conclude that human immortality is a fact, or at least a probability, our conclusion must rest on some basis more substantial than mere desirability.

We shall therefore begin our analysis by considering several meanings of the term "immortality," for few frequently discussed subjects are more likely to have their key terms understood differently by the several parties concerned. It would be too much to hope that we can arrive at any final definition of the term which will satisfy all readers, but it is both possible and necessary that we establish working definitions that shall hold for purposes of discussion. If nothing else, we can reduce the number of possible meanings to the term, leaving only those which are defensible on intellectual grounds. Such a reduction should bring some clarification to what is at best a confused philosophical problem.

The Several Types of Immortality

1. *Biological.* At least three separable varieties of experience are covered by the single term *immortality*. First, there is *biological* immortality, which is so obvious that its existence can hardly be a controversial issue. This type merely means that we survive our own death in the persons of our children, grandchildren, and grandchildren's children down through the generations. Ordinarily there is no implication of any personal survival in this statement of racial continuity; it should perhaps be called a "continuation" rather than a "survival." Those who emphasize this continuation claim nothing for humanity that does not hold true for all forms of life. A human being is neither more nor less immortal than the other members of the animal kingdom; in handing on the torch of life, all hand on something of themselves. None, however, hands on that peculiar uniqueness that makes this particular dog "Fido" or this particular man "John H. Smith." Dealing in strictly biological concepts, this view of immortality stresses the fact that each living organism is only a temporary repository for the germ plasm; the individual's life is merely a stewardship, which upon his death is surrendered and handed over to his sons and daughters.

2. *Social.* A second kind of immortality, almost as obvious and noncontroversial as species-survival, is *social* survival. In this case survival consists of our continued existence after death in the memories of our family and friends. Such a view emphasizes that those individuals who contribute most to society are the ones who survive longest socially. There

is thus a certain rough justice in the situation: our survival depends upon how worthy we are—that is, whether we have made social contributions that merit remembrance after our death. In any case, whatever we have done in the way of goodness and kindness survives our lifetime, and those who have been the recipients of our good will shall rise up to keep our memory green and to call us blessed. Those who have led great and useful lives automatically become members of George Eliot's "Choir Invisible":

> O may I join the choir invisible
> Of those immortal dead who live again
> In minds made better by their presence . . .
> To make undying music in the world.

3. *Moral.* There is a variant of this social immortality that has considerable attraction for modern religious liberals who find it impossible to believe in a heaven of harps and golden streets, but who find it even harder to believe that a lifetime of moral struggle and social good will have its only end in the grave. This view might be called *moral* immortality. It usually implies an ethical dualism, in which life is regarded as an unceasing struggle between the forces of good and the forces of evil. In this agelong battle the individual is like a soldier who, although he cannot win the war single-handed, can fight the good fight and perhaps gain a small bit of ground by defeating some of the enemy. Another analogy, popular with exponents of this viewpoint, compares human existence with the sea and its ceaseless erosion of the shore. Each oncoming wave, formed for a moment out of the vast ocean, makes the attack, bites out a small bit of earth or loosens one small rock, and then is swallowed up again by the parent sea. In the same manner a human being, rising as an individual from out the vast sea of humanity, courageously makes his brief attack upon the slowly crumbling mass of evil, then sinks back into the parent race. In this return he relinquishes his individuality and personal identity, but that bit of evil which he eliminated remains as a permanent memorial to him and to his effort. Returning to personal anonymity, he nonetheless has not lived in vain; by this enduring contribution his life has been given a dignity and purpose which redeems it from futility and elevates it to a level that is distinctly human and permanently significant.

The Traditional Position

It hardly need be said that few people have any such concepts as the foregoing in mind when they use the term "immortality." In popular use the word ordinarily means a personal survival of some sort, a state in which we continue our individual existence as a unique personality. To most persons the belief in immortality means a belief that they will continue to live after death as distinct individuals, whose hopes and worthwhile activities will be much the same as when they were on earth. To persons who believe thus (and they undoubtedly constitute a majority in the Western world) a pale form of survival such as biological, social or moral immortality is hardly worth considering. Unless our postmortal existence is one in which individuality and personality survive, and in which there is a continuation of purpose and achievement, this existence will not be survival in any significant sense. *Identity* and *continuity* are the central ideas here. Unless both are maintained, most persons feel there is no real immortality. Certainly both identity and continuity have been implied by the term as men have ordinarily employed it; when the poets and seers of all the ages have voiced the eternal dream of humanity, it is of a personal survival that they have spoken.

Because the historical and the popular meaning of the term "immortality" has implied this personal survival, the philosopher usually confines his analysis to this view. With the rest of mankind he asks whether men survive death, and if so, under what conditions. For instance, what is the relation between such survival and individual conduct before death? Is all survival dependent upon leading a moral life in this world, or does the morality of our earthly life determine only the *kind* of survival we shall have? Or is it possible that life beyond the grave is independent of moral consideration, so that both the good man and the wicked survive in the same state?

Relation Between Survival and Morality. As might be expected, there have been innumerable answers to these searching questions. The doctrines have been so numerous and so varied that any classification is difficult. As far as Western thought is concerned, however, we can make several valid generalizations. In the first place, since the late Greek period there has been a tendency to regard certain actions, certain beliefs, or particular patterns of conduct as prerequisite to personal survival. In other words, the state in which one survives, and perhaps any survival at all, has been held to depend upon either what a person believes, or the kind of life he leads, or both. The powerful influence of Christianity is plainly evident here. The acceptance of certain theological doctrines, together with a life lived according to the Ten Commandments, has always been regarded by the Church as indispensable to salvation. Few thinkers in the Western world have been able to formulate a positive doctrine of immortality that did not reveal the influence of this tradition. Even today, when theological belief has lost much of its power over men's minds, it is still almost impossible to find a contemporary doctrine of immortality that postulates survival for all men in the same state, regardless of their moral deserts. We are so conditioned by Christian thought that an immortality without relation to morality is almost inconceivable. If the next world is not a place where the just are rewarded and the unjust punished, or where moral effort bears some kind of fruit, then for most of us it is nothing.

The Greek Attitude. It is frequently something of a shock to beginning students of philosophy to learn that the ancient Greeks had little idea of the afterlife as something that had to be earned by moral struggle. Most students today can understand that the Greek concept of survival had no relation to the individual's *belief*, but they find it hard to understand that postmortal existence also had little relation to one's *conduct*. Even if we no longer think in terms of a traditional "Heaven" and "Hell," the idea of a future life which gives all men the same relative status as before death impresses us as illogical. The only rejoinder is an historical one: to the Greeks it apparently seemed quite logical. To most of us, however, whether it is logical or illogical, such a situation appears definitely unmoral. Our moral sense is disturbed by such a view; we would prefer to take our chances in a universe in which survival somehow depends upon our worthiness to survive. We feel that if immortality is to have any significance at all, it must first have ethical significance.

An ancient Greek or a modern ethical skeptic would probably argue that this modern attitude is not morally mature. For it implies the question, "Why be good if immortality falls equally to the just and the unjust?" which in turn suggests that all good conduct should be motivated by hope of a reward. The ethically mature person, it is argued, will do what he does because it is right, and not as an installment payment on Heaven or as a bribe to escape extinction. To most people, however, the afterlife, whatever form it may take, must be an existence that justifies and complements earthly life; it must be a state in which moral aspirations are realized. It must be a realm where the search for the good culminates in success, and where man's ethical life is completely fulfilled. Rather than any mere *continuation* of our lives, immortality must also mean their *completion* and their *fulfillment*.

Contrast Between the Naturalistic and Idealistic Positions

It is obvious that these "musts" which immortality is supposed to fulfill are compelling only if the universe is the embodiment of, or has a concern for, moral values—in short, if it meets the idealist's requirements of what a "good" universe should be. Clearly, if the world-order is a moral order, then an afterlife of some kind seems required for the further realization and the ultimate preservation of moral values. For it is all too evident that our moral aspirations are rarely realized here in this life; "the good die young" all too often, and even when they don't, the comparative ineffectuality of many noble lives is apparent. The wicked prosper all too often, and even when they don't, they often seem to get much more fun out of life than do many saints. There are innumerable moments in any person's life when circumstances seem to frustrate our best intentions, and when what started out as an act of good will is transmuted under our very eyes into baser metal. We can logically hold the universe to be a moral order only if we postulate a time of ultimate equity, when our good intentions will finally bear the fruit they were supposed to bear.

At this point it is interesting to note that many thinkers who do not believe in a personal survival nonetheless hold that the universe is concerned with the realization and preservation of values—that it operates in the direction of the good. Such a view represents an extension of the social view of immortaltiy which we have already discussed. Those who hold this doctrine are necessarily somewhat vague as to how such contributions as we make to the good are caught up and preserved in the cosmic order; all are in agreement, however, that values are the most precious things in the universe which is organized to assure their realization and to guarantee their survival, regardless of what becomes of us as individuals.

It should be noted that this doctrine of the survival of values involves more than a mere social preservation of individual contributions. It is conceivable that society might turn its back on values which the race has laboriously realized, as happened in the Dark Ages of early medieval Europe, but the doctrine under discussion holds that these aspects of the good are not annihilated but only suspended, either to re-emerge at a later date (as occurred after the Dark Ages) or as permanent contributions to the total good in the universe.

Both this view and the preceding doctrine of immortality as a fruition of moral values are characteristic expressions of an idealistic metaphysics. Both views imply an ultimate reality which is either identical with the good or has goodness as a major component, and both postulate a world-order that is definitely *moral* rather than *mechanical*. Both doctrines imply a universe which is friendly to man and all that is highest in his nature, and both guarantee that this highest shall be realized and preserved permanently.

It need hardly be said that a naturalistic metaphysics undercuts all such views. The naturalist does not need to postulate immortality in order to complete his system either logically or morally. Holding that the universe is indifferent to human values, and that there is no necessary relation between the real and the good—that is, between what exists and what we wish to exist—the naturalist cannot admit the force of those "musts" which the idealist holds that immortality logically fulfills. Since the human mind is the only thing in the naturalist's universe that is concerned with the realization of values, how can it be argued that the moral struggle has significance only in survival? In other words, the idealist argues that unless there is a postmortal existence to complete the moral effort, then moral values have no cosmic significance. "Exactly!" replies the naturalist. "All this grandiose talk of cosmic values is merely man's attempt to give importance to his own desires and aspirations. Undeniably, it is comforting and even flattering to believe that the universe sees things as we do, that its dreams are our dreams, its purposes our purposes, its ideals our ideals. Admittedly, it would be wonderful if this were so." But, as always, the naturalist reminds us that the desirability of such a situation has nothing whatever to do with its reality, nor has its *logicality* anything to do with its *factuality*; in short, this idealistic attempt to link human aspirations to the train of the cosmos is only a refinement of anthropomorphism.

Attitude of the Naturalist. Does all this mean that the naturalist has no belief in immortality? If we use the term to mean anything more than racial continuity or social survival, it logically follows from the naturalistic position that there can be no such thing. In sum, just as the idealist is compelled by the logic of his system to conclude that there probably is personal survival, so the naturalist is required by the logic of *his* position to doubt, if not deny outright, any such possibility. The naturalist admittedly has little warrant for certainty in the matter, and usually his attitude is agnostic rather than dogmatic. It is clear, however, that while he cannot deny survival with any certainty, the whole logic of his system is such as to make belief in immortality both unnecessary and illogical. We are in the same situation here as when dealing with the problem of God's existence. On neither question is there empirical evidence nor intellectual proof; the only basis for belief is a kind of moral logic, as Kant and many other modern philosophers have been free to admit. To deny the existence of God and the immortality of the soul has seemed to imply that there can be no objective or absolute moral order in the universe. This implication, acknowledged by both the great rival schools of philosophical thought, has been freely accepted by the naturalist and incorporated into his world-view. To the idealist, the idea is intolerable. Indeed, it is difficult to see how it could be accepted by the idealist without threatening the whole structure of idealistic thought.

Idealism's Great Hope

Since it is the idealist who carries the burden of establishing the survival of the personality, it will be only fair to conclude our discussion of immortality with a sympathetic summary of his reasoning. The moral argument we need not repeat, since we have just concluded our presentation of it. It is the metaphysical-ontological argument that requires our attention here, for many idealists appear to regard this as even stronger than the moral evidence. It will be recalled that the generalized essence of idealistic metaphysics is a belief that ultimate reality is mental or spiritual in nature, and that the objective order of physical existence—the natural world—has a derived or secondary reality. To quote again a phrase of Hocking's, for idealism the apparent self-sufficiency of nature is an illusion; nature depends for its being upon something beyond, behind or above it. This something is Mind. As we have seen in Chapter 3, the subjective (Berkeleian) and the objective (Hegelian) idealisms do not entirely agree in their methods for grounding existence in Mind. All types of idealistic thought would probably agree, however, that matter and the whole world of physical objects derives its meaning, and ultimately its existence, from a supersensuous realm of Mind or Ideas. All schools of idealism consequently deny the primacy of matter, and instead accord all primacy—logical, ontological, and chronological—to a nonmaterial order of being.

The implications of such a view for immortality are plain. If "mind," "thought," "spirit," or "intelligence" is primary, and the physical world derives its meaning (and ultimately its existence) from this nonphysical source, it is clear that we as minds, spirits, or personalities may be able to exist apart from our physical organisms. For (according to idealistic ontology) mind might logically exist apart from body, since it belongs to a more primary and more "real" order of being. The reverse would not be possible, however; the body may continue to exist temporarily apart from the mind or soul it has recently housed, but it cannot exist even temporarily independent of all mind—that is, independent of the Divine Mind or the Absolute. Thus, contends the idealist, the postmortal or postphysical survival of the personality is not only possible but even probable. Indeed, the logic of idealism would make this survival almost certain. If, as we have seen in Chapter 3, bodies exist primarily as a bridge for communication between minds, it is conceivable that these same minds could exist independent of *any* physical organism. Once we assume the primacy of the mental or spiritual, nothing is precluded as impossible in the direction of immortality. Granted this basic postulate of idealism, the survival of the human personality is more than merely plausible; it becomes a wonderful probability.

The Problem of Ultimate Belief

What, then, can we believe? By now the answer appears clear: we can believe whatever is not ruled out by empirical evidence *and is also allowed by our fundamental philosophical position.* Consequently in no other problems that philosophy touches does the split between idealism and naturalism appear so marked as here on the subject of God and immortality. Since we are dealing with problems on which little or no empirical evidence exists, there is no belief that is definitely ruled out on empirical grounds—and of course none that is clearly ruled in. In the last analysis, therefore, what we believe will necessarily be conditioned by our general philosophical world-view—unless, of course, we are inconsistent in our thinking and hold contradictory beliefs. Assuming, however, that our beliefs are consistent, our views on such ultimate issues as the existence of God and personal survival will be those which harmonize with our philosophical system as a whole. We will believe whatever we can believe within the framework established by that system. More accurately, we will hold whatever beliefs are required to complete our system and make it all of one piece. And here, as nowhere else, the idealist and the naturalist part company with dramatic finality. In order to make his world-view consistent and complete, each must follow the implications of his basic postulates through to their logical end, with every step taking him farther away from his philosophical opponent.

1. *For the Idealist.* For the idealist, with the ideational aspect of existence primary and the realm of spirit ultimate, "nothing is foreclosed as impossible in the direction of man's highest aspirations."[1] While there are probably not many members of this school who believe in "the resurrection of the body and the life everlasting" in the conventional theological sense, a majority do accept a survival of some sort, particularly a survival of the more rational and moral elements of man's nature. Here, as on so many other issues, the general mood and attitude of the idealist is strongly sympathetic to the mood and attitude of religion. Although he is perhaps more critical (and certainly more analytical) than most religious minds, the idealist nevertheless finds himself a willing fellow traveler with them. Speaking usually in terms of "the Absolute" rather than of "God," and "the conservation of values" rather than "Heaven," the chief point of separation between the idealistic philosopher and the religionist lies in the emphasis which the former gives to the theoretical as against the practical aspects of these ultimate issues.

2. *For the Naturalist.* And the naturalist? As the answers he gives to these problems run directly counter to human hopes and aspirations, it

[1] Hocking, *Types of Philosophy,* p. 334.

is difficult to present the naturalist's reply in a way that will appeal to many readers. In fact, the burden of *emotional* proof is definitely on the naturalist, wherever the burden of logical or empirical proof may fall. His answer seems too harsh, too stark, too "realistic" for most people. For the popular attitude is usually something as follows: since we cannot prove our answers in any way, and we consequently have the right to believe either viewpoint, surely it is better to hold that which yields greater assurance and makes life more worth living—which obviously means the idealistic view.

We shall have more to say regarding this attitude in a moment, but first it will be well to give a brief statement of the naturalistic position. We can judge how tolerable it is only if we understand the position thoroughly.

It will be recalled that while the naturalist is willing to wait for science to settle the question of the ultimate "stuff" out of which the universe is made, he is certain that the general nature of the world-order is physical. By this he does not necessarily mean that the universe is "nothing but a vast machine," but rather that its processes are physical processes, its forces are physical forces, and its laws are physical laws. As a corollary to this, there can be only one order of existence—in other words, everything which exists or functions is part of the order of nature. This explicitly excludes anything supernatural or transcendental from the category of objective existence; the physical or natural order encompasses all that exists.

The Contributions of Science. Like the scientist, from whom he draws both the bulk of his data and the general mood of his thought, the naturalist holds that physical operations and the laws governing them are sufficient to account for all phenomena. Where the principles involved are as yet unknown, the naturalist assumes that, when they are discovered, they will prove to be as physical and "naturalistic" as those principles which science has already established. In view of the steady extension of natural explanations into field after field of human experience, it requires considerable hardihood to challenge this assumption; so many phenomena formerly regarded as mysterious and even supernatural have yielded to scientific analysis that the person who argues that some particular phenomenon is impervious to scientific explanation in physical terms must assume a tremendous burden of proof. Postulating the natural status of all phenomena, the naturalist cannot logically admit exceptions to this all-inclusive order of things and processes.

Among these natural processes, those studied by the various biological sciences (including psychology) loom large in any intellectual consideration of immortality. For the biologist also has extended the rule of physio-chemical laws and naturalistic explanations over nearly all his field. More recently, the psychologist has carried this extension into what was long regarded as the very citadel of the supernatural and transcendental: the human personality or "soul." As the scientist and the naturalist long ago boldly predicted, neither biology nor psychology have discovered any contradictions to the naturalistic postulates. Discovery after discovery has served to confirm the basic scientific theory of causal relations describable in quantitative terms, until today it is possible to hope that psychology may eventually be able to give adequate naturalistic explanations for all human behavior.

Among the most significant generalizations which the biological scientist has formulated is this: no life exists apart from an organism, *and no mind, thought, or consciousness exists apart from a physical, neural structure of some kind.* In simpler language, biology says that it can discover no instance of such a thing as nonorganic life or disembodied mind. Psychology expresses this same idea by announcing that as far as it can discover, all psychological change—all mental events—are either preceded or accompanied by neural (that is, physical) changes, which of course implies the existence of a neural structure. Since the psychologist can discover no exception to this neural basis for mental activity, he has logically extended it into a postulate of his science, which can be phrased thus: All psychological occurrence presupposes—and presumably depends upon—neural occurrence in the form of energy changes within groups of nerve cells. Although the psychologist becomes embarrassed when people outside his field attempt to pin the label "materialist" upon him, it is easy to understand how this central postulate lends itself to a materialistic interpretation—and why the tough-minded schools of philosophy often call the psychologist as an unwilling expert witness to testify in behalf of their anti-idealism and antispiritualism.

The Functional View. It should be pointed out that these generalizations of the biological sciences are in keeping with the practice of most scientists, who adopt a functional view of phenomena whenever possible. As concerns life and the mind, this means a nonsubstantive approach to biological phenomena. More simply, it means that both life and mind are considered as "functions of organisms" and not as entities in themselves. "Life" is to the biologist merely a convenient term for the sum total of certain assimilative, adaptive, reproductive *processes,* and not a stuff or substance which is poured into the organism at birth and which flows out at death. An analogy from the field of mechanics may be helpful. Motion is defined by the physicist as a function of bodies, representing the expenditure of energy; it is not an entity or substance in itself. As it is only the expenditure of energy, when this has all been spent in friction the object ceases to function as a moving object—that is, it stops. Where has the motion gone? If we mean "motion" as an expenditure of energy, it has been dissipated as energy. However, if we mean "motion" as a stuff or substance which was present in the object, "it" has not gone anywhere, for "it" never existed. To take an even more simple analogy, consider the perennial puzzle for children's minds: Where does your lap go when you stand up? The answer is of course "nowhere," for your lap is not an entity or part of your body that has independent existence, such as your nose has. It is rather a relationship between certain parts of your body when they are in certain positions, relative both to each other and to the horizontal and vertical planes.

The Functional vs. the Substantive View. When we are driving along in an automobile and an insect suddenly smashes against the windshield, it is natural enough for us to wonder where that tiny life has gone. The change from a complete organism in full function to a mere blob of matter is so tremendous that it is hard not to feel that some "thing" or "stuff" or "substance" has been eliminated. When a human being is killed before our eyes in a similar violent and instantaneous manner, this conviction is even stronger. Recalling the functional view of the biologist, however, we remember that "life" is only the capacity for, or sum of, certain processes—notably self-reproduction, self-repairing, and adaptation to environment. When from natural causes (such as old age) or injury the organic structure is shattered, obviously it is no longer functioning— which is to say it is no longer "living." Where has "life" gone? Using the term in the functional sense as science does, "life" has not "gone" anywhere. Functional capacity is no longer present, but that no more means it has "gone" somewhere than the disappearance of your lap when you stand up means that it has "gone" anywhere. In other words, once we have rid our thinking of a substantive view of life, much of the mystery and transcendence commonly associated with the phenomenon of death immediately disappears.

The same is true of "mind," "consciousness," or "personality." If we hold a substantive view of personality, then naturally we feel that we must account for its disappearance at death; we quite logically ask what has become of it, and feel impelled to postulate a "heaven" or afterworld of some kind as the locale of its presumed survival. However, when we adopt the functional view of mind as held by contemporary psychology, such an assumption becomes not only unnecessary but even illogical. Regarding "mind" as merely a convenient name for the sum total of an individual's capacities and experiences—or, to be even more technical, of his actual and potential neural reactions—we have no problem involved in the disappearance of that "mind" at death. The capacity for reaction, consisting of latent neural energy, has undergone a change no more mysterious than any energy change in nature. And the accumulated neural reactions, which we call "habit-patterns" and "memories"? Representing as they do a permanent or semipermanent alteration in neural structure, with the decomposition of that particular nervous system, or a transformation in its molecular structure, these alterations also disappear. In other words, the question "Where has the mind or personality gone?" becomes similar to the question "Where does the form or structure of a plant go when it dies and decomposes?" The "form" of the plant and the "structure" of the mind both constitute an *organization,* and only that. Modern psychology comes around to Aristotle's view here: the mind is the *form* (or, as we prefer to say, the *function*) of the organism, particularly of its brain and central nervous system. When through decay, injury, or shock this function is fatally impaired or stopped altogether, we have the end of "mind" or "personality."

The Basic Incompatibility of the Two Views. It is apparent that the naturalistic view, with its co-mortality of body and mind, is based upon the anti-idealist postulate that the physical order is primary. More specific to the problem before us, the naturalist holds that the mind is completely dependent upon the physical (and more particularly, the neural) structure of the body. In other words, the body is not a mere housing or instrument for an independent "soul." On the contrary, the mind is not only entirely dependent upon the physical organism for its existence, but is itself merely the functioning of that organism, particularly its functioning accompanied by consciousness. We have seen that idealism believes that the mind has a dignity, value, and importance far greater than any which the body can ever have. We have also seen that the idealist regards the body as the servant or instrument of the mind which temporarily inhabits it. Thus the basic incompatibility of the two viewpoints is manifest: each, beginning with its particular postulates, can logically arrive at only certain conclusions. If mind is primary in the world-order, and if consciousness, character, and personality are the most important elements in that order, then logically mind can and must survive. If, on the contrary, the physical or material world is primary, and mind is a development of matter and wholly dependent upon matter for its existence, then just as logically our individual consciousness cannot survive the death of the physical organism.

The Implications of Immortality

The student whose background, if not temperament, has always been idealistic usually finds it difficult to believe that life can be tolerable without the hope of immortality. The naturalistic view, permitting nothing more than racial or social survival, impresses many as not only unacceptable personally, but impossible both socially and morally. Such persons often find it hard to see how anyone would be moral without reference to the next world. They are inclined to quote a variation of Voltaire's famous remark concerning God: if there were no immortality, it would be necessary to invent one—the implication being that society can hold together under law and order only if men believe in a future life. More significant than this reaction is the popular idealistic contention that life here and now is not enough; it does not in itself offer enough to be worth the living. There is a religious corollary to this view which impresses the naturalist as particularly unfortunate: human life can never be satisfying enough to be self-justifying. This implication that efforts toward social advancement, scientific and technological improvement, and greater sharing in the good things of life are all fundamentally a waste of time strikes the naturalist as defeatism and fatalism of the worst kind. It explains the naturalist's charge that much religious and idealistic thought is reactionary, since it tends to disparage social amelioration by implying that such improvement is not really important. In sum, the naturalist feels that all belief in personal survival contains the seeds of what he considers the unforgivable sin, otherworldliness. Any slighting of this very real life here and now for the sake of a purely hypothetical future existence impresses the naturalist as not only shortsighted but socially irresponsible. He agrees completely with Matthew Arnold's "Empedocles on Etna," which answers those who belittle earthly life thus:

> Is it so small a thing
> To have enjoyed the sun,
> To have lived light in the spring,
> To have loved, to have thought, to have done;
> To have advanced true friends, and beat down baffling foes—

> That we must feign a bliss
> Of doubtful future date,
> And while we dream on this,
> Lose all our present state,
> And relegate to worlds yet distant our repose?

The argument is the old familiar one: one side says, "This life is all we know for sure; let us therefore work together to make it as decent and satisfying as possible for all men." The other says, "Yes and no; this life cannot be all there is, for never in itself could it justify the toil and tears, the unceasing moral struggle, and the persistent hunger for righteousness that lies deep in human hearts. Man's ultimate home must be elsewhere, for his unrealized capacities and unattained moral aspirations are too great for any possible earthly fulfillment."

Since the naturalist finds the idealistic belief in immortality contains implications of a paralyzing otherworldliness, it is not surprising that the idealist should find in naturalism the seeds of worldliness. He believes it inevitable that such an emphasis upon the satisfactions of this world will lead to materialism, sensuality, and a philosophy of pleasure. Idealism finds it hard to see how the denial of immortality can avoid inspiring a mood of "eat, drink and be merry, for tomorrow ye die," or, "gather ye roses while ye may." The idealist argues that if this life is all, we cannot logically escape practicing an ethics of *carpe diem*—seize the day, and crowd into it everything you can. Omar Khayyám seems to the idealist to preach the only logical alternative to a life lived in expectation of personal survival:

> While you live,
> Drink!—for once dead, you never shall return.

> Ah, take the cash, and let the credit go,
> Nor heed the rumble of a distant Drum.

> Ah, make the most of what we yet may spend,
> Before we too into the Dust descend.
> Dust into Dust, and under Dust, to lie,
> Sans Wine, sans Song, sans Singer, and—sans end!

The Naturalist's Reply. The naturalist replies that the idealist grossly slanders human nature.[2] Naturalism does preach a doctrine of *carpe diem,* but this in no way implies sensuality or a philosophy of pleasure. It is admitted that the logical course of action to follow, if one cannot believe in a future life, is to find as much of meaning and satisfaction in this life as we can, *but who can seriously argue that the maximum of satisfaction lies in sensual pleasure?* The naturalist is just as aware as the idealist of the enormous capacities for satisfaction and self-realization that are latent in human beings, and he too knows that a large majority of these are definitely not on the sensual level. Naturalism, particularly in the subschool known as humanism, places a powerful emphasis upon the complexity and variety of human potentialities, and urges that we realize as many of these as possible. It is thus the idealist who appears to impute a basic sensuality to human nature. For the naturalist, humanity is not basically anything, except infinite in potentiality. Therefore naturalism not only admits but even insists that "this-worldliness" is the logical result of rejecting belief in personal immortality. The naturalist vigorously denies, however, any implication that the organization of life around the maximum realization of *all* human values leads to the degradation of life, or to a gospel of "eat, drink and be merry." The naturalist believes that it is only by turning our back on the idea of an afterworld and devoting ourselves wholeheartedly to the realization of "heaven on earth" that humanity can be elevated to its highest level. The doctrine of "pie in

---

[2] We have met this reply before, in Mill's defense of utilitarianism (Chapter 13).

the sky," says naturalist, has been one of the greatest barriers to human progress. As long as men are encouraged to put their hopes on the next world, regarding it as their true home, just so long will they continue to consider their earthly sojourn an exile. And of course no exiled person can have the same interest in his surroundings and their improvement as the individual who has freely chosen his dwelling place.[3] In sum, our loyalties cannot be divided; it is only as we give our loyalty wholly to life here, and to all that it can offer in possibilities of human development, that we will ever find either personal or social salvation. "Man cannot live by bread alone"—but who, demands the naturalist, can argue that our earthly existence offers only bread? And, even if it did, surely that is more nourishing than "pie in the sky."

The Foundations of Belief

"What then can we believe?" As regards God, immortality, and other such ultimate questions that perplex men, it is evident that our situation here is the universal one wherever belief is concerned: what we can believe, whether it be concerning God or the ultimate nature of anything in human experience will depend upon the kind of universe we believe in. If we can accept the universe portrayed by idealistic metaphysics, then we can believe many things that are necessarily foreclosed to us if we reject such a world-view. The acceptance of idealism inevitably affects our perspective: in viewing the universe through the eyes of the idealist, we see everything as possessing significance and moral value; we see Purpose lurking in the wings and Intelligence brooding over all as Director of the vast spectacle. For the naturalist, things appear very differently: there is no back drop of "meaning" or "purpose," and such meaning as things and events have is conferred on them by our reactions and our attitudes toward them.

Why Not Believe? At this point in any discussion regarding belief a further question usually arises. Since the idealistic view makes the world seem a friendlier place to live in, and gives a cosmic significance to human destiny, why does not everybody (including the naturalist) hold this

[3] Cf. Montague, *Ways of Knowing*, p. 62.

view? It need hardly be said that it is always an idealist or religionist who raises such a question, but this does not necessarily invalidate the inquiry. Assuming that the questioner is not merely asking, naively, "Why doesn't everyone believe as I do?" the demand is a natural one, for it is admitted that idealism does a better job than naturalism of meeting the demands of *both* the head and the heart; the idealist has an assurance and a comfort that the naturalist can never know. Thus it seems almost perverse for anyone to refuse this heart-warming assurance. As is often remarked, it doesn't *cost* anything to believe, so why not?

Here again it is William James who probably expresses this attitude most clearly and most famously. His celebrated essay, "The Will to Believe," is a long pragmatic elaboration of this same question: since it is more satisfying to believe in God and immortality, and as this belief involves no risk but only great possible gain, why not believe? The French philosopher of the seventeenth century, Blaise Pascal, formulated what has come to be known as "Pascal's wager," and James admits he merely extends this. Let us begin with Pascal's own words:

> "Either God is or is not," we can say. But to which side shall we incline? Reason cannot help us. There is an infinite gulf fixed between creature and creator. What will you wager? It is like a game in which heads or tails may come up. There is no reason for backing either the one possibility or the other. You cannot reasonably argue in favor of either.
>
> If you know nothing either way, it might be argued, the true course is not to wager at all. But you must wager; that does not depend on your will. You are embarked in this business. Which will you choose?
>
> Let us see. Since you must choose, your reason is no more affronted in choosing one way than the other. That point is clear. But what of your happiness? Let us weigh the gain and loss in wagering that God does exist. If you wager that He does and He does, you gain all. If you wager that He does and He does not, you lose nothing. If you win, you take all; if you lose, you lose nothing. Wager then, without hesitation, that He does exist.[4]

James agrees with Pascal that reason cannot settle the question of God and immortality. But he is not satisfied to argue from our need for God to the existence of God, as Pascal had done before proposing his "wager" as an additional argument for persons whose need for God was

[4] *Pensées*, number 223.

less urgent than his own. Instead James elaborates another idea made famous by Pascal: "The heart has reasons which the head knows not."

James defends the right of what he calls our "passional nature" and its demands, which are roughly equivalent to what the contemporary psychologist calls our emotional needs. But James goes farther than merely asserting that all men require emotional satisfactions as well as those of the intellect. He argues that in the last analysis all vital decisions and judgments, even when they seem most rational and logically grounded, are actually emotional choices made by our "passional nature." Let us take for example the scientist's or philosopher's well-known belief that truth is the supreme value, and that the findings of our intelligence or reason are always to be preferred to the promptings of our desires. But, asks James, what about those situations—some of them greatly significant for human happiness—where intelligence can discover no "truth"? Take our present problem, the existence of God and immortality. Neither science nor logic can give us definitive answers; if we must depend upon them we are and probably ever shall be in the dark.

So what should we do? The skeptic or agnostic says, "Suspend judgment; make no choice; neither affirm nor deny." The more toughminded may go so far as to insist that we should not believe anything we can doubt. They may demand that we *never* believe on insufficient evidence, and even argue that it is immoral to do so. James quotes Clifford, a well-known skeptic of his own day, upon this point.

> Belief is desecrated when given to unproved and unquestioned statements for the solace and private pleasure of the believer. . . . If a belief has been accepted on insufficient evidence, even though the belief be true, the pleasure is a stolen one. It is sinful because it is stolen in defiance of our duty to mankind. That duty is to guard ourselves from such beliefs as from a pestilence which may shortly master our body and then spread to the rest of the town. It is wrong, always, everywhere, and for everyone, to believe anything upon insufficient evidences.[5]

But, James cleverly asks, is this viewpoint of an arch-skeptic like Clifford not a very passional position based solely upon an emotional choice? What the person who holds it is really saying is that he prefers the risk of

[5] *The Will to Believe and Other Essays in Popular Philosophy*, p. 8.

losing something good by refusing to believe what might be true, rather than the risk of believing something which might not be true.

James thinks that the skeptic-agnostic is so afraid of being duped by hope that he flies to the other extreme and becomes duped by fear. To James this is absurd: if we are forced to choose between risks, he asks on what grounds should anyone select the risk offering no gain and all loss as against the one offering no loss and great possible gain. This brings us back to Pascal's wager; or, in James's characteristic language:

> Dupery for dupery, what proof is there that dupery through hope is so much worse than dupery through fear? I, for one, can see no proof; and I simply refuse to imitate the skeptic's option in a case where my own stake is important enough to give me the right to choose my own form of risk.[6]

And so we come full circle: risk is involved whenever we make choices on insufficient evidence; but in living we often have to take these risks, and certainly a decision regarding God and immortality is the supreme example of such a forced choice. And in the last analysis there is nothing except our temperament or private need to decide which dupery—that of hope or that of fear—we prefer to risk. So why not believe, concludes the theist and idealist, since it costs nothing and may yield enormous dividends in both present peace of mind and postmortal happiness?

The Naturalist's Apologia. The naturalist's answer is usually as incomprehensible (to the idealist) as his original attitude. He replies, "I do not accept the belief because I cannot. You are quite wrong when you say that such assurance costs nothing; it would cost me my most cherished possession, my intellectual integrity." It should be noted immediately that this answer is never intended as a reflection on the intellectual honesty of the idealist; it is merely a statement that the naturalist himself cannot hold such a conviction except at this heavy price.

It may be argued that, as we have already agreed, both world-views are probably on a par as concerns their logic. If this is true, then how is any less mental rigor required to find the idealistic system acceptable? The naturalist explains: "I am not referring to my opponent's logic when I allude to intellectual integrity; I am referring only to the postulates

---

[6] *Ibid.*, p. 27.

upon which his logical structure is built. It is these basic assumptions which I cannot accept, for they are not justified by either my experience or what I believe to be the consensus of empirical evidence generally. If the idealist wishes to accept these assumptions, or must accept them to find the universe a tolerable environment for human life, that is his affair. Perhaps he has had personal experiences that lead him to believe the ultimate real is spiritual, or which warrant his taking this belief as the major postulate of his system. If he can do so, well and good; I for one cannot."

Whence Come Such Differences? It is plain that we cannot carry this discussion much further without becoming involved in a treatise on the psychology of belief. We can hardly bury the issue, however, without a final word. One of the most puzzling questions in human experience concerns just this point: How can two persons share the same experience and have opposite reactions to it? We raised the question at the conclusion of Chapter 4, and we are now brought back to it. "Difference in the background which individuals bring to the common experience," is the usual answer. But when we have noted the strikingly divergent reactions of individuals who are the same age and from similar general backgrounds, as for instance, members of a closely knit family or lifelong intimate friends, we come to feel that this answer is too simple. A person who has been in long close association with two brothers, for example, and has observed how consistently one may read idealistic implications into everything that occurs while the other reacts just as inevitably in a naturalistic direction, feels impelled to probe deeper.

The only answer that promises to meet any scientific test holds that such divergence is due in part to individual difference in inheritance and equipment—differences in neural structure, sensory sensitivity, glandular function, and even digestion! The psychological result of our basic neural and glandular functions is usually called "temperament," and the term is widely used to describe an individual's psychophysical predisposition. Our question may therefore now be asked in revised form: How far do temperamental differences lead to differences in philosophical viewpoint? Is the battle between the idealist and the naturalist "all a matter of glands," to use a well-known phrase?

The Problem of Temperament. William James is probably responsible for the modern attempt to connect temperament and metaphysics;

we have already referred to his celebrated contrast between the "tender-minded" idealist and the "tough-minded" naturalist.[7] The English poet Coleridge, writing nearly a century and a half ago, expressed much the same idea when he described all men as either Platonists or Aristotelians. In our day, with the rise of the so-called glandular theory of personality, the view that one's world-view is closely tied up with one's organic functions has gained considerable acceptance. As might be expected, the naturalist, with his emphasis upon the physical realm as primary, finds nothing illogical (and certainly nothing shocking) in such a theory. He is not in the least disturbed when someone suggests that he holds the system he does, and particularly the original postulates upon which the system is built, because of a certain glandular balance—or more likely, imbalance. Indeed, our original prejudice in favor of certain postulates is likely to impress the naturalist as best explained in terms of a deep-seated temperamental preference; he may even wonder how else to account for it.

Not so the idealist. Any physical theory of personality is disturbing enough, but the extension of such a view to philosophy is intolerable. In fact, there are probably few theories that are so certain to arouse the idealist to combat as this. The naturalist sometimes likes to taunt his opponent with the charge that the idealist regards all views other than idealism as not only false, but wicked. This is undoubtedly an exaggeration, but in the case of the present theory regarding the sources of temperament it comes rather close to the truth. For such a theory, if it could be established experimentally, would seriously endanger the whole structure of idealistic metaphysics. Could it be proved that persons of a certain glandular balance, for example, tend to gravitate toward one major pole of thought as against the other, what would become of the basic postulate that "mind" or "thought" is primary in the universe? If what we think is determined by what we eat or how our pituitary is behaving, then obviously "matter" or the physical realm is ultimate. However logical or significant or inspiring idealism may be, the verification of this theory of temperament would leave the idealistic philosophy up in the air with no support, and little except a certain esthetic charm to justify its existence.

[7] James himself did not use the terms "idealist" and "naturalist" in his contrast, but the close affiliation between his classification and the ideological dichotomy we have stressed throughout this book is accepted generally.

We have thus come full circle: what we can believe about God and immortality appears to be determined by what we can believe about the nature of the world in general—which in turn is seen to depend upon what we can believe regarding the sources or determinants of belief itself.

The circularity of such a conclusion must mean that it will be less than completely satisfying. But within the framework of our present knowledge, it is hard to see what other conclusion is possible. In the last analysis we believe what we can; but this in turn is dependent upon such a multiplicity of factors, which vary so widely from individual to individual, that each mind will have its own particular possibilities of belief.

CHAPTER 19

HUMANISM AND EXISTENTIALISM

AMONG THE PHILOSOPHIES OF OUR DAY ARE TWO WHICH OCCUPY A peculiar position. Both stand on the borderline between technical systems and popular "philosophies of life," and both have been of greater interest to writers and "intellectuals" than to professional philosophers. Both have—or at least imply—abstract metaphysical theories, but both are known almost exclusively for their explicit ethical judgments and their concrete views regarding the human situation. Both philosophies seem peculiarly and strikingly modern (in spite of the fact that each has roots running back one or more centuries). For both express moods and attitudes that can only be called "contemporary."

It is almost certain that the student will have heard of these philosophies; if he picked up any philosophical terms at all, prior to beginning his formal study of the field, "humanism" and "existentialism" are probably among the first he acquired. It is possible that both schools owe their popularity to the fact that they have intrigued writers, particularly novelists and playwrights, rather than to any special importance they have in the intellectual scheme of things. But, regardless of whether history will show these philosophies to have been profound or merely well publicized, their influence during the middle third of the twentieth century will still have been very significant. The exact relation between humanism and existentialism cannot be discussed fruitfully until we have considered the two separately. We will begin with the older, humanism.

Renaissance Humanism. The term "humanism" has an extended history and like most long-used terms it has carried a variety of meanings. Three connotations have been particularly important. The oldest meaning is literary and cultural, growing out of literary criticism and the cultivated study of literature incidental to the Renaissance. Here the word was used to indicate the thought and writing, particularly of the sixteenth century, which had as its primary subject-matter mankind—that is, man's interests and activities in this world, particularly his intellectual and esthetic activities. The ideal man, according to these early humanist writers, was the fully developed individual, all of whose capacities were realized to the maximum. The philosophy of self-realization became dominant at this time.

As is well known, much of the living and thinking of the Renaissance was a conscious revolt against the monastic ideals of the Middle Ages. The man of the Renaissance was no longer willing to sacrifice a large part of his humanity for the sake of other-worldly rewards, and the monks and nuns (who were presumed to have made notable sacrifices in this direction) became objects of ridicule and scorn among many writers and thinkers of the period. The awakened interest in, and recovery of, much material from classical civilization brought to men of the fifteenth and sixteenth centuries a poignant sense of what humanity can be at its best. The Renaissance mind saw Greek and Roman life as the ideal product of humanistic development, and it despaired of ever reaching such heights again. But the fact that classical man had done so much in the world of here and now, showing little concern for the next world and its supposed rewards and punishments, encouraged men of the Renaissance to attempt a fuller realization of human capacities than had been sought during the middle ages.

It is the reflection of this effort in literature, literary criticism, and art which constitutes "humanism" in its first and oldest sense. This Renaissance movement also establishes the root meaning of the term—namely, a constant focus upon man, his earthly existence, and the magnificent potentialities of that existence. It should be pointed out that this original humanism did not reject religion as a component of the good life. But it did specifically repudiate monasticism, fanaticism, and all attempts to make religious values supreme, particularly if such supremacy meant sacrificing any part of man's essential humanity.

Modern Meanings of "Humanism"

The other principal meanings of "humanism" are of more recent origin, having developed largely within the present century. Each represents a particular emphasis upon some fragment of the over-all meaning of the term. There is, for example, a type of pragmatic philosophy developed by the leading British pragmatist, F. C. S. Schiller, which he specifically labeled "humanism." Schiller's basic position is summarized in his favorite quotation from Protagoras, a contemporary of Socrates and Plato: "Man is the measure of all things." However as Schiller's main interest was epistemological and logical, rather than ethical, he naturally stressed the pragmatic and humanistic criteria for "truth" and "validity," rather than for "good." In general he believed that any talk of absolute, transcendental, or a priori truths is futile. We know what we know as a result of our strictly human experience, and because this experience changes from one generation to the next we must expect our knowledge and our truths to change too.

Although Schiller did his work in the early 1900's before modern logical empiricism reached its present development, it is easy to see certain relations between this British humanism and the contemporary positivistic thought which we discussed in Chapter 11. The two schools would agree, for example, that there is no means by which man can transcend his experience to gain knowledge of a supposed transempirical reality. Hence any talk of "eternal verities" or "absolute truth" is nonsense. Admittedly we can dream about such unknowable essences, and certainly we may wish we could prove that they exist. But since such existence cannot be established—for it could be established only by experience, and there is no possible way we can get outside experience to find what exists "outside experience"—any statement which pretends to express transempirical, nonhuman truth is meaningless. As Schiller was never tired of reminding us, "Man is the measure of all things—*of that which is that it is, and that which is not that it is not.*" Only human experience can tell us what exists and what does not; from no other source can we get knowledge regarding either the fact or the character of actual existence. Modern positivism and what we may call "epistemological humanism" both take this as the most basic brute fact of our mental life, and both agree in condemning the innumerable philosophical and theological schools which ignore this brute fact.

Religious Humanism

A far better known, and certainly more controversial, type of humanism is generally called *religious humanism*. Unfortunately this term also suffers from considerable ambiguity, since even the many persons calling themselves religious humanists are not agreed on what is involved. The one thing all such humanists do agree upon is an opposition to the more orthodox, fundamentalistic, and Calvinistic forms of Christianity. The humanists are particularly opposed to the emphasis these sects give to original sin, human depravity, or man's hopelessness without divine aid. But, after repudiating these more extreme doctrines which stress God's infinite perfection and man's infinite imperfection, religious humanists seldom agree concerning the content of the religion they propose.

The most serious difficulty they face arises from the definitions, and even the concepts, of "God" and "religion." By and large these religious humanists have tried to decrease the supernatural element in religion, and some have expressly eliminated all supernaturalism whatever. This has of course meant a complete redefinition of "religion," since as far as the Western world is concerned, supernaturalism and religion have been inseparable. In some cases, this elimination or de-emphasizing of supernaturalism has involved a parallel elimination of God, but in other cases it has meant a redefinition of that term. It must be admitted, however, that this redefinition has frequently been so drastic that God has been eliminated indirectly and surreptitiously, rather than frankly and directly.

The Definition of "God." There is a tendency for religious humanists to define God wholly in terms of human ideals and social principles. Corliss Lamont, a well-known American writer on humanism, has collected samples of these socially-oriented definitions of deity, and I can do no better than to borrow a few from this source.[1] For instance, Durant Drake writes, "God is the universal self in each of us, our good will and

---

[1] *Humanism as a Philosophy*, second edition (New York: Philosophical Library, 1949). All quotations are from this edition. The book can be recommended to anyone wanting more information on humanism.

idealism and intelligence which binds us together and drives us on by inner compulsion toward that ideal life for which in our better moments we strive." Jesse H. Holmes describes God as the unifying element within that moves us to unity in a brotherly world. Henry Nelson Wiemann, who is particularly well known for his efforts to define God in humanistic terms, writes as follows: "God is that interaction between individuals, groups and ages which generates and promotes the greatest possible mutuality of good."

It hardly needs to be pointed out that, however noble these concepts of God may be, they certainly have almost nothing in common with traditional definitions of deity. For example, there is no relation between them and the various concepts of God discussed in our earlier chapter on theism. In fact it is difficult to see how a theist and a humanist, even with abundant goodwill on both sides, could avoid confusion and ambiguity if they tried to have intelligent discourse on the general subject of deity. This is not to imply that theists are "right" and humanists "wrong" in their respective concepts, but rather to remind humanists that the burden of semantic proof falls on them if they choose to retain a word which has for centuries had one general meaning, while insisting on using this word to convey a different connotation. Any speaker or writer has the right to define his terms as he pleases, but religious humanists are often accused of making heavy demands on their readers or listeners when they employ a conventional term in a most unconventional sense, and then expect the reader to make the semantic adjustment each time the term appears.

The Definition of "Religion." The humanistic concept of "religion" involves many of the same semantic issues. By insisting that religion is a matter of *attitude*, rather than of *content*, some of the humanists have classified such phenomena as communism and even atheism as "religions." As Lamont very well says, "Some of these redefinitions would by implication assign the name of religion to any socially organized enterprise that succeeds in winning the devotion and emotions of men. On this basis football, trade unions, political parties, armies, and even poetry societies all become forms of religious endeavor."[2]

In short, religious humanists have sought to retain the term "religion" for all high-minded and socially-oriented activity, regardless of whether or not any transcendental or supernatural element is involved.

[2] *Op. cit.*, p. 181.

This has the obvious advantage that they can consider their own humanistic activities "religious," and can affirm to the world that humanists, like most people, have a religion. But it has the obvious disadvantage of creating confusion and ambiguity, since transcendentalism of some sort has always been central in religion, at least within the Western world.

Probably the most famous document produced by American humanism was the celebrated *Humanist Manifesto* set forth in 1933 and signed by many intellectual and religious leaders of the liberal type. The statements contained in this fascinating little document attempted to include several varieties of humanism under one general heading, so naturally religious humanism was included. But, since the group of signers numbered several well-known agnostics, compromise was inevitable. The result was a definition of religion which most religious persons will probably find as astonishing as irreligious persons did at the time of publication: "Religion consists of those actions, purposes and experiences which are humanly significant." As the critics of religious humanism point out, it is hard to see what this definition does *not* include, since most human activities are humanly significant. Certainly it includes art, education, social service, politics, trade unionism, jurisprudence, science, and the like. But everyone who seeks to communicate accurately has discovered that any definition which includes everything has no meaning. So in this particular instance most persons gain little understanding from the definition.

It must be acknowledged that religious humanism has set itself an almost impossible task, so we can be sympathetic when it appears to meet difficulties. It attempts to set up a view of human life and human destiny which runs counter to Christian theism at nearly every point. But, since this same Christian theism is what most people in Europe and America mean by "religion," it is impossible for most of us to shift semantic gears every time we hear the word "religion." However this is just what religious humanism asks us to do. It employs the terms "religion" and "religious" very freely, just as it does the terms "God" and "divine." Yet we are expected to make a mental shift every time the words appear—which is certainly more work than most of us are able to perform easily as we read or listen.

In short, the religious humanist attempts to build a religion which specifically leaves out most of the content of traditional religion. He believes in God—meaning a summation of all the social aspirations of the race and the ideational forces operating in history. He believes in immortality—meaning the social conservation of each individual's contribution toward human progress. Most importantly, he believes in man, particularly man's idealistic aims and achievements. Whatever contributes to human welfare is divine, and all activities which advance mankind's highest development are religious activities. Such is the gospel according to contemporary religious humanism.

Naturalistic Humanism

The last major variety of humanism we shall consider is probably best called *naturalistic humanism*, although the term *scientific humanism* is more popular. As both terms suggest, this philosophy has close affiliations with both philosophic naturalism, which we studied at length in Chapter 4, and with the generalized scientific world-view. In fact it would be accurate to regard this type of humanism as the ethical theory, or philosophy of value, that is most logically derived from naturalism. It might be called "applied naturalism" without doing violence to either humanism or naturalism.

The most significant doctrine in naturalistic humanism is undoubtedly its specific repudiation of every form of supernaturalism. This philosophy holds instead that there is only one order of existence—namely, the natural world—and that man is a wholly natural creature whose welfare and happiness come solely from his own unaided efforts. As we saw from the chapter on naturalism, the universe is seen as indifferent to humanity, just as it is to all life. Nature provides us with only the potential raw materials, as it were, out of which we can build a satisfying existence for ourselves and perhaps for our descendants. But nature guarantees us nothing. We are on our own, in an environment which has no plans, no moral preferences, and makes no promises.

The naturalistic humanist is equally specific in rejecting what he considers the "illusion of immortality." He believes that "This life is all and is enough." He does not deny that the yearning for survival is widespread, and hence must be considered natural. But this has no relation to the possibility of survival—that is, we cannot argue that because men have this yearning, therefore it must be satisfied. The humanist's real emphasis, however, is not upon the negative implications of this central doctrine, but rather upon showing that life here and now can be satisfying enough to make the prospect of death acceptable psychologically. Whether or not he succeeds in this effort is of course a decision that depends upon how tough- or tender-minded his reader-listener happens to be. Naturalists, materialists, and the like find no difficulty accepting the humanist arguments on this point, but of course other schools of thought disagree violently. A naturalistic humanist holds that all the many efforts to prove the existence of either God or immortality involve wishful thinking, and he regards all these as evidence of emotional and intellectual immaturity in whoever makes such efforts.

From even this brief sketch of naturalistic humanism we can see that it primarily makes explicit some of the implications within the general naturalistic world-view presented earlier. There are, however, some less obvious (and perhaps less negative) implications of naturalism that are elaborated by humanism. Since it is these that give humanism its particular contemporary character we must examine them in some detail.

Humanism's Ideal Society

It will be well at this point to listen again to Lamont as he gives a summary statement of naturalistic humanism:

> Humanism is the viewpoint that man have but one life to lead and should make the most of it in terms of creative work and happiness; that human happiness is its own justification and requires no sanction or support from supernatural sources; that in any case the supernatural, usually conceived of in the form of heavenly gods or immortal heavens, does not exist; and that human beings, using their own intelligence and cooperating liberally with one another, can build an enduring citadel of peace and beauty upon this earth.
>
> It is true that no people has yet come near to establishing the ideal society. Yet Humanism asserts that man's own reason and efforts are man's best and, indeed, only hope; and that man's refusal to recognize this point is one of the chief causes of his failures throughout history. In times of confusion and disintegration like the present, men face the temptation of fleeing to some compensatory realm of make-believe or supernatural solace. Humanism stands uncompromisingly against this

tendency, which both expresses and encourages defeatism. The Humanist philosophy persistently strives to remind men that their only home is in the mundane world. There is no use of our searching elsewhere for happiness and fulfilment, for there is no place else to go. We human beings must find our destiny and our promised land in the here and now, or not at all.[3]

If one accepts this humanistic ideal of the good life and the good society, what are some of the practical implications—and applications? It appears that the following implications would have to be acknowledged. First, this humanistic ideal for society would seem to mean that religion in virtually all its present forms would die out. A humanist society, assuming its members were intellectually consistent, would have no use for religion as the term is generally understood, and no employment for those who preach doctrines involving supernaturalism, other-worldly standards, or postmortal rewards and punishments.

Humanism and Social Controls. Secondly, a society living by naturalistic humanism would necessarily have to shift its ethics from the foundations they have had for centuries—namely, the "will of God" or "divine commands." This would be a radical shift indeed, for there is a very widespread belief, even among agnostics and atheists, that faith in God is necessary for most men in order to keep them moral and socially responsible. This belief is expressed in the well-known saying we have already quoted: "If God did not exist it would be necessary to invent Him." It is also expressed in the remark of the Earl of Shaftesbury, popularized by Disraeli and others: "All wise men have the same religion [*i.e.*, skepticism or atheism], but wise men never tell." The implications of such statements are obvious: "It is all right for me and my fellow-intellectuals to live without religious beliefs, because we are intelligent men of good will who do not need the promise of heaven or the threat of hell to keep us virtuous. But the man in the street is a simple animal who has to be manipulated for his own good, by dangling such lures or threatening such tortures. We elite can live without supernatural sanctions, but we must discreetly retain them in order to keep the majority of mankind in line."

A humanistic society would reject this intellectual double standard. It would instead encourage *all* its members to live by a single standard, that of human welfare in this world of here and now. A humanistic ethics

[3] *Op. cit.*, pp. 21 f.

would base its values entirely upon the nature of man and the logic of human relationships. Its only sanctions would be social and legal; social ostracism and legal penalties would be the sole instruments utilized for maintaining order. But humanists believe that the willing cooperation of all members of society could be secured by educating them to realize that their own personal welfare is inescapably linked to the fair enforcement of these social and legal codes.

It has been my experience that even the most optimistic and enthusiastic humanist seldom minimizes the difficulty of such an educational program. Nor does he underestimate the complexities involved in making a transfer from our present ethical system, grounded in supernaturalism, to one which cuts free from any transcendental supports. But he believes this can be achieved, and he holds that it must be achieved if men are ever to live as free, mature individuals. The establishment of such an ethical culture is a central goal of all proposed humanistic "revolutions," and it is not hard to see why. Since Christian theism in its many forms has been the most obvious social cement in western society, it is admittedly radical to propose that this old cement be dug out and some new type of mortarless building material be substituted. The humanist believes he possesses this new material, which he calls variously "education," "ethical culture," "social conditioning," and so forth. The antihumanists are skeptical of this claim—to say the least; they prefer to trust the old-fashioned cement of supernaturalism.

Humanism and Science. The third important implication of the humanist philosophy is more intellectual than ethical. If life in this world is all we have, then knowledge of this world and how it works is our most important knowledge. And since the most reliable source of such knowledge is scientific research, it follows that science provides us with the knowledge which is most humanly significant. Thus it is not surprising that humanists have the utmost respect for science, nor is it surprising that they urge the extension of scientific method into every possible area of experience. The sciences of man (that is, the social sciences) are particularly important to humanism, and its exponents insist that these fields must be developed as rapidly as possible.

It will be recalled that philosophical naturalism places the same emphasis upon the importance of science. This common emphasis reveals the close relation between humanism and naturalism. In fact it is at just this point that the two schools merge; "scientific method" (and the worship of this method) provides the ever-open doorway through which naturalists and humanists not only intercommunicate, but easily pass from one school into another. This facile passage back and forth between the two positions, with no passports required, contributes a good deal to the popular impression that humanism is merely "applied naturalism."

Naturalists prefer their intellectual world-view to be judged apart from any humanistic applications, especially as not all humanists make the same applications. In fact, humanists have usually been more eager to claim affiliations with naturalism than vice versa. For naturalists sometimes find humanists naive or starry-eyed. And naturalists have on occasion resented some humanistic claims that naturalism implies a particular social program, or supports a particular political party, or entails some particular economic reform. But, all in all, the two schools have worked together surprisingly well, in spite of the fact that their basic interests are divergent. Naturalism's interests remain theoretical or intellectual, whereas humanism concentrates largely upon the ethical field, and is therefore essentially practical rather than theoretical.

Humanism, Naturalism, and Idealism. These various implications of humanism indicate the difference between the tough- and tender-minded views of the world. In fact they emphasize the contrast even more than do the parallel differences between naturalism and idealism, which we stressed in earlier chapters. Naturalism, for example, stops with an over-all world-view that is antisupernatural; it does not go on to consider the popular question, "Can such a view ever be made satisfying?" The naturalist usually considers this an irrelevant question. He is likely to react to it somewhat as follows: "The question is not whether my viewpoint is satisfying or not, but whether it is *true* or not. If it is true, then men have got to learn to live with it, regardless of whether it satisfies or pleases or flatters them." The opposing schools, on the other hand, such as idealism, usually take this question of "satisfaction" very seriously. Even when they do not openly state that the demand for satisfaction is one which we have the right to make of any world-view, their criticisms of the naturalistic position reveal that "satisfaction" is a major aim of their own position. Their objections to materialism, naturalism, and agnosticism usually concentrate upon the supposed fact that these views are "intolerable," "repugnant," "dreary," or "coldly depressing," rather than upon any logical weakness they may contain.

Humanism, however, differs from both the idealistic attitude and the naturalist's proclaimed indifference to whether or not his viewpoint can be satisfying. The humanist boldly argues that life in an indifferent universe is not only all there can be for man (thus far agreeing with naturalism), but then goes on to proclaim that such a life is enough. "Life can be beautiful—without supernatural origin, support, or destiny." Such is the basic doctrine of naturalistic humanism. But the humanist realizes that life can be beautiful only if there can first be a major reorientation in both the attitudes and the ethical foundations of our whole society. Consequently most of his practical efforts are aimed at bringing about just such a reorientation.

Existentialism

One of the most provocative thought movements of recent years, existentialism, is frequently considered a first cousin of naturalistic humanism, although neither all humanists nor all existentialists are happy with the assigned kinship. The two movements certainly have much in common, particularly in the eyes of their critics. It would perhaps not be unfair to describe existentialism as extreme humanism, or humanism carried through to its farthest implications. However, in this carrying-through process, the character of the philosophy changes profoundly; humanism is essentially optimistic in its view of the human condition and man's fate, but existentialism is basically pessimistic, and only one small ray of hope is permitted to lighten the general gloom.[4]

The existentialist asks this central question: "Since God does not exist, what then? What are the full implications?" However, it is more than a denial of God's existence which gives existentialism its base; there is an additional denial of *all* purpose, logic, plan, and meaning in the universe. And, the existentialist holds, there is no purpose or meaning

---

[4] There is a Christian form of existentialism which is currently quite influential in Protestantism, particularly in America. However it is not actually new, but rather a revival of some of the darker phases of Calvinistic theology—hence the term "neo-orthodoxy" usually applied to the movement. So far the movement has remained influential largely within the seminaries, rather than among the masses of Protestant laymen. It is certain that most Americans, particularly those under thirty years of age, who hear the term "existentialism" think immediately of the atheistic or humanistic type, not of that linked with neo-orthodoxy. We shall use the term throughout the remainder of the chapter to indicate the atheistic type.

in human life. To use the existentialist's favorite descriptions, existence is contingent and absurd, and all human beings are supernumerary and superfluous—not to mention dispensable and replaceable. But these are large and somewhat vague terms, so let us see what meaning the existentialist gives them and how this links him with humanism.

When the naturalistic humanist says "Man is the measure of all things," he is speaking of man as a species, not of men as individuals. When he says "We are alone in an indifferent universe," he again means mankind in general, and he immediately introduces the positive and hopeful idea that men as individuals are not alone, but are naturally social creatures capable of sharing and cooperating with their fellow-humans to advance both their individual welfare and that of the whole race. The humanist finds in mankind's isolated uniqueness a dynamic force that can be utilized to inculcate greater social awareness and mutual helpfulness among individuals. In this way he converts what impresses most people as an unfortunate aspect of the human situation, man's cosmic aloneness, into a potential source of human good.

To an existentialist, however, the phrase, "Man is the measure" (to him a pompous and platitudinous phrase), would certainly not mean mankind as a whole. A central doctrine of existentialism proclaims that the individual alone is the measure of all things, particularly of all values. Life is a continuous process of making choices, and all choices, in the final analysis, are personal and individual. Each one of us chooses his life, so to speak, by the unending series of day-by-day, hour-by-hour, and even minute-by-minute decisions he makes. Each chooses what he will give his attention to, what he will spend his income for, what he will give his time and energies to. A man's life is a project, and each of us is his own architect and builder.

The Responsibility Is Ours Alone. Existentialism emphasizes that there is no escape from wholly individual responsibility. We may delude ourselves by thinking we can evade this total responsibility by trying to put the burden of choice off on some other person or some institution: we may join an authoritarian church or political movement which requires complete surrender to its orders, but this does not free us from the responsibility. We choose the church or party, or the leader or hero whom we will follow, *and this is a continuing choice,* existing at every minute; we can always leave the church or party, or elect to follow a new authority of some kind. Even if we were born into a certain religious faith or into a certain society requiring extreme conformity, it is still our choice, renewed every instant, whether we will remain in that faith or society. There is no escape from responsibility: the choice is ours, and ours alone.

It is immediately clear that existentialism contradicts determinism as the latter doctrine is usually formulated. It equally contradicts fatalism, predestination, and all similar doctrines which make external compulsion responsible for most human choices. And it has very little sympathy with psychoanalytic theories that picture man as a collection of complexes and conditioned reflexes, set up during the individual's formative years, which largely motivate him. In short, existentialism believes man has freedom—total freedom, even "dreadful freedom"; and this school accepts as an authentic person—that is, as a real man—only those individuals who are aware of this complete responsibility and all its implications.

Existence Precedes Essence. The name "existentialism" emphasizes this same idea. It is derived from an implied contrast with the western view of human nature as developed in the eighteenth century and transmitted to the present by innumerable philosophers, poets, theologians, novelists, and playwrights. This traditional view holds that there is an essential human nature, present in each individual and setting both the upper limit to his achievement and the lower limit to his possible degradation. The "essence" of man was supposedly something that could be altered very little by environment or individual choice. And, since it was regarded as innate, it was present potentially at birth and completely throughout adult life.

Existentialism believes that man has no "essence" in this sense of something that precedes individual existence. There is no such thing as "man in general" or an abstract "mankind." In short, there is no Platonic man. There are only *men*: individual creatures existing at a specific time and place in history who come into this world bearing no "essence," actual or potential. The most basic concept in the whole existentialist philosophy is simply this: *existence precedes essence,* not vice versa as in the traditional theory of man outlined above. We make our own essence—each of us individually and exclusively—and we are making it every moment of our lifetime. This explains the existential statement that we do not acquire an "essence" until the moment of our death, when no further choices are possible and the "project" is finished. Therefore a whole lifetime of existence precedes the acquisition of an "essence." And even when at death we have completed the project and thus acquired this "essence," it is still strictly individual, even unique. The character we have achieved, the personality we have developed, the individual history we have made by living through certain events—all these are personal and wholly individual. We still do not become a segment of "essential mankind," even after death.

The existentialist acknowledges that the full realization of this freedom, and awareness of our complete responsibility for all choices we make, produces serious malaise and anxiety in most people. But the authentic person cannot escape this "ethical anxiety," and any psychotherapy that existentialism sponsors attempts to help the individual live with the anxiety, rather than seek ways to eliminate it. For the anxiety is inescapable, once we realize fully the consequences of our choices. This "ethical anxiety" is not the usual worry of conscientious or devout persons that they will do something "wrong." It is something far more profound and terrifying: it is the perpetual awareness that *every* choice is significant, rather than just the conventional moral choices. Because every choice carries this implication of our complete personal responsibility, and every choice thus becomes part of our history and permanent "essence."

To heighten the tension and increase "ethical anxiety" still more, existentialism pictures a universe which—as far as our separate life experiences are concerned—is wholly contingent. As a result, life is inescapably absurd, and all individuals are supernumerary. This brings us back to our big, vague terms again, but now we are better prepared to analyze them in a meaningful way. The remainder of our discussion of existentialism will be given to this analysis.

Existence Is Contingent. Any individual, household, or organization that operates on a budget set up for months in advance must allot a percentage of its expected income to "contingency funds." This is an acknowledgment that even the most careful planning is not capable of predicting future needs exactly. There must be some reserve set aside to take care of the unforeseen, unpredictable, or emergency situations that inevitably arise in the lives of both organisms and organizations. These are the "contingencies."

When the existentialist states that "All existence is contingent," he is not denying the reliability of natural laws or the possibility of scientific prediction and control. Nature may be as rigidly deterministic and regular as nineteenth-century science pictured it; or it may have indeterminism at its nuclear core, as contemporary physics seems to find. For existentialism this is irrelevant. What is important for men—as for all animate creatures—is the basic fact that, *as far as their individual life histories are concerned, the universe is utterly contingent.* Anything can happen to anybody, and regardless of how great the predictive power of science may someday become, this basic situation will not be altered. In terms of generalized probabilities, science (both natural and social) can be quite exact. For example, it can say that a person driving his car at eighty miles an hour who has an accident is x-times more likely to be killed than if he were driving at thirty miles an hour. Or it can say that a driver who consistently exceeds speed limits by fifty percent is more likely to have an accident than are nonspeeders. But in terms of the individual driver—the actual human being, and not just a generalized "fast driver"—it can tell us nothing regarding his accident probability or life expectancy. Slow drivers also have accidents, and even get killed in them. The probabilities are less, but the possibility remains. Anything can happen to anybody. A person who doesn't even drive can be killed the first time he gets inside of an automobile.

To existentialism, a life history is nothing but a series of contingent occurrences. The people we meet, become friends with, fall in love with or fight with, all are met contingently. Lovers often try to persuade themselves that they were destined to meet—"marriages are made in heaven"—but this is a delusion. People move into a certain house in a certain neighborhood and find happiness or unhappiness there. If chance had set them down in the next block, surrounded by other neighbors and other potential friends or lovers, they might have found the opposite.

Existentialism carries this idea through to the bitter end. In a scene in one of Sartre's novels, the hero is sitting in a park. He suddenly realizes the total contingency of the situation: his being in the park at that particular moment, the shape of a tree root protruding from an earth bank nearby, his even being alive at that particular epoch. Events could just as easily have put him at some other place at that instant, the root could have been some other shape or grown in such a way that the excavated earth would not have exposed it. And the hero's being alive at that moment, instead of in some past or future century, is the most fortuitous event of all. His having been conceived at all—that particular sperm fertilizing that particular ovum—was an absolutely random occurrence. And why was he born in a particular town, when his parents could just as easily have been living elsewhere? And why has he escaped all the hazards of living to reach maturity, and escaped all the hazards of war in which so many of his contemporaries died?

Many persons can persuade themselves that all this seeming randomness in a life-history is only apparent: they believe that there is a hidden purpose or logic or design that saves all occurrences from being "merely contingent." Existentialism utterly rejects such "delusions," and employs the harshest terms to characterize persons who hold or preach these "fairy tales." At most we (or an outside observer) can only say that such-and-such happened to us because we decided to do thus-and-so. But what made us decide to do thus-and-so, when there was just as much possibility of our deciding to something else that would not have produced the such-and-such event as a consequence? The theist can say that it was "God's will"; the fatalist can say that "It was written," "in the cards," or "in the stars." Even the determinist, so opposed to theism in many ways, can say that the event was part of an unbroken (and unbreakable) chain of cause-and-effect relations stretching back in time in an infinite regress. But the existentialist rejects all of these as pseudo-explanations. He does not deify "chance" or "randomness," but he does regard it as the most basic characteristic of all existence.

Life Is Absurd. Of all existentialism's general doctrines, probably none repels more people than the statement, "Life is absurd." However, if we accept the preceding idea that all existence is contingent, then it is hard to see how we can avoid acknowledging the absurdity of life. We must remember, though, that the strict meaning of "absurd" is "inconsistent with truth," "illogical," or "irrational." "Absurdity" is a logical judgment, rather than a loose term meaning "crazy," "wild," "socially undesirable," or "morally unsound." In popular use the term often carries some or all of these latter meanings, or else means simply, "What I don't like or agree with." The existentialist employs the term primarily in its original logical meaning. Thus if we grant that the universe is completely contingent in the sense that anything can happen to a person, then it is obviously absurd (that is, inconsistent, illogical) to continue believing and acting as if life had any general purpose, plan, or order. In a universe in which occurrences, in so far as they affect our individual lives, remain random and unpredictable, we necessarily live always on a razor's edge of uncertainty. Consequently there is no security in relying on nature or the cosmos to arrange events into an order that promotes our happiness or makes a logical pattern.

Here again the contrast between existentialism and theism is enlightening. Theists (and most idealists) hold that an over-all purpose or plan exists, which includes our individual lives and the events affecting these lives. These schools seldom claim that the plan is known to us, particularly in its day-by-day details, but they insist that a plan is there. Various arguments are advanced to prove the existence of such a cosmic design, but the most general and basic argument is this: There *must* be a plan, else the universe would be meaningless and human life would be absurd. To which the existentialist answers, "I am glad we agree; unless there were a plan and purpose, the universe would be meaningless and life absurd. Since there is no evidence that this 'necessary' plan exists, I am forced to conclude the absurdity of life. Anyone who reaches the opposite conclusion is operating on blind faith motivated solely by wishful thinking."

Existentialism's Way Out: The Commitment. It was pointed out above that existentialism is not completely pessimistic or defeatist, and we shall conclude with a brief statement regarding the way of salvation that this school allows. To begin with, existentialism attacks only the doctrine that assumes an over-all, cosmic, or objective design in the universe and in human lives. It in no way denies the possibility that individual men and women can formulate individual goals and find subjective purposes in living. The key word here is "subjective." Theism and idealism hold that an *objective* plan exists, even if we cannot discover it— that is, the design exists in the same sense that the physical universe exists. Existentialism, on the contrary, holds that not only are all values purely personal and individual (as we saw earlier), but so are all plans and purposes. Life can therefore be made meaningful only if we can find, *for ourselves and in ourselves,* significance and satisfaction in certain activities or goals. This involves making commitments, and it is these commitments which make life livable.

A commitment is any interest or project to which we give ourselves wholeheartedly. The term used by French existentialists to indicate a committed individual—*un homme engagée*—is indicative when translated literally. In English, "an engaged man" usually means one who has made the major commitment of pledging his troth to a woman. Existentialists believe that life can and should contain many commitments that are as passionate and wholehearted as this type of engagement usually is. However, unlike the ideal marriage engagement, these other commitments need not be long-lasting and fixed. They can change, and in fact do change during most lives. The devotions and intense interests of one season or period of our life give way to others, but durability is not the main thing determining their importance in our personal histories. It is rather their intensity and the scope they have in our lives while they endure that count in making our otherwise meaningless lives meaningful. But, once again, this meaningfulness is strictly subjective. It is the grand delusion to believe that the universe is concerned with our commitments and the satisfactions they produce. It is almost as great a delusion to believe that "society" or "people" are really concerned either. In this as in all things, existentialism claims, each of us is alone. There may be other individuals who share the same project and work for the same goals, but if we dropped out of the activity (or out of existence, for that matter) they would close ranks and life would go on. In this sense we are each superfluous and dispensable. As the characters in Sartre's writings often point out, when an individual dies, the subways remain crowded, the restaurants full, and heads crammed to bursting with little problems. Even a great war, killing millions, leaves the world little changed. The populations soon expand to more than fill up the vacancies, and the world continues to go "nowhere"—nowhere, that is, in the sense of toward some goal.[5]

The Human Situation. It is obvious that the existentialist has no inflated idea concerning the cosmic significance of the human race. On the contrary, he probably has the lowest opinion of man's importance ever formulated into a philosophical system. But, and this is important, this deflation of man's cosmic status in no way diminishes the subjective importance of each individual's decisions, commitments, and satisfactions. The central thesis of contemporary existentialism regarding the human condition could be summed up in the same words that have been used to summarize the viewpoint of one of the founders of Christian existentialism, Pascal: "What am I? Unto the universe, nothing; unto

[5] These two examples are borrowed from Alfred Stern, *Sartre: His Philosophy and Psychoanalysis* (New York, 1953), pp. 22-23. The first is from Sartre's *Mort's sans Sépulture* and the second from his *Le Sursis*. This book of Stern's remains the best introduction to existentialism I have discovered, particularly for the student with some knowledge of philosophy.

myself, everything!" What the individual does with his life, once he has recognized this most basic fact regarding his own existence, is crucial. If he is an atheistic existentialist he will not waste time trying to prove that the universe really does care about him. He will instead make his commitments and initiate his projects in full awareness that he is surrounded by a universe which is infinite in time, space, and indifference to his existence or his happiness. He will, in short, go it alone.

Viewing man's situation in the vast cosmos, the theist concludes, "We are alone, except for God." The idealist says, "We are alone, except as our finite minds share in the thoughts of the Infinite Mind." The humanist states, "We are alone, except for the companionship of nature and our fellow men." The existentialist insists, "We are alone, period." Regarding the source of value, theism says, " 'Good' is what is harmonious with the will of God." For idealism, "good" is what is consistent with the thinking of the Absolute Mind. Humanism believes that "good" means whatever promotes human welfare. For existentialism, the "good" is whatever an individual finds or makes good by his interest or his devotion. We have already quoted Hobbes, writing in the seventeenth century, on this point: "Whatsoever is the object of any man's appetite or desire; that it is, which he for his part calleth *good.*" However, the existentialist theory of value goes even farther than this, declaring that what a man *calls* "good" and what *is* good are one and the same. All valuation is personal, since it is the result of a unique individual history and the expression of an individual life project.

It is obvious that contemporary existentialism constitutes a radical theory of values. In the same way that logical empiricism, with its antimetaphysical drive, subverts most of traditional philosophy, so existentialism subverts most traditional ethical systems. Where traditional ethics has sought universal norms of value and conduct, existentialism flatly denies that any such norms exist; where traditional ethics has, intentionally or unintentionally, largely supported conventional moral standards and the approved social behavior, existentialism has specifically attacked most of these same standards. Where traditionalists have been on the side of the angels, so to speak, and humanists on the side of man at his ideal best, existentialism has been on the side of *men*—in all their individual weaknesses and strengths, wisdom and stupidities, good actions and bad. Whether, by thus repudiating the usual concept of an ideal human nature and ideal standards of conduct, existentialism has degraded man or instead produced the first genuinely honest system of values, is a question that must be left to each reader—and to the judgment of history.

L'Envoie

The writer or teacher of philosophy always feels qualms of responsibility when he brings his readers or students up to his point and then suddenly turns them out into the philosophical night with a cheery, "Well, from here on you are on your own. Good-by, and good luck!" However, there appears to be no escape from such a parting; for ultimately each human being must decide, strictly by and for himself, what he can believe—indeed, what he must believe if life is to be lived with any satisfaction. There is no philosophical alternative to making this most important of decisions. We may postpone it for a while, or even seek to avoid it altogether by following authority of some sort; but, as we have seen from our discussion of epistemology, neither course enables us permanently to avoid the issue. Even if we articulate no belief in so many words, we must act as if we regarded certain things to be true; our actions will imply a certain belief, whether or not we make it explicit. If we seek to escape the responsibility for our metaphysical thinking by following some authority, we have the new responsibility of deciding which authority to follow, and how far to follow it. These various evasions are futile; in determining ultimate beliefs, the philosophical implications are clear: whether we realize it or not, we each make our own decisions regarding the nature of ultimate reality and the kind of world we believe we inhabit. The essence of wisdom is therefore to make these decisions as intelligent as possible, in order that our individual world-view may be as true, as workable, as rewarding and as enduring as possible. For, as Aristotle said long ago and as we emphasized when first our philosophical journey together began, whether we will philosophize or whether we won't, we *must* philosophize. The mere fact of membership in the race imposes this burden upon us; the only question is how well or how badly we bear it.

GLOSSARY OF TERMS

The chief sources used in the preparation of this glossary have been Baldwin's *Dictionary of Philosophy and Psychology,* Runes' *Dictionary of Philosophy* and Lalande's *Vocabulaire de la Philosophie.* The list of terms is not meant to be exhaustive. In general the words defined are those which appear in the text. A few additional terms have been included for the sake of completeness and as an aid to the student who may be puzzled by the technical vocabulary of books used for collateral reading.

ABSOLUTE—That which is nonrelative. As used in philosophy, wholly complete, perfect, independent, unconditioned, and ultimate. In a more popular sense, without reservation (*e.g.,* "absolute truth"). *The Absolute* may mean the ultimate principle or explanation, the world ground or first cause, or the all-experiencing Subject who perceives the universe as its total object.

ACTUALISM—The view, commonly associated with the name of Hume, that the mind is not a unified, independent entity, but only a succession of experiences or conscious states. There is no spiritual bond of unity that ties these together. They are haphazardly joined by the laws of association, but the result is not a substantial self. Opposed to the much older and more widely accepted *substantive view* of mind.

AGNOSTICISM—The doctrine that it is not possible to attain knowledge of a subject, usually God. Popularly confused with *skepticism* (in epistemology) and *atheism* (in theology). The term was coined by Thomas Huxley to denote a modest ignorance and a state of suspended judgment regarding ultimate issues.

A POSTERIORI—Knowledge or reasoning that is derived from, or based upon, experience. In logic, *a posteriori* reasoning is synonymous with *induction.* Opposed to *a priori.*

APPEARANCE—Strictly, anything which is presented to, or observable by, a

433

perceiving subject. As ordinarily used in philosophy, the sensuous aspect of things, in contrast to what they actually are. This makes appearance synonymous with *phenomenon,* as opposed to the *noumenon* or thing-in-itself. In some systems of idealism, appearance is regarded as a degree, fragment, or partial aspect of reality.

A PRIORI—Knowledge that is logically prior to experience, or reasoning based upon such knowledge. Hence, knowledge which is innate (and therefore universal) as contrasted with that derived from sensation. *A priori* reasoning is loosely synonymous with *deduction.* Opposed to *a posteriori.*

ARCHETYPE—The original pattern or model, of which a class of things are copies. A key word in Platonism, where the Forms constitute ideal patterns of earthly objects.

ATHEISM—Used to mean either a denial of the existence of any Deity, or only the existence of a personal (*i.e.,* theistic) God. The first meaning is far more common in popular thought. Frequently confused with *agnosticism* and even *skepticism.*

ATOMISM—The view that reality consists of indivisible, discrete particles or entities. These may be either material or spiritual, although the former view has been far more common historically. If material, they are usually regarded as exceedingly minute and infinite in number.

AUTHORITARIANISM—The view that the ultimate or most valid source of knowledge is authority of some type. This authority may be an institution (*e.g.,* the Church), a text (the Bible), a moral or civil code, or a person.

AXIOLOGY—The systematic study of *value—i.e.,* the theory of the desirable or the good. In philosophy, most discussion of ethics and esthetics presupposes some axiological theory. Particularly important are questions regarding the criteria and the nature of value, although the metaphysical thinker is usually more interested in determining the status of value in the universe.

BEHAVIORISM—The doctrine that the science of psychology should be built upon the objective observation of behavior, rather than upon the subjective study of "states of consciousness" (as in introspective psychology). The term "behavior" is broadly defined by this school to include all observable actions, ranging all the way from violent bodily activity to highly abstract speech.

BEING—Whatever exists, may exist, or have reality. In logic, the most general class, inclusive of everything whatsoever.

CARTESIAN—Referring to the views of René Descartes (1596-1650) and his followers. Usually it is his metaphysical dualism, with its division of reality into the contrasting realms of "thought" and "extension" (*i.e.,* matter), that is implied.

CATEGORICAL IMPERATIVE—The key term in Kant's ethical thought, denoting the supreme moral law. It is unconditional, admitting of no exceptions, and absolute, since it is in no way relative to some further end.

CATEGORY—Technically, one of the ultimate modes (*i.e.*, conditions or classes) of being, or (in Kant) one of the fundamental forms of the understanding. More broadly, one of the most basic or inclusive classes to which objects or experiences can be reduced. A fundamental classification within knowledge.

CAUSALITY—The relation between cause and effect. The *principle of causality* (or *causal principle*) is the basic assumption that nothing happens without a cause, or that every event in the universe is governed by the cause and effect relation.

COGNITION—The act of knowing or perceiving. The adjective *cognitive* is widely used in philosophy in place of the nonexistent adjectival form of "knowledge"—*e.g.*, when an object enters a "cognitive" relation it becomes known or perceived.

COHERENCE (or Coherence Theory of Truth)—The view that the truth of any statement (or proposition or judgment) is determined by its coherence with the rest of our judgments. Thus "truth" constitutes a completely integrated system, and a statement is to be tested in terms of its consistency with this inclusive system. The principal rival view is the *correspondence theory* of truth.

COMMON SENSE—That body of fact and opinion that is supposed to belong to all men as a result of universal human experience—fire burns, water wets, unsupported objects fall, and so forth. Such knowledge is contrasted with both the systematic knowledge of science and the doctrines of some particular school of thought.

CONCEPT—A general idea of any class of objects. Synonymous with *universal* (as a noun) and closely related to *generalization*. Contrasted with *percept*. Any common noun denotes a concept.

COSMOLOGICAL ARGUMENT—The attempt to prove God's existence by the principle of causality. All causes presuppose antecedent causes, but the regress must end somewhere. Obviously this can only be in something which is itself uncaused, and therefore eternal—*i.e.*, God. More briefly, the argument that the universe requires a cause.

COSMOLOGY—The subdivision of philosophy which studies the origin and constitution of the universe as a whole. Contrasted with *ontology*, which seeks to discover the nature of being as such. Often confused with *cosmogony*, a view (usually pictorial) as to the creation of the universe or world.

CYNICISM—A negative attitude toward all or nearly all values; a lack of faith in disinterested motives; a pervasive doubt regarding either the validity or the effectiveness of human ideals. Opposed to *ethical idealism*.

DEDUCTION—The reasoning process in which conclusions are drawn from accepted premises. Ordinarily the premises are more general than the conclusion, so deduction is popularly defined as reasoning from the whole down to the part, or from the general to the particular. Mathematical reasoning and the operations of formal (or Aristotelian) logic are both deductive in character. Opposed to *induction*.

DEISM—The doctrine that God is the creator and lawgiver of the universe, but nothing more. He is not the source of goodness, nor can He be described as a moral being. Further, He has no direct relation with the world, but is essentially an "absentee landlord." Hence there can be no communication between man and God, so both prayer and worship are futile. Historically, deism denotes a view popular in eighteenth-century England and France, where its exponents attempted to establish religion on a natural basis by eliminating revelation and dogma.

DETERMINISM—The view that every event in the universe is completely dependent and conditioned by its cause or causes—*i.e.*, that the causal principle is universal. More specifically, the doctrine that human behavior (including all judgments and choices) is determined by physical or psychical antecedents which are its causes. Opposed to *indeterminism* (the belief in complete freedom of the will) and to be distinguished from *fatalism* (the belief that events are predetermined or predestined, and therefore inevitable regardless of our efforts to prevent their occurrence).

DIALECTIC—In contemporary usage, the critical examination of principles and concepts in an effort to determine their meaning, presuppositions, and implications. Unfortunately the term has several specialized and largely unrelated meanings, particularly when used by Plato, Kant, Hegel and Marx. In popular usage, "dialectics" is the art of reasoning and argumentation.

DICHOTOMY—In logic, the division of any class into two contradictory (that is, mutually exclusive) subclasses, such as objects into "animate" and "inanimate." More loosely, any fundamental division, usually with the implication that the separation represents a permanent aspect of the nature of things.

DOUBLE-ASPECT THEORY—The doctrine (traditionally associated with Spinoza) that the material and the mental (more specifically, body and mind) are only the contrasting aspects of a single ultimate "substance." In psychology the doctrine is known as *psychophysical parallelism*, while in metaphysics it is often called *neutral monism*, in contrast to the psychic monism of *spiritualism* and the physical monism of *materialism*.

DUALISM—Any viewpoint or system that reduces its field to *two* independent ultimates, neither of which can be reduced to the other. It is necessary to distinguish between metaphysical or ontological dualism, which divides reality into "mind" and "matter" (or "thought" and "extension") and epistemological dualism, which makes its basic dichotomy between the real object and the image (the sense datum or "idea" of the object) present to the mind.

EGOCENTRIC PREDICAMENT—Term used by R. B. Perry to denote the epistemological predicament of the mind, which finds it impossible to get outside the circle of its own sensations and ideas to know the external world directly. Such subjective idealists as Berkeley take this situation to be indicative of the nature of Reality; they thus hold that *esse est percipi*, "to be is to be perceived." The realist, on the contrary, regards the situation as only an unfortunate intellectual predicament, epistemologically serious but without ontological implications.

ÉLAN VITAL—Literally, "vital impetus." Term used by Bergson to indicate the source of evolution in the biological sphere. More loosely, the biological urge which manifests itself in all organic activity.

EMERGENCE—Broadly, the doctrine that "life" and "mind" have both come from inorganic matter. *Emergent evolution* holds that life represents a novel quality that emerged from the nonliving as a consequence of the latter having attained a certain level of organization. *Emergent mentalism* maintains the same for mind: when the nonmental attains a new level of complexity (*i.e.*, a more highly developed brain and nervous system), mind or consciousness appears.

The general doctrine of emergence is also known as the *theory of levels*.

EMPIRICISM—The epistemological doctrine that the only valid source of knowledge is *experience*. Building firmly upon the position that knowledge cannot extend beyond experience, empiricism is opposed to *a priorism* of any kind, particularly the claims of *rationalism* that the mind can discover truths which are "innate" or which in some way transcend experience.

ENTELECHY—In Aristotle, the actuality of a thing as opposed to its potentiality —*i.e.*, the essence of a thing, or in some contexts, its essential function. Thus the soul is the "entelechy" of the body, just as vision is the "entelechy" of the eye (Aristotle). In modern philosophy, the term is used by some vitalists to denote the nonmaterial vital something (also called "psychoid") which distinguishes living processes from those which are inorganic.

EPICUREANISM—The system of moderate and refined *hedonism* taught by Epicurus (342-270 B.C.). It advocates the pursuit of the joys of friendship and of the mind, rather than those of the body, since the latter are more violent and consequently more difficult to control. The highest good for the Epicurean is *ataraxia*, "serenity" or "peace of mind," rather than positive pleasure. Hence the doctrine can be described as essentially a *negative hedonism*.

EPIPHENOMENALISM—The doctrine of mind-body relation in which mind is regarded as a by-product or incidental effect of the brain processes. This implies that all mental activity is basically physical change, and that consciousness has no causal influence on the physical realm.

EPISTEMOLOGY—That subdivision of philosophy which studies the nature, the sources, the possibilities, and the limitations of knowledge. Loosely, the "theory of knowledge."

ESSENCE—The necessary nature of a thing, in contrast with its non-necessary (*i.e.*, "nonessential") qualities or accidents, and regarded independently of its "existence" or actual being. Popularly, that which makes a thing what it is.

ESTHETICS (also AESTHETICS)—Traditionally, the study of beauty in art and nature. The modern use of the term usually includes much more, such as the nature of the esthetic experience, types of artistic expression, the "psychology of art" (either the creative or the appreciative process, or both), and the like.

ETHICS—That subdivision of philosophy which studies the nature of the good, the right, obligation, or the ideal in human conduct. As such it is also a subdivision of *axiology*, the theoretical study of *value*.

EUDAEMONISM—The word *eudaemonia* (usually translated "happiness" or "well-being") was used by Aristotle to indicate the highest good for man, which he held to consist in the active exercise of human abilities in accordance with reason.

The tendency in post-Aristotelian ethical thought was to make eudaemonism practically synonymous with *hedonism*, although this does considerable violence to Aristotle's doctrine.

EVIL (PROBLEM OF EVIL)—The problem (particularly burdensome in all idealistic systems) of how to explain the existence of evil in a universe supposedly created and governed by Mind, Reason, Purpose, or some other power. The problem is even more acute in most forms of theism, since the Deity is usually regarded as infinite in power, wisdom, and goodness—capacities which seem incompatible with the continued existence of evil in the world.

EXISTENTIALISM—The contemporary philosophy (primarily ethical) which holds that there is no essential human nature common to all men. Instead each individual creates his own essence or character throughout his lifetime by his choice of interests and actions. Thus "existence" precedes "essence," since the latter is not completed until life and its endless series of choices is terminated by death.

EXPERIENCE—One of philosophy's most important and most ambiguous terms. Loosely, anything which is undergone or lived through, particularly if the process involves consciousness or awareness. Also, the highest or most inclusive class, to which anything must belong before it can be referred to in any way. Any more precise definition necessarily involves a metaphysical view or theoretical standpoint; thus the realist will define "experience" in terms unacceptable to the idealist, and vice versa.

FATALISM—The view, far more common in Oriental thought than in Western philosophy, that all events are predetermined or predestined for the time, place, and manner of their occurrence. Applied particularly to human affairs, especially the time of one's death.

FORMALISM—Term used to denote two different but related ethical doctrines: (*a*) the view that the fundamental principle for the determination of duty is purely formal—*e.g.*, Kant; (*b*) the view, more accurately called *intuitionism*, that the rightness or wrongness of any action may be determined by direct intuition, without regard for the consequences and without the aid of discursive reason. The doctrine implies the existence of a "faculty" or organ which gives this immediate insight, usually identified with the *conscience*.

FREE-WILL—More accurately, *freedom of the will*. The doctrine that man's will or capacity for choice is independent of all antecedent conditions whatsoever—*i.e.*, that the human will is free from the causal principle which binds the rest of the universe. Synonymous with *indeterminism* and opposed to both *determinism* and *fatalism*. The *free-will controversy* centers around the validity of the indeterminist position.

GOD—In philosophy, the highest or ultimate Being. Probably the chief difference between the metaphysical and theological views of Deity arises from the fact that the philosophers cannot take the existence of God on the basis of authority or revelation. While many metaphysical systems do culminate in (or at least include) God, this existence is demonstrated rationally and not held as a tenet of faith.

GOOD—That which possesses worth or value of any kind. In axiology the concept of good is largely built around the distinction between that which has value in itself (*intrinsic* good), and that which has value only as a means to some other object or end (*extrinsic* or *instrumental* good).

HEDONIC CALCULUS—The view of Jeremy Bentham, that we can establish the goals of conduct by weighing the pleasure that will result against the pain involved. If there is a preponderance of pleasure, the act is good; if pain outweighs pleasure, it is bad.

HEDONISM—The doctrine that the ultimate good (and therefore the criterion of all value) is *pleasure*. It is customary to distinguish between *ethical hedonism*, which holds that only pleasure has positive ultimate value, and *psychological hedonism*, the belief that all behavior (both human and animal) is motivated by the pursuit of pleasure or the avoidance of pain.

HUMANISM—The term has so many meanings that a single definition is impossible. All do have one thing in common, however: an interest in and a focus upon human welfare, particularly in terms of life here and now. In technical philosophy, the term was adopted by F. C. S. Schiller to describe his particular type of *pragmatism*.

HYLOZOISM—The doctrine that nature is alive or that matter has spiritual qualities. The view was widespread in early Greek thought, but indicates not so much a positive doctrine as a failure to realize what we regard as one of the most fundamental dichotomies in experience, that between animate and inanimate nature.

IDEALISM—Technically, any system which reduces all existence to mind or thought. This may be either a single, absolute mind or thinker (*e.g.*, Hegel's "the Absolute") or a plurality of minds (pluralistic idealism, as in Berkeley). More loosely, any system or viewpoint that is formulated in terms of the ideal, and which stresses the mental or spiritual aspects of experience. Opposed to *naturalism* and in a broader sense, to *naturalism*.

IDEOLOGY—Any group of general ideas, particularly in the social or politico-economic realm. In current usage, the term usually implies a solid *Weltanschauung* that is held unconsciously, as when a Marxist speaks of "bourgeois ideology." Occasionally used in the sense of a set of ineffectual ideals or standards which are opposed to truly effective causes (usually economic).

IMMANENCE—The metaphysical and theological view that God is an indwelling Being who does not exist apart from (or outside of) the universe. Thus God and the world are identical and presumably co-eternal. Synonymous with *pantheism,* and opposed to the doctrine of *transcendence.*

INDETERMINISM—Synonymous with *freedom of the will.* The doctrine that man's will or capacity for choice is independent of all determination whatsoever, and thus functions in a noncausal vacuum. Opposed to *determinism.*

INDUCTION—The reasoning process in which generalizations, laws, or principles are formed from the observation of particular cases. Popularly, that reasoning which moves from the part to the whole, or from particular to general. Most human knowledge is inductive or empirical in character, since it consists of generalizations on our sense experience. Opposed to *deduction.*

INSTRUMENTALISM—That subschool of pragmatism associated with John Dewey. The word is best understood as an epistemological *operationalism*, in which terms, concepts, ideas, are regarded as "tools" or "instruments" for transforming an indeterminate situation into a determinate one. Thus truth would exist only when it is usable as an instrument, serving ultimately to advance the welfare of the individual or social group.

INTERACTIONISM—A widely influential view of mind-body relation formulated by Descartes and still accepted by many thinkers. Eminently dualistic in character, it assumes a mutual causal influence of the physical and the mental upon one another.

INTUITION—Direct or immediate apprehension. *Intuitionism* in epistemology is the theory that direct (*i.e.*, nonmediated or nondiscursive) awareness is the most valid source of knowledge. This is usually accompanied by the theory that man possesses a separate "faculty," neither sensory nor rationalistic in character, which is capable of apprehending "truth" or "Reality" directly. *Ethical intuitionism* likewise builds upon the theory that man has a special faculty (usually identified with the *conscience*) which is able to make absolute moral judgments. Both *absolutism* and *formalism* in ethics usually include intuitionism as a basic doctrine.

LOGIC—Technically, that subdivision of philosophy which studies the laws of valid inference. Popularly, the "art" of reasoning. Logic is traditionally divided into (1) formal, deductive, or Aristotelian and (2) inductive logic or scientific method. It is usually the former which is meant when the term is used in general philosophical discourse.

LOGICAL EMPIRICISM—An extremely influential epistemological view which holds that the determination of meaning is the crucial problem in all philosophical discourse. The school acknowledges only two kinds of meaning, factual and formal. The former is established by sensory verification, the latter by the rules of logic and syntax. Statements which cannot be verified in one of these two ways are meaningless or "nonsense." This includes all metaphysical propositions—*e.g.*, any statement regarding the character of reality in general or as a whole—so the logical empiricist movement has been very critical of much traditional philosophy. Related to *positivism*, and sometimes called *logical positivism*.

MACROCOSM (and MICROCOSM)—The whole universe or "great world" in contrast to some part of the whole which is regarded as reflecting or epitomizing it. This *microcosm*, or "world in miniature," is usually man, whose inner complexity is supposed to be analogous to the outer order of nature. The two terms always imply one another.

MATERIALISM—The view that everything in the universe, including life and mind, can be reduced to, and explained in terms of, matter and motion. Thus only matter and motion have existence or ultimate reality. This implies that all mental processes and properties are physical in origin and completely dependent upon matter for existence. Thus conscious events are, like all phenomena, reduced to the transformation, or spatial rearrangement, of material atoms. Although the three concepts overlap, materialism should be distinguished from both *mechanism* and *epiphenomenalism*.

MATTER—As one of the most fundamental categories of experience, matter is difficult to define. It is that which has as its most important characteristics "extension" and "impenetrability," although "mass," "weight," "permanence," and so forth, are almost as basic to the concept. Matter is also regarded as the extramental cause of sensory experience. But whether we give matter the status of an appearance or regard it as the only reality will depend upon our general philosophical position.

MECHANISM—Broadly, the view that all phenomena can be accounted for by mechanical principles—*i.e.*, by the laws of matter and motion. In a narrower sense, the doctrine that organic processes are continuous with inorganic; hence living behavior is explicable in mechanical terms, and biology is an extension of physics and chemistry. This makes biological mechanism the opposite of *vitalism*.

MELIORISM—A term originated by George Eliot to indicate the view that lies between *optimism* and *pessimism*. It holds that the world is basically neither bad nor good, but capable of change in either direction. Thus the good can be increased, notably by human effort. As ordinarily used, the term implies that such continuous improvement is a fundamental part of the evolutionary process.

METAPHYSICS—Broadly, the science or study of being as such, as contrasted with the investigation of being in some particular form (*e.g.*, physical science). Sometimes the term is used in a restricted sense as synonymous with *ontology*, but the more common practice is to use it as including both *ontology* and *cosmology*. In a more literary sense, metaphysics is the study of the ultimate real, and hence constitutes the central query of traditional philosophy.

METHODOLOGY—Technically, that subdivision of logic which systematically analyzes the principles and processes which should guide inquiry in a particular field. More loosely, the means by which activity in any field is either organized or carried on, although it is probable that the term can properly be used in this broad way only in intellectual pursuits.

MIND—One of the ultimate categories of experience, used in general opposition to *matter*. The term may refer to (1) the individual subject or consciousness; (2) the entirety of psychic experience; (3) the conscious element in the universe; (4) all three of these. In systems of monistic idealism the term is usually written with a capital letter to denote the ultimate real.

MONAD—The term comes from the view that the universe is composed of elementary units of some kind. However these are not physical (as in ordinary atomism) but rather metaphysical, or (in some systems) both corporeal and spiritual. The term has become associated particularly with the thought of Leibniz, whose *monadology* postulates an infinite number of beings pursuing their own development according to an inner law in complete isolation from, but in pre-established harmony with, one another. For Leibniz, monads lack extension, shape, divisibility and penetrability.

MONISM—The metaphysical position which views reality as the manifestation of a single principle or substance. This ultimate principle may be psychical and spiritualistic (as in idealism) or material (materialism) or neutral (*e.g.*, the neutral monism of Spinoza). *Epistemological monism* is the doctrine that the object and the idea of it are identical. This is in opposition to the far more common *epistemological dualism*, which holds object and idea to be numerically two separate (and usually, qualitatively different) entities.

MYSTICISM—The doctrine that ultimate truth is attained through intuition rather than from either reason or ordinary sense experience. The mystic usually regards intuition as an independent organ or channel of communication which gives immediate knowledge, as contrasted with that knowledge which is mediated by sense or reason. While the context of the mystical experience varies widely, it usually involves an intense awareness of God's presence or a direct communion with Him, although this Being is likely to be the ineffable "One" rather than the personal Deity of most theists.

NATURALISM—The metaphysical view that the universe is self-sufficient, without supernatural cause or control, and capable of explanation in purely natural terms. The most radical aspect of the view is its belief that life and mind are in no way exceptional, but are rather an integral part of the natural order. This implies that man's values and ideas are the product of evolution, and therefore only an expression of the needs of the human species in the world of here and now.

NOMINALISM—The view (originally medieval) that only individual objects have an objective reality, and that concepts or universals are only "names" (*nomina*). Thus concepts have no extramental existence. Opposed to medieval or Platonic *realism*, which regards universals or class terms as having objective existence. (Note: Medieval realism should not be confused with modern realism, which is in many ways its complete opposite.)

NORMATIVE—That which constitutes (or relates to) a standard or regulative ideal. Thus a "normative judgment" is one which expresses a preference or evaluation, in contrast to a cognitive or factual judgment. Thus "The book is on the table" is not a normative judgment, while "This is a good book" expresses such a judgment.

NOUMENON (plural NOUMENA)—Kant's term, now used generally in philosophy, to denote the "thing-in-itself," as contrasted with *phenomenon*, or the appearance of a thing to the senses. Kant held that noumena are unknowable, since sense data can report only the appearance of objects.

OBJECTIVE—That which exists outside the mind, independent of perception and (usually) independent of the existence of a conscious subject. More broadly, that which exists in the world of common experience and is therefore capable of being perceived by all observers. Opposed to *subjective*.

OCCASIONALISM—An extreme form of *parallelism*, more theological than philosophical. It holds that mind and body do not affect each other directly, but that every occurrence in either the mental or the physical realm is the "occasion" for God to intervene to bring about a corresponding change in the other realm.

ONTOLOGICAL ARGUMENT—The most rationalistic of the so-called "intellectual proofs" of God's existence. It holds that the existence of God follows inescapably from the very concept of Deity. The idea of God is that of the most perfect Being; if this Being did not exist, then there would be other beings which (since they do exist) would be more perfect. The argument is stated in various other ways, often in terms of a "most real Being" (*ens realissimum*), which clearly must exist to be such. First formulated by Anselm (c. 1100), the argument has been used in modified form by many theologians and philosophers, notably Duns Scotus, Descartes, and Leibniz. The most notable attack on the argument was made by Kant.

ONTOLOGY—Sometimes taken as synonymous with *metaphysics,* but more accurately that subdivision of the latter which studies "Being" in its most abstract form: What is the nature of "Being" as such? Or, What does "to exist" mean?

PANPSYCHISM—The view that all nature, including matter, is psychical or has psychical attributes. In its classical form, the monadology of Leibniz, nature is composed of centers of perception comparable to the human mind. The doctrine represents a modern revival of ancient hylozoism, and is a form of idealism.

PANTHEISM—The doctrine that God and the universe are identical. It thus is synonymous with the doctrine of *immanence,* and is opposed to the *transcendence* view of Deity. The Church has always regarded pantheism as heresy, and the foremost exponent of the view, Giordano Bruno, was burned for his belief (1600).

PARALLELISM (PSYCHOPHYSICAL)—A theory of mind-body relation which holds that there is a one-to-one correspondence between psychic events and bodily changes—that every event in either realm is accompanied by a synchronous change in the other. Ordinarily the theory denies any causal connection between the parallel series, although causation *within* both series is acknowledged. The doctrine is closely related to *neutral monism* and the *double-aspect theory* (e.g., Spinoza).

PARSIMONY, LAW OF—The postulate, basic to scientific thought, that explanatory factors are not to be multiplied beyond necessity—that is, that the simplest adequate explanation is to be taken as true. Thus science allows only the indispensable number of assumptions to be made in explaining any phenomenon, and the simpler of two hypotheses is always to be preferred—all else being equal. The implication of the law is that there is a corresponding principle of simplicity in nature—"nature uses the simplest means possible." Also called "Occam's Razor," after its fourteenth-century formulator, William of Occam.

PERFECTIONISM—The ethical doctrine, often called *idealistic perfectionism,* which holds that the highest good consists in the attainment of perfection. Sometimes this state is described in terms of moral perfection or complete virtue, but more often it is taken to mean the maximum realization of our capacities and potentialities, or at least those which are highest and most characteristically human. The modern term *self-realization* is now preferred by many ethical thinkers to indicate this doctrine.

PHENOMENON (plural PHENOMENA)—That which appears to consciousness or can be perceived. The appearance of a thing in contrast to the *noumenon* or "thing-in-itself." Thus phenomena, as studied by science, are things as they are for man, rather than as they are for themselves.

PLURALISM—The view that reality is composed of a multiplicity of distinct, independent, and ultimate substances or entities. Technically, any world-view which postulates more than two ultimates would be a pluralism; historically, however, pluralistic systems have nearly all argued for many reals, usually an infinite number. These may be material (*e.g.*, the atomists), spiritual (Leibniz) or neutral (Herbart).

POSITIVISM—The view, first given organized expression by Comte about 1840, that the only certain knowledge is knowledge of phenomena, particularly as afforded by science. The doctrine usually includes a denial of the possibility of ultimate knowledge—that is, that which transcends experience—particularly where final causes are concerned. Very loosely, positivism is an emphasis upon scientific facts as opposed to metaphysical speculations.

POSTULATE—An indemonstrable statement taken as a basis for deductive reasoning. The *verb* often has a somewhat broader meaning: to state something which must be assumed or taken for granted in order to prove something else. Sometimes used as synonymous with *axiom*, although the best usage regards the latter as more universal in scope and more plainly self-evident in character.

PRAGMATISM—A recent movement associated particularly with the name of William James, John Dewey, and F. C. S. Schiller. While the various members of the school emphasize different problems, all agree in opposition to absolutism of any kind, particularly absolute idealism. Pragmatism builds generally around the following points: (1) the meanings of all conceptions are to be found in their practical bearings; (2) the function of thought is to serve as an instrument of adaptation and as a guide to action (Dewey); (3) the primary test of truth is the practical consequences of our belief. The chief significance of pragmatism has been its critical, analytical activity, rather than its metaphysical formulations.

PRE-ESTABLISHED HARMONY—The term used by Leibniz to explain the relation between mind and body and (more precisely) between the monads which make up his system. These are connected by means of a divinely established eternal harmony or synchronization so that, without causal relation of any kind, changes in one realm are paralleled by changes in the other.

RATIONALISM—The doctrine (primarily epistemological) that knowledge and truth are ultimately to be tested by intellectual and deductive rather than sensory methods. Rationalists usually regard "reason" as a separate source of knowledge, in no way dependent upon experience. Opposed to *empiricism*.

REALISM—The term has several separate meanings. *Epistemological realism* is the view that (1) concepts or universals have an objective or extramental existence (usually called "Platonic" or "medieval" realism) or that (2) it is possible for us to have a direct and valid knowledge of the external world by means of sense experience. *Metaphysical realism* is the view which denies that the universe can be reduced to "mind" or "thought." This implies that the universe has an independent or "real" existence which is in no way dependent upon perception or consciousness. Opposed to *idealism*.

RELATIVISM—The position that there is no objective, absolute, or final truth; truth is always relative to the locale, the time, the group or the individual. Far more common is the doctrine of *ethical relativism*, which holds that "rightness" and "goodness" vary from age to age, group to group, and so forth. Opposed to *absolutism*.

SELF—Loosely, the ego, subject, or I of experience. Due to the development of psychology, there is an increasing tendency to use the term as synonymous with the *personality* as viewed by other observers. Historically, the self has often been given a metaphysical meaning: it is the principle of unity that underlies subjective experience, and hence in many idealistic systems is the most significant thing in the universe.

SELF-DETERMINISM—A compromise position between the extremes of *determinism* and *indeterminism*. The advocates of self-determinism hold that our actions are indeed determined, but not by external forces or conditions of any kind. It is the nature of the self (usually its psychic elements only) which controls our choices, and this "causality of a permanent spiritual self" is regarded as our guarantee of our essential moral freedom.

SELF-EVIDENCE—The property of being clear to the understanding without need of proof or demonstration. Applicable to any statement, the truth of which is immediately apparent by direct inspection.

SELF-REALIZATION (Doctrine of)—The ethical doctrine that man's highest good lies in the maximum realization of his potentialities and capacities. Under the name *perfectionism*, it is the higher human capacities that are emphasized, while other thinkers (notably Aristotle) have stressed the development of what is unique in man, specifically his ability to organize his activities in accordance with reason. Also called *eudaimonism* and *energism*.

SKEPTICISM—The epistemological belief that the human mind cannot attain certain or absolute knowledge, or if it could, would not be able to recognize that knowledge as certain. This denial of absolute knowledge may apply only to certain fields or subjects (*e.g.*, God, immortality, the nature of the self or the ultimate real, etc.) or it may be extended to include all subjects whatsoever. The term should be carefully distinguished from *cynicism. Agnosticism* and skepticism are loosely synonymous, except that the former is more a confession of ignorance than a doubt of possible knowledge. Further, agnosticism is often used only where knowledge of God is concerned.

SOLIPSISM—The most extreme form of subjective idealism. It maintains that the mind can know nothing except its own experiences, and therefore cannot prove the objective existence of anything extramental. When extended to metaphysics, the doctrine holds that only my self (*i.e.*, my mind) and its perceptions or conscious states exist. All physical objects, as well as all other persons, depend upon my consciousness for their existence.

SPIRITUALISM—In philosophy, the metaphysical doctrine that the ultimate reality is Spirit, Mind, or Reason. This may be either single or plural. The term is loosely synonymous with *idealism,* but is more accurately used to denote that extreme form of idealistic thought which holds that nothing but spirit exists. Opposed to *materialism.*

STOICISM—One of the great ethical systems of the ancient (particularly Roman) world. Its chief doctrines were (1) the pursuit of happiness within oneself by the cultivation of apathy or independence of the external world; (2) living "according to nature," which means both to follow *reason* (as the highest principle in human nature) and to obey the all-pervading law of the "Logos" or World-Reason. Thus living according to these laws becomes the highest duty of man.

SUBJECTIVE—That which is concerned with, or arises from, the mental processes of the individual, in contrast to that which exists in the external environment. Opposed to *objective,* and loosely synonymous with *personal* (feelings, values, etc.) and *introspective* (method, study, etc.).

SUBSISTENCE—As used in modern philosophy, the term indicates the kind of being, neither mental nor physical, that is supposedly possessed by essences, universals, logical propositions, and (for some thinkers) values. Such being is in contrast to *existence* as possessed by concrete objects.

SUBSTANCE—The essential nature or reality that underlies the properties of anything. Usually employed in the inclusive sense to mean that which is conceived of as existing in and by itself—the permanent cause underlying phenomena. Hence it is that which receives modifications, but is not itself a modification of anything else.

SUMMUM BONUM—Literally, "highest (or supreme) good." The theoretical ultimate goal of human conduct, which, of highest intrinsic value itself, is the supposed end or reason for all decisions and actions. There have been many candidates for this ethical ideal, among them happiness, pleasure, virtue, obedience to duty, self-realization, power, and so forth.

SUPERNATURALISM—In philosophy, the doctrine that the universe is the creation of an outside source or agency which rules it. This agency is usually God, who transcends His creation, and who is both the author of all being and the source of all value. Opposed to *naturalism,* particularly to the naturalistic doctrine that the existence and operation of the universe can be explained in terms of natural forces within it.

SYLLOGISM—A form of deductive reasoning involving two propositions (called "premises") that are related to one another so as to imply a third (the conclusion). The traditional example is

> All men are mortal
> Socrates is a man
> Therefore Socrates is mortal.

SYNOPTIC—That which gives a general view of a whole and all its parts, the whole being seen in its entirety and the parts in their necessary relations with each other and within the whole.

TELEOLOGICAL ARGUMENT—One of the intellectual "proofs" for the existence of God. Known also as the *argument from design,* it holds that the universe as a whole reveals evidence of adaptation to ends, which is in turn evidence of conscious purpose, or Creative Intelligence. A great favorite of theologians in the eighteenth and early nineteenth centuries, the argument has been virtually eliminated from philosophy by the natural selection theory of Darwinian evolution.

TELEOLOGY—The doctrine of final causes, which holds that the universe is ordered by ends and purposes. Thus events are to be explained not by their antecedents ("efficient causes") but by their results ("final causes"). More popularly, the view that everything that exists or occurs has a purpose, and thus is to be explained in relation to the future, rather than in terms of the past. Directly opposed to *mechanism,* which seeks to explain all phenomena solely in terms of antecedent events.

THEISM—Very loosely, the belief in the existence of a god or gods; hence the logical opposite of *atheism,* which denies such existence. More properly, the doctrine that God is single, personal, infinite, and both transcendent (in essence) and immanent (in presence and activity). The theistic concept usually includes eternality, omnipotence, omniscience, omnibenevolence, and omnipresence. Theism has also usually included the concept of God as both creator and moral center of the universe. When we add to these characteristics the capacity to hear and answer prayer, the theistic Deity becomes synonymous with the traditional God of Christendom. As such the concept is opposed to both *deism* and *pantheism.*

THEOLOGY—The systematic study of God: His existence, nature, powers, laws, and relations—particularly to man and the world. Often the study includes an analysis of the grounds and limits of our knowledge of Deity, in which case the speculation may be more philosophical than theological in the strict sense. The study may be purely theoretical, having no necessary connection with religion, but this is not common.

TRANSCENDENT—That which lies beyond experience and hence is unknowable. Used particularly by Kant. In general, the term is applicable to all thought systems which regard experience as regulated by a priori forms and principles. In a more popular sense, the term is used interchangeably with *transcendental* to indicate anything that is "out of this world." In theology it denotes the doctrine that God is outside of Nature, and is thus opposed to *immanent*.

TYCHISM—The doctrine that chance has an objective existence and plays an effective role in the world process. Thus "chance" is not a mere name for our ignorance regarding causes, but an actual existence.

UTILITARIANISM—The doctrine that the ideal end of human conduct should be the greatest good for the greatest number—"good" being defined in terms of pleasure or happiness. The viewpoint, given classic formulation by Jeremy Bentham and the two Mills, is essentially a *social* (as contrasted with an egoistic) *hedonism*. Opposed to ethical *intuitionism* or *formalism*.

VALIDITY—The property of being legitimately derived from premises by logical inference. Thus a valid conclusion is one which is inferred from antecedent premises. Validity should be distinguished from *truth* (or more precisely, *truth to fact*).

VALUE—Broadly, that which makes anything worth possessing or realizing. The numerous controversies concerning the source and status of value, as well as its relation to human conduct, make the term one of the most ambiguous within philosophy. All schools, however, seem to agree that values can be divided into "intrinsic" and "instrumental," and that judgments of value must be distinguished from judgments of fact (*e.g.*, "This is a good book," as contrasted with "The book is on the table."). Probably the greatest controversy centers on the question of whether values are objective or subjective, absolute or relative.

VITALISM—The biological doctrine that organic processes are not explicable in physiochemical terms, but can be accounted for only by assuming an unknowable, nonmaterial entity or substance, called variously the "psychoid," "entelechy," "*élan vital*" or "vital principle." Opposed to *mechanism*.

WELTANSCHAUUNG (or WELTANSICHT)—An all-inclusive world-view or outlook. A somewhat poetic German term to indicate either an articulated system of philosophy, or a more or less unconscious attitude toward life and the world—*e.g.*, "the Platonic *Weltanschauung*" or "the medieval *Weltanschauung*."

WORLD—In philosophy, a realm or sphere of either existence or experience.

The term usually implies a relatively unified self-contained whole, as, for example, the "world of nature," the "world of music," the "world of dreams," etc. The term should not be confused with the earth—*i.e.*, the planet on which we live. "World" frequently means our total environment, or even the whole universe regarded as an object of experience. Such a meaning is exemplified in the statement, "Man seeks to understand his world."

INDEX

Index of Topics

Index of Names

Note: (n) = *note;* (q) = *quoted.*